Understanding Habermas

To Ånund Haga
and Jon Hellesnes

Understanding Habermas

Communicative Action and Deliberative Democracy

Erik Oddvar Eriksen and Jarle Weigård

continuum
LONDON • NEW YORK

Continuum

The Tower Building, 11 York Road, London SE1 7NX

370 Lexington Avenue, New York, NY 10017-6503

www.continuumbooks.com

British Library Cataloguing-in-Publication Data
A catalogue record for this book is available from the British Library.

ISBN: 0–8264–6064–X (hardback)
ISBN: 0-8264-7179-X (paperback)

Figures 2.1 and 2.2 are taken from *The Theory of Communicative Action Volume 1: Reason and the Rationalization of Society* by Jürgen Habermas
Introduction and English translation © Beacon Press 1984
German text © Suhrkamp Verlag, Frankfurt am Main 1981
Reprinted by permission of Beacon Press, Boston

Figures 3.2, 5.1, 5.2 and 5.3 are taken from *The Theory of Communicative Action Volume 2: Lifeworld and System: A Critique of Functionalist Reason* by Jürgen Habermas
Translator's preface and translation © Beacon Press 1987
Originally published as *Theorie des kommunikativen Handelns, Band 2: Zur Kritik der funktionalistischen Vernunft*, © Suhrkamp Verlag, Frankfurt am Main 1981
Reprinted by permission of Beacon Press, Boston

Typeset in Sabon by RefineCatch Limited, Bungay, Suffolk
Printed and bound in Great Britain by Biddles Ltd, Guildford and King's Lynn

CONTENTS

PREFACE

Jürgen Habermas is the author of one of the most comprehensive, ambitious and debated projects in social theory of the twentieth century. His deep-seated theory and his penetrating analysis seem to arouse attention in ever wider circles. At the same time it is a fact that Habermas's own books and articles are not always easily accessible. Apart from the impressive volume of some of his most important works, both content and presentation style are often characterised by great complexity and require prior knowledge to get in. These are the reasons why we endeavoured to synthesise the most important theoretical contributions of Habermas. The book is particularly aimed at students of politics and society and primarily undergraduate and graduate students who specialise in sociological, political, legal and philosophical subjects.

This is a revised and expanded edition of a book which first appeared in Norwegian in 1999. The main difference between the two versions is the final chapter (Chapter 11 'A World Domestic Policy'), which has been added in the present edition and which deals with international affairs. This is a topic to which Habermas (alongside many other political theorists) has devoted much of his attention in recent years, and we find it important to discuss the discourse-theoretical achievements regarding such questions. We also have made some alterations to Chapter 4 and in general updated and made adjustments to the text in the remaining chapters.

Some remarks about the intentions behind the present volume might be in order. First of all it is obvious that even though we have tried to cover several parts of Habermas's work (some would say that this is the core of his theoretical production), his intellectual contributions are so far-reaching that there are still many areas we have not touched upon or only marginally. This applies to, for example, his early contributions on epistemology in connection with the positivist debate, his many debates with different philosophical opponents, and not least his innumerable comments to political events and topical social questions. Instead, we have focused two main areas: the basic categories of social action, i.e., the theory of communicative action, including some adjacent moral-philosophical questions and a model of the modern social formation (the book's Part 1), and his later work on a discourse theory of law and politics, including international relations and post-national democracy (Part 2).

Secondly, although the book is written as an introduction, we cannot claim to have removed every obstacle to the full understanding of Habermas's theoretical work. To dwell into the subtleness of his thinking will always be time and energy consuming. His theoretical insights *are* compound and that is to a large extent what makes them interesting. We expect readers to find some parts easier than others, and we believe that especially Chapters 7 and 11 probably are a bit more difficult to grasp than the rest. Besides, both Habermas's own theory and the present book are constructed in such a way that an optimal benefit from reading Part 2 presupposes knowledge of the content of Part 1.

Thirdly, the book is not only an introduction to Habermas's work but also in some respects an attempt to employ his theory more independently. Hence, the presentation in some sections goes beyond what can be derived from Habermas's own writings. Our ambition is to derive implications from the general theoretical framework with regard to more specific problems. Primarily this applies to

Chapters 10 and 11 of Part 2, the first of which discusses the possibilities of application in institutional design and which falls outside of Habermas's own project. The same goes in part for Chapter 11, which outlines the discourse-theoretical reconstruction of international relations and cosmopolitan democracy.

The book has come about as a cooperative undertaking between two writers who from the outset each had responsibility for different chapters: Weigård for the Introduction and the four chapters of Part 1, Eriksen for the six chapters of Part 2. We have, of course, also benefited greatly from various kinds of input from many friends and colleagues, and we would like to express our gratitude to them. First of all, we think of colleagues at the different institutions we have been linked to during the creation process; that is the Faculty of Social Science at the University of Tromsø, the LOS-Centre and the Centre for the Study of the Sciences and the Humanities at the University of Bergen, as well as the ARENA-Program at the University of Oslo. Many have read and made valuable comments to drafts to one or more of the chapters. We would especially like to mention Lars Blichner, Ole Brekke, the late David R. Doublet, John Erik Fossum, Willy Guneriussen, Hans-Kristian Hernes, Agustin José Menéndez, Bjørn Erik Rasch, Helene Sjursen, Marit Skivenes, Marianne Takle and – in particular – Gunnar Skirbekk. In addition we would like to thank the reviewer for our Norwegian publisher, Heine Andersen, and the three anonymous reviewers for Continuum. Most of all, however, we would like to thank Anders Molander. He has read the chapters not only once but some of them several times, and through the whole process made invaluable suggestions to improvements of the text.

Frøydis Wiik and Kristin Killie have translated most of the original text, and Anne Elizabeth Stie and the authors the rest. Regarding technical matters, the authors have received qualified help from Maila Solheim in getting the manuscript in shape, not least in the puzzle of keeping track of the many references. Economically, the Norwegian Research Council, the ARENA-Program, and the Department of Political Science at the University of Tromsø have supported the publication.

We dedicate this book to the professors in philosophy at the University of Tromsø, Ånund Haga and Jon Hellesnes, who by their seminars and other forms of contact from the late 1970s onwards aroused our interest for this outstanding social and political theorist.

Erik Oddvar Eriksen and Jarle Weigård
Oslo/Tromsø
September 2002

CHAPTER 1

Introduction

HABERMAS AND HIS CONCEPTION OF RATIONALITY

The 'Modern Age' is an elastic concept. With the speed with which things are changing today, we tend to regard many things as being out-of-date even after a few years. However, if we look at it from a historical perspective, it is usually the past three to five centuries which are referred to as the Modern Age. In this period, the spiritual contributions and scientific insights of Antiquity, which were rediscovered in the Renaissance, were combined with a desire to control and manipulate nature. This linkage formed the basis for the development of an empirically oriented natural science. In conjunction with the great geographical discoveries and a developing market economy, it was the prerequisite for the emergence and dominance of our modern Western civilisation. Our Western society is first and foremost a civilisation of *rationality*. A rational world view based on enlightenment and knowledge, a rational exploitation of nature based on scientific insight, and a rational form of social interaction based on the capitalist entrepreneur's calculating attitude towards his environment – these are all typical expressions of the new spirit of the times. The shift of attention towards the subject of rationality during this period is evident in the philosophy of René Descartes (1596–1650), the pioneer philosopher of early modernity.

While there is widespread consensus that our modern society is a civilisation with clear rationalist elements, the question of how this condition can be described in more detail, and what one should think of it, is more controversial. Some positions in this debate have attracted a great deal of attention and are hence well known. On the one hand, *logical positivism* expressed the pursuit of the rationalist ideal, which was premised on mathematical language and the scientific approach to the objects of study. On the opposite side we find the *Romantic movement*, whose roots date back to Rousseau, who rejected the rationalist ideal of the Enlightenment. According to the Romanticists, we should not let ourselves be led by externally acquired knowledge but behave expressively by listening to the 'voice of nature' inside us, to our authentic humanness. We gain access to our 'selves' through sensitivity and an 'unassuming' attitude, rather than through cool intellect and rational insight. Subjectivity replaces the rationalist belief in objectivity. *Post-modernism* represents a third position and a different way of rejecting rationalism. According to Post-modernism, the claim that rationalism represents objectively valid standards is false, as such standards do not exist. All theories pretending that they are objective should be deconstructed and revealed as just a blind for hidden interests and power motives.

The specifically modern form of civilisation and the idea that has promoted it – rationalism and the belief in enlightenment – are, in other words, controversial. The leading exponent of the modern ambivalence towards rationalism is Max

Weber (1864–1920). Rationalism is at the same time our blessing and our curse. It is our blessing because it has made our Western civilisation unique in world history. In many areas it has provided us with things that we regard as expressions of 'progress' and the goods in life. It is our curse because it threatens to dehumanise our existence and confine us to an 'iron cage of rationality'.

It is against the background of the debate on rationality and 'modernity' that Jürgen Habermas's authorship is perhaps best understood. Whether he is speaking as an epistemologist, a moral and social philosopher, a sociologist, a political theorist, or if he is commenting on current political developments, the problem of rationality is always present, either directly as a topic, or as an underlying premise. In this debate Habermas makes his mark as a critical upholder of the rationalist idea. He is critical, as he is satisfied neither with the dominating epistemological view of rationality – represented by positivism – nor with the way the idea of modernity has been realised in capitalist society. He is nevertheless an upholder of the ideas of rationality and modernity, as he believes there is an alternative interpretation of these concepts, which is more adequate in the epistemological as well as in the political sense. To him, modernity is still an unfinished project,[1] whose realisation is well worth striving for, as it can be done in a better and more comprehensive way than has been the case so far. Thus he not only turns against those who view rationality in a positivist and instrumentalist manner. His criticism is just as much aimed at various types of sceptics, who, like the Romanticists and Postmodernists, question the idea that our rational capacity may be used both to establish valid standards and to answer the more difficult questions in life.

In Habermas's view, the problem with the traditional scientific view of rationality is that it has one-sidedly emphasised the cognitive aspects of reason: in the Cartesian paradigm, the individual subject uses all his or her rational ability to interpret events and facts, in an attempt to relate optimally to a changing external world. On the one hand, this is an expression of what Habermas refers to as a *philosophy of consciousness*. In this approach, rationality is viewed as a characteristic of an active, thinking subject, who receives information about a world that consists of objects. On the other hand, this paradigm has led to an instrumental understanding of rationality, where rationality is defined in terms of the individual actor's capacity to use his knowledge in order to achieve his goals. Rationality, then, is a measure of effectiveness by which one can adjust to or manipulate one's surroundings in order to realise subjective preferences. In Habermas's view, this one-sided understanding is also reflected in the rationalisation of modern society. The reason why our civilisation has become only a limited success (as claimed by Weber), is that the emphasis has been too one-sidedly on gaining control over nature and people, and on the production of material goods.

Jürgen Habermas

Born in 1929, Habermas grew up in the little town of Gummersbach, east of Cologne, Germany. He studied at the universities in Göttingen, Zurich, and finally in Bonn, where he took his doctorate in 1954 with a treatise on the philosopher F. W. J. Schelling. After working as a journalist, in 1956 he was employed as an assistant to Theodor W. Adorno at the Institute of Social Research in Frankfurt. Here he participated in an empirical study of political awareness among students. In 1961 he completed his treatise *Structural Transformation of the Public Sphere* (English translation: Habermas 1989a), which qualified him for a chair at German universities. It was a study on the political significance of the public sphere in bourgeois society, its development and alleged decline. From 1961 to 1964 Habermas taught philosophy at the University of Heidelberg, and in 1964 he succeeded Max Horkheimer as professor of sociology and philosophy at the University of Frankfurt.

Other important publications from the 1960s include a collection of articles titled *Theory and Practice* (1963; English translation: Habermas 1973) and the epistemological work *On the Logic of the Social Sciences* (1967; English translation: Habermas 1988), where he addresses the positivist normative relativism and argues for the distinctive character of the social sciences. The discussions on the relation between epistemology and social theory continued in two books published in 1968 – a collection of articles titled *Technik und Wissenschaft als 'Ideologie'* (Habermas 1968; English (partly) translation: Habermas 1971a) and the larger work *Knowledge and Human Interest* (English version: Habermas 1971b). In 1971 he became director of the Max Planck Institute in Starnberg, where he continued his very productive authorship with titles such as *Legitimation Crises* (1973; English version: 1975), *Zur Rekonstruktion des Historischen Materialismus* (Habermas 1976; English (partly) translation: Habermas 1979a) and – his main work in two volumes – *The Theory of Communicative Action* (1981; English version: Habermas 1984 (volume 1)/1987a (volume 2)).

In 1982 he returned to his old professorate in Frankfurt, where he is still working. During the 1980s and 1990s and into the new millennium, he has produced an even flow of new collections of articles with topics such as moral philosophy (Habermas 1990a, 1993a, 2003), political theory (Habermas 1998a), epistemology (Habermas 1999a), analyses of modernity (Habermas 1987b, 1992a) and comments on the political situation (Habermas 1989b, 1990g, 1994b, 1997a, 2001a, 2001g). His greatest work from this period is his discussion of law and political theory, *Between Facts and Norms* (1992; English translation: Habermas 1996a).

THE THEORY OF COMMUNICATIVE ACTION

According to Habermas, there is another aspect to rationality, which he refers to as *communicative rationality*. This kind of rationality is not tied to the subject–object relation of a cognising and monologically acting individual, but to a subject–subject relation between communicating and interacting individuals. This aspect of rationality is necessary in order to maintain society as a social fabric regulated by norms, institutions and conventions, a place where new insights and knowledge can be developed and transferred, and where individuals can be socialised into fully developed personalities. Rationality not only answers questions about facts, but also so-called practical questions about further action, i.e. ethical and moral dilemmas. Reason also has its limitations and weak spots for Habermas, but he still believes that rational insights are a better ground to build on than, e.g. intuition and emotions, the ideals of Romanticism. According to him, we can obtain a degree of rational certainty that will prevent us from ending up in a state of scepticism and value nihilism. This state has tended to become the result of the radical critique of modernity that has been carried out in the tradition from Friedrich Nietzsche (1844–1900) to postmodernists such as Michel Foucault (1926–84) and Jacques Derrida (1930–).

Habermas's belief in rationality does not imply a dogmatic faith in any estab-lished set of substantial knowledge. On the contrary, all knowledge is in principle fallible and conclusions must therefore be regarded as revisable. Habermas's per-spective rather implies a *procedural view of rationality*, where it is not our con-clusions but the manner in which we arrive at them which are permanent and in a way above criticism. The procedure involves maintaining a form of openness around the conclusions; they can always be challenged, criticised and tried again. What is rational, then, is that position or claim which is supported by the weightiest arguments. A procedural approach to rationality does not guarantee that we will arrive at the right answers in all cases, but it guarantees that we can continuously test the answers again if there is reason to doubt their correctness.

This perspective forms the basis for Habermas's theory of communicative action. The main tenet of this theory is that our communication through lin-guistic utterances may be regarded as 'speech acts'. The theory implies that we continuously have to take a yes or no position to specific validity claims which are implicit in the utterances. By this he wants to point out that human communica-tion is a medium of a rationally binding character. It has the capacity to function in an action-coordinating manner, which means that agents' actions will depend on how they evaluate the statements of other agents. According to Habermas, this is human rationality 'proper', i.e. the ability to let one's actions be guided by a common understanding of reality, a consensus established through linguistic dialogue. By the term *communicative action*, then, he thinks of action which is linked to such linguistic validity claims, i.e. action which is oriented towards interaction on the basis of a consensus about those claims (cf. Habermas 1984: 101). However, this rationality potential, which follows from the rationally bind-ing power that language has is far from being realised all the time, and here we are back to the critical aspect of the theory. For in addition to the communicative type of rationality, there are other forms of rationality and logic of action that fill a natural and necessary function especially in modern society. Of particular importance is *purposive rationality*, which is highly instrumental in the economic

The Frankfurt School

Jürgen Habermas's intellectual and academic career is linked to the so-called Frankfurt School, also known as the 'critical theory' tradition. The former term refers to an interdisciplinary milieu which was established about 1930 around the Institut für Sozialforschung (Institute of Social Research) at the University of Frankfurt, and which included names such as Max Horkheimer (1895–1973), Theodor W. Adorno (1903–69) and Herbert Marcuse (1898–1979).* When Hitler seized power in 1933, the institute had to move to the USA, but it was partly re-established in Frankfurt in the post-war period. The continuity between the first and second generations of the Frankfurt School is symbolised by the fact that Habermas was at first Adorno's assistant, then later took over Horkheimer's professorate. However, theoretically, there are significant differences between Habermas and the older members of the Frankfurt School.

The concept of critical theory refers to the ideological roots of the school, and links it to the Marxist tradition. It was nevertheless in clear opposition to the dogmatic and 'official' Leninist 'communist party Marxism' of the inter-war period. However, the founders also wanted to establish an alternative to what they regarded as a 'bourgeois' attitude within the social sciences, i.e. the traditional way of interpreting and using theories of social relations in a capitalist society. Briefly, the Frankfurt School was inclined to claim that there is no *neutral* description of social phenomena (in contrast to, for example, the claims of positivism). Social theories will either be critical, i.e. they will reveal illegitimate power relations, or they will obscure suppressive conditions. In contrast to the objects under study by the natural sciences, the social sciences study objects that are also potential subjects. If they are made aware of those relations which govern their lives, people may take action to change those relations. Social conditions are hence not only objective facts, i.e. conditions that we have to adapt to. They are relations which we can analyse from within, relate to, and perhaps move beyond through solidarity of action. The factuality of a condition may as well be an expression of a perverted condition as of a 'natural' condition. A neutral social science is impossible because the researcher must always choose either to present a condition which is empirically given as self-evident, or to contrast it with a potential state of affairs, i.e. with those conditions that could also have been realised.

The programme of the Frankfurt circle has been to throw critical light on hidden power relations and other kinds of illegitimate social phenomena, on the basis of what has been referred to by Habermas as the 'emancipatory knowledge-interest' of the social sciences. Here the ultimate goal is the autonomous human being and a free society (Horkheimer 1972, Adorno 1976, Habermas 1971b). Habermas's break with early critical theory is expressed among other things in his wish to revise Marx's old substructure–superstructure model completely, and assign independent meaning to 'superstructure phenomena' such as arguments, norms and scientific truths (Habermas 1979b). Another sign of this break is the fact that Habermas has distanced himself from the cultural pessimism which gradually came to characterise the older Frankfurt generation.

*For a general introduction to the history and ideas of the Frankfurt School, cf. Held 1980 and Wiggershaus 1994.

sector and in various kinds of formal organisations. The problem, however, in Habermas's view is that these other standards of rationality have a tendency to impose themselves on or 'colonise' areas that ought to be dominated by communicative rationality. The consequence is that relations which should be based on personal commitment, common understanding and involvement, are instead regulated on an impersonal basis, with alienation, disintegration of social responsibility and decline of legitimacy as results. Habermas, therefore, wants to make it the critical goal of the social sciences to reveal and analyse such developing tendencies.

With his concept of communicative action, Habermas wants to distance himself from the cultural pessimism which has characterised many of those who have studied the modern Enlightenment project from the time of the Renaissance onwards. This concerns first of all Max Weber (1978), who saw an effective, but totally dehumanised social ideal in the breakthrough of the modern, calculating, purposive rationality. It also concerns Habermas's predecessors at the Frankfurt School, Horkheimer and Adorno, who in light of their experiences with the Nazi monstrosities in Europe, and during their exile in the USA, also with what they perceived as the conformist, uncritical American society, in the course of the wartime came to draw conclusions which in many ways continued and reinforced Weber's views: the ideals of the Enlightenment turn into their own opposites as they end up in the total, manipulative dominion of instrumental reason (Horkheimer and Adorno 1972, Horkheimer 1947). With his theory of communicative action, Habermas wants to show that there is a more positive way of interpreting modern societies. Rationalisation is not necessarily equivalent to instrumental, strategic, purpose or system rationalisation. *Communicative* rationality also constitutes a possibility – a possibility which may in fact contribute to increasing the scope of rationality and freedom (Habermas 1984). 'Modernity' implies not only an increase in our ability to control nature; it also implies the development of moral and legal norms which make possible new forms of civilised, humanist resolutions of conflicts.

COMMUNICATIVE ACTION AND POLITICAL THEORY

The conditions for political action have always been a major topic in Habermas's works. The normative approach of the theory of communicative action, which is based on the rationality potential which is assumed to exist in speech acts, makes it particularly relevant to the study of modern, constitutional democracies. To be sure, there is no general agreement as to what forms the basis of democracy today, i.e. in what sense democracy involves government by the people, and what particular factors make us respect political decisions as authoritative and legitimate.

Here we can speak of at least two main approaches to the study of politics. The approach which today has become dominant in Western understanding of politics goes back to the Renaissance philosopher Niccolò Machiavelli (1469–1527). He insisted that politics must be analysed as an endless struggle for power, where the actions of the different agents are governed by a desire to have one's own interests realised. This is the view known as *'realpolitik'*, of which we find elements in several of the schools of the twentieth century. One of them is legal positivism, represented by Carl Schmitt (1888–1985), who viewed politics as a struggle between friend and foe, and who claimed that the validity of the law ultimately rests on an arbitrary decision on the part of the rulers (Schmitt 1988). Also in the theories of Max Weber, the theme of power has a central position. He characterised the specifically modern form of government as a legal domination or authority. Thus, legitimacy is a result of legality; the laws are considered to be legitimate if they have been sanctioned by way of the correct formal procedures of representation and decision-making. Both Weber and the economist and political theorist Joseph Schumpeter (1883–1950) maintained that democracy in reality would and should be confined to the election of leaders. In other words, they envisaged a system where different political elites would compete for the favour of the electorate, and where the influence of the people would be limited to choosing its rulers (Weber 1978, Schumpeter 1942). Others have emphasised that democracy must be regarded as a channel for the aggregation of voter preferences, based on the voters' subjective wishes and interests (Downs 1957). Furthermore, it is the strength of the votes, expressed by the decisive power of the majority will, which first and foremost characterises modern 'polyarchies', and which ensures their legitimacy (Dahl 1971). To the systems theorist and sociologist Niklas Luhmann (1983), it is the functionality of the law in governing society which secures its legitimacy.

What unites these schools is the view that the legitimacy of politics is based on power rather than on the content of decisions; right is in the final instance derived from power. Legitimacy is ensured by us following prescribed procedures in the decision-making process, and it does not depend on any normative or moral component in politics. This view can be contrasted with a view that goes all the way back to Aristotle (384–322 BC), and which defines politics as a strive to form a society which is good for everyone (Aristotle 1957). According to this approach, the goal of political efforts is not the realisation of self-interest, but of the common good. Here legitimacy is linked not to procedures, but to content, which means that policies are legitimate to the extent that they result in solutions that are in the best interest of society. Morality and ethics thus become the main aspects of politics. These are views that can be ascribed to the main part of the *republican* school within political theory (cf. Arendt 1958, 1990; Walzer 1983; Sunstein 1988b, 1993; Sandel 1996), or more generally to the so-called *communitarians* within American social philosophy and sociology in particular (MacIntyre 1985; Sandel 1998; Bellah *et al.* 1986, 1991; Taylor 1989; Bell 1993).

To Habermas there is some truth in both these approaches. As already mentioned, he himself is a proceduralist in his view of rationality. He is also a proceduralist in his view on how political questions should be solved. However, in contrast to the view of the *realpolitik*, Habermas does not think validity is secured if procedures simply produce results which are in accordance with the prevailing power relations and with subjective expressions of will. As far as possible, procedures must ensure that the content of the chosen solutions are rational. This is where his communicative basis plays in, for as there is no a priori blueprint for the best solutions, the issue has to be decided through a deliberate process, where all the involved parties have the same fundamental right to have their voices heard. It is the institutionalisation of such *argumentative procedures* which ensures the legitimacy of democracy.

Hence, we need forums where it can be discussed and decided what the common good really is, and what is to be regarded as collective obligations. Habermas focused on this issue as early as in 1962, in his treatise *The Structural Transformation of the Public Sphere*, where he studied the properties of the new social phenomenon known as the political and cultural public. The phenomenon developed when political questions gained a broader social interest and relevance in the eighteenth and nineteenth centuries (Habermas 1989a). Through public discussion and reasoning different views on political questions may be subjected to criticism, and the public sphere is hence a necessary channel for establishing democratic legitimacy.

Habermas's main conclusion in this early work was nevertheless that since the middle of the nineteenth century, the public sphere has lost much of its critical function. (In this respect he may be said to be in agreement with the culture-pessimistic post-war attitude of the older generation within the Frankfurt School). This development was primarily caused by the transition to a more power-based politics, linked to the emergence of organised interest groups and party competition. This again led to the spread of phenomena such as political propaganda, marketing and cultural industry. Rather than enlightening people's consciousness, the tendency is that public statements are increasingly used to manipulate public opinion; however, Habermas does not claim that the potential for critical reasoning has altogether disappeared. Accordingly, in his greatest social theoretical monograph – *The Theory of Communicative Action*, which first appeared in German in 1981 – his analysis is that the political sphere in modern societies is divided between a socially integrated and a system-integrated sphere. In the socially integrated sphere, i.e. the public sphere, the logic of communicative action prevails. Here our cultural identity, as well as our political opinions are created. However, the decision-making level belongs in the system-integrated sphere, which Habermas calls the administrative system (in that part inspired by Talcott Parsons and Niklas Luhmann). In this system we find both the actual administration (bureaucracy, the power structures) and the politics exerted by modern political parties and interest organisations. Here the basis for the coordination of action is not consensus formation, but rather the use of the 'steering medium' of power, to which the actors can relate in a strategically rational way.

In other words, Habermas gives a description which in its empirical approach is not radically different from that of the followers of the *realpolitik* model and the 'economic' model of politics: power and strategic interests play the leading part in the coordination of political processes today, not dialogic, communicative action. However, in contrast to the defenders of these other positions, Habermas maintains that the framework within which the exercise of power and strategies takes place must nevertheless be kept together by an underlying consensus and approval of the system. The strategic processes cannot legitimise themselves.

However, in *Between Facts and Norms* (German edition of 1992), it may be said that Habermas aims to carry out an analysis of the legitimation basis of law and politics in a more positive sense. Here he concludes that our representative democracy to a large extent represents precisely a *deliberative* model of politics, in spite of the fact that much political activity takes the form of power struggles and strategic play. Politics nevertheless has a dual normative foundation. First of all it has a normative basis in the legal institutionalisation which surrounds it, and whose procedures also ensure that strategically motivated actions take place under conditions which are reasonable and morally acceptable. The legal discourse is a type of normative discourse, i.e. a discussion about how things should be. The second normative basis of politics is its connection to a public political discussion, which takes place both in the public room and in representative assemblies. Here different questions are addressed directly, for example what matters should be on the agenda, what should be done, and what solutions are good and just. As long as the decision-making process is not immune against impulses of this kind, it has not completely lost its deliberative, democratic core.

One basic problem in the monograph under discussion is the attempt to dissolve the paradox that lies in the concept of a *democratic constitutional state*. The paradox consists in the fact that according to the democratic principle the people (or its representatives) have the authority to pass the laws of society, including constitutional provisions. On the other hand, the principle of the constitutional state gives the individual constitutional protection against any encroachment the state may make on his or her personal freedom. Thus, *political power is bound and limited by the law, which secures the rights of the individual, while at the same time it is politics that authorises the law*. This is a fundamental dilemma in political theory. Habermas's solution is that rather than seeing the individuals' personal autonomy (as legal subjects) and their public autonomy (as political citizens) as mutual limitations, we should regard them as conditions for each other: democracy cannot survive in a society where individuals do not enjoy personal autonomy in the form of, among other things, legal security, just as personal autonomy does not have a secure foundation in a society which is not democratic (i.e. where citizens can make use of their political rights to decide the rules of their intercourse).

THE STATUS OF THE THEORY OF COMMUNICATIVE ACTION

It is natural also to comment on what pretensions lie behind the theory of communicative action, i.e. in which contexts it is meant to be a useful aid.

First and foremost it represents a quite ambitious attempt to create a general social theory – a theory of social and political integration – which embodies central insights from a series of sociological and philosophical schools. Here the most important components are:

- Max Weber's theory about the rationalisation of the Western cultural sphere.

- The critical 'Western' Marxist tradition, with the emphasis on reification and human alienation in modern society (Karl Marx, Georg Lukács, Theodor W. Adorno and Max Horkheimer).

- The analytical tradition of the philosophy of language (Ludwig Wittgenstein, John L. Austin, John R. Searle).

- George Herbert Mead's foundation of a social-psychological theory on symbolically mediated interaction.

- Emile Durkheim's normative theory of society founded on the sociology of religion.
- Talcott Parsons's and Niklas Luhmann's construction of a system-theoretical social science.
- Philosophy of right in the traditions of Rousseau, Kant, Hegel and Carl Schmitt.
- John Rawls's and Ronald Dworkin's contributions to the interpretation of liberal political theory.

It goes without saying that this is going to be a relatively complex theoretical concept. Most competing paradigms of social science offer theories which are constructed around much simpler basic assumptions than is the theory of communicative action. In all theory formation there will be a trade-off between simplicity and analytical scope and depth. If the theory is too complicated, it is difficult to handle; if it is made too simple, it will produce explanations of limited relevance. Communicative action theory aims to explain or provide an understanding of a wide spectrum of social conditions, which means that it is of a very general character. At the same time it aspires to provide a profound understanding of these relations, among other things by putting the different phenomena into a larger context.[2] However, this may undoubtedly be at the expense of simplicity, elegance and precision in analyses and conclusions.

This becomes evident if we compare the theory with a set of theories which jointly have become a very important school of thought within Western (and especially American) social research, viz. economically inspired social theories. They have different names, such as game theory, rational choice, public choice, social exchange theory and transaction analysis; however, the core of these theories are relatively similar. Plainly, the main presupposition is that we have to do with monologically acting agents; they make their action plans without seeking any acceptance from other agents involved. Their action involves choosing between different alternatives in order to maximise utility, on the basis of a preference scale that is considered to be exogenously given, which means that the theory does not aspire to explain how the relevant preferences are formed. This type of conventionalised presuppositions often provides a basis for operationalisations in the form of a very concise conceptual apparatus, by means of which relatively complex action situations can be described through brief formulas or equations, as we know it also from economic theory.[3] The methodological strength of this type of theoretical approach should be obvious; it provides concisely formulated hypotheses which may be (relatively) easily tested, and which have unambiguous conclusions. However, this methodological elegance naturally has its costs as well. There is often reason to ask whether the representation of social conditions and human motivations are not unduly simplified by these theories. We may also suspect that the conceptual apparatus of these theories are rather too precise in view of the reality it is assumed to describe, so that the results of the analyses provide a picture not so much of the empirical realities, but rather more of the internal relation between the presuppositions of the theories. For example, we may well ask how often human actions are rational to the extent and in the manner which models resulting from these theories normally presuppose.

These few critical remarks are not stated here in order to show that economically inspired theories are irrelevant or without interest in other social sciences. We do not by any means hold that opinion. Among adherents to and active users of such theories there will of course be different opinions about the paradigm's status and area of use. Some seem to mean that all social behaviour can and should be analysed as chains of individual utility maximising actions, and that the economic paradigm is therefore the only theoretical tool which is needed in the social sciences. Others take a much more pragmatic approach, and claim that such models can be useful tools in many kinds of analyses, without putting forth the postulate that this type of theory may explain everything, or that other theories are superfluous.

Habermas's own position on the matter seems clear. He recognises that the number of areas which are dominated by what Weber called purposive-rational action has increased radically in modern society, and that these areas may to a large extent be regarded as a kind of *norm-free sociality*, where particular steering media (money, power) have increasingly replaced, or relieved, communication oriented towards reaching understanding. This is primarily the case within the 'subsystems' of market economy and (as already mentioned) public administration. For the main part we may reconstruct these areas on the presupposition that agents act strategically. However, outside of – and as a premise for – these areas of strategic action, there are spheres which are still dominated by social integration and communicative action, and which hence cannot be satisfactorily analysed as arenas of strategic interaction. Thus, when it comes to understanding the very basis of social life, i.e. what makes society possible at all, Habermas maintains that the economic paradigm does not represent an adequate approach.

Admittedly, we have seen that a main hypothesis in Habermas's work from 1981 is that the purposive-rational model of action is gradually dominating more areas, i.e. a 'colonisation' is taking place, through which spheres that were earlier characterised by social integration are gradually invaded by imperatives linked to the logic of system integration. So maybe those who claim that economic models of analysis are a superior paradigm for the social sciences can lean back and conclude that eventually they will be proved right after all, even on the terms of the communicative perspective? That is a conclusion against which Habermas would have strong reservations, for what he wants with his colonisation thesis is primarily to warn against the pathological consequences of the development just described. He wants to demonstrate that many social processes can not be transformed from communicative to purposive-rational action, and that the form of integration which is required to maintain fundamental social relations will simply break down if we allow this trend to continue uninterrupted. Thus, more than anything, Habermas's position represents a critique of the many theoretical schools which are premised on an instrumental view of all social relations. His main point of criticism is that they do not have any corrective to this perspective, and that any tendency in the direction of more instrumentality in the real world can therefore never be understood by these schools as anything but a matter of course. As a rival to the empiricist theoretical approaches, Habermas therefore proposes a *critical* alternative. While the former approaches confine themselves to describing and explaining social developments, critical theory in addition aims to warn against developments that represent a perversion of fundamental social institutions.

ORGANISATION OF THE FURTHER PRESENTATION

Part 1 discusses Habermas's theories of rationality, action and society. The discussion opens, in Chapter 2, with an account of that concept of rational action which is at the basis of the communicative understanding of society and politics. Here the communicative concept of rationality is compared to two other concepts, viz. purposive and contextual rationality. What is special about the communicative concept of rationality is that it makes possible three different ways of experiencing reality, described in terms of Habermas's 'three worlds'. Chapter 3 focuses on the concept of communicative action. We discuss the implications of the concept and how the emergence of this form of social coordination can be explained. Central here is the concept of validity claims, which, according to Habermas, is implicitly raised in connection with all speech acts oriented to reaching understanding. The topic of Chapter 4 is the normative theory of the communicative perspective, i.e. what is referred to as 'discourse ethics'. Here we discuss some of the problems which are raised in attempts to justify choices of actions in a morally valid way. Chapter 5 discusses Habermas's attempt to understand modern society in a combined system and action perspective, i.e. as characterised by both system and lifeworld relations at the same time. In addition we will discuss what he regards as tendencies that are currently threatening the relationship between system and lifeworld, viz. the system's alleged expansion at the cost of the lifeworld.

Part 2 is concerned with Habermas's more specifically political theory, especially the relation he establishes between law and politics – between the constitutional state and democracy. In Chapter 6 we draw the contours of this model of democracy by sketching Habermas's discourse-theoretical concept of deliberative democracy. We do that by at the same time contrasting it with a liberalistic and a republican model. Chapter 7 discusses Habermas's discourse-theoretical concept of law. The law is analysed as a medium of integration in modern societies, and on the basis of its normative as well as its instrumental aspect: it has a connection with morally valid argumentation, while at the same time it makes it possible for the individual to act strategically within its frames. Chapter 8 discusses the structure of the political decision-making process in today's representative democracies. Habermas's main point is that the democratic formation of will and opinion is filtered and takes form through a set of different discourses, which may vary according to the nature of the problem in question. The question which is in focus in Chapter 9 is the role of the public sphere in the political process. Here Habermas claims that the citizens have no means of controlling directly formal decisions through the informal discussions that take place in the public room, but that these discussions are nevertheless an important deliverer of premises for the relevant decisions. Thus, even today the public has its necessary function as a source of legitimacy and a critical supervisor of the democratic process. Chapter 10 discusses the possible constructive implications that may be derived from discourse theory through principles for the communicative design of institutions. How can political, administrative or professional institutions be designed in order to maximise the potential for communicative rationality in the decision-making processes? Even if the possibilities are explored which lie in the use of such a design perspective, the chapter also warns against the dangers that a technocratic misuse of the theory represents. And finally, in Chapter 11 we outline the discourse-theoretical reconstruction of international relations and cosmopolitan democracy. Due both to globalisation, which challenge the capability of the nation state, and to the non-institutionalised form of human rights politics, political institutions beyond the nation state are called for. Politico-judicial bodies on the supra-national level are required in order to catch up with economic globalisation and to secure impartial law enforcement in case of human rights violations. However, Habermas at the same time has reservations with regard to the possibility of a world polity with a government, as proposed by some cosmopolitans. Does that mean that only varying degrees of democratic integration are possible at the national, the regional, the transnational and the world level, respectively?

Notes

1. Cf. his 1980 lecture 'Modernity: An Unfinished Project' (Habermas 1996b).
2. The theory of communicative action builds on an explicitly *hermeneutic* view of science, which is in sharp contrast to the positivist view. To hermeneutic approaches, an overall perspective is fundamental because such approaches base their theories on an *interpretation* of social phenomena in their context. Like everybody else, social researchers gain access to their objects through *participating* in society (Habermas 1988a, 1990e).
3. Cf. for example Buchanan and Tollison (eds) 1984.

PART 1

ACTION THEORY AND SOCIAL THEORY

CHAPTER 2

Rationality and action

INTRODUCTION

There are different opinions with respect to what should be the starting point of theory formation in the social sciences, i.e. what constitutes the elementary building blocks in the explanation of social life. However, there is a large but heterogeneous school which insists that social science must be based on action theory, i.e. its explanations must refer to actors who act consciously and intentionally. This school is founded on Max Weber's methodology, and today it first and foremost includes social scientists who concentrate on Weber's so-called purposive-rational action type, such as game theorists and others with a basis in economic theory formation. However, the school also includes various hermeneutically oriented theorists, who claim that we must try to understand an action on the basis of the meaning that the actors themselves put into it. Jürgen Habermas may also be placed in this latter category of scientists, although he crosses several borders with his concept of communicative action and his theory about modern society. It is important to note, however, that his primary building block is not the concept of purposive rationality, but rather other elements from action theory, developed by Weber as well as by others.

What distinguishes the different concepts of action is mainly that they build on rather different understandings of human rationality. Admittedly, the different approaches also have a common rationality foundation as they all rest on the basic assumptions that agents seek to realise an intention or purpose through their actions, and that the rationality of an action is tied to those factors which motivate agents to act in a particular way. However, there is strong disagreement with respect to what factors are taken into consideration when agents are planning their actions. Here we find a dividing line between those approaches whose main presumption is the lonely, monologically acting individual, and those that presuppose that several interacting agents coordinate their action plans through prior linguistic communication.

SCIENCE AND RATIONALITY

Rationality, or reason, has always been a central concept in all scientific cognition. Although there have been different opinions as to how the concept should be defined, most scientists have regarded their work as grounded on rationality premises. On the one hand we have the premise that the cognitive process itself, as well as the scientific method, must comply with particular rationality requirements. This requirement has been common to the humanities, the natural and the social sciences. A second premise is that rationality may also be found in the object under study. The status of the latter premise has, of course, varied according to what kinds of objects each branch of the sciences have had as their domain. However, also within disciplines that study more or less the same object, such as the social sciences, different approaches and schools have disagreed about this premise.

Science allows us to understand and explain reality by simplifying it and creating order in apparent chaos. In order to do this, we need to find an ordering principle or pattern which makes seemingly random factors fit into a system. Rational explanations are basically attempts to find such ordering principles which may help us understand observations of reality. One way of categorising the various theoretical traditions within sociology and other social sciences is through a 'Social Facts Paradigm' (Emile Durkheim), a 'Social Definition Paradigm' (Max Weber), and a 'Social Behaviour Paradigm' (B. F. Skinner) (Ritzer 1980). Of these, the first and third paradigm share a structural similarity with the explanatory models of the natural sciences: the systematic relations and the rational explanation pattern are normally visible only to the researcher, while they are hidden to the social agents who produce them. Thus, in the *social facts paradigm* it is objectified social entities (social 'facts' in Durkheim's own terminology) which influence each other causally or functionally[1] on a macro-level, while the actors, who operate on a micro-level, are not conscious of what is 'really' happening. In the *social behaviour paradigm* there are normally particular 'stimuli', i.e. some kind of external influence, which trigger a particular 'response' in the 'respondent'.[2] This relation between trigger and effect is not normally assumed known to anybody but the researcher.

The *social definition paradigm* (which may also be understood as the action-theoretic paradigm), is based on the assumption that social reality is rationally structured through the actions of intentional agents. The main aim of social science is to reconstruct that structure. Rationality has to do with the agents' relationship to the world, i.e. how they perceive and relate to their surroundings. There is a necessary conceptual connection between action and rationality. Actors may give their grounds for behaving in a particular way, and others may understand (or maybe not understand) those grounds. In other words, the main thesis of this paradigm is that the key to understanding social reality can be found by studying people in their capacity as agents who act according to how they define their situation. The world should be described 'from the actor's point of view'. Consequently, in order to detect a pattern in social reality, one has to understand the meaning that the agents put into their actions, i.e. what they seek to achieve by or express through their actions. In contrast to the other two paradigms, the methodical starting point is here that to explain an action, one should not look for the explanation behind the agents' back, but rather try to understand the relevant action by seeing it from the agent's own perspective.[3] The assumption that agents act rationally thus implies the belief that the intentions of the various agents coincide – more or less perfectly – with certain principles which the researcher may reveal and reconstruct.[4]

According to Habermas (1990e: 23), any meaningful human expression – be it a processed object, a social institution or a verbal utterance – can be approached from two different angles: either as a phenomenon or event that can be observed, or as an understandable objectification of meaning. Thus a tool may be described both with respect to its external characteristics, such as measure and weight, and with respect to what it is made for, i.e. what function it is meant to have. The latter involves an attempt to understand the meaning embedded in the object, and this can only be done if we can view it from the same perspective as the person who produced it. Similarly, we can measure a verbal expression in any language with regard to its volume and pitch; however, it is only utterances which are formed in a language we know that we can interpret with respect to meaning, i.e. the significance which the speaker has attached to the utterances. To understand the meaning of an expression, we must, according to Habermas, enter into a (real or imaginary) communicative relation with the sender. This is the essence of the *hermeneutic* approach, which in Habermas's opinion should be the primary method within the social sciences, and which he has given his own design through his theory of communicative action.

In our daily social coexistence we all have to strive to understand each other's meaningful expressions; however, this activity is not regarded as science. The question is hence what separates this 'everyday hermeneutics' from the alleged scientific hermeneutics, which Habermas claims should form the basis of theory formation in the social sciences and the humanities. His answer is that what these sciences must aim at is a *rational reconstruction of the know-how which is spontaneously expressed in the everyday practice of subjects who are capable of speech and action* (Habermas 1990e: 31). What characterises this practice is that it frequently follows particular rules which are often unknown to or unreflected by the actors themselves, and which therefore need to be reconstructed scientifically in order to be properly understood. Language is a good example in this respect. For thousands of years human beings have used language in accordance with intricate and complicated grammatical rules, often with a number of inflected forms for verbs, nouns, and other categories. Language was thus in use long before the emergence of a linguistic science which could reconstruct and interpret these rule systems to us. In the same way, it is not the mathematicians who have 'decided' that two plus two makes four; people have related to such rules long before mathematics was established in order to systematise mathematical rules.

In Habermas's view, the same methodological principles may be successfully adopted also in other areas of research. Just as we in our use of language follow grammatical and semantic rules, we also follow argumentation or pragmatic rules, i.e. rules that prescribe how we carry out *speech acts* (cf. the next chapter). And just as we follow certain instrumental rules when we act, in order for tasks to be carried through as efficiently as possible, we also adhere to *ethical* and *moral rules* which prescribe what behaviour is regarded as appropriate or acceptable in various situations. Indeed, Habermas even believes that it can be proved which principles we go by when we make *new* rules (cf. Chapter 4). To Habermas the point is that we within all these areas can obtain scientific cognition through a rational reconstruction of the pre-theoretical knowledge which is expressed in everyday practice, and which that practice is intuitively founded on. Since it is the rule systems behind the practice that we aim to reconstruct, we have to be able to distinguish correct behaviour from incorrect behaviour, for just as there are frequent examples of individuals who sin against grammatical rules or make mistakes when they carry out mathematical operations, we must assume that people break argumentation rules and normative rules. In the attempt to establish argumentation theory and moral theory as reconstructive disciplines, the greatest theoretical challenge may be precisely to identify the borderline between the compliance and breach of rules in these areas.

Action-oriented and behaviour-oriented researchers have often disagreed about the realism of the assumption that agents act rationally. From the perspective of behavioural theory or systems theory, we may also ask why it is so important to hold on to the notion of the rational actor. After all, it is frequently almost impossible to relate complex social realities to the specific intentions of specific actors. From the point of view of action theory, and on the basis of what has just been said about a rational reconstruction of action rules, it is easier to understand that this starting point is an important principle. If the key to understanding social phenomena is that meaning which the actors express through their actions, any understanding of the phenomenon depends on the assumption that the actors do not act randomly, but in a manner that can be identified as a rule, pattern or principle. Such principles can be described precisely as particular forms of rationality logic. The greater parts of observed social action patterns that are consistent with such principles of rational action, the closer one gets to a comprehensive understanding of these action patterns. If a certain sequence of observed actions is at odds with a particular rationality logic, it is possible that the researcher has used the 'wrong' rationality logic, and that the problem should be approached from the point of view of a different logic. Much of the theoretical debate within the action theoretical paradigm can thus be understood as a controversy about which rationality logic (or logics) is best suited as a tool for studying social reality. Briefly, the question is which concept(s) of rationality should be used in the social sciences, or how should rationality be defined within these sciences. In what follows we will explain in some more detail the various positions in this debate.

WEBER'S RATIONALITY AND ACTION MODEL

Max Weber is regarded as the founder of the paradigm referred to as action theory. The basic ambition of his research was to understand the so-called Occidental rationalisation. In specific, he wanted to find out which particular factors have produced and have continued to characterise our modern Western civilisation compared to other advanced civilisations in history. In this connection Weber found it necessary to distinguish between various types of action and rationality.

First, he establishes that 'action' should be understood as all human behaviour to which the individual attaches *subjective meaning* (Weber 1978: 4). By this he means behaviour which takes place consciously and intentionally. Weber's categorisation of actions is based on the solitary subject, an agent who acts in order to achieve an imagined goal (teleological action) (Habermas 1984: 279). The concept of *social* action, which involves several actors, is derived from the basic model of the solitary actor. A social action is one that takes the behaviour of others into consideration and is oriented towards that behaviour. The various agents involved must mutually adjust their actions to each other (Weber 1978: 4, 26). On the basis of these considerations he then introduces a distinction between four types of action, which includes social as well as non-social actions. Crucial here is the extent to which actions can be regarded as rational.

The first category is *purposive-rational* (zweckrational) action, which involves that expectations of the behaviour of external objects or individuals serve as 'conditions' or 'means' of a rational, success-oriented striving for personal ends. The next category is *value-rational* (wertrational) action. It concerns the conscious belief in the (ethical, aesthetic, religious, etc.) unconditional *intrinsic* value of a certain mode of behaviour, independently of its prospects of success. The third type is referred to by Weber as *affectual*, especially *emotional*, action. It is determined by the actor's current affections and emotional states. Finally we have the *traditional* type of action, which is behaviour controlled by ingrained habits resulting from long-term habituation (Weber 1978: 24 f.). Regarding the two latter types, viz. affectual and traditional actions, Weber points out that they lie close to the borderline of what can be referred to as meaningfully oriented action. Although many of our daily activities fit well into the description of traditional actions in particular (habitual, routinised activity), it is nevertheless clear that Weber is first and foremost interested in the purposive-rational and the value-rational types of action.

From Weber's description we understand that his concept of purposive-rational action involves agents who are fully conscious of their subjective values, and who on this basis choose their ends and the means which are necessary to achieve those ends. At the same time they must consider the consequences of various choices. As mentioned above, the value-rational form of action – of which the attitude to action of the Kantian ethic of conviction constitutes the model example (Habermas 1984: 282) – completely disregards the consequences of actions, while attention is paid to values as well as to ends and the means which are used. By contrast, the affectual type of action leaves us no control with the values which form the basis of our actions, while we may still choose our goals and means. Finally, in the traditional form of action, we control our means only, while the ends are taken to be beyond rational consideration. These relations are illustrated in Figure 2.1.

From the purposive-rational to the traditional type of action, there is, according to Weber's reasoning, a step-by-step abandonment of the actor's rational control over the action. Thus it is clear that at least in one sense it is the purposive-rational type which is Weber's rational ideal, and which constitutes the standard also for the rest of the typology. This is of central importance to his main purpose, which was, as mentioned above, to understand the specifically

Types of action in descending order of rationality	Subjective meaning covers the following elements:			
	Means	Ends	Values	Consequences
Purposive-rational	+	+	+	+
Value-rational	+	+	+	−
Affectual	+	+	−	−
Traditional	+	−	−	−

Figure 2.1 *Weber's typology of action*

Source: Habermas 1984: 282.

Western (Occidental) form of rationalisation. According to Weber, what characterises our modern Western rationalisation is precisely the frequent use of the purposive-rational action type, where we consider our ends and means, while at the same time we calculate the consequences of our actions. It is this kind of rationalisation which has given us our well-organised, functional society with high material standards. On the other hand, it is also the widespread use of this kind of rationality which Weber sees as the danger of modern society. It is this ideal which leads us into the 'iron cage of rationality'; a potentially dehumanised society where people struggle to find meaning in life. Habermas's predecessors in the tradition of critical theory, Horkheimer and Adorno (1972), also claimed that this was the inevitable consequence of the modern form of rationality, i.e. of the expansion of instrumental reason. To Habermas, by contrast, it has been a main aim to be able to show that the modern form of rationality makes it possible to realise other values as well to those which are in focus in the purposive-rational action model.

PURPOSIVE AND COMMUNICATIVE RATIONALITY

Within the action theoretical tradition, it is first and foremost Weber's emphasis on the purposive-rational type of action which has been followed up by later researchers. Moreover, it has become more cultivated. Specifically, while Weber to a certain extent emphasised that also our values and the way those values influence our priorities are subjected to rational consideration (Weber 1978: 26), later theory development concentrates on the rational choice of *means* relative to an end, which has been regarded as given independently (exogenously) of the rationality model. Nevertheless, the premises for this delimitation is still found in Weber's own work, for with the conception of the monologically and teleologically acting agent as his point of departure, it is only the effectiveness with which a means can be used to reach a certain end (or the truth of the assumptions about the relation between ends and means) which can be objectively assessed (cf. Habermas 1984: 281).

In Weber's concept of the purposive-rational type of action, the more recently developed distinction between *parametric* rationality (or in Habermas's terminology: *instrumental* rationality) and *strategic* rationality is not yet established. As claimed by Weber (1978: 24) in his definition, the attitude of the individual actor is to reduce objects as well as other people to the same level, i.e. as a 'condition' for or a 'means' to realise the goals of one's own actions. In other words, the perspective is a utilitarian one, where the purpose of the action is to maximise those values that are ranked highest by the actor, whether they are expressed by terms such as 'utility', 'self-interest', or by way of some other concept. The premise that people in the action environment can also be reduced to objects creates a basis for regarding the environment as parametric or constant. Such simplified assumptions also make it easier to arrive at clear and unambiguous rules for rational behaviour in various situations. The problem is that this very assumption will itself be irrational in many situations, since other people who are included in the action environment do not act as static objects, but as dynamic agents with their own action plans (cf. Elster 1984: 117). Therefore, this model is strictly speaking valid only in very simple social situations, where a single human agent is surrounded exclusively by material objects, for example a craftsman working on an object.

Most action environments include several participants, however, and purposive-rational action theory therefore took a long step towards greater realism when in the 1940s other strategically acting agents were introduced into the model as a dynamic element. This represented the beginning of the development of *game theory* as a separate discipline.[5] The idea that rational action is strategic choices made under the uncertainty created by the choices of other rational actors has been introduced into social science under names such as *rational choice, collective choice, public choice, social choice* and *social exchange theory*.[6] As already mentioned, the strategic version of the purposive-rational model has considerably improved the predictive power of the model; however, the increased realism has also caused some of the limitations of the model to appear. Under strategic conditions it is not always possible to identify one way of acting as better than all others; many games have no solution, or perhaps several solutions that appear to be equally good (Elster 1984: 117 ff.).

A more fundamental question is whether the category purposive-rational action may be said to give an exhaustive picture of social interaction, even under modern, Western conditions. Even though many agree with Weber that the tendency is towards a greater use of this type of action, his own attempt to define three alternative categories nevertheless shows that he never meant to say that purposive rationality reigns supreme. However, this seems to be the position of many of his successors within this tradition, at least if we judge by their use of theory and concepts. The above-mentioned schools (game theory and the various schools within choice and exchange theory) have in fact focused exclusively on the means–ends model, frequently claiming that social science can be built on this paradigm alone.

To Habermas, as well as to other social scientists, it is nevertheless clear that the purposive-rational model is not adequate when we wish to reconstruct society by way of action theory. According to Habermas, this way of interpreting the coordination of social acts has one serious limitation, viz. that rationality and subjective meaning are seen as something which arises from the consciousness of each individual, rather than from the communicative relation which is always present and which is always recreated between several individuals. If we wish to understand the social fabric which holds society together, it is not sufficient to assume that the various actors regard each other as conditions and means to one's own ends (as claimed by Weber). A coordination of actions does not take place only in those cases where the actors relate to each other as strategic opponents in a game where the aim is to obtain individual results. Games of this kind must take place within social frames which cannot themselves be explained as products of strategic games, but which have to be seen as symbolic constructs, formed through linguistically mediated communicative interaction. Examples of such social constructs are formal or informal institutions, laws, rules, norms and conventions. For such constructs to be created, the actors must be able to reach a mutual understanding of conditions in the social reality. To do this, the different participants must not regard each other as opponents, but as partners, all wanting to realise a common goal.

Action orientation / Action situation	Oriented to success	Oriented to reaching understanding
Nonsocial	Instrumental action	____
Social	Strategic action	Communicative action

Figure 2.2 *Habermas's typology of action*
Source: Habermas 1984: 285.

Habermas therefore deems it necessary to introduce the category *communicative action*, alongside the purposive-rational categories referred to as instrumental and strategic action (cf. Figure 2.2). The difference between the categories lies in their action orientation: while purposive-rational action is coordinated by an *orientation to success*, communicative action is *oriented to reaching understanding*. Success-oriented actors will act on the basis of their respective calculations as to how they can best reach their individual goals. By contrast, to understanding-oriented actors the pursuit of one's own goals is subordinate to trying to reach a common understanding with other actors with respect to what should be done in the relevant situation. The distinction between a strategic and a communicative attitude can thus be said to correspond to the distinction made by Kant in his formulation of the categorical imperative, viz. that between treating people as a means to an end, or to treat them as an end in themselves (cf. White 1988: 45).

We may ask whether it is legitimate to use the concepts 'rational' and 'rationality' to refer both to actors who interfere strategically with the external world, and to actors who try to reach an agreement through communication oriented towards understanding. Is there anything that ties these situations together, and that can hence be said to characterise the phenomenon of rationality in general? According to Habermas's communicative frame of interpretation, the same standard of rationality applies in the two cases. We may on one hand think of a businessman who carries out the success-oriented action of buying stocks in a particular company in order to increase the yield of his capital. Was this a rational thing for him to do? We must at least assume that he himself in the actual situation believed that this was a sensible move, given his objective. If he did not judge the situation in this way, we cannot say that he acted with purpose. The question is how an independent observer can judge whether the action was rational. According to Habermas, this can only be done by looking at the arguments which can be adduced for and against the claim that the action was an effective means to realise the objective. In the same vein, we may on the other hand imagine a market analyst who carries out the understanding-oriented action of putting forth an assertion that the share price of the company in which the businessman invested has entered a long-term period of decline. Judging the rationality of such an assertion involves judging the truth content of that statement. Again, this involves taking into account those arguments that can be adduced to support the claim, as well as the objections that can be raised against it.

> These reflections point in the direction of basing the rationality of an expression on its being susceptible of criticism and grounding: An expression satisfies the precondition for rationality if and insofar as it embodies fallible knowledge and therewith has a relation to the objective world (that is, a relation to the facts) and is open to objective judgement. A judgement can be objective if it is undertaken on a basis of a *transsubjective* validity claim that has the same meaning for observers and nonparticipants as it has for the acting subject himself. Truth and efficiency are claims of this kind.
>
> (Habermas 1984:9).

What is rational, then, is that which can be convincingly grounded, and, as will be shown in the next chapter, the possibility of intersubjective judgement of rationality depends on the fact that all kinds of utterances are linked to certain validity claims, which have the same meaning to everyone involved. Whether we are dealing with purposive or communicative rationality, the same rationality criterion is used: The actor must have relevant knowledge of the situation, and that knowledge must in an adequate manner be connected to what is done or said. According to Habermas (1984: 11), the difference lies in the way the relevant knowledge is used in the two cases. In the example with the stock buyer, we have instrumental usage, i.e. the agent is acting purposely in accordance with an individual action plan. To be able to say that he acts in a rational manner, we must presuppose that he has good reasons to act as he does; however, the success of his actions does not depend on the fact that others accept his reasons (but rather on whether the value of the shares increases or decreases). This is in contrast to the market analyst, whose actions are communicative and understanding-oriented, and who with his assertion appeals directly (if implicitly) to his audience to have his knowledge accepted as valid. The aim of the (speech) act is in this case to create an intersubjective agreement that things are really what they are claimed to be. If the claim is not immediately accepted as true by the receivers, the action will only be successful if the sender is prepared (and able) to give additional – and convincing – reasons that his or her contention is correct.

These two examples nevertheless represent only one dimension of the way that we relate rationally to the world, viz. as a totality of objective facts or relations. Habermas maintains that we must also consider other kinds of relations as relevant in a rationality perspective:

> In contexts of communicative action, we call someone rational not only if he is able to put forward an assertion and, when criticized, to provide grounds for it by pointing to appropriate evidence, but also if he is following an established norm and is able, when criticized, to justify his action by explicating the given situation in light of legitimate expectations. We even call someone rational if he makes known a desire or an intention, expresses a feeling or a mood, shares a secret, confesses a deed, etc., and is then able to reassure critics in regard to the revealed experience by drawing practical consequences from it and behaving consistently thereafter.
>
> (Habermas 1984: 15)

In addition to the distinction between a success-oriented, purposive-rational and an understanding-oriented, communicative attitude, we must distinguish between different kinds of communicative attitude, all depending on what kind of actor–world relation we are discussing. To illustrate the significance of different rationality perspectives, we may look at an example which contrasts a purposive-rational attitude with a normativistic, understanding-oriented one. The example takes as its starting point a problem which has engaged many theorists, especially within the rational choice school: why do (so many) citizens participate in political elections? To the individual voter, the chance that precisely his or her vote is going to tip the balance is so small that it is out of proportion with the costs of showing up at the polling station. In this perspective voting hardly seems worthwhile. Thus to the rationally calculating actor there is hardly any other option than being an abstainer.[7] Rational choice theorists have launched a number of different (though hardly any satisfactory) explanations of this fact (cf. Green and Shapiro 1994: 47 ff.), and some of them virtually admit that this is an example which shows that not *all* social behaviour *is* rational: people vote because they think that their vote is more influential than it actually is.

However, this explanation has several weaknesses. Firstly, it is not very convincing, as it does not explain how a widespread social practice such as voting can be maintained over a long period of time, if it only rests on a bluff that never seems to be revealed, viz. the bluff of the individual voter's political influence. Secondly, the phenomenon in question becomes inaccessible to analysis when it is put into the drawer of 'irrationality'. What is irrational is that which we cannot understand, and when we are told that participating in elections is an expression of irrational behaviour, it is difficult to comprehend when, how and why voters are motivated either to vote or to abstain from voting. It is therefore tempting to look for alternative explanatory models.

CONTEXTUAL RATIONALITY

By using a different standard of rationality we may perhaps shed new light on the problem in question. Perhaps the rationality connected with voting is not tied to influence on the result, but to the act of voting itself. To vote may be seen as a way of expressing an attitude (White 1988: 18): by 'doing our civic duty' we want to show that we support our democratic system, a political party or a specific policy. The action can be seen as rational because it meets those *normative expectations* which the citizens of a democratic state are faced with. By voting we wish to demonstrate, to ourselves and our fellow citizens, that we do not belong to the category of politically indifferent people. By voting or not voting we may thus manifest what kind of person we want to be, in relation to different sets of social expectations.

We have now defined a kind of rationality which largely coincides with Weber's second important action type, viz. his *value rational* action. Taking part in the election is important to us because we are bound by particular values, not because we judge it to be the best way of spending our time with a view to the maximising of interests against a general value horizon. This form of rationality may be more precisely referred to as *contextual* rationality,[8] and while Weber's value rationality was formulated on a purely monological, subjective basis, the more recent contextual rationality represents a more intersubjective turn. Rationality is here understood as norm-conformative action. Thus, an action is regarded as rational to the extent that it conforms to current normative structures in the relevant society. The meaning of an action must in other words be derived from its role in relation to the prevailing normative views of the social context of which it is a part (White 1988: 18). The concept of contextual rationality also creates a clear connection between Weber's action-theoretical and Durkheim's social-fact approach. The contextually rational agents act intentionally, just like Weber's agents, but their actions are carried out relatively to and limited by the normative guidelines they live under, as Durkheim assumed.

It seems evident that the contextual approach may help us better to understand many action situations which the strategic model leaves unexplained. In general, it gives us insight into the way in which actions may contribute to reproducing the symbolic structures of a society, and how these in turn maintain a social world which gives meaning in life to each individual. Nevertheless, this position is also fraught with certain obvious weaknesses. In the following we will mention three such problems (cf. White 1988: 20 f.). The first problem concerns the explanatory status of the theory, i.e. to what extent it succeeds in explaining actual social conditions; the other two problems have to do with the normative status of the theory, i.e. to what extent it is able to defend its analytical scheme against objections of a normative kind.

The first objection is one that is very often raised against explanatory models of a 'norm sociological' kind, namely that they have difficulty in explaining how fundamental changes can take place in a society where actions are governed by normative expectations. If the standard of correct action all the time is to adapt one's behaviour to the current normative structure, we first have to ask where those norms come from, how they arose and how they came to take their present form, and secondly, how they can be changed and developed over time. This kind of theory does not seem to be able to answer any of these questions in a convincing manner. By extension, we may raise a normative objection. What should we think of the kind of ideological power which may be exerted in such societies when particular people or groups – a priesthood, in a literal or figurative sense – control the content of the norms? Generally, there is every reason to ask where the legitimate limit of the norm-conformative type of action really goes. About a society where all actions express conformity to current norms it at least has to be said that personal freedom is badly situated. Contextualist theorists have not come up with a satisfactory answer to this problem either. A similar question may, by the way, also be aimed at the strategic model: where does the limit go for the legitimate spread of this type of action, before we find ourselves in the iron cage of rationality, as feared by Weber? This is a problem which seems to be completely disregarded by modern strategic-rational theory.

The second normative objection which needs to be raised against the contextualist theory concerns its relativistic nature. As one of the main tenets of this theory is that actions are meaningful and valid only in relation to the normative structure of the concrete society in which they take place, it follows that there is no supra-local or universal standard against which we can measure these actions. To put small children out to the wolves, to burn witches or hang heretics or even try to extinguish a whole people in gas chambers, these are all actions which are irreproachable if they are in agreement with the norms and laws of the society in question. There will in fact be no basis for a debate about what is acceptable or unacceptable in such norms, as, according to contextualist theory, these norms themselves represent the highest premise of evaluation.

One of the main aims of Habermas's concept of communicative action is to overcome all the weaknesses of both the contextual and the strategic rationality models which we have just discussed. In the concept of communicative action both these types of rationality are, however, included as important elements.

HABERMAS'S THREE WORLDS

Habermas's general point is that the relations between actors and their environment are more complex than what has been captured by on the one hand a purposive-rational – and thus in an epistemological sense *positivist* – approach, and on the other hand by a contextualist-interpretative – and thus in an epistemological sense *hermeneutic* – approach. He claims that we must rather introduce a concept of rationality which is complex enough to distinguish between three different forms of reality experience, or three spheres of validity. Using Karl Popper's terminology, he refers to them as three *worlds*: the objective, the social and the subjective world (cf. Habermas 1984: 85–94).

In the *objective world* the actor relates to his environment as existing states of affairs or facts, either in their present form or in the form they may be given through manipulative intervention. To this world belongs a teleological or purposive-rational model of action, which means that actions in relation to this world are intentional interventions, carried out to realise a desired state of affairs. Action rationality in this case consists in a maximally effective employment of means in order to reach clearly defined goals. This normally involves making the optimal choice between several possible courses of action. The objective world does not contain only material objects as well as the relations between these (for example natural laws) and between the actor and the objects. It may also comprise other agents and their action plans (strategies), in addition to the agent's own action plans. In this case we are dealing with strategic action. The point is that the objective world includes everything to which the agent takes an objectifying attitude. The starting point is thus the monologically acting agent, i.e. an agent who lays his or her action plans without prior mutual coordination with other agents.

Instead of an action-oriented approach, the actor may take a purely cognising attitude to the objective world. The relation between actor and environment is thus of a *cognitive* kind; instead of effectiveness the criterion of rationality is the epistemological requirement that the actor's understanding of the objective states of affairs is true, i.e. that it corresponds to the factual situation.

By contrast, the *social world* represents a normative context which establishes which forms of interaction belong to the totality of legitimate interpersonal relations. In this case the actors are members of a social group, and their actions are oriented towards some shared values. In those situations in which a particular norm applies, the individual agent will through his actions either adhere to or break the norm. To the extent that a set of norms is valid to the members of a group, they express an existing agreement that they have the right to expect from each other that they in particular situations will carry out prescribed actions or abstain from carrying out forbidden actions. To adhere to a norm thus involves fulfilling a generalised behavioural expectation.

There may be two reasons why we follow a norm. On the one hand we may choose to obey the (legal) norm not to exceed the 50 mph speed limit on a stretch of road where we know that there are automatic speed checks. We may perhaps do this only to avoid getting fined, even if we personally think that the speed limit in the relevant area should have been higher, or even if we have no personal opinion as to how fast it is safe to drive on that particular stretch of the road. At any rate, in this case we relate to the speed limit as a fact which we choose to respect, i.e. as a state of affairs in the objective world. Most of us relate differently to the norm (also a legal statute) that we should not take somebody's life. Even if we imagine a situation where killing somebody did no longer send us to prison, there is reason to assume that most members of society would abstain from doing it, simply because it conflicts with some fundamental values that are shared by the large majority. Murder is a kind of behaviour which we are not willing to accept, from ourselves or from others; we regard it as an atrocious crime. Thus, the norm not to kill may be said to have *moral validity* to us, in addition to its legal validity. We believe that society rightly expects us to comply with it. These are the kind of relations which constitute the social world: expectations to our behaviour which are maintained because the members of the group personally accept their moral-practical validity. This means that the norms in question are of an imperative or 'should' character to the members.

The distinction just discussed also shows that while a teleologically acting agent only has to relate to one world, viz. the objective world, a norm-following agent needs to take two worlds into account – the objective and the social world. This means that a socially competent agent must be able to distinguish between the factual and normative elements of an action situation, i.e. to distinguish between having to relate to 'circumstances' and having to relate to values (so that we do not treat people as things and vice versa). It is nevertheless clear that the norm-following agent orients his actions primarily in relation to the social world.

Two things can be tested with respect to normative validity. On the one hand, we may ask if an agent's motives and actions are in accordance or at odds with the prevailing norms. On the other hand, we may ask whether these prevailing norms really deserve to be recognised as valid norms. Traditionally, many schools (from Max Weber via Talcott Parsons to Peter Winch and other 'contextualists') have maintained that the only way to test this latter condition rationally is to hold a derived or subordinate norm up against a more fundamental norm of a society, and then examine if the two are consistent or not. However, the validity of these fundamental norms of a society or culture cannot themselves be tested against some more fundamental principle. This position is referred to as ethical *non-cognitivism* and involves that normative values are not based on a truth content and can hence not be tested by way of reason. Habermas nevertheless wants to demonstrate that actors also have intuitive access to certain universal principles, against which the validity of all context-dependent norms can be tested. His 'test' is derived from that established by Kant in his categorical imperative: is a specific norm an expression of universalisable interests? In other words, can the actors without contradiction wish the norm to be made into a general law? According to Habermas, this type of test points to the rational core which moral-practical problems also possess. It is a central, but controversial element of communicative action theory. The topic will be discussed in more detail in Chapter 4.

The *subjective world* is the sphere of inner, personal experience – intentions, thoughts, attitudes, wishes, feelings, etc. – to which each subject has a privileged access. This sphere is made accessible when an actor meets 'the others' as an audience and through dramaturgical action gives them a picture of his/her subjectivity: a self-presentation.[9] The form of this dramaturgical type of action is expressive utterances. The model is obviously taken from the world of theatre, with two main differences. On the one hand, the 'actors' do not primarily relate to an 'external', acquired part; rather, they play their own part of their own life, expressing their own selves. On the other hand, the agents constantly switch between being an actor and being the audience. However, it may vary considerably to what extent we actually express ourselves in such situations, and to what extent we are influenced by the environment. To put it differently, it may vary to what degree we reveal the feelings, wishes and opinions that we really have, or if we mainly express those inner experiences that we wish our audience to believe that we have. Precisely this is the central question in connection with the dramaturgical action type and an objective approach to the subjective world: do the actors really say what they feel/want, etc., or is it all a deceit? There is also a third possibility, viz. that actors have become the victim of a self-deceit. The persons in question may actually believe that those feelings, wishes and attitudes which they express are genuinely personal experiences and are well founded. However, by penetrating deeper into their own personality, sometimes with the help of others, they may gain new insight and come to change their opinions. For example, we may in certain situations unconsciously suppress our actual feelings towards specific persons, or an advertisement may cause us to believe that we have a strong need for a product which we, when we think about it, hardly need at all. We may also, through one-sided political propaganda, come to take up attitudes which we, upon closer consideration, conclude that we cannot defend.

With respect to the first aspect, i.e. whether the actors express their real opinions or try to deceive their audiences, the requirement which has to be met for this type of utterance to be regarded as valid is that it represents a truthful expression of the actors' inner experiences. In the other case, i.e. whether the agents have fallen victim to self-deceit or are able to express genuinely personal experiences, there is an authenticity requirement, i.e. the utterances must be expressions of the real self.

We may ask whether it is at all possible for other people to judge either truthfulness or authenticity. It is clear that if there is no such possibility, we cannot judge the rationality of the dramaturgical type of action. However, Habermas maintains that there are certain options also in this area. With regard to the truthfulness requirement, we should watch out for inconsistencies, either between different things a person says, or between what the person says and does. The authenticity claim is more difficult to handle in every way. First and foremost, it raises a puzzle with political undertones: who else than I should be allowed to judge what my true self is? Within the tradition of liberalism one has therefore always on principle claimed that only the individual actor can be the judge of her own interests, wishes, opinions, etc., while more authoritarian schools have not been afraid to maintain that the 'people' must be given the 'right' opinions on these matters from outside (for example from Lenin's cadre party). The latter position may well lead to unacceptable forms of paternalism.

On the other hand, it is difficult to deny the fact that we all under certain circumstances may have misconceptions which we in some cases may need the help of others to overcome (cf. Taylor 1985b). To Habermas the authenticity requirement seems to be inspired by Sigmund Freud's psychoanalytical method, where a patient through conversations with a therapist comes to gain greater insight into his own psyche (cf. Habermas 1971b). This model example is referred to by Habermas as a *therapeutic discourse*. An actor's authenticity or inauthenticity in the presentation of inner experiences is thus not something others can judge about independently of the person in question, but something that the actor in the end him or herself must bring to clarity – perhaps with the help of others.

If we are dealing with an actor who, through a conscious form of dramaturgy, tries to manipulate an audience into believing that (s)he has other attitudes/feelings etc. than the actual ones, this type of action belongs in the grey zone between action oriented to success and action oriented to reaching understanding, according to Habermas. It is related to the success-oriented type insofar as the actor uses a strategy to which the audience in a certain sense falls victim. On the other hand, its understanding-oriented character consists in the fact that the actor cannot openly show that his/her message is a strategy. On the contrary, the audience has to be made to interpret it as a genuine expression of something which the actor represents. This demands an understanding-oriented attitude for both parties, even if it happens under false premises.

Dramaturgically acting agents must relate to at least two worlds, viz. the inner (subjective) and the outer world, where in the latter one does not necessarily distinguish between an objective and a social world. The subjective world is nevertheless the primary world in relation to this type of action.

We hence see an interesting difference between the action models of Weber and Habermas. To Weber the purposive action attitude, which he saw as ideal-typical of the modern culture, is the most complex one, in that it allows the actor to take into account her own values, ends and means, as well as the consequences of different choices of action. To Habermas, by contrast, the success-oriented action attitude is the least complex, as it is only capable of incorporating objectified states of affair. The teleologically acting agent is only able to relate to one world (the objective world), while the norm-conformatively and the expressively acting agent both have to relate to at least two worlds. Thus, the rationalisation which is possible within the success-oriented paradigm is, according to Habermas, a very one-sided form of rationalisation, which disregards fundamental and dynamic developmental processes in society. However, Habermas is not satisfied with such concepts of action which include two of the three worlds either. He finds that to be adequate, the social sciences must have at their disposal a theory which includes all three worlds. This is what he wants to demonstrate by explicating his communicative action model, which is the topic of the next chapter. Figure 2.3 summarises some main features of the three worlds.

Characteristics / World concept	Content	Actor attitudes	Actor–world relations	Criteria of rationality	Action orientation
Objective	existing states of affairs	objectivating	cognitive	truth	oriented to reaching understanding
			teleological	effectiveness	oriented to success
Social	norm-guided relations	norm-conformative	norm-regulated	rightness	oriented to reaching understanding
Subjective	inner experiences	expressive	dramaturgical	truthfulness/authenticity	oriented to reaching understanding

Figure 2.3 *Characteristics of Habermas's three worlds*

CONCLUSION

There is no general agreement within the social sciences about which presuppositions can be made regarding human rationality, or what systematic place agents' actions should have in social analysis. The school which emphasises these two concepts the most is the so-called interpretative or action-theoretical social science, which is founded on Max Weber's basic position that sociology must try to understand social relations by taking the perspective of the acting agents. Within the action-theoretical paradigm, there is disagreement between those who, like Weber, primarily regard human actions as motivated by purposive-rational calculations, and those who for example interpret these actions as responses to those norms and values which are prevailing in the agent's social environment or context. Habermas wants to create a meaning-interpretative social science, which is based on a rational reconstruction of that know-how which is expressed through the everyday practice of subjects who are competent of speaking and acting. The criterion of rationality is if something can be defended by way of good reasons. This leads him in the direction of a model which is able to capture not only the ends–means relation, but also other aspects of the rationality of action. Reality is therefore divided into three 'worlds' or validity spheres: the *objective* world, which consists of existing states of affairs or facts; the *social* world, which consists of our norm-guided relations to other people, and the *subjective* world, which consists of our inner experiences, to which we have privileged access. On the basis of this multi-dimensional concept of rationality, he proceeds to explicate a concept of communicative action, at the same time as he explains the conditions under which agents are able to coordinate their actions through mutual understanding and agreement.

Notes

1. Cf. the so-called *structural functionalist* and *systems theoretical* schools.

2. The concept of *actor* would be ill-placed within this paradigm, as it implies the idea of self-determined actions, which, strictly speaking, does not belong here.

3. A (normative) advantage of such an approach is that it becomes less alienating and potentially more liberating in relation to the individuals who are the objects of study of the social sciences. Explanations can more easily be communicated back to the objects of study, who can compare them to their own intuitive understanding. They may perhaps use this knowledge to understand their own situation better, and hence perhaps also act in order to change that situation.

4. The distinction between behaviour-theoretical and action-theoretical orientations is nevertheless not very clear in practice. Particularly during the past 40–50 years, many schools which are premised on (Weberian, purposive-rational) action theory have been strongly influenced by behavioural theory. There has been a 'behavioural revolution' within the social sciences (Almond 1990). One example is Herbert Simon's (1976) revision of the classical micro-economic rationality model, which has been applied to the study of modern organisations. His conclusion was that the ideal rationality presuppositions of the model were not met in real organisational behaviour. These presuppositions thus had to be modified through the introduction of the concept of *bounded rationality*. Another way of meeting the demand of more 'realistic' analyses has been to keep the formal rationality presuppositions of the model, while in practice one has deviated from the requirement that the point of departure should be the 'actor's point of view'. This has been a common solution e.g. within the rational choice school. Instead of offering explanations which are based on those justifications that the actors involved would actually have given, so-called 'as if' explanations are offered. This means that an observed social pattern is reconstructed *as if* the agents had acted on the basis of motivations which it is intuitively unlikely that they may have had.

5. John von Neumann is regarded as the leading pioneer in this field (see Neumann and Morgenstern 1944).

6. Basic studies within this tradition are, among others, Arrow 1963; Downs 1957; Black 1958; Buchanan and Tullock 1962; Riker 1962; Blau 1964; Olson 1965, and Coleman 1974.

7. This is a conclusion which may, with some reservations, be derived from Anthony Down's (1957) classical discussion of 'the paradox of voter turnout'. By contrast, on the basis of strict game theoretical premises, it is just as rational to vote as to abstain from voting; the model has no equilibrium point, the game no solution. This is explained by the fact that game theoretical models build on the formal presupposition that all actors are equally rational. Consequently, if we accept that one actor arrives at a 'clever' solution (such as staying at home on election day), one has to presuppose that everyone else manages to do that as well. However, in that situation the paradox arises that if everybody abstains from voting because they expect to be just one more voter without any influence, it will all of a sudden be very rational to be the one who actually gives his or her vote, and who is thus able to determine the outcome of the election all alone. In practice (given the psychological 'inertia'

we must generally expect in social behaviour) this is a rather unrealistic pre-supposition. He/she who on the day of election is considering whether it will 'pay' to vote, may usually take it for granted that the turnout rate is going to be approximately the same as in the previous election (which means that his/her vote is not likely to tip the scale).

8. It is primarily Peter Winch that has given this model its content and made it relevant to the social sciences (see Winch 1958, 1964).

9. This concept and a great deal of the theory behind it was first developed by the sociologist Erving Goffman (1959).

CHAPTER 3

The communicative concept of action

INTRODUCTION

The communicative perspective represents a break with a century-long tradition which has tried to derive the premises for human rationality from the subject's mental activity or thought processes. This *consciousness-philosophical* paradigm has its origins in René Descartes's (1596–1650) epistemology, where introspection into (i.e. 'inner observation of') the conscious life of the individual was made the basis of our knowledge of human rational capacity. There are still many scientific approaches which implicitly or explicitly build on this interpretative framework; however, from the late 1800s and throughout the 1900s there have been several parallel movements in the direction of what we may refer to as a *communication theoretical paradigm*. Here the aim has been to reach an understanding of the rationality problem by moving the focus away from the subject's consciousness and on to the intersubjectivity which is formed between several persons who participate in a communicative relationship. Among other things, this change of perspective has made an extension of the rationality aspect possible: from including only questions relating to objective states of affair, it now also includes normative and expressive conditions.

We can distinguish three main roots of Habermas's communicative theory of action. One is the *analytical philosophy of language*. It is founded on Ludwig Wittgenstein's (1889–1951) concept of *language game*, and is further developed by John L. Austin (1911–60) and John R. Searle (1932—), among others, through the development of *speech act theory*. The second influence is the so-called *phenomenological* tradition, represented by the philosopher Edmund Husserl (1859–1938) and his student, the sociologist Alfred Schütz (1899–1959). They developed the theory of a socially shared *lifeworld* ('Lebenswelt') as a basis for human knowledge. The third influence is a specifically American tradition, represented first and foremost by the philosopher Charles Sanders Peirce (1839–1914), the founder of the school called *pragmatism*, and the social psychologist George Herbert Mead (1863–1931). Mead (inspired by Peirce) founded *symbolic interactionism*, which emphasises the uniqueness of the human linguistic capability, and how language structures the way in which we relate to the world. These three elements of Habermas's theory will be discussed in the present chapter. However, first we give a presentation of some fundamental concepts of the theory.

FORMAL PRAGMATICS AND VALIDITY CLAIMS

The concept of *communicative action* refers to at least two subjects who are capable of speech and action, and who establish (by verbal or extra-verbal means) an interpersonal relation. They try to achieve a mutual understanding of a specific action situation, in order to be able to coordinate their action plans and thus their actions. This is done by means of linguistic communication. In the course of the communicative process, both have the opportunity to present their respective interpretations of the situation, as the aim is to negotiate common definitions of the situation, i.e. a demonstration that they understand things in the same way (Habermas 1984: 86). The objects of this interpretation process, i.e. the issues which they are negotiating, will always be conditions in the objective, social or subjective world. The respective interpretations of things belonging to the three worlds will have to be presented as criticisable utterances, i.e. utterances which the other participants in the interaction can either accept as valid without reservation or deny the validity of. If the participants can establish that their starting points are different, i.e. that they do not have the same definition of the situation they are faced with, they will try to influence one another to adjust their interpretations by presenting new criticisable utterances. The goal is all the time to arrive at a definition of the situation which is shared by everyone and which they thus can answer for personally.

This is the basic tenet of what Habermas refers to as *formal pragmatics*. In brief, it is a theory about how certain formal qualities of language and the relations which are established when we use it implicitly have an action coordinating and thus a socially coordinating function. The effect comes about because aspects of our language use in conversations rationally commit the actors to behave in a particular manner. The starting point for the argumentation is as follows: in order for a normal conversation to be perceived as meaningful, the utterances must have certain built-in validity claims. This means that by expressing a concrete meaning content, the speaker also implicitly puts forth certain claims regarding the status of what is said, and that the audience, in order to take the utterance seriously, implicitly expects that these claims are put forth. More precisely, there are three different validity claims which Habermas claims are implicit in speech acts:

a) that the statement is *true*;

b) that the speech act is *right* in relation to the current normative context; and

c) that the speaker's manifest intention is *meant* as it is expressed.

(Habermas 1984: 99)

The three validity claims thus coincide with the three rationality criteria that are connected to the objective, the social and the subjective world respectively, viz. objective truth, normative rightness and subjective truthfulness. Although all three claims play a role in connection with all types of utterances, one of them will be dominant or more prominent in connection with some types of sentence, depending on which world the content is primarily related to (Habermas 1984: 308). To take an example, imagine a skipper on a fishing vessel who one morning says to his crew: 'The weather is too bad to draw the nets today.' By saying this in that particular situation, we must assume that he implicitly means three things in addition to the statement itself, namely:

a) 'What I am saying is true!' (the weather is [too] bad);

b) 'It is legitimate for me to say this!' (as a skipper and experienced fisherman I have both the authority and knowledge to judge whether we should go out to sea); and

c) 'I mean what I say!' (it is really my judgement that we cannot draw the nets since the weather is so bad).

The skipper's definition of the situation (that the weather is too bad for the nets to be drawn) may be immediately accepted by the rest of the crew, either because they themselves make the same judgement, or because they trust that the skipper with his long experience makes the right judgement. However, it is also possible that one of the crew does *not* without reservation accept the skipper's definition of the situation. He may for example oppose it with the following statement: 'It is just a strong breeze; it is quite possible to draw the nets today!'[1] To the extent that this utterance is to be taken seriously as well, the same three validity claims must implicitly be linked to it. It is reasonable to expect that the skipper, faced with this challenge, will attempt to meet the validity claims implied in his utterance, and which now have been questioned. He may, for example, try to refer to the fact that the weather conditions are much worse at the fishing ground than in the harbour where they are at the moment, that the wind is expected to increase during the day, etc. In this way they may continue their discussion until they agree on a common understanding of the situation, or until the skipper uses his authority to overrule all objections and make the final decision himself.

According to Habermas, it is exactly these validity claims, which are implicit in the typical speech act, as well as the speaker's commitment to meet them with arguments which gives language its rational action coordinating power. Since we in all situations where we use language makes these claims that the utterances are valid, the basis is laid for potential bonds between speaker and hearer which may commit both parties rationally. 'Silence gives consent', is a common expression. In this lies the expectation that the individual who has had the opportunity to raise objections against a statement without doing it, in reality has accepted the speaker's validity claims and consequently will behave accordingly. Thus it is presupposed that speaker and hearer agree on the definition of the situation, and that this mutual understanding forms the basis for a coordination of their actions. Normal, everyday language use is geared to achieving such common definitions of the situation. If such agreement is not present from the start, the rational way of obtaining it is to give decisive weight to the objective power of conviction in the various arguments. In other words, the process must be based on open argumentation, without the use of external or concealed forms of coercion. However, even if the goal may be stable and clear agreement as a basis for the coordination of action, that goal is not necessarily obtained. According to Habermas (1984: 100 f.), this is rather the exception in the communicative practice of everyday life; an ideal which functions as a starting point to and a guiding line in the communicative process, but it is hardly ever fully realised (cf. Hohengarten 1992: xi). Actual communication processes are rather characterised by unclear and weak definitions of situations, which have to be reinterpreted constantly. The common understanding which has been obtained is frequently of a highly temporary character; it is threatened both by pure misunderstandings and by power-based imperatives. Yet we are constantly compelled to make new efforts in order to maintain this agreement, to be able to solve the small and great challenges we are constantly faced with as social beings.

SPEECH ACTS

It has been argued that Habermas strictly speaking only *presumes* that validity claims exist, but that he does not argue for it in a convincing way (cf. Johnson 1993: 76). However, with respect to theories at this level of abstraction, we may question what type of 'evidence' is possible. The strongest form of 'evidence' in this case is probably the open, transcendental philosophical[2] challenge to the critics and the sceptics: are you capable of reconstructing human language use and its social role in a logically consistent manner *without* presupposing that such validity claims exist? Until this has been done in a convincing manner, one may at least maintain that there is a presumptive basis for accepting Habermas's version.

There have also been objections to Habermas's distinction between an attitude oriented to reaching understanding, which is linked to communication, and an attitude oriented to success, which is linked to instrumental and strategic action. For example, Jon Elster (1992), has emphasised that our use of communication may actually in many cases be strategically motivated; language becomes a means to reach the (often selfish) goals which we have set ourselves beforehand. Among other things, we may make a proposal because it serves our own narrow interests; however, we may well justify it by means of arguments that have a general and impartial character and which are hence likely to gain support from wide groups. Do we not frequently use language in this and similar ways in order to get the results we want? If so, where does the distinction go between the orientation to reaching understanding and the orientation to success?

In justifying this distinction, Habermas primarily builds on the development of the so-called *speech act theory* within (primarily British) analytical philosophy. The theory was founded by John L. Austin (1962) and further developed by John R. Searle (1969). It represented a new way of regarding linguistic utterances. Earlier the general assumption was that action is one thing, whereas speech primarily serves to describe actions and other real phenomena. However, Austin maintained that speech very often *is* action. By this he meant that the use of linguistic utterances is a fundamental element in human interaction, and that social conditions are to a great extent formed and transformed through the use of language. This happens when our language use is characterised by a so-called *performative* attitude, as when we say 'I promise you to come tomorrow.' When we make such a statement, we have not only *said* that we promise something, we have also carried out the (symbolic) *act* it is to make a promise. A similar act is performed by a clergyman who at the baptismal font says: 'I baptise thee in the name of the Father and of the Son and of the Holy Ghost' and with these words carries out the act of christening someone. Hence, our utterances do not exclusively or primarily serve to describe events or actions; they themselves become actions that bind us, as they have consequences, like other types of action.

Austin's main point is that a linguistic utterance has several aspects and must therefore be analysed on several levels, and that we by making an utterance in fact perform several actions simultaneously. In order to describe the different levels of speech acts, Austin distinguishes between *locutionary, illocutionary* and *perlocutionary* speech acts. A *locutionary* action is simply expressing states of affairs – particular words with a particular meaning. The action aspect lies in the fact that something is being said. By contrast, an *illocutionary* action is an action which we carry out in expressing particular words or utterances, such as making a request, a contention, an ascertainment, a promise, a warning, an order etc. Finally, a *perlocutionary* action is what we do through or by making an utterance. Through an utterance we may, for example, insult, please, irritate, persuade or reassure someone in regard to something, or we may stimulate someone to do something or prevent them from doing it. The perlocutionary aspect of the speech act is hence the effect it has on the hearer, and thus also on some condition of the external world.

For our purposes it is primarily the relation between the illocutionary and the perlocutionary aspect of speech acts which is of interest, since this distinction corresponds to Habermas's distinction between a communicative, understanding-oriented, and a teleological, success-oriented use of language. The illocutionary aim of a speaker is always and only to get the hearer(s) to understand the meaning of what is said. This means on the one hand to understand the literal (locutionary) content of the utterance, and on the other to understand it as a particular type of symbolic action – a congratulation, a request, an explanation, a warning, a command, etc. This is the manifest content of the speech act, and in order to succeed in making the listener(s) understand that content, the speaker must be able to express it as clearly as possible according to established conventions of language use.

By contrast, the perlocutionary aim of the speaker is to bring about a concrete language-external result, by way of language. To achieve this, the speaker must to a varying extent also take into account the illocutionary aspect. Most speech acts have both illocutionary and perlocutionary effects. Their perlocutionary effects can be more or less intentional on the part of the speaker. The perlocutionary aims can be obvious or veiled, and they can be more or less dominant in relation to the illocutionary aims (Habermas 1998g: 330). Examples of situations where the illocutionary aspects are dominant are when a request is complied with because it is regarded as valid or reasonable by the addressee, or when we do something we have promised to do because we feel bound by our promise. Here the perlocutionary effects are dependent on a mutual agreement between speaker and hearer about what kind of behaviour it is reasonable to expect.

It is quite a different matter if we should say to another person: 'You are behaving like a swine.' Here it is the speaker's perlocutionary aim to insult or reproach the other which has become dominant. To be sure, the perlocutionary effect is also in this case dependent on the fact that the addressee is able to understand the utterance at the illocutionary level, i.e. as an insult or reproach. However, the relevant effect does not rest on a mutual understanding in a deeper sense: the addressee does not have to look at himself as a swine in order to feel the unpleasantness in knowing that this is the way the speaker sees him. The latter example thus belongs to the category of *perlocutions*, which is a class of speech acts where the success-oriented, perlocutionary objectives of the speaker are dominant in relation to the understanding-oriented, illocutionary aims (Habermas 1998g: 332). Hence, perlocutions are prototypes of strategic language use: the speaker can one-sidedly pursue his own goals, even if the hearer does not acknowledge his terms as valid. One type of speech act which may function as a perlocution is threats, which consist of an announcement of a conditional negative sanction, such as: 'If the balance due to us is not paid immediately, there will be a debt collection.' In such cases the illocutionary aim of the speech act, i.e. to inform the debtor about what might happen, can most of the times be said to be subordinate to the perlocutionary objective, which is to 'scare' the debtor into paying the amount (s)he owes.

As pointed out by Elster, among others, it is important to be aware that communication may also be used on the basis of an orientation to success. However, what we may primarily learn from speech act theory is that there exists a different form of language use, which is genuinely oriented to reaching understanding. This understanding-oriented way of using language is logically primary to success-oriented language use, since it is only when we have learnt to master the illocutionary side of language, and are thus able to communicate a message to others, that we may use language in a success-oriented way. Hence, we normally do not have the choice between using language in a success-oriented *or* in an understanding-oriented manner, as nothing can replace the understanding-oriented attitude.

STRONG AND WEAK COMMUNICATIVE ACTION

While Habermas was previously (cf. Habermas 1984) inclined to emphasise strategic and communicative use of language as two clearly distinct and exhaustive categories, he has more recently (cf. Habermas 1998g) come to the conclusion that there are intermediate categories as well, which combine the success-oriented and the communicative attitude into a more complex picture. As mentioned before, the starting point of the concept of communicative action is that actors attempt to come to an agreement about the definition of a situation, i.e. to reach a mutual understanding of how a given situation should be described. It has been taken for granted that there is a close relationship between the concepts of agreement and understanding, in the sense that both involve seeing things the same way. Indeed, understanding presupposes agreement to some extent. However, according to Habermas (1998g: 320 f.), it is quite possible to understand each other's intentions without necessarily sharing the premises of these intentions; thus, one has to distinguish between *Verständigung* and *Einverständnis*. The latter indicates an agreement or consensus which arises when actors can accept a validity claim for the same reasons. An understanding in a more narrow sense is what we have when one actor is able to see that another actor, *on the basis of her specific preferences* and under given circumstances, may have good reasons to act in a particular way, without the former actor, on the basis of *his* own preferences, wanting to make those reasons his own. Consequently, we may distinguish between actor-independent and actor-relative justifications of action, where the former category provides a basis for a stronger form of co-understanding than does the latter. There is also a distinction as to what types of validity claim are activated in the two cases. The only requirements for a simple understanding to arise are that a hearer believes that the speaker (a) has a realistic *understanding* of reality, and (b) actually expresses his true beliefs and opinions; in other words, he must meet the claims of truth and truthfulness. These are the conditions that have to be met for the actors to be able to interact in a success-oriented and strategic manner, while at the same time they pursue understanding-oriented, illocutionary goals (i.e. a different form of language use than the perlocutions that we just discussed). In order to bring about *agreement* it is, in addition to truth and truthfulness, also required that the actors are able to view the normative rightness of the action in the same way. Thus, the action is not only to be understood as (purposive) rational from the actor's subjective perspective, but as normatively valid from an intersubjective perspective as well.

On this background Habermas (1998g) makes a distinction between two versions of communicative action, viz. communicative action in a strong and a weak sense (cf. Figure 3.1). By communicative action in a *strong* sense, Habermas means action which is coordinated through the actors' agreement about the basis for the cooperation. This means that they let their will be bound by intersubjectively shared value orientations, which are set to be superior to private preferences in the choice of goals. They accept validity claims on the basis of corresponding, actor-independent reasons. By contrast, what characterises the *weak* form of communicative action is that the actors merely recognise and understand each other's respective, actor-relative reasons for acting in a particular way. In order to illustrate the implications of this distinction, we need to look at some examples. We may for example imagine an actor (A) who says:

'I'm going to leave tomorrow.'

This is not meant as anything else than a one-sided announcement of A's action plans, and thus it cannot be regarded as an attempt to bring about a consensus

Action type	Dominant speech act mode	Validity claims raised concerning . . .			Orientation of language use	Form of interaction made possible
		Truth	Rightness	Truth-fulness		
perlocutions	perlocutionary	no	no	no	oriented toward success	strategic
'weak' communicative action	illocutionary	yes	no	yes	oriented toward reaching under-standing	conditionally strategic
'strong' communicative action	illocutionary	yes	yes	yes	oriented toward agreement	communi-cative

Figure 3.1 *Properties of three types of linguistically mediated interaction*

with other actors. The person who wants to make up his mind regarding the illocutionary content of the utterance in its literal interpretation needs to consider two questions:

(1) Is it *possible* for actor A to realise such an intention? In other words, the question is if A has a rational view of the objective world, and if the utterance thus meets the truth requirement. If A is on an isolated island that does not have any boat calls until two days later, or serves a life sentence in an escape-proof prison, there is reason to doubt that the statement is an expression of a rational purpose. Consequently, one may choose *not* to take it seriously.

(2) Is it reasonable to think that this is A's true intention? The problem, which must be judged in relation to the relevant context, is whether A lets us take part in his real action plans, or if the statement is meant as a joke or as a consciously misleading manoeuvre. In other words, is it a truthful expression of the agent's subjective world?

Another actor (B) makes the following statement:

'Give me the money!'

This statement is not consensus-oriented either, but has the form of an imperative. Yet it also has an illocutionary content which the addressee can and must give a critical examination. In principle it is the same two types of questions that have to be asked here as in the previous example:

(1) Does B have any reason to believe that I should comply with such a demand? If it is a robbery situation, if B is armed or if he is tall and strong, it is obvious that such reasons may exist. On its own given terms, one may then say that B's statement reflects a realistic and rational attitude to the objective environment, and that B thus seems to meet the truth requirement. Should B, however, attempt to get money from me without having any sanctions to enforce his claim, the statement most likely demonstrates an irrational attitude to the objective realities. The action plans are based on insufficient facts, and the implicit truth premise of the utterance has not been met.

(2) Is B really interested in getting money from me? Is B sincerely expressing his intentions, or is the statement meant as a joke? If B is a child playing a robber, there is reason to take it as a joke; if on the contrary, B *is* a robber, the utterance should definitely be taken seriously.

Both these utterances are, then, examples of what Habermas referred to as communicative action of the weak type, where only the requirements of truth and truthfulness, and not the requirement of rightness apply. What the addressee must take a position to in these situations, is whether it from the perspective of the speaker may be good reasons for leaving the next day or demanding money from the addressee, respectively. However, it is also possible to imagine a situation where an addressee can respond to these two utterances by asking another type of question:

(1) Is it *right* for A to leave tomorrow? This problem may for example arise if A has promised to visit his old parents for a whole week during his summer vacation, but decides to leave after only two days.

(2) Does B have a *legitimate right* to demand money from me? Such a question may arise for example if B is an old friend of the addressee who asks for a 'loan' in return for previous services.

In both cases the question arises on the background of the speakers' assumed obligations in relation to the same norm and value foundation which the addressees have. In other words, the presumption is a shared social world of interpersonal relations, to which it is questionable whether the speakers relate in an adequate way. In this case we have communicative action of the strong type, where it is presupposed that a speaker implicitly claims his utterance to meet also the prevailing standards of normative rightness, not only of truth and truthfulness. Speaker and hearer should then be able to assess the utterance on the basis of the same premises and use the same arguments to justify its validity (or lack of such). This requires that they do not only understand each other's perspectives, but that they in fact also agree about a common perspective – a common definition of the situation – on the basis of which the utterance can be judged.

As illustrated by our examples, the literal content of the utterance does not have to be different depending on whether it is included in a communicative action of the weak or the strong type. Whether it is of the former or the latter type is fully dependent on the context in which it is uttered. If A is a guest at a hotel who is informing the staff about her plans to leave, it would normally not be natural to question her decision from a normative point of view. However, if A's utterance falls in a family context, this type of question seems quite reasonable. Likewise, if B is an armed robber, there is no reason to think that the order is pronounced as an utterance which claims legitimacy, or which in that particular situation should be evaluated from that perspective. It must be understood as a simple, power-based imperative. If B is an old friend, however, the utterance may be interpreted as a demand for just treatment. The order may then be understood as a 'normatively authorised' request.

This discussion consequently shows that it is not possible to establish a simple dichotomy between success-oriented use of language, which is included in strategic interaction, and language use oriented to reaching understanding, which is included in communicative interaction.[3] There is also a mixed type, which is neither fully strategic nor exclusively designed to create a basis for agreement. In this weak form of communicative action, the speaker does not raise any normative validity claim in connection with her utterance. The parties only need to have one normative expectation to each other, viz. that their utterances are not meant to mislead or deceive the other party, i.e. that both abstain from turning the speech acts themselves into strategic actions (cf. Habermas 1998g: 327). If language is used as a means in strategic games, communication soon becomes impossible and meaningless. If we constantly lie or are insincere in order to gain short-term strategic advantages over our opponents, we must assume that the opponents realise this and cease to attach any importance to what is said.[4] In certain situations characterised by intense tension and suspicion, such as the Cuban missile crisis in 1962, this condition may be a critical factor. The Americans were facing the difficulties of communicating convincingly to the Russians that they really intended to use the military means which they *said* they were going to use, and that their statements were not empty threats. In most other political situations which involve strategic action, this problem does not become as acute as in this case, as one does not behave unconditionally strategically, but strategically within certain institutional and normative frames that guarantee a basis for true communication.[5]

THE ATTITUDE ORIENTED TO REACHING UNDERSTANDING

In its weak as well as in its strong form, the concept of communicative action presupposes that the agents are able to reach a mutual understanding, although this understanding has to be deeper in the case of 'strong' communicative action. According to Habermas *we understand a speech act when we know what makes it acceptable*; and it is acceptable when those conditions are met which allow the hearer to take a 'yes' position on the validity claim raised by the speaker (Habermas 1984: 297 f.). If an old friend comes to us with a plea for money, two requirements must be met in order for us to say that we have understood his plea (in addition to us understanding its literal linguistic content). First of all we must understand what we are actually asked to do, for example the size and the terms of our contribution. Secondly, we must have an opinion about what circumstances would make us regard such a request as justified, and why our friend may have reason to think that the relevant circumstances obtain in that particular situation. In other words, the presumption is that speaker and hearer share some values in light of which the request could appear as justified. However, if the hearer does not see any reasons which the speaker could use to justify the request for money, we may not say that the speech act has been understood. While the speaker claims to have made a request with which the hearer should comply because it is supported by strong arguments, the hearer cannot find that there are any such arguments. Thus to the hearer the speaker's demand becomes incomprehensible as a rational, normatively authorised request.

The situation is, of course, quite different if we imagine that the speaker is an armed robber and the request is not supported normatively, but by means of power. The hearer can then be said to have understood the speaker's request for money as a rationally founded claim if the hearer believes that the speaker has such means at his disposal (and the will to use them) which the hearer believes the speaker would regard to be sufficient to motivate the hearer to comply with the request. Both in relation to actor-independent appeals to normative justification and in relation to actor-relative references to private preferences and means of power, the action-coordinating power of communication does not depend on the validity of what is said, but on the implicit *warranty* that the speaker takes upon herself to redeem her validity claims if the hearer should require it (Habermas 1984: 302). In many cases, this is sufficient. We assume that a speaker is capable of redeeming, by means of convincing arguments, the validity claims that have been raised, without claiming that the arguments should actually be presented. Only if the validity of what is said in one way or another appears problematic to a hearer, it may be necessary to challenge the speaker into stating her reasons. Sometimes this will reveal that the speaker does not have sufficiently good arguments to support her utterances. However, this is not enough to undermine language as a medium of coordination, as long as we know that our communication partners *on the whole* (a) believe that they have good grounds for saying what they are saying, (b) are willing to present these grounds if they are asked to do so, and (c) actually turn out to be reliable in most cases. Habermas (1996a: 4) maintains that in our daily use of language, we make certain *idealisations*, i.e. that we generally presuppose that utterances have more validity than what they subsequently turn out to have. However, it is precisely such idealised presuppositions that make meaningful communication possible. The mistakes that we inevitably make when reality does not correspond to our presuppositions are mistakes which we can only try to correct and learn from as they are revealed.

It is important to realise that only communicative action in the *strong* sense is a fully 'adequate' form of communicative rationality, in the sense that it is only this type of communicative action that raises all the three validity claims that are linked to communication oriented to understanding. The weak variant can in this respect be described as a normatively reduced version of the concept, a version which presupposes and refers to the strong version. Because on a deeper level there has to be a normatively based trust and agreement between the parties with respect to the premises for the communication itself (viz. that one should not lie and cheat). This is necessary if we want to use language in a form of interaction oriented to success without perverting the communication itself.

The distinction between communicative and strategic action exists, but it is not as easy to draw the line between the two as one might think at a first glance. This is due to the fact that the speech act itself is tied both to the mental processes that precede the utterances, and to the physical, action-related processes that the utterances may induce. Hence, in some cases language use which is actually communicative can be misinterpreted as strategic action. Elster makes himself guilty of precisely this kind of misunderstanding when he, as mentioned earlier, claims it to be strategic language use when actors try to convince others that a proposal is positive judged from a *general* interest viewpoint, while their real reason for supporting it is that it takes care of their own interests. However, the theory of communicative action does not ask about the actors' motives, but rather about how they coordinate their actions with other people's actions. The criterion of communicative rationality is that we pursue our goals *to the extent this receives qualified acceptance from others*, in other words, the maximising of interests is subordinated to and conditioned by a communicatively obtained agreement. The crucial point here is that agents make their action plans depend on the fact that their interaction partners can be convinced by means of good grounds. If the argumentation is truthful and sincere, the use of language is oriented to reaching understanding and (strongly) communicative, not strategic (cf. Eriksen and Weigård 1997).

On the other hand, some types of language use *are* to be described as strategic and not as communicative action. This is quite clear in situations where an actor through his or her utterances lies, misleads, and blurs the actual facts in order to gain strategic advantages. However, as already mentioned, this is a use of language which can only give short-term profit, and which is parasitic in relation to the sincere, understanding-oriented use of language. In other words, its existence presupposes the existence of a legitimate, general expectation that we can trust each other's utterances. The consciously perlocutionary use of language is also strategic, which means the speaker's primary aim is not to reach a mutual understanding of some affair, but to obtain a result by (one-sidedly) provoking a particular reaction from the hearer. Nonetheless, here also the outcome presupposes that speaker and hearer are able to communicate in an illocutionary sense, i.e. that they as a starting point understand each other.

Finally we have the category of weak communicative action, where the actors' use of language creates an understanding-oriented relationship, but where this at the same time makes it possible for them to interact in a success-oriented manner through their non-linguistic actions and their general attitudes.

THE LIFEWORLD – OUR HORIZON OF BACKGROUND KNOWLEDGE

The concept of a lifeworld has a central position in Habermas's theory of action and society. He analyses the concept both from an internal participant perspective and from an external social-theoretical spectator perspective. From the participant perspective, the concept is an explanatory element in the representation of the communicative action attitude. It is used in addition to and complementary to the concepts of validity claims and the objective, social and subjective world, as a tool to explain how an approach oriented toward reaching understanding is possible and consensus obtainable. In this connection we may say that the concept has a kind of *cognitive* status: it covers an epistemological fellowship and a cultural reservoir of which we, as members of a society, are always a part. It is this aspect we will concentrate on here. Regarding the external approach, Habermas links the concept of lifeworld to the structural components (culture, society, personality) and the social spheres (private sphere, public sphere) which he believes are to a great extent maintained by an understanding-oriented attitude and by means of communicatively governed interaction. Here the lifeworld is synonymous with the concept of *civil society*, as it is used by Habermas himself and others (cf. Cohen and Arato 1992). In this connection he places the lifeworld in opposition to the 'subsystems' of economy and administration, which are characterised by a success-oriented attitude to action. We will return to this aspect of the concept in Chapter 5.

The concept of lifeworld was first used by Edmund Husserl, in a science-critical sense. He contrasted the concept of a pre-scientific lifeworld, which forms the basis for our natural and immediate everyday experience, with what he saw as the artificially constructed objective world view of science. This is the way Alfred Schütz uses the concept as well, although his aim is primarily sociological rather than epistemological. Hence the lifeworld becomes the framework of the individuals' lives. It is a culturally transmitted framework, which thus binds together the individual and society. It communicates a common stock of ideas which gives (a mutual) identity to the individual and the collective. This line of thinking is also Habermas's fundamental reason for implementing the lifeworld ('Lebenswelt') into his communicative theory of action.

In one sense we can say that Habermas needs the lifeworld concept in order to demonstrate that the communicative coordination of action is not an impracticable project. As mentioned before, he presupposes that in order to coordinate their actions, agents must have a common definition of the situation (i.e. an understanding of how things are). However, if actors in every new interaction situation had to start almost from scratch and negotiate a completely new definition of the situation, the communication medium would soon be overloaded and show itself to be unsuitable for coordination purposes. As we know, this is normally not the case; on the contrary, actors may frequently assume that they share all the important presuppositions which are involved in the description of the situation. When one of them makes a statement with an implicit claim to truth, rightness and truthfulness, these validity claims are therefore not challenged by the other actors. And if one element of the statement *is* challenged after all, the agents can nevertheless start their discussions on a solid foundation of shared presuppositions and concentrate on the actual point of dispute. What is the explanation of such a fundamental common understanding? It is here that the lifeworld comes in. The lifeworld is the reservoir of taken-for-granted and shared knowledge that we as members of a society all have a part of, and which ensures that we see many things in more or less the same way.

Consequently, there is something naive and unproblematised in our relation to the lifeworld knowledge. As long as it remains in its lifeworld context, we are not conscious of having it, and if we are to relate to it in a conscious and critical manner, it has to be brought out of this context. This may happen if we find ourselves in a new situation, where things which we have previously taken for granted suddenly become a salient point and thus put under critical scrutiny. The lifeworld can therefore be referred to as a horizon of experiences and knowledge that we implicitly control, but which we explicitly become aware of in bits and pieces, as the situation brings new things into focus. Hence, we will always stay within our lifeworld context. We cannot decide to set it aside, disregard it or remain generally critical to it. When we interpret the world, it is always on the basis of preconceived convictions that the lifeworld supplies us with (Habermas 1987a: 125). However, this does not mean that we are hopelessly trapped and determined by the pre-programmed interpretation patterns of our lifeworld. As mentioned before, *elements* of the lifeworld content can at all times be subjected to critical examination and re-evaluation. In this way that meaning relation which the lifeworld constitutes can be changed gradually, but we cannot change everything at once.

According to Habermas (1987a: 124), we may think of the lifeworld as a culturally transmitted and linguistically organised stock of interpretive patterns. Our language and our cultural background are dimensions of our existence which we can never leave behind. In other words, we can never set them aside in order to find out what the world looks like without linguistic or cultural presuppositions. They are what we call *transcendentally given* entities. Hence, the lifeworld can also be understood as a common context, where agents, on the basis of linguistically and culturally transmitted knowledge, can establish processes for obtaining agreement about problematised issues. In these processes they identify matters as related to the objective, the social or the subjective world. However, this type of differentiation has no relevance to the unproblematised stock of knowledge of the lifeworld, as shown in Figure 3.2. Here the lifeworld is presented as an arena of communication where two actors, on the basis of their language and culture and through understanding-oriented utterances (CA), reach an understanding of relations which belong to the three worlds.

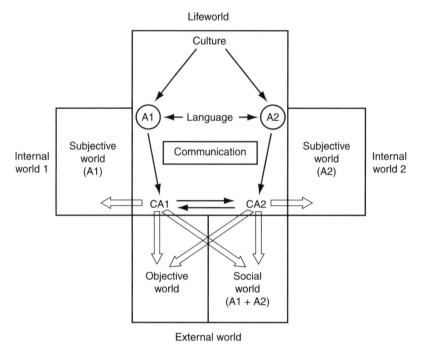

Figure 3.2 *World-relations of communicative acts (CA)*
The double arrows indicate the world-relations that actors (A) establish with their utterances (CA).
Source: Habermas 1987: 127.

MEAD'S THEORY OF LINGUISTIC DEVELOPMENT

So far, the communicative concept of action has been studied from the 'inside', i.e. as an internal, logical relation between classes of linguistic utterances and classes of action. However, communicative action should also be understood from a social point of view, i.e. as a system of linguistic symbols which we as a species have acquired the competence to master through a long history of evolution, and which each individual through socialisation must acquire anew. This was the perspective that George Herbert Mead, the founder of social psychology, took in his discussion of the conditions for the action coordinating function of language in everyday life.

To understand better Mead's point of departure, we should briefly mention his epistemological–philosophical source of inspiration, C. S. Peirce. Here we find the first clear break with the Cartesian paradigm of a philosophy of consciousness. While the old paradigm presumed that cognition was a dyadic relation between a cognising subject and a cognised object, Peirce placed the *sign* between subject and object (Gullvåg 1972: 47). Our cognition never has direct access to objects; it is always mediated through signs, or symbols. The central category of such signs or symbols is language. This means that the basis for our cognition can not be anything private or individual (as previously assumed); rather it has to be something social and collective:

> Peirce maintains that to the extent thinking is cognitive, it has to be linguistic or symbolic – it has to presuppose communication by means of signs. The communicable meaning of signs must be something social: it cannot consist in individual reactions or private sensation, which are incommunicable, but rather in something which is public and general, viz. action habits. If language is to have cognitive meaning, it has to be defined by the ways in which it is used in communication.
>
> (Gullvåg 1972: 18 f.)

This was the basis for Mead's development of a theory about symbolically mediated interaction. What he tried to understand was how we, by means of language, are able to develop into the kind of beings who can participate in the specifically human form of social life. In order to explain this, he starts by observing the simplest form of communication, i.e. the communication type that animals and humans have in common, and which consists of *gestures*, i.e. bodily expressions. Mead's primary example is a dogfight (Mead 1962: 42 f.). When two dogs meet in a fighting situation, they will watch each other's movements. If one of them moves, the other will respond with an adjusting movement to avoid getting into a more unfavourable position. Each movement becomes a stimulus which triggers a particular response from the opposite party.[6] We have a similar situation when two boxers move around in the ring, trying to 'read' the opponent's next move before it comes, in order to make their own countermoves, such as dodging a hit, making a counterattack, etc.

Thus, gestures, or body language, contain information which may be useful to other 'organisms'; gestures are bearers of *meaning*. However, this is so-called natural meaning; it is not a message which is consciously adapted by the 'sender', but rather the 'receiver's' interpretation of the 'sender's' success-oriented behaviour. Hence, the gestures in question do not have the same meaning to the two parties. The two dogs are not conscious of how their respective movements are interpreted by the other party. Neither does a boxer who moves his right hand in order to find an opening in his opponent's guard do this in order to inform his opponent. The difference between humans and animals becomes clearer if we move a step forward in the communicative development, to so-called *signal languages*. The behavioural pattern of many species of animals and birds is that they post a guard that observes the environment while the rest of the flock is grazing or relaxing. This guard will then start to run/fly or cry out an alarm call as soon as a danger appears, which to the rest of the flock will be a signal to get away. In the same vein, if somebody cries 'fire' or the fire alarm is released, it will be a signal of imminent danger to our fellow humans. However, while the cry of warning or the reaction to it is a biologically conditioned, instinctive *behaviour* on the part of the birds, the cry of fire and the reaction to it will be meaningful, socially acquired *action* on our part. It is only from our spectator position that we can say that the guard in the flock of birds cries 'in order to', i.e. with the intention to, warn the others. Biologically, the cry is only an instinctively released reaction to the sensed danger, and the function of this reaction is that it warns the flock, which reacts just as instinctively when they hear the cry.

According to Mead, what separates humans from animals is that such signals among humans release (or may release) *the same reaction in the 'sender' as in the* 'receiver', while that is not the case with animals (Mead 1962: 190 f.). This is because people have a unique capability of placing themselves in the position of others, or taking the attitude of the other, which animals lack. Put differently, humans can observe themselves and their behaviour from the outside, and thus have *self-consciousness*, which animals do not have. The alarm bird is not capable of imagining how its cry is interpreted by the others, and the other birds are on their part just as incapable of putting themselves in the warning bird's position as it cries (for example, by imagining what kind of observation may have triggered the warning). When *we* on the other hand hear someone cry 'fire!', we know what this means precisely because we can place ourselves in the warning person's position; we can think that he or she must have seen flames or smoke, etc. And the person who sounds the alarm can use this signal consciously just because he or she knows that it will call forth images of flames and smoke in the listeners, precisely because it calls forth the same images in the person him- or herself. Thus, the cry of fire and the fire alarm are examples of what Mead refers to as *significant symbols*, something corresponding signals of warning among animals are *not*. He uses the term to refer to gestures or other signs which are representations of some idea or meaning, and where there is general agreement that this particular sign represents this particular content.

> Gestures become significant symbols when they implicitly arouse in an individual making them the same responses which they explicitly arouse, or are supposed to arouse, in other individuals, the individuals to whom they are addressed . . . In this way every gesture comes within a given social group or community to stand for a particular act or response, namely, the act or response which it calls forth explicitly in the individual to whom it is addressed, and implicitly in the individual who makes it; and this particular act or response for which it stands is its meaning as a significant symbol.
>
> (Mead 1962: 47)

Hence, it is the ability to see the situation from the other's point of view, taking the attitude of the other, which in Mead's opinion conditions the development of human languages or systems of significant symbols. What happens is that we start using such symbols towards each other, with specific expectations as to how the other(s) will understand them and consequently react to them. If the reaction is different from what we had expected, i.e. if speaker and hearer misunderstand each other, they initiate a process in which they mutually adjust the relevant meaning conventions until they arrive at an identical linguistic practice. Through such a process of trial and error, we manage to find a well-functioning linguistic meaning, according to Mead.

Habermas views Mead's work as an important element in the foundation of the communication theoretical model. He is nevertheless able to detect weaknesses and faults in the way in which Mead carries through his project. In Habermas's opinion, Mead is not able to make full use of the insights which are made accessible by an approach through the philosophy of language. He does not understand the importance of the grammatical differentiation of the language, i.e. the fact that grammatical distinctions are inextricably linked to our ability to relate to our environment in different ways. For example, we may relate in an objectifying manner to a world of factual relations, and in a normative manner to a world of social relations. Mead does not seem to realise that this differentiation is a prerequisite for our ability to use language in a way which is oriented to reaching understanding (Habermas 1987a: 23/25). The result is that Mead uses a cognitivistic way of explanation in areas that require normative explanations.

One example of this is his account of the transition from communication via natural gestures to the development of significant symbols. According to Mead, this transition takes place when each 'organism' hypothetically takes the other's perspective in the form of a *prognostisised* understanding of his or her attitude: as senders, we have certain expectations – or a prognosis – that an addressee will interpret the message in the way it was intended by the sender. This would explain that there is a (varying degree of) similarity between different actors' use of a communicative symbol. However, Habermas claims it is not this which character-ises our use of linguistic expressions, but rather the fact that we assign a common or identical meaning to these expressions. To make this possible, a standard must be established, in relation to which we may criticise what is conceived of as an incorrect use of symbols. In other words, there must be a distinction between right and wrong use of symbols: 'There is an identical meaning when ego knows how alter *should* respond to a significant gesture; it is not sufficient to expect that alter *will* respond in a certain way,' (Habermas 1987a: 14). In practice, though, two persons may never put exactly the same meaning into a concept, and in more serious cases this may, as we know, lead to misunderstandings. However, the word 'misunderstanding' presupposes that there is a correct understanding which the misunderstanding can be adjusted in relation to. And the presupposition that we are capable of using concepts in their correct meaning, and that different individuals will assign the same meaning to them, belongs to the idealisations that our daily use of language cannot do without (Habermas 1996a: 19). To establish a system of significant symbols between actors who take a purely observatory, cognitive and objectifying attitude to each other is therefore not possible, con-trary to what Mead believed. It is rather a project for intersubjectively cooperat-ing agents, who are able to reach the normative aim of establishing standards of right and wrong, on the basis of a common and shared lifeworld. According to Habermas, this principle is implied in Wittgenstein's concept of a rule: establish-ing a system of significant symbols involves establishing a set of rules that prescribe what is and what is not correct use of language, with corresponding possibilities for criticism of deviating practice. However, Mead's theory neverthe-less contains elements that make it possible to understand social interaction as anchored in a normative attitude. We will return to this topic in Chapter 4.

CONCLUSION

To act communicatively means to act in order to obtain agreement, or to act on the basis of an already obtained mutual agreement with other actors with respect to what is the purpose of the action. This presupposes that agents arrive at a common definition of the situation, which again presupposes that they mutually accept the validity claims which are implicit in the relevant utterances (viz. to truth, rightness and truthfulness). However, the concept of communicative action is relevant also in a weaker sense, where only the validity claims to truth and truthfulness apply, but not to normative validity. This form of linguistic co-ordination allows the agents to establish a success-oriented perspective on the interaction. The distinction between an understanding-oriented and a success-oriented use of language largely corresponds to the distinction between illocutionary and perlocutionary speech acts, where the concept of communicative action is tied to the understanding-oriented and illocutionary mode of language use. The different types of speech acts can be linked to various forms of linguistically mediated interaction, as well as to the concepts of an objective, a social and a subjective world. However, these must be complemented by the concept of the lifeworld, which represent the constitutional basis for using language in an understanding-oriented way. The lifeworld is the horizon of knowledge which we as members of a society share and naively take for granted. It constitutes our common stock of culturally transmitted and linguistically organised patterns for the interpretation of reality. What is special about the human language, according to Mead, is that particular symbols represent a particular meaning content, which is common to everyone within a linguistic community. This makes them into 'significant symbols'. A system of significant symbols can come about because of the unique human ability to take the attitude of the other and thus see oneself from the outside.

Notes

1. This objection is raised against validity claim (a), viz. the requirement that the statement must be true. However, there may also be objections against the other two validity claims. With respect to point (b), which concerns the normative rightness or legitimacy of the utterance, an objection may be: 'This is not a matter for you to decide on your own.' And to point (c), viz. the speaker's truthfulness or sincerity: 'You cannot possibly mean that. You are just making fun of us.'
2. We will return to the transcendental form of justification in Chapter 4.
3. Habermas has been criticised for contradicting himself when, in *The Theory of Communicative Action* he understands so-called simple imperatives ('Give me the money!') as being understanding-oriented and communicative and at the same time success-oriented and strategic speech acts (cf. Skjei 1985). Habermas himself has admitted to making mistakes on this point (Habermas 1985b: 112; cf. Apel 1998: 710 ff.). The introduction of the category weak communicative action must probably be understood, among other things, as an attempt to solve this paradox.
4. This is a limitation which concerns the weak form of communicative action. It does not have the same significance in connection with perlocutions, as these are not presented with a claim to truth and truthfulness, and thus cannot be said to deceive anybody.
5. Cf. the political form of decision-making that Habermas calls 'procedurally regulated bargaining' which is discussed in Chapter 8.
6. Mead regarded himself as a 'social behaviourist', and whether he discussed animal or human behaviour, he made frequent use of general concepts and metaphors which belong to this school of thought. The basic model is that one 'organism' receives 'stimuli' from another 'organism', which in turn releases a 'response' in the first 'organism'. Behaviourism in general has been accused (by those who belong to the meaning-interpretive school) of being blind to the principal difference that exists between social, human action and the

behaviour of rats used for experimental purposes. What is noteworthy about Mead's theory in this respect is that he, by taking the behaviour of animals as a starting point and then subsequently demonstrating what distinguishes it from human behaviour, is to a large extent able to show what is fundamental and unique about human action and interaction.

CHAPTER 4

Discourse ethics

INTRODUCTION

The dominant schools within the social sciences have in general paid little attention to normative questions. Most probably, this is mainly because they have operated with only a two-world model: an objective world of generally accessible facts, which can be analysed by way of reason, and a subjective world of inexplicable and irrational individual feelings, ideas and values, which consequently is not characterised by the kind of system or regularity which scientific analysis requires. Behind this distinction we also find the distinction between *is* and *ought*, i.e. between reality as it is – which is the legitimate province of science – and the question of what ought to be – which belongs to the domain of personal will. When normative phenomena are pressed into this scheme, they will on the one hand be perceived as objective facts, as facts which science must somehow relate to because they exist, since individuals operate with normative rules and let their behaviour be regulated by them. If on the other hand we ask about the content of these norms, it is immediately understood as a product of subjective tastes, which is consequently impenetrable to rational analysis.

As we have seen, Habermas's contribution here is that he brings in a third, *social* world. By introducing this world, he does not have to try to reduce norms neither to objective facts nor to subjective statements of will. Rather, the social world is understood as an intersubjective sphere of validity in its own right. As already mentioned, Habermas does not deny that there are important differences between norms and facts, but he maintains that also norms and normative problems can be made the object of rational evaluation and analysis. Thus he positions himself as a normative *cognitivist*, i.e. he claims that our normative judgements and standpoints rest on a foundation of knowledge. Even though norms are not true or false in a literal sense, as are claims of fact, they have what Habermas refers to as 'truth-analogue' qualities. This means that just as we can test if a claim of fact is true or false, we can test if a norm is morally valid (that is, *right*) or not. However, this is a task which he thinks must be carried out by members of society in their daily practice. It is *not* a task for social science or philosophy to provide us with 'answers' to the many existential normative problems that we constantly come across. As usual, the contribution of the social sciences and philosophy is to reconstruct – and thus help us understand – how we in our social practice already have the resources to deal with this type of challenge in a rational manner.

As we will see in the present chapter, Habermas draws a connection between his theory and the social psychological and sociological theorists who have linked together the development of linguistic competence and the development of moral consciousness. This naturally leads to a type of moral theory that builds on a Kantian foundation. However, this rigid formalist foundation in itself creates a basis for new problems, which Habermas in recent years has developed and expanded his theory in order to deal with.

'THE GENERALISED OTHER' AS A MODEL FOR NORM-REGULATED BEHAVIOUR

As mentioned in the previous chapter, Mead believes that our human ability to imagine our interaction partners' perspective on the world enables us to develop a set of linguistic symbols with a particular meaning content. But according to Mead, this ability to put ourselves in the position of 'the other' explains not only the ability to coordinate interaction through the use of significant symbols; it also explains the more complex form of action regulation which takes place on the basis of *social norms*. This is something every individual learns through socialisation as it grows up, and Mead describes how it happens when we 'take on' different roles (ideal role-taking). The development takes place in two stages. Mead illustrates it by referring to the challenges children meet in the world of play. In the early stages, children, through ordinary play, enter into different roles (one at a time), for example by playing cops and robbers. Later on, they are faced with more complex challenges, as when they through games in an ideal (imaginary) sense must enter into different roles simultaneously. Thus, in order to master sports such as baseball or football (i.e. in order to master its own role in the game), the child at the same time must be able to 'take' (i.e. 'be conscious of') the roles played by several of the other participants of the game, because what it needs to do itself all the time depends on what the others do (Mead 1962: 152 ff.). However, just as I have expectations with respect to what each participant is going to do in his or her role, I am also aware that each participant has his or her own expectations with regard to what I am going to do in my role. Such expectations more or less control the way I play my role. Moreover, they do not remain diverging individual expectations; rather, in my consciousness they merge into the team's expectation about how I should play my role in a system of roles.

It is this collective expectation which is referred to by Mead as 'the generalised other', and which he uses to draw some important theoretical conclusions. For he sees such an ideal taking over of roles as the basis of norm-regulated, social behaviour. The first step in this process is that the child, who relate to a specific other, in general a care-taking person, experience that there are demands and expectations tied to its behaviour. It realises that it may pay to live up to such expectations, while if it does not do this, it can be met with sanctions. By internalising the expectations in question, children learn to adapt to the role of child in relation to the complementary role of (for example) parent. In the next step the developing child experiences that it is met with such behavioural expectations from all quarters, and that it itself also forms corresponding expectations with respect to how others should behave. Children learn to see the many expectations in terms of the social group's or society's generalised expectations about what is correct behaviour in different situations. The expectations are hence to be understood as a social norm. By internalising these expectations, the socialised individual has learned to see itself from the position of the generalised other. It has turned the collective expectations into its own, i.e. into expectations it has to its own behaviour as well. For this to be possible, the person must be able to take into consideration the fact that the social situation does not only involve the roles of *ego* and *alter* – speaker and hearer, oneself and one's opponent; it also involves *a neutral third party* – a listener or an onlooker. It is only when we learn to see the situation from the perspective of this neutral observer that we are able to distinguish between the opponent's particular expectation to our behaviour and the generalised expectation represented by the third party.

In discussing this issue, however, Mead runs into problems which are similar to those he experienced in explaining how societies develop language systems with a common meaning. He tries to understand norm development from a purely cognitive perspective as well, and doing this, he loses sight of that which makes norms morally binding. Mead's point of departure is that through socialisation, individuals are made to behave in conformity with the norms because they experience that if they deviate from the norm they are exposed to the group's sanctioning potential. The norm itself merely has the character of a social fact. It is a behavioural expectation which has for some reason become generally accepted, and violation of it is more or less likely to be punished with sanctions of some kind. However, young people gradually internalise social norms, i.e. they make them a part of their own personality. To Habermas, it becomes a problem to explain this last part of the process if the normative element is in the final instance given a purely arbitrary, empirical foundation: 'The authority of the group consists simply in the fact that it can threaten to carry out sanctions in case interests are violated,' (Habermas 1987a: 38). However, moral authority must build on something more than just the threat of sanctions, as it is not this threat we internalise, but the feeling that the norm represents a *right* prohibition or obligation. How else can we explain that norms are followed even in situations where the threat of sanctions does not exist? Mead also realises that the moral attitude which we develop cannot be based on force. He therefore presupposes that 'the generalised other' is a bearer of a normative authority which deserves respect in itself, independently of any sanctions. The question is then: how has society become integrated into a collective level of consciousness, in which its common will ('the generalised other') to the members represents a morally binding authority? On what does this binding character of collective commands depend? Mead has no answer to this. Habermas therefore maintains that Mead lacks a valid explanation of why factual norms are experienced as *valid* norms.

However, Mead has other insights to contribute to the understanding of morality. As we have seen, he links the formation of our self-consciousness and personality to the ability to see ourselves from the perspective of the concrete or generalised other. On the other hand, personality cannot be reduced to this ability to see ourselves through the eyes of others. In that case, each personality would only be a reflex of any other, and nothing new or distinctive would enter into social interaction. Instead, the formation of personality takes place in the tension between socialisation and individuation, i.e. between the internalisation of standards that are common to the social group, and the development of each individual's unique character and ability to behave autonomously. Mead attempts to express this idea by separating the personality into one social component, which he refers to as 'me', and one individual component referred to as 'I':

> The 'I' is the response of the organism to the attitudes of the others; the 'me' is the organized set of attitudes of others which one himself assumes. The attitudes of the others constitute the organized 'me', and then one reacts toward that as an 'I'.
>
> (Mead 1962: 175)

In this way we can say that 'I' is what makes each person a creative and special being; it is what gives him or her a purely personal identity, as well as freedom and the initiative to act. We nevertheless need to ask the following question: given that 'me' is formed as an imprint of society or our social environment, where do we get our 'I' from? Is it an ability to react which is programmed into our genes already from birth? Mead does not think so. He believes that this too is an ability that we acquire through our lives as users of language in a society, but it nevertheless involves a totally different type of property than 'me'. Through 'me', we internalise concrete behavioural expectations in the form of roles or norms, so that we know what the environment demands from us. By contrast, 'I' is the expression of a behavioural expectation at a higher level, i.e. an expectation that we should be able to make independent decisions and realise ourselves as unique individuals. This is not a social expectation which has made itself felt with the same force everywhere and at all times; it has become particularly widespread in modern societies.

What does individualisation involve, then? Is it a kind of *carte blanche* that allows each individual to act as 'weirdly' and idiosyncratically as they may possibly want to, only guided by impulse and without reference to external standards? According to Habermas's (1992b) interpretation of Mead, this is not what 'I' is all about. 'I' does not cut off the connection to our social basis, but opens up the opportunity to put into parenthesis those expectations that our current context normally involves. We are thus able to attach ourselves to the expectations of the abstract, universal community of language-using subjects, with which we may hypothetically communicate through an imaginary discourse. This community is not limited in time or space, which is why we may sometimes either trust or fear that 'history's judgement' of a person or action will be different from that which is passed in our own times. In the area of morality, individualism involves that each individual is expected to have the ability to judge whether current social expectations deserve to be respected, or if they are perhaps idiosyncratic themselves. This is done by taking a universal perspective, and asking what is right based on quite general principles for human action. Thus we move from a concrete morality led by norms, to an abstract morality led by principles. Correspondingly, the development of an ego-identity is characterised by a marked turn towards greater individualism. In traditional societies, people typically obtain the respect and recognition of others by entering into a role which is defined in advance, and which is related to class and position in society. By contrast, it is typically modern to demand universal recognition of a role that we have defined for ourselves, based on who we want to be and how we understand ourselves (cf. Taylor 1994). In neither case does the individualistic dimension involve individuals who are shut off from the outer world; on the contrary, it involves individuals who are able to take a broader perspective which includes all other individuals. Individualism hence emerges as the other side of universalism (Habermas 1992b: 186). As we will see, Mead's ideas of moral development are supported by recent researchers within the tradition of communicative theory.

STAGES IN THE DEVELOPMENT OF MORAL CONSCIOUSNESS

One of these researchers is the American psychologist Lawrence Kohlberg (1927–87). The essence of his theory (which he attempted to confirm through empirical studies) is that from childhood to adult age, humans pass through several successive stages, which all reflect various degrees of moral maturity. This developmental process (and the stages of consciousness that it involves) is universal and can hence be traced in different cultures. Habermas[1] has for a long time been interested in the theory, not least because it represents a rare attempt to test hypotheses which form the basis of his own discourse ethics. However, in formulating his psychological theory, Kohlberg has incorporated elements from other cognitivistic theories of morality, first and foremost the theories of Mead and John Rawls. Thus, he may to some extent be said to presuppose that which is to be proved. Thus, Habermas (1990b: 118) admits that Kohlberg's empirical findings cannot be regarded as independent confirmation of any such theories of morality (for example discourse ethics). He nevertheless finds that this fact does not make Kohlberg's psychological theory in principle unfit as an aid to test the normative theory, since all empirical testing must take certain theoretical presuppositions for granted. We may still use such methods to determine which theoretical claims and empirical data are compatible, and which are not.

Kohlberg (1981: 409 ff.) maintains that from infancy to the transition between adolescence and adult age, the individual goes through three levels of moral development, viz. the *preconventional*, *conventional*, and *postconventional* levels. In order to create a more precise scale, each of the three levels is again split into two stages. Consequently, the model all in all operates with six hierarchical stages, where each stage includes the content of the previous stage, while at the same time it replaces it.

Stage 1 is referred to as *the stage of punishment and obedience*. It is characterised by relations with authority persons and their rules. What is right is here taken to be synonymous with the attempt to avoid breaking rules and to obey in order to escape punishment. Stage 2 is referred to as *the stage of individual instrumental purpose and exchange*. What characterises it is that we become more aware of the fact that we have our own interests to protect, while at the same time we recognise that other individuals also have their own interests to look after. Hence, what is right at this stage is to seek to protect our own interests and to accept other people's right to protect theirs. A right outcome of a transaction is thus understood as a fair outcome, i.e. an equal exchange or an agreement which is balanced and reasonable to both parties.

The conventional level can be said to correspond to Mead's 'me' perspective. First we have stage 3, viz. the *stage of mutual interpersonal expectations, relationships, and conformity*, which reflects the attitude which is, according to Mead, expressed in 'play'. A 'good boy' attitude is here prevalent. What is right here is to live up to the expectations of our closest environment, to be loyal in our different complementary roles with others, and to generally show consideration. We feel a need to be 'good' in the eyes of ourselves and others, and when we put ourselves in the position of others, this is the kind of behaviour we would have wanted. The next stage, viz. stage 4, is referred to as *the stage of social system and conscience maintenance*. It expresses much of the same attitude that Mead found in 'game'. Here we find a 'law and order' attitude. That loyalty and conscientiousness towards those nearest to us which was expressed at stage 3 is at this stage transferred to society. We do the right thing by observing the law and serving the community, and in doing so, we retain our self-respect and our good conscience.

What is characteristic of the postconventional level is that our moral decisions are made on the basis of superior rights, values or principles about which everybody can potentially agree. Here we are touching on Mead's 'I' perspective. Stage 5, *the stage of prior rights and social contract or utility*, is characterised by a natural right approach. We acknowledge that we are bound by certain principles which rank above the relative values and regulations on which the laws and norm systems of a particular society are based. Most often the latter type of norm will be derived from and be in harmony with the former, but if the two are in conflict, the right thing to do is to let the superior principles apply. We are bound by fundamental values such as life and freedom, and by the 'contracts' that we have entered into, which involve the community, family, friends and work. It is also important that those laws and obligations that we build on are designed in such a way that they lead to the highest possible degree of 'utility' to society as a whole. Finally, stage 6 is *the stage of universal ethical principles*. The right thing to do here is to follow such universal principles that we think all of humanity should follow; i.e. universal principles of justice which involve equality of human rights and respect for people's dignity as individuals. This obligation is based on a rational insight into which principles are the right ones.

The model discussed here seems roughly to correspond to, and thus in a way to confirm, the kind of moral attitudes on which discourse ethics builds. On the other hand, Habermas (1990b: 120) finds that Kohlberg's theory of developmental psychology itself needs moral-philosophical support to be able to give a satisfactory explanation of how and why such learning processes in consciousness takes place. Not surprisingly, he believes that with respect to this problem, his own communication theoretical platform is more useful than is Rawls's theory, which was Kohlberg's primary foundation. Habermas maintains that the moral maturation process described by Kohlberg can best be explained on the basis of the more differentiated ability to take different perspectives which turns us into individuals capable of speech and action. What characterises the preconventional level is on the one hand the fact that the child does not have a perspective which includes all the three worlds described by Habermas; it only distinguishes between an internal and an external world. On the communicative side, it has developed a perspective that includes the roles of speaker and hearer only, i.e. an I–thou relationship. What happens in the transition to the conventional level, is that the child develops an observer or onlooker perspective. The child learns to take an outside look at the situation, including its own role in it. Thus from a communicative point of view, a division arises between the grammatical roles of first, second and third person. As far as world perspective is concerned, the introduction of an observer role makes it possible to distinguish between a subjective world, an objective world and a social world of generalised expectations to behaviour, as noted by Mead (Habermas 1990b: 139 ff.).

In the transition from the conventional to the postconventional level, a further development of perspective takes place. At the conventional level we relate to objective, subjective, and social states of affairs as given entities, in a rather naive way. By contrast, at the postconventional level we learn to relate to these things in a reflected and hypothetical manner, as something which may and may not be as it is presented. While the previous level involves an implicit relation to validity claims, those claims are made the explicit object of a discursive exchange of arguments at the postconventional level. Correspondingly, the speaker perspective has changed from integrating the participant and onlooker perspectives at the conventional level, to the development of the roles of proponent and opponent who defend and criticise validity claims in a discourse at the postconventional level (Habermas 1990b: 158 ff.).

At the preconventional level we can clearly distinguish two sources of motivation that control the individual's actions. On the one hand, we have the (normative) *authority* that the child must relate to in the form of demands that are made on it from relevant reference persons. On the other hand, there is the child's experience of having *interests* that can be realised in different degrees, depending on behaviour. Habermas (1990b: 149 ff.) claims that at the conventional level, the two sources of motivation result in two different types of action: the norm-regulated, understanding-oriented, and communicative type of action, and the interest-based, success-oriented and strategic type of action. However, at the postconventional level this division is surmounted, as discourse is a form of interaction where the success orientation is included in a comprehensive attitude oriented toward reaching understanding. We so to speak participate in an *competition with arguments*, where the aim is to convince each other and thereby obtain consensus (Habermas 1990b: 160).

In Habermas's reformulated version of Kohlberg's theory, moral consciousness at the preconventional level is influenced by the fact that the premises for correct action are external, in the sense that they lie in the form of reciprocity that links the child to the action environment. At stage 1, this means the complementarity between command and obedience which characterises the relation between the child and authority persons. At stage 2 it means the symmetry in exchange relations or the fair compensation that is aimed at in the child's exchange relations with the environment. At the conventional level the requirements for correct action are internalised in the individual's own personality structure. At stage 3 it happens in that the child identifies itself with a particular role and internalises the expectations that are linked to it; at stage 4 in that it identifies with the general norm system of the society in question. However, when the adolescent reaches the postconventional level, this 'natural' identification dissolves through what is referred to by Habermas as the moralisation of society. The point here is that it is not until we reach this level that it is possible to regard normative questions as moral evaluations which are in principle open. Thus, at stage 5 we realise that also established norms must be tested rationally in relation to superior principles of justice. At stage 6 we take a step further and establish that norms can only be legitimised through a procedure which in itself can be given independent justification (to Habermas, this in practice involves the universalisation test of discourse ethics, which we will discuss later in this chapter). However, at all stages, it is the reciprocity in interpersonal interaction which is the point of departure when we try to find out what is the right thing to do (Habermas 1990b:165 ff.). The main characteristics of this model are summarised in Figure 4.1.

Level of moral consciousness	Form of interaction	Speaker perspective	World perspective	Premises for right action	Basis for conception of justice	Developmental stage	Corresponding concepts in Mead	
pre-conventional	authority/ interest based action	I–thou relation	internal/ external	adaptation to external circumstances	complementarity command/obedience	1		
					symmetric compensation	2		
conventional	communicative/ strategic action	system of first, second and third person	three-world system	internalised expectations to behaviour	role conformity	3	play	me
					norm conformity	4	game	
post-conventional	discourse	proponent/ opponent	reflective, hypothetical	rational knowledge	principles of justice	5		
					procedures for justification of norms	6		I

Figure 4.1 *Moral-cognitive stages of development*

Habermas is the first to emphasise that this theory still has an uncertain and hypothetical status, and that much more research is required before we can even begin to talk about real empirical confirmation. The relation between Kohlberg's theoretical scheme and his empirical data is not unproblematic either. We will briefly mention two of the discussions that this has given rise to, and which Habermas comments on.

The first debate concerns how stage 6 of the model should be understood. It was triggered by the fact that Kohlberg in his later revisions of the theory felt compelled to exclude the highest stage, simply because he did not find sufficient empirical evidence that people develop a moral consciousness that corresponds to this stage. He therefore came to regard the universalistic moral attitude more as a philosophical construct than as a 'natural' psychological stage of development which people in general experience. However, to Habermas (1990b: 172 ff.) this is the wrong way of formulating the problem. We have seen that at the post-conventional level, individuals have acquired a *reflective* attitude. In other words, they not only give expression to and practise implicitly acquired knowledge and attitudes, but are able to reflect on what should be their attitude if they are faced with a certain problem. This means that in a psychological investigation of such topics, a test person at this level will not give a naive response to the psychologist's questions; he or she will be capable of entering into a moral theoretical debate with the psychologist on an – in principle – equal basis. At this level there is also a basis for debate, as there is still no generally accepted answer to the philosophical question of which types of principles should form the foundation of moral theory.[2] Therefore, postconventional moral thinking expresses a type of competence that makes the distinction between natural psychological development and philosophical consciousness disappear. Even though we may agree with Habermas at this point, it still remains to prove empirically to what extent people really obtain such a level of reflection. This must still be a fundamental criterion for a reconstructive theory of morality.

The second debate focused considerable attention around Kohlberg's theory. The discussion was triggered by his American colleague Carol Gilligan (1982), who questioned whether the premises for Kohlberg's developmental model were neutral with respect to gender. According to Gilligan, Kohlberg's material contained an over-representation of female respondents, who intuitively seemed to have a reflective attitude to moral questions, but who were nevertheless ranked as low as stage 3. The reason was that in many contexts they put decisive emphasis on behaving in such a way that they lived up to expectations and toned down conflicts in the action environment. In Gilligan's opinion, this was not an expression of a defect in their understanding of moral questions; rather, it reflected different, i.e. female, values. Gilligan therefore suggested that above or next to the masculine understanding of morality, which is oriented towards rights and justice (and which is expressed at the postconventional level in Kohlberg's model), we would have to place a specifically female ethics which is context related and based on a philosophy of responsibility and care.

Kohlberg met these objections by rejecting their empirical foundation; i.e. he denied the fact that there was a disproportionate number of female respondents at the lower levels of the model. Regardless of who is right, Habermas (1990b: 175 ff.) has found that Gilligan's contribution raises problems which cannot be overlooked, and as we will soon see, he has attempted to develop his own theory of morality so that it cope with these problems in a better way. He agrees with Gilligan that normative questions also involve context relative considerations. However, he believes it is wrong to try to isolate this as a separate stage in the development of moral consciousness. Instead, concrete values such as care and responsibility for one's immediate family and friends are said to relate to what he refers to as the *ethical* aspects of normative questions, which always arise when norms are realised. But when different value standards are to be compared and conflicts are to be solved, there is a need for a reflective procedure which he defines as *morality*, and it is the ability to think in such a way which is characteristic of the postconventional level. Thus, Habermas maintains the view that moral justice is an aspect of practical reason that also in a cognitive sense is superior to the aspect of ethical value, even though both elements are equally important in real action situations.

THE FOUNDATION OF MORALITY IN THE SACRED

Although Mead noted that the forms of moral consciousness seem to have been going through a development between traditional and modern society, both he and Kohlberg, both being psychologists, were primarily concerned with a different history of development, viz. that which takes place within the single individual from childhood to adult. This is referred to as the *ontogenetic* perspective. Thus, Habermas has to look elsewhere for an explanation of how the development of morality has been going on as a social evolution throughout the history of the human species – the so-called *phylogenetic* perspective. This brings him to the sociologist Emile Durkheim (1858–1917) and his explanation of how moral attitudes have their origins in the sacred. Moreover, he finds that Durkheim explains the morally binding character of norms in a better way than Mead.

Through his study of so-called primitive religions, primarily Australian totemism, Durkheim (1976) was able to establish that there is a distinct structural similarity between fundamental religious attitudes and moral attitudes. First, both are characterised by an orientation towards the collective and impersonal and hence a renunciation of immediate individual interests. When we enter into the religious sphere, it is in company with others, and our respect for the religious is a respect for an impersonal and super-individual power. In the same way we can say that our respect for moral standards is oriented towards the collective and impersonal, and has priority over personal considerations of utility. Secondly, Durkheim maintained that the authority linked to holiness and the authority linked to morality both contain the same strange duality and contradiction: they are at the same time something that we fear and something we experience as positive and wish to live up to. Just as believers find joy in fulfilling their religious duties, and thus see a value in fulfilling them for their own sake, so morally acting agents most often have a positive feeling when they comply with social norms because the norms are perceived as superior principles. This led Durkheim to believe that the basis of morality must be sought in the sacred. The explanation of why moral commands are obeyed even when they are not linked to sanctions is to be found in a binding power that they ultimately take from the religious sphere. It is because norms possess a moral authority that society punishes breaches of them; not the other way around, as many have claimed, that punishment gives authority to the norm. When breaking moral norms makes us feel guilt and shame, it is a reaction which was originally triggered by offences against the sacred (Habermas 1987a: 48 ff.).

This respect for the sacred, i.e. for religious symbols, has been developed and maintained through ritual practice. According to Durkheim, what characterised such traditional societies was on the one hand that they built on a type of world view which was in all its basic features founded on religious conceptions, and on the other hand, that there was no great difference between the collective identity of society and the individual identity of its members. The participation in religious rites has served several functions. First, it has helped carry on society's world view – i.e. the distinction between what is profane and what is sacred and between what is permitted and what is not permitted. Secondly, the collective identity and solidarity of society has been secured. Thirdly, this collective identity has also been socialised into an integral part of the members' identity. The worship of the same symbols, the compliance with the same taboos, signified a normative kind of consensus which also defined the individual as a member of society (Habermas 1987a: 52 f.). In Durkheim's opinion, the binding nature of morality thus depends on the fact that we respect morality as something (in a broad sense) sacred. He therefore has absolutely no faith in the possibility of basing morality for example on utilitarian considerations.

Even if we accept that the moral attitude has such a source, it is still a far cry from the mythical world views of traditional societies to the views that make themselves felt in our modern societies. The next question is therefore how we got from there to where we are now, i.e. how norms have managed to keep their binding character in spite of the fact that they have been freed from their religious slough. Habermas's (1987a: 77) answer – which he finds support of in Durkheim and Mead – is that there has been going on what he calls a *linguistification of the sacred*. Language has developed as a medium of communication and entered into an increasing number of social contexts. As a consequence, it has become both possible and necessary critically to evaluate more and more aspects of life, and to take less of what has been passed on for granted. This involves what has been referred to as an increasing risk of dissent, and it has led to the dissolution of the uniform religious world picture in favour of more secular frames of interpretation, such as the scientific one. At the same time, the individual has to a greater extent separated itself from the collective identity and developed a more subjective personality. In the normative area, the consensus that was previously handed down ritually and guaranteed by religious conceptions has gradually been replaced by the form of consensus that must be achieved through exchange of arguments and voluntary, critical approval.

First, a separation takes place between informal moral norms and formal laws. Regarding the development of the system of laws, criminal laws came first, while private law is of a more recent date. Therefore, according to Durkheim, the links to the sacred origins of the law are most obvious in criminal law. Criminal law was originally society's ritual reaction against profanation and breach of taboos; it was a demand that committed sins must be expiated. In principle, there is not a big difference whether the reaction is aimed at profanation of holy objects or misdeeds such as rape or murder. It is more difficult to explain how the regulations of private law can have a binding function as well, as their sole function is normally to balance purely profane private interests, based on a concept of private ownership. The basic institution in the regulation of private legal interests is the *contract*, and the question which has been posed by theorists from Thomas Hobbes to Herbert Spencer and Max Weber is why contractual obligations actually are met. These theorists have answered the question by referring to the power potential of the state: contracts are fulfilled because violations of them are punished by the state. At the same time this form of enforcement is perceived as legitimate, because the contract has been entered into voluntarily, and because everybody knows that in the long run it is in their common interest that the state exercises this kind of force. In fact, the Hobbesian tradition has maintained that the entire state can be understood precisely as a contract between the members of society. The members have entered into this social contract because they find it is in their own interest to have a superior body which makes sure that all private contracts between the citizens are fulfilled.

Durkheim (cf. 1964: 211 ff.) does not find this explanation satisfactory, however, because it does not explain why a number of completely atomised individuals should have enough trust in each other to enter into the original social contract. Hence, society cannot be the result of a contract. On the contrary, orderly social conditions are a prerequisite for contract-making to be possible at all, and such conditions can only have been brought about through the normative integration of society. Thus, the coercive power of the state, as well as the contract institution itself, also rest on an element which is in the final instance normative. It is this element Durkheim refers to as the *non-contractual in the contract*. When society, through the state, takes upon itself to make sure that contracts are complied with, it is because contracts are regarded as legitimate, in so far as they protect a general interest. However, the condition for this to be the case is not only that the contract has been signed voluntarily, but also that its content can be justified from this perspective. More precisely, the content of the contract must be *just*, which means that the contract partners appear in an equal relationship.[3] The parties may well enter into the contract with a view to their respective particular interests only, but society's conditions for approving and sanctioning the contract are universal and general. What gives the contract its binding character is that the framework conditions that constitute it either have been, or would have been, approved by the members of society, because they are felt to be reasonable and just. Under modern conditions, this is a type of agreement that must be ensured through the democratic opinion-forming processes that spring from the political public sphere: 'To the degree that the basic religious consensus gets dissolved and the power of the state loses its sacred supports, the unity of the collectivity can be established and maintained only as the unity of a communication community, that is to say, only by way of a consensus arrived at communicatively in the public sphere,' (Habermas 1987a: 82).

The situation is similar when it comes to modern morality, i.e. those aspects of social life and action which are still regulated by informal normative guidelines, after some of the norms have been formalised into laws with appurtenant penal provisions. As people began to ask questions regarding the traditional, inherited guidelines for what is right and wrong, these had to be replaced by new ones. The new guidelines could only come about as a result of the social process in which the members themselves exchange attitudes and arguments regarding such subjects. Hence, this kind of morality, which is formed through *discourse*, emerges as a kind of rational consensus, i.e. as a result which everyone can freely accept, because they recognise the reasonable grounds on which it is based. Both Durkheim and Mead noted that such a morality would have to be based on universalistic principles. This means that it would have to view conflict situations from a neutral perspective and treat all cases which fall under the same category in the same way. The same condition is implied also in Kant's principle of morality, the categorical imperative. But how it is in practice possible to arrive at a universalisable standpoint is only comprehensible if we as a starting point take Mead's concept of seeing the world from the perspective of the generalised other, and link it to the idea of an open community of communication. Mead (1962: 379 ff.) also realised that it is precisely through discussions with others about common problems that a position such as the generalised other can be formed and expressed, since our personal wishes must here yield in the search for commonly acceptable solutions.

According to Habermas (1987a: 93), the common will, also when it has been formed through rational, linguistic discourse, has managed to keep the respect and binding authority that it gains from its original connection with religious conceptions. Still, in more recent years, Habermas has also underscored that a morality detached from its religious foundation and re-established on a purely rational basis will lead to a motivational deficit. A religious person, who might believe that his or her personal salvation depends on doing the right thing, will have a very strong motive to do so. On the other hand, a moral cognitivist who believes a certain moral command should be followed simply because it is the right thing to do, will have a much weaker motivation for actually acting upon his conviction. To know what is right for epistemic reasons does not mean that other motives will not prevail. 'There is no direct route from discursively achieved consensus to action,' (Habermas 1998b: 35).

THE MORAL PERSPECTIVE

The theories of Mead, Kohlberg, and Durkheim about moral development in individuals and society constitute the most important empirical points of reference to Habermas in his long-lasting work with his own moral theory, the so-called discourse ethics. Philosophically, it belongs to those theories of morality that begin with Immanuel Kant's (1724–1804) concept of *practical reason*. According to Habermas (1990d: 196 f.), this tradition has four basic characteristics: it is

- deontological

- cognitivist

- formalist

- universalist.

That it is *deontological* (from Greek *deon* = duty) means that it aims to explain which qualities give commands and action norms their binding character, i.e. why we feel a moral incitement to follow them. This is related to the fact that they are an expression of right or just principles, principles that everyone can agree with on a rational basis. The *cognitivist* character of the theory is closely related to this fact, as it emphasises that moral actions rest on rational moral insights, and that moral rightness is to be regarded as a 'truth-analogue' quality (i.e. it is not synonymous with truth, but resembles it). That the theory is *formalist* means that it does not attempt to specify the content of moral 'truths'. It does not have any answer as to which goods we should strive for; it is not substantial or teleological, as is, for example, utilitarianism and Aristotelian ethics. Instead it attempts to demonstrate which principles and procedures we must apply in order to arrive at morally tenable results. Finally, the *universalist* character of the theory involves the claim that not all normative principles are relative in relation to time and space, and that it itself builds on principles which are universally valid, i.e. everywhere and at all times.

Habermas maintains that a moral theory based on these four qualities both can be defended and is the best suited tool in trying to understand what the moral attitude really consists in. Our greatest challenge is to substantiate for one thing that moral judgements have a cognitive character, which means that they build on rational insight, and secondly, that these judgements also have universal validity. It is not immediately clear what could constitute the basis for these assessments. For example, if a psychologist through his/her professional methods concludes that a test person has this or that moral view, it is a cognitive statement. However, this is a statement which must be related to a theoretical discourse; it is either true or untrue that the person has these views. But what basis do we have for approaching the question of whether these opinions are normatively valid, i.e. a problem which belongs to a moral-practical discourse? Is there any kind of independent basis to which normative statements can be compared – in the same way as statements about objective conditions can be compared to the state of the objective world[4] – or are they just an expression of the single individual's arbitrary, personal opinions and subjective feelings?

The Kantian tradition has generally presupposed that people's everyday experiences with morality constitute a basis of reference for moral judgements. That all of us have an *intuitive experience of a moral dimension of life* is not only an objective fact; it is also a point of departure for a philosophical reconstruction of a specific normative logic. If moral philosophy can demonstrate that there is a rational pattern in people's moral actions, i.e. that they follow a particular principle when they comply with moral judgements, then it has also demonstrated that normative perceptions are not arbitrary and purely subjective, but that they have a well-considered, intersubjective, and cognitive core. It was such a principle Kant believed he had found by the formulation of the categorical imperative – a principle that people already practise or attempt to practise in action. It is also this kind of principle that discourse ethics seeks to formulate.

Habermas (1990c: 28 ff.) here refers to an article by the British philosopher P. F. Strawson (1919—), who discusses what our immediate experience can tell us about morality as a phenomenon. According to Strawson (1968), it is correct that we respond to moral offence – a committed injustice – by an emotional reaction. However, such emotional reactions are different from, for example, fear or rage, which are spontaneous, unpremeditated, and uncontrollable. Our reaction to actions which are regarded as morally wrong is resentment or indignation, or – if it is an injustice committed by ourselves – a feeling of guilt or shame. These reactions show that we believe we have *reasons* to feel the way we do; that we consider ourselves to be entitled to take this attitude, or that others are entitled to take a condemning attitude if we ourselves have caused the injustice in question. This shows that morality has a cognitive basis. Moral feelings are also different from those feelings that we have in connection with incidents to which we take an objectifying attitude. Our despair may be equally deep in the two situations; however, we do not blame natural forces if our house burns down as a result of lightning, in the way that we may blame our neighbours if their careless way of burning rubbish is the cause of the fire. What makes us feel moral indignation towards someone, or assume that someone feels the same way towards us, is no doubt the fact that we expect these others to be capable of identifying something as an offence in the same way as we do. We feel indignation because we think that those who caused the injustice should have known that their action would be regarded as an offence, but they nevertheless performed it. Correspondingly, we can be well aware of it if we have ourselves committed an action which is an offence, in our own as well as other people's eyes. Thus, morality must necessarily have an intersubjective basis, i.e. it rests on a system of *common normative expectations*, which is not only shared by ego and alter but by society as a whole.[5]

However, ethical non-cognitivists have not accepted this as a final proof. They can accept the description above as one that broadly gives a correct description of our intuitive understanding of normative questions, but they nevertheless claim that that understanding must be rejected as false; critical scrutiny shows that it is an illusion which is unfounded. What appears to us as moral reasons for doing this or that, is in reality only camouflaged expressions of our subjective choice between different purposes, which cannot in themselves be justified (Habermas 1990c: 55). The main argument of ethical non-cognitivists is that normative statements can never be verified or falsified, in the way that descriptive statements can. The lack of reality basis in normative questions is shown in the fact that it is rarely possible to agree on basic moral questions. In order to get on the offensive in this debate, then, the cognitivists must refer to a principle which can form the basis for normative agreement. However, the requirement must be stricter than that. Not only must the principle allow people to agree; it must also make sure that this agreement builds on morally tenable premises.

> We must distinguish between the social fact that a norm is intersubjectively recognized and its worthiness to be recognized. There may be good reasons to consider the validity claim raised in a socially accepted norm to be unjustified. Conversely, a norm whose claim to validity is in fact redeemable does not necessarily meet with actual recognition or approval.
>
> (Habermas 1990c: 61)

Thus, an empirical test does not suffice; we must be able to distinguish social validity from normative validity. That we aim at a reconstruction of people's intuitive understanding and practice in normative questions does not mean that the only factor that we need to take into consideration is how people actually behave in a given situation. Instead, the approach involves a certain idealisation, in the sense that we try to look 'behind' concrete practices, in an attempt to articulate those basic principles that are perhaps only imperfectly expressed in established norms and individual actions. What we are trying to reconstruct is thus an ideal formulation of those normative principles that on logical consistent terms can be derived from our everyday interpretation of morality.

THE PRINCIPLE OF UNIVERSALISATION

All attempts at formulating cognitivist theories of morality have concluded that the only principle which can make it possible to create agreement about normative questions, and which can be said to be implicit in people's moral practice, is some version of the idea which lies behind the categorical imperative. 'This bridging principle, which makes consensus possible, ensures that only those norms are accepted as valid that express a *general will*. As Kant noted time and again, moral norms must be suitable for expression as 'universal laws',' (Habermas 1990c: 63). In other words, the principle involves that norms are only valid if they can be made *universal*. That formulation of the principle which Habermas has found most adequate is built into the so-called *principle of universalisation*, which states that any norm must meet the following conditions in order to be valid:

> *(U)* *All* affected can accept the consequences and the side effects its *general* observance can be anticipated to have for the satisfaction of *everyone's* interests (and these consequences are preferred to those of known alternative possibilities for regulation).
>
> (Habermas 1990c: 65)[6]

According to Habermas (1990c: 65), what distinguishes (U) from most other formulations of the idea of universalisability, is that here each and everyone is required to view a matter from the perspectives of each of the other people involved. This is precisely what Mead was alluding to with his concepts of ideal role-taking and of taking the perspective of the generalised other. To Habermas, the point is that such a goal can in practice only be reached through an open discourse, where each and everyone can present their own version. In such a discourse, the arguments will show whether the norm in question damages some people's interests more than others', or if it deserves intersubjective recognition because it expresses a genuinely common and impartial interest.[7]

However, so far we have given the reader no reason to assume that (U) takes such a unique universal position, i.e. that the principle is equally valid across every cultural and historical dividing line. Even if (U) agrees with *our* intuitive understanding of how we think and act morally, this may be because we are all part of modern Western culture. After all, we do run into many different value conceptions when we move about in social and historical space. To be sure, we may maintain that even though other principles of morality can be established which are incompatible with the Kantian point of departure, it may nevertheless be possible to argue convincingly that the Kantian position is superior to the others in one way or the other. However, a question that must be answered in that case is: from what position would such an argumentation take place? For the test to be real, our position must be independent of both the Kantian and the competing moral perspectives. Otherwise we would presuppose exactly that which was to be proved. However, it is difficult to imagine what such a neutral meta-position would be like. The attempt to justify (U) as a universally valid moral point of departure therefore fails, at least for the moment. Proponents of the non-cognitivist perspective (Albert 1985) have maintained that all attempts to justify a universalist morality have resulted in a 'Münchhausen trilemma',[8] where we are finally faced with a choice between three solutions that are all equally dissatisfying. First, we may try to justify a norm by deriving it from a superior norm, which must again be derived from a norm at an even more principal level etc. in an infinite regress. Secondly, we may interrupt this regress at an arbitrary point and decide to turn a particular moral principle into the unfounded starting point, from which other principles must be derived. Thirdly, we may argue in a circle. If we start out by presupposing that certain premises are valid, we can in the next instance be able to justify the same premises (cf. Habermas 1990c: 79).

However, the Münchhausen trilemma only arises if a deductive justification strategy is regarded as the sole way of supporting a universalistic moral theory. But Habermas's friend and colleague through many years, Karl-Otto Apel (1922—), who has played at least as great a role as Habermas himself in the development of discourse ethics, has demonstrated that it is possible to use a different, indirect form of justification instead, the so-called *transcendental-pragmatic* form (Apel 1980). In short, its main tenet is that if the validity of a disputed moral principle cannot be denied without committing a *performative contradiction*, the principle in question must be regarded as valid. A performative contradiction occurs when a claim is presented which is in opposition to something that must be presupposed in order to present the claim. Apel's classical example is a person who says: 'I do not exist.' The person has then committed a performative contradiction if we presuppose that existence is a necessary condition for giving a statement. Correspondingly, Apel and Habermas maintain, the argumentative practice based on communication oriented to reaching understanding itself presupposes that there is equality and symmetry between the parties. The purpose of an argument is to convince the participants in the discussion, and people cannot be truly convinced unless they, on an independent basis and without force, determine to accept some argument as valid. He or she who attempts to convince their audience that they are rationally irresponsible beings, and that their views should therefore not be taken into account, commits a performative contradiction, for just by venturing into an exchange of arguments with these people, the speaker has implicitly accepted them as in principle equal to (her-)himself as far as mental abilities are concerned.

What will the situation be like for somebody who wants to argue *against* the universal validity of (U)? Again we have to look at the implicit presuppositions that lie in the concepts of arguing and convincing. For example, it would go against the basic meaning of these concepts if we try to obtain agreement by excluding relevant counter-arguments, either by shutting out potential participants, or by somehow preventing them from presenting their views. Thus, they who want to argue that the principle of universalisation lacks validity have just by entering into the argumentation presupposed its validity. For in the same way as, according to (U), the validity of any norm depends on its acceptance by everyone who is affected by it, so the validity of any argument presupposes that it can be accepted, on a free and rational basis, by all relevant participants in a discourse (Habermas 1990c: 86 ff.). Thus, it appears that the symmetry or equality which is a fundamental characteristic of the relation between the parties in understanding-oriented communication has normative implications as well. It would be an example of a performative contradiction if we try to justify the legitimacy of a norm that does not have such qualities that it would be accepted through a communicative procedure. This is reflected in what Habermas (1990c: 93) refers to as the *principle of discourse ethics*:

> *(D)* Only those norms can claim to be valid that meet (or could meet) with the approval of all affected in their capacity as participants in a practical discourse.

(D) is meant to express the basic idea of discourse ethics; it summarises the core content of the theory. By contrast, (U) has a more 'active' status as a *rule of argumentation*. This implies that to be in harmony with the insights of discourse ethics, the discourse participants must comply with this rule in discussing the validity of norms (Habermas 1990c: 93).[9]

However, the universal validity of discourse ethics is still not fully established, for if this validity is justified with reference to an argumentative practice, we know that the scope of this kind of practice has varied greatly between different types of human society. This form of interaction has perhaps been cultivated to a particular extent in our own scientific civilisation. This fact is acknowledged also by Habermas, but he nevertheless maintains that in some form and to some extent, argumentation seems to be a common feature of all cultures.

> This is why there is no form of sociocultural life that is not at least implicitly geared to maintaining communicative action by means of argument, be the actual form of argumentation ever so rudimentary and the institutionalization of discursive consensus building ever so inchoate.
>
> (Habermas 1990c: 100)

The implication here is that it is possible to argue, on the basis of the cultural self-understanding of any society, that a consistent practising of this self-understanding involves that (U) must be accepted as valid. Hence, in deciding questions with normative implications, the interests and views of all affected members must be given equal weight. That this principle is not yet followed universally, and that it is in fact not consistently followed in any society, can according to discourse ethics only be explained by the fact that people do not act consistently and rationally in all practical situations. The reason may perhaps be that they have not reflexively realised what they have already implicitly accepted by entering into argumentation.

A disagreement has, however, emerged between Apel and Habermas with regard to the scientific-logical status of discourse ethics. Apel claims that by deriving the principle of universalisation from the general precondition for argumentation, we have been able to establish a completely secure, a priori basis for a cognitive theory of morality, a so-called *ultimate justification* of moral judgements. He claims that this represents a solution to the Münchhausen trilemma, and that the principle of universalisation constitutes an unshakable basis against which concrete norms can be tested. However, Habermas has reservations against this way of understanding discourse ethics. First, he claims that even though it may be demonstrated that (U) is a necessary condition for meaningful argumentation, it does not automatically follow that actors are rationally committed to treat each other as equals also in their general interaction. The rules to which we are subjected as discourse participants are not necessarily transferred to our role as actors. Therefore, the validity of concrete action norms cannot be inferred from the existence of these general preconditions for argumentation. Such validity can only result from agreement obtained in a practical discourse. However, in such practical discourses (where the validity of norms is discussed), the members of any society would have to build on particular rules of argumentation[10] (concerning free participation and exchange of opinion, etc.), and it is from *these* rules that (U) must be derived in order to become a universally valid principle for the justification of moral norms, according to Habermas (1990c: 85 f.).[11] Thus, Habermas wants to tie the discourse ethical claim to universal validity much closer to the factual normative argumentation that takes place within the framework of the individual historical lifeworld context (cf. Apel 1992a: 128). His point seems to be that the moral status of people is more or less given from their status as lifeworld participants; we cannot choose to disregard this background.[12]

This has to be seen in the light of the previously mentioned distinction between ethics and morality, between the contextual and universal aspects of norms. Habermas (1990c: 108 f.) realises that the establishment or rejection of norms always takes place within the ethical context of a concrete lifeworld, and that there is not very much we can say about this theme on a general, non-contextual moral basis. Is it, for example, right to allow euthanasia? The question can hardly be given a universally valid answer on purely moral premises. The truth is rather that all societies have some traditionally handed-down value judgements which will strongly influence the discussion of the issue. Still, when such questions are raised in the form of a moral-practical discourse, people are nevertheless able to problematise the traditional views in order to find an answer as to what is the right thing to do, all things considered and given new knowledge and a new situation. The only practical contribution from the moral theory is a reminder that when such decisions are made, all parties must be allowed to participate in the discussion on equal terms, and the interests of all parties must be given equal weight when a decision is made. Thus, Habermas conceives of discourse theory as a purely procedural theory to an even higher degree than does Apel.[13] Habermas's version suggests a procedure that must be followed in order for norms to be regarded as morally valid, but it does not say anything about the content of these norms.

Secondly, Habermas will not (in contrast to Apel) give (U) status as an 'ultimate justification' of moral argumentation, i.e. as a priori principle that can never be questioned or falsified. To be sure, he does not find either that there is any alternative to accepting (U) as a necessary premise, if we want to enter into what we understand as argumentative practice. He nevertheless claims that in principle we must be open to the possibility that somebody may at some stage approach the question from a different conceptual perspective than has been done so far, and hence arrive at a different result. Therefore, we cannot refer to (U) as a priori knowledge, but rather as something which can and should be tested empirically (Habermas 1990c: 95 ff.).[14] Will this weaken the cognitivistic pretensions of discourse ethics? Habermas (1990c: 98), at least, does not think so. In his view, we rather get a theory of morality that is more in line with empirical sciences as far as cognitive status is concerned, as its attempt to reconstruct existing normative conceptions can now to a greater extent be made the object of testing. The descriptions of discourse ethics may in this connection be regarded as a competitor to the reconstruction proposals of other moral theories, in the same way as different theories compete within other disciplines.

PRAGMATIC, ETHICAL, AND MORAL DISCOURSES

Although Habermas originally placed himself safely within the Kantian tradition of moral philosophy, it has become increasingly clear to him over the years that the question of what is *right action* in a given situation involves a wide area of problems, which contains more dimensions than those captured by the universalism and formalism of the Kantian theory. In order to expand the perspective, Habermas has included also two other well-established approaches to normative questions. Consequently, he now (Habermas 1993c) refers to the *pragmatic*, the *ethical*, and the *moral* application of practical reason.

He relates the *pragmatic* dimension of practical reason to the utilitarian tradition within moral philosophy. Its founder, Jeremy Bentham (1748–1832), maintained that there existed no other standard for moral values than what was appreciated by each individual. In other words, what is a moral good is a purely subjective question. In Bentham's view, the only general statement we can make about this topic is that humans will, by nature, try to act in a way that maximises the feeling of pleasure or happiness and minimises the feeling of pain. This should be the starting point of politics and legislation as well: society must be arranged in a manner which makes it possible to maximise the total amount of happiness or utility, as those concepts are defined by each individual. This goal, Bentham thought, could best be reached through a liberal policy, which gives the individual the greatest possible freedom of choice in as many areas as possible. As it is not possible collectively to define any general ideal values (in the substantial sense) that the morally good action should realise, the practical-philosophical question of what should be done is here reduced to a pure consideration of expediency, and must be decided on the basis of the individual's subjective 'preferences'.

According to the utilitarian view, it is unnecessary and useless to consider or discuss these preferences, since we must assume that people know what they want and because the criteria for making such choices are of a purely personal character. What can be discussed, however, is which concrete goals can be said in the best possible way to realise the supposedly given preferences, or which means can most effectively realise the chosen goals. This is what pragmatic[15] considerations are all about. Many everyday decisions are indeed of such a character that this type of consideration is sufficient. Whether the question is how we should proceed in order to repair a bicycle or cure an illness, where we want to go on vacation, or which type of education we must choose in order to realise our career plans, the starting point is always that we know what we want to achieve. What must be decided through a rational choice is how we can best achieve it.[16]

> As long as the question 'What should I do?' has such pragmatic tasks in view, observations, investigations, comparisons, and assessments undertaken on the basis of empirical data with a view to efficiency or with the aid of other decision rules are

appropriate. Practical reflection here proceeds within the horizon of purposive rationality, its goal being to discover appropriate techniques, strategies, or programs.

(Habermas 1993c: 3)

The Aristotelian tradition within normative philosophy is also oriented towards the search for happiness or for the good life, but it gives a far more existential interpretation of this question than does utilitarianism. Indeed, Aristotelian ethics does not presuppose that individuals know from the start what they want to do with their lives, and that the only problem is to find ways of realising their goals. On the contrary, it is the task of ethics to contribute to clarifying what is a good life, and which type of conduct is required in order to achieve it. Here ends and means become one, and to plot the right course in life requires *phronesis* or practical wisdom, which is something very different from theoretical or calculating rationality, according to Aristotle. To make the right choices becomes a question of finding our identity, i.e. who we are and who we want to be. For example, if we take different educations to be not only more or less efficient means of obtaining a career, but a question of what we want to do with our lives, the choices we make in this connection come into an entirely different perspective. It becomes an example of what Habermas understands as an *ethical* problem, that is, a type of problem that involves value judgements.

Habermas links the distinction between pragmatic and ethical questions to Charles Taylor's (1985a) distinction between *weak* and *strong evaluations*.[17] What characterises pragmatic questions and weak evaluations in this respect, is that we may choose one alternative instead of another simply because we prefer it, without having to justify this preference to ourselves or to others. When we wish to buy one brand of car instead of another, or to spend our holiday in the south instead of in the north, these are examples of choices that we constantly have to make, but where one of the alternatives in no way appears (normatively) superior to the other. However, according to the Aristotelian tradition (to which Taylor may be said to belong), certain types of questions are different in the sense that some alternatives can be claimed to be better than others in a qualitative sense. For example, an action may be characterised as cowardly, mean or ill-considered, while we could instead have chosen to act bravely, nobly or sensibly in the relevant situation. When we act in situations where our choices can be described as either commendable or reprehensible, they are based on what Taylor refers to as strong evaluations, and it is this type of considerations that in Habermas's view are involved in ethical questions. Such choices have to do with our identity and self-understanding, i.e. who we want to be in our own eyes, as well as in the eyes of others. Habermas describes ethical questions as *clinical*. This means that by clarifying such questions, we can gain greater insight into those goals that we really want to realise, and hence we can avoid making important value choices which are based on self-delusion. The function of ethics here is to help ensure that our life project does not fail, but instead becomes an authentic realisation of our possibilities and ambitions.

In the Kantian tradition, there is a third way of understanding normative questions, viz. in terms of how we can reasonably be expected to behave when our actions affect other people's interests. Such situations involve problems of justice, i.e. what Habermas defines as *moral* questions. From a pragmatic point of view, it is impossible to identify anything as a moral dilemma, as an actor here acts monologically, i.e. other actors are perceived merely as means or obstacles in the realisation of his or her own, individual action plans.

> If I can secure a loan only by concealing pertinent information, then from a pragmatic point of view all that counts is the probability of my deception's succeeding. Someone who raises the issue of its permissibility is posing a *different* kind of question – the moral question of whether we all could will that anyone in my situation should act in accordance with the same maxim.
>
> (Habermas 1993c: 6)

Neither from an ethical perspective is it possible to regard normative problems as intersubjective questions of justice. To be sure, ethics also sees the need for rules that regulate our interaction with other people. However, its approach is to a greater extent based on the fact that we all live in societies founded on particular traditions, and this among other things concerns rules for behaviour. If I violate such rules, it may of course influence both other people's respect for me and my self-respect, and in the end even contribute to the destruction of the social order. Thus, if we omit to follow the normative codex of society, it will easily come into conflict with the aim of realising a good life for myself and my fellow citizens. We should therefore take established rules of conduct into consideration, thereby showing that we respect our fellow beings and the traditions of society. However, the moral perspective does not ask if it is wise of *me* to act in a particular way in a particular situation, but whether *we all* can rationally wish everyone to act in the same way in all corresponding situations, i.e. that the maxim of the action should be turned into a general law. This principle follows from a 'communicative-theoretical transformation' of Kant's categorical imperative.[18] Thus, while ethical problems have a subjective and particular point of departure, this is transformed into an intersubjective and universal problematic in the moral case. The moral attitude is consequently expressed in the duty we all have to act justly towards other individuals.

It should be clear from the discussion so far that it would not be in the spirit of Habermas to assume that new practical knowledge is developed primarily through silent contemplation in the consciousness of individual subjects. He is instead concerned with how such processes take place through the exchange of arguments between people in discourses. Habermas (1990b: 130) describes discourses as a continuation of communicative action by other means. When we, in our daily communicative coordination of actions, get to a point where the basis for the mutual interaction appears to be problematic, perhaps because we disagree about elements in the action context, we often need to remove the point of disagreement from its immediate context and attempt to solve the problems through systematic argumentation which aims at creating a basis for new agreement. However, such discourses will be different depending on whether the problems are of pragmatic, ethical or moral nature.

In Figure 4.2 we have tried to summarise some of the characteristic features of the various types of discourse, especially how they relate to Habermas's three world concepts.[19] First of all, we must distinguish between theoretical discourses, which relates to questions about how things are – correct descriptions, and practical discourses, which relates to questions about what I/we should do – right action. The theoretical discourse has the scientific debate as its model example and in this perspective the world is always seen as an objectively existing reality.

Type of discourse	World perspective involved in . . .		Content of discourse	Aim of discourse	Cognitive/ Normative Ideal	Corresponding Concept of Action Rationality
	Problem formulation	Problem solving				
theoretical	objective world	objective world	theories, descriptions	reveal facts	truth	——
pragmatic (practical)	subjective world	objective world	technologies, strategies	indicate rational choices	utility, expediency	purposive (instrumental/ strategic)
ethical- existential (practical)	subjective world	social world	values, principles for life conduct	give clinical guidance aimed at personal self- realisation	the good	contextual
moral (practical)	social world	social world (ideal, universal)	norms, obligations	find just solutions to normative conflicts	the right	communicative

Figure 4.2 *Discourse-theoretical properties related to a three-world perspective*

What the discourse is all about is formulating correct theories and giving adequate descriptions to represent this objective world. The aim is thus to reveal relevant facts and establish true statements about the subject being discussed.

In this chapter we are, however, more interested in the discourses that relate to right action or the use of practical reason. If we start with the pragmatic type of discourse it has as its raw material, so to speak, each individual's preferences and purposes, i.e. things to which he or she has a privileged access as part of their subjective world. The start of the problem that we try to solve by means of a pragmatic discourse is always: 'what does s/he (we) want?' As mentioned, these subjective goals are not worth discussing, according to this perspective and must be taken for granted. What can be discussed is how such personal preferences may best be realised, and that is exactly what the pragmatic discourse tries to establish. In the effort to find such solutions the world is seen as an objectively existing relationship between various phenomena, where the most efficient means can and must be chosen to realise the given ends. The content of the discussion is typically which technologies or strategies that might be best suited to make this happen. The aim is thus to single out the most rational choice among the existing alternatives, based on a normative ideal where utility or expediency is viewed as the ultimate value. The underlying rationality concept is purposive rationality, either in its instrumental or in its strategic version (cf. Chapter 2).

Even the ethical-existential discourse starts out from the first person perspective and thereby from a subjective type of questioning: 'who I am and who I would like to be, or how I should lead my life' (Habermas 1998b: 26). But in order to answer such questions satisfactorily, we will need the assistance of other individuals with whom we share our lifeworld. They may 'assume the catalyzing role of impartial critics in processes of self-clarification' (Habermas 1993c: 11).

> The attractiveness of the values in light of which I understand myself and my life cannot be explained within the limits of the world of subjective experiences to which I have privileged access. From the ethical point of view, my preferences and goals are no longer simply given but are themselves open to discussion; since they depend on my self-understanding, they can undergo reasoned change through reflection on what has intrinsic value *for us* within the horizon of our shared social world.
>
> (Habermas 1998b: 26 f.)

Unlike the preferences that appear in pragmatic discourses, ethical preferences are not of a pre-rational and pre-reflective nature and can therefore be altered through an exchange of arguments. Solutions to ethical-existential problems thus involve the individual's social world. The themes open to discursive reflection will here typically be which values are really good and which principles should be chosen to guide one's life conduct. The aim is to help the individual to make the right choices in order to achieve the best possible realisation of personal potentials. Normative standard is the belief that some substantive values are better than others and that the aim of human existence is to strive for a good life. Standards of rationality – what values are good or bad – are seen as collective properties inherent in and unique to each society, which implies a contextual concept of rationality (cf. Chapter 2).

When we get to the moral type of discourse, the formulation of the problem reflects from the outset awareness of a social world, a world consisting of 'a normative context that lays down which interactions belong to the totality of legitimate interpersonal relations' (Habermas 1984: 88). In this instance the question is what kind of behaviour we are justified to expect from our fellow members of society, and what they are equally justified to expect from us. But in answering such questions it is not always sufficient to refer to existing moral norms in the particular community to which we belong, because these socially accepted norms may well be flawed from an ideal point of view. The point of the moral discourse, as Habermas sees it, is exactly to test such norms and maxims from the perspective of a *universal* social world. This ideal moral community consists of all individuals who have been socialised into any communicative form of life.

> Every concrete community depends on the moral community as its 'better self,' so to speak. As members of this community, individuals expect to be treated equally, while it is assumed at the same time that each person regards every other person as 'one of us.'
>
> (Habermas 1998b: 29)

The content of a moral-practical discourse is which norms and moral obligations are legitimate because they give equal consideration to the interest of all affected. The practical aim is obviously to point to just solutions to normative conflicts, where the standard is set by the validity claim of rightness. And in order to test for universal moral validity the participants need a communicative concept of rationality.

THE GOOD AND THE RIGHT – CONTEXTUALISM AND UNIVERSALISM

With his tripartite division between pragmatic, ethical, and moral discourses, Habermas attempts to communicate a more complex picture of practical reason than he has done previously. He will still insist that the most fundamental question in normative theory is the question of what is right, of giving our fellow beings a just treatment, with the principle of equality as a starting point (implying the claim of universalisability). This puts the moral use of practical reason in a unique position.[20] On the other hand, Habermas emphasises that normative questions are so complex that we also need the pragmatic and ethical approaches, and that the utilitarian, Aristotelian, and Kantian traditions may all contribute in solving normative problems. In addition to the question of what is right, the normative approach thus also has to discuss the question of what is good, i.e. which values are worth striving for, as well as the kinds of questions which must be answered on the basis of subjective preferences and empirically based knowledge of the circumstances (viz. the pragmatic dimension).

During the past 30 years, there has been an extensive and intense debate between those who think the search for 'the good' and those who think the search for 'the right' should be the primary objective of normative theory.[21] This can also be described as a choice between putting solidarity or justice first. The supporters of solidarity place primary emphasis on the preservation of those structures that keep society intact as a collective. These are often emotional bonds, which naturally tie us more closely to those we associate with and to whom we, in a concrete sense, have a relationship as fellow human beings. By contrast, the supporters of justice particularly emphasise the equal respect that each human being deserves as an individual (Habermas 1990d: 200). As we have seen, feminist theorists such as Carol Gilligan (1982) (and, for example, Iris M. Young (1990)) have criticised the justice-based moral theory on the basis of such a solidarity consideration. They claim that abstract, principled reason can not be used in relation to many types of question which are involved in normative evaluations. There is a need for a more contextualistic perspective, which captures those interpersonal relations and the compassion and care that are present in practical interaction situations. As claimed by Gilligan, it is rather a question of being able to view the situation from the perspective of the concrete other than from the perspective of Mead's generalised other. This is not only true in specific friendship and love relations, but generally in situations where the compassion, consideration and solidarity of the citizens are called for, and which are hence relevant from a moral perspective (cf. Lévinas 1969; Benhabib 1987, 1992; Honneth 1995; Skirbekk 1993).

It may seem reasonable that a concept of justice must hold a central position in a normative theory. The question is nevertheless how far we can get with the type of universalistic and formalistic approach to moral questions for which Kant was a spokesman (cf. Bernstein 1995). Hegel was the first to criticise Kant's idea that moral actions could spring from a general principle of reason, such as the categorical imperative. In Hegel's view, the categorical imperative can justify about everything and nothing when it comes to concrete actions. What really governs people's actions is *Sittlichkeit* or 'ethical life', i.e. those customs and practices into which people have been socialised through their social affiliation. Here Hegel is in line with today's feminists and neo-Aristotelians, who also emphasise that good actions must be motivated by something substantial and concrete which we can relate to (for example national sentiment). Therefore, the standards for what is regarded as good are bound to differ according to (cultural, social) context.

A slightly different type of criticism has come from another proponent of the critical theory tradition, viz. Albrecht Wellmer (1986, 1991). His criticism is also directed towards the stringent formalism and universalism of discourse ethics. Among other things, Wellmer maintains that the principle of universalisation makes unrealistic demands on the cognitive and moral competence of the citizens; thus, it is difficult to use it to derive clear consequences.[22] The conditions that are made in the principle of universalisation (U) lead to a series of questions that need to be answered. For example, we need to ask who is really affected by a decision, who are relevant and competent participants, to what extent should they participate, and what can be demanded of them. Further, to hear all those who are affected by a decision involves practical problems, and there is limited knowledge about consequences, power relations, and the interpretation of needs, etc. Thus this strong formulation of discourse theory may potentially lead us into a series of problems, especially if we expect it to tell us what is the correct action in different situations.

Habermas (1990d) has in part wanted to demonstrate that these forms of criticism do not affect discourse ethics, but his primary response has been to realise that the theory must be reformulated in order to stand up to such objections. First, he believes that the theory does not have to make a choice between justice and solidarity – between the abstract, equal rights of every individual and the emotional bonds that tie people together in groups and communities. Instead, the theory must presuppose a combination of these considerations, as a cooperative search for agreement depends on individuals who are on the one hand autonomous, but who are at the same time able to cooperate and feel responsibility and respect for each other. This point is taken care of through the fact that the moral type of discourse has been supplemented by the ethical type. The fundamental normative question, he now confirms, can indeed be interpreted as the Aristotelian, ethical problem of what is good – the good life and the good society. However, we cannot let the question rest with every single group or cultural community and their definition of what is good according to their specific values. As such groups meet and confront each other, the question must be extended to ever wider circles: what is equally good for all? Then we have reached the level of justice, which can be understood as an idealising extension of the ethical problem of the good. Rather than interpreting them as opposites, Habermas now (1998b: 29) recognises the 'remnant of the good at the core of the right'. But even if he sees the question for the good as the (in one way) fundamental normative question, he still regards the question for the right as the superior question; he maintains the priority of the right over the good (Habermas 1998b: 28).

Secondly, he believes that Hegel's critique of Kant partly misses its target, and to the extent that it affects Kant's theory, it nevertheless does not affect the discourse ethics of today. For example, he maintains that the formal and universalistic character of this theory does not turn it into an empty scheme, from which no moral insights can be extracted, as was claimed by Hegel. He nevertheless admits that there may be problematic aspects to a universalistic approach. For example, universalistic principles can, under the cover of 'equal treatment', be abused in order to defend the suppression of weak groups, which perhaps cannot obtain real equality without some form of special treatment. Habermas (1993c: 15) maintains that today as before, such imbalances can only be removed by means of social and political mobilisation on the part of the suppressed. In the same vein, he emphasises that even though universalism basically employs the same standard in relation to everything and everyone, nobody is entitled in the name of universalism to deprive anybody of the right to be different. The autonomy of the individual, which is an absolutely necessary condition for a universalistic morality, implies not least the right to choose our own course in life.[23]

However, other theorists have also contributed to mediating the tension between universalism and contextualism. Not least, the legal theorist Klaus Günther, in his book *The Sense of Appropriateness*, has proposed a distinction between a *discourse of justification* and a *discourse of application*. While the former asks for a norm's universalisability, the latter asks what norm is appropriate in a given case of norm conflict (Günther 1993: 212). For example, a norm that says 'you shall not lie' may in certain cases collide with a norm which states that 'everything must be done to save lives'. Which one we should choose depends on how the situation is best described. In any complete description of a practical situation, conflicts of norms will inevitably arise. The problem can only be solved by taking into consideration all potentially relevant norms, comparing and contrasting them in a process that includes all affected parties. Here it is important to be able to defend our selection of specific features of the situation as normatively relevant. The function of the discourse of application is to point out as many moral perspectives as possible, subsequently to deduce the suitable norm from them (Günther 1990: 204). In such a debate, the validity of the relevant norms is not considered. The question is rather *if* a particular rule should be followed in the present circumstances, and in case of yes, how this should be done.[24]

Habermas here follows the direction pointed out by Günther. The principle of universalisation is sufficient to justify or give grounds for norms on a general basis, but it is not suited to give directions for what should be done in a concrete situation. The test of universalisability can be used to rule out certain norms of action if it turns out that they are not universalisable. However, when we in a given context are faced with several universalisable norms that have conflicting content, a different type of discourse is needed to clarify the application aspect.

> the *application* of norms calls for argumentative clarification in its own right. In this case, the impartiality of judgment cannot again be secured through a principle of universalization; rather, in addressing questions of context-sensitive application, practical reason must be informed by a principle of appropriateness (*Angemessenheit*). What must be determined here is which of the norms already accepted as valid is appropriate in a given case in the light of all the relevant features of the situation conceived as exhaustively as possible.
>
> (Habermas 1993c: 13 f.)

Thus, Habermas to a large extent admits that the critics are right in some of their objections to the Kantian point of departure, viz. that the question of universalisability of norms is a specialised and narrow – if important – aspect of practical reason (Habermas 1990d: 206/210). In order for moral considerations to be relevant to a real action situation, concrete aspects of the situation must also be considered. Secondly, also the norm-testing element is now given a more context-sensitive design. This is done by supplying justification discourses with a knowledge and time index: a moral norm is only valid to the extent that it incorporates a common interest at the current time and in relation to the current level of knowledge.[25] Correspondingly, the principle of universalisation (U) is given a formulation which is less absolute and more contextually dependent than is the old one. Now it says that

> (U) A norm is valid when the foreseeable consequences and the side effects of its general observance for the interests and value-orientations of *each individual* could be *jointly* accepted by *all* concerned without coercion.
> (Habermas 1998b: 42)

What is new here is primarily that the basis for accepting norms as just also is seen in relation to the value orientation of each individual (in addition to their interests). Although this does not constitute a dramatic change, it is nevertheless a sign that the rigour of discourse theory has been reduced, and that there is greater room for situational insight and practical judgement. Admittedly, this formulation of (U) does not solve the objections raised by Wellmer either, but this is to a considerable extent done through the knowledge and time index that Günther links to justification discourses. The total result is that it is not only the abstract, deontological, and impartial justifications that constitute what is normatively relevant in the theory of morality, but also the demands made by solidarity and common sense. In other words, a moral rule can be quite right in principle, but in practice there may be good reasons for making exceptions when we consider what is at stake for particular groups and individuals. When conditions are activated which concern compassion, care, and empathy, other justified moral norms may also be relevant. However, such discussions of what is a sensible and appropriate application of norms in a given situation take place under conditions of limited time and imperfect knowledge.

CONCLUSION

In Habermas's view, moral questions are open to rational assessment in a similar (but not the same) way as factual questions are. His starting point is Mead's analysis of how we develop norm-regulated behaviour by learning to view our own actions from the perspective of the collective we belong to, i.e. what he refers to as taking the attitude of the generalised other. It is a further step when we develop the ability not to take existing normative expectations for granted, but to take an independent and critical attitude towards them, based on the perspective of the universal community of communication to which we also belong ('I' as opposed to 'me'). Kohlberg studied the same process as a development of personality, from the preconventional via the conventional to the postconventional level of morality. The reason why moral norms have such authority is, according to

Durkheim, that they were originally linked to religious rites and conceptions. However, through the linguistification of the sacred, the religious basis has been replaced by a rational basis. We have respect for norms and regulations because and to the extent we consider them to express a general interest, i.e. a principle of justice.

Discourse ethics is basically a Kantian theory of morality, i.e. it is deontological, cognitivist, formalist and universalist. Normative questions are of a cognitive nature, as there may be more or less good reasons for different attitudes to such questions. The decisive test when it comes to the rightness of norms, is if they can be universalised, i.e. if we, without contradiction, can want them to be followed generally. This must be decided by the affected parties through a practical discourse. However, the question of what is the right action in various situations has several aspects. Habermas consequently makes a distinction between pragmatic, ethical and moral discourses, which ask what is useful, what is good, and what is right, respectively. Although the moral aspect of practical reason remains superior, it is necessary to consider concrete elements of the situation, as well as the pragmatic and ethical perspectives, when norms are applied. A new distinction has therefore been made between discourses of justification and discourses of application, where the first type tests norms' formal universalisability, while the second tests which norm is most appropriate to apply in a certain situation.

Notes

1. Cf. Habermas 1979c, 1990b, 1990f, and 1993d in particular.
2. It should be mentioned that Kohlberg and Habermas disagree with respect to how the stages in the model should be formulated and interpreted, especially at the postconventional level. Kohlberg attempted to construct the model in such a way that the various moral-philosophical positions would correspond to a particular stage in the development of consciousness. Hence, utilitarianism and the understanding of morality found in the natural right approach would be located to stage 5, while the Kantian form of moral thinking would correspond to stage 6. However, to Habermas this is an example of a typical 'naturalistic' misconception within developmental psychology. In his view, the distinction should be formulated in a way that would only mirror different degrees of reflection. Thus, stage 5 corresponds to a line of thinking where it is deemed necessary to justify action norms by referring to superior principles, but not to justify the principles themselves. By contrast, stage 6 expresses the understanding that such principles need justification as well. As we will see later, this is the case in connection with the attempt of discourse ethics to derive the validity of the universalisation principle from the universal community of communication (Habermas 1990b: 172 f., cf. Habermas 1990f).
3. It might perhaps be argued that no individual with concern for his or her own interests would voluntarily enter into a contract that was not just and fair to both parties. However, this is not always true, since people may find themselves in a desperate situation, which can make them enter into

contracts and transactions that are not fair. For this reason, society does not accept such contracts, e.g. about selling oneself as a slave, even if people have entered into them 'voluntarily' (cf. Walzer 1983: 100).

4. Habermas (and many with him) would be certain to underscore that there is no way that we can *directly* compare statements about objective conditions to the objective world itself either. All we can really do is compare different statements about objective conditions with each other, because we do not have any experience of the objective world that is not symbolically mediated and filtered through linguistic statements. This is a type of insight that goes back to Kant's theoretical philosophy.

5. Cf. the discussion on the emotional basis of morality in Vetlesen 1994.

6. Habermas has used different formulations of the principle of universalisation in different contexts, for example this somewhat simplified version: 'For a norm to be valid, the consequences and side effects of its general observance for the satisfaction of each person's particular interests must be acceptable to all,' (Habermas 1990d: 197).

7. We may ask: 'What if a participant who in reality wants special treatment for strategic reasons refuses to accept that a norm treats everyone equally and is thus just, although he in his own mind realises that this is actually the case?' The simplest answer in our context would be that this participant does not take a moral attitude, but a strategic one. The case in question therefore falls outside the scope of what is discussed here, viz. which principles determine explicitly *moral* actions. However, in reality we have to take into account that such participants may appear, and ideally a discourse situation should be sufficient to reveal these actors, because they are not capable of presenting a convincing rational justification for their standpoints.

8. After the fairytale character Baron von Münchhausen who, when he got into a scrape, solved the situation by lifting himself by the hair.

9. However, whether there is really a fundamental difference between (D) and (U) is a point that is still being vigorously debated. Apel (1998: 733 ff.) thus maintains that (D) can only be regarded as a variation of (U), and cannot be given the status of a purely formal principle, which is indefinite with respect to content, as was intended by Habermas. According to Apel, this is because the presupposition that all participants are equal, autonomous, and rational is built into (D) as well; thus the principle is morally charged.

10. Cf. Chapter 10, p. 217; see also p. 207.

11. However, there is well-founded doubt as to whether the way in which Habermas himself undertakes this derivation is logically valid, or whether it is rather based on circular argumentation (cf. Rehg 1994: 56 ff.).

12. For this more Hegelian aspect of Habermas's philosophy, cf. Bernstein 1995.

13. Cf. the formulation of (D), as well as Apel's objection in note 9 above.

14. This can be related to the criterion of falsification (developed by Karl Popper) which is used within the empirical disciplines. Thus, a universal statement such as 'All ravens are black' only has status as a not yet falsified hypothesis. Although no one has so far seen a white or a blue raven, we cannot *in principle* rule out the possibility that such a raven might fly by some day. Habermas wants to use this principle within discourse ethics as well.

15. The words 'pragmatic' and 'pragmatics' come from the Greek *pragma*, which means 'what has been done', 'deed', 'fact'. In modern use, the terms

have acquired two slightly different meanings. Habermas uses them both, and this may create confusion. On the one hand, the terms are used here in connection with pragmatic discourses, where the meaning is close to that which we find in everyday speech, which involves an emphasis on what is useful or expedient. On the other hand, we have the meaning that goes back to C. S. Peirce's foundation of pragmatism as a philosophical school. This meaning emphasises that what an utterance or an understanding is worth when it comes to truth content must be decided by looking at its practical consequences. A continuation of this school is found in speech act theory, which puts the main emphasis on the practical *use* of language (as opposed to what words *mean* in a semantic sense). It has further inspired the theories of Apel (transcendental pragmatics) and Habermas (universal/formal pragmatics) about what kind of knowledge can be derived from the fact that we are *language using subjects*, as discussed in this and the previous chapter.

16. Because its adherents conceive of utilitarianism as a complete moral-theoretical alternative, they have tried to apply its consequence-ethical principle to a broader set of questions than this one, viz. the question of what is the right distribution of goods and burdens between several individuals or groups. The answer offered by utilitarianism is that the right distribution is that which yields the best result or the greatest utility from a collective perspective. It thus clashes with the Kantian principle of morality (because maximising of total utility is not necessarily consistent with unconditional respect for each individual). In Habermas's opinion, utilitarianism 'does not permit an adequate reconstruction of the meaning of normativity in general' (Habermas 1998b: 11 f.). Unlike utilitarians, then, he believes that we can never give the full answer to normative dilemmas based on the consequences that actions have in realising individuals' subjective preferences. Such considerations can only be one *part* of an adequate moral solution.

17. This is again a development of Harry Frankfurt's (1971) distinction between first and second-order desires. In addition to their immediate first-order desires, individuals can also form second-order desires. This involves the ability to *evaluate* their own wants and needs, regarding some as desirable and others as undesirable, the human species being a self-interpreting species.

18. 'Do not do unto others what you would not have them do unto you' is a principle that goes by the name of the *Golden Rule*, and which is known, among other things, from Christian ethics. However from a universalisation perspective, the rule has the limitation that it views the question from an egocentric perspective, the starting point being how *each subject* would like to be treated. Compared to the golden rule, Kant's categorical imperative represents an expanded perspective, since he claims that an action maxim is only valid if it is possible for *everybody* to want it generally to be followed. Discourse ethics represents a 'transformation' of this view in the sense that it recognises that what everybody can want is not something each of us can know by trying hypothetically to put ourselves in other people's shoes, as presupposed by Kant. This is something that can only be clarified through a real discourse where all potential parties may express what they really want (Habermas 1993c: 7 f.).

19. A point apart from this is, of course, that discourses *in themselves* are intersubjective undertakings and therefore in that respect always related to

the social world. Our aim here is not, however, to characterise the praxis of discussing according to world relation but rather to indicate what world concepts are involved in the perspectives that are raised through the various types of discourses.

20. It would thus have been more precise to refer to this theory as a 'discourse theory of *morality*'. However, Habermas chooses to hold on to the term 'discourse ethics', which is already firmly established and was so long before he introduced his distinction between ethics and morality (Habermas 1993b: vii).

21. The opposing sides of this debate are the so-called communitarians or neo-Aristotelians on the one hand (with Michael Sandel (1996, 1998) as a prominent representative), and the liberals or neo-Kantians on the other (their leading figure being John Rawls (1971, 1993)). For an introduction to this debate, cf. Mulhall and Swift (1996) and Forst (2002).

22. Cf. also McCarthy 1991a, Rehg 1994, Höffe 1996, and Hösle 1997.

23. 'nobody may be excluded in the name of moral universalism – neither unprivileged classes nor exploited nations, neither domesticated women nor marginalized minorities. Someone who in the name of universalism excludes another who has the right to *remain* alien or other betrays his own guiding idea. The universalism of equal respect for all and of solidarity with everything that bears the mark of humanity is first put to the test by radical freedom in the choice of individual life histories and particular forms of life,' (Habermas 1993c: 15).

24. 'The norms that are eclipsed by the norm actually applied in a given case do not thereby lose their validity but form a *coherent normative order* together with all other valid rules. From the standpoint of coherence, the relations within this order shift with each new case that leads to the selection of the 'single appropriate norm.' Thus, it is the system of rules as a whole that ideally permits just one correct solution for every situation of application. Conversely, it is the particular situation whose appropriate interpretation first confers the determinate shape of a coherent order on the unordered mass of valid norms,' (Habermas 1993e: 38).

25. 'A norm is valid if the consequences and side effects arising for the interests of each individual as a result of this norm's general observance under unchanging circumstances can be accepted by everyone,' (Günther 1993: 35).

CHAPTER 5

System and lifeworld

INTRODUCTION

In Chapter 2 we mentioned that Habermas is among the theorists who favours an action-theoretical approach in the social sciences. In Chapter 3 we demonstrated how he has pursued this ambition by developing a concept of communicative action, based on an attitude oriented to reaching understanding. Subsequently, in Chapter 4, we established a connection between this understanding-oriented attitude and ethical cognitivism, i.e. a theory which claims that also the normative aspects of social life can be subjected to rational analysis. However, in the present chapter we will see that Habermas also makes considerable reservations with respect to what aspects of society he believes can be fruitfully studied from an action-theoretical point of view. In this respect he makes use of another theoretical tradition – the systems theory – as it has been developed primarily by the American Talcott Parsons (1902–79) and continued by Habermas's fellow-countryman Niklas Luhmann (1927–98).

Habermas maintains that what characterises modern society is that actions within comprehensive areas, such as market economy and the political-administrative apparatus in general, are relieved from the demands of justification which are otherwise implicit in the validity claims that are raised in communication oriented to reaching understanding. Within these areas, we do not have to justify our actions through good reasons. Instead, relatively autonomous systems of action have been developed which are coordinated through the actors' *success-oriented* behaviour, and which are responsible for the material reproduction of society – as it is ideal typically expressed through the profit and utility maximising behaviour of the actors in the market. Therefore, Habermas has found that the approach of the systems theory is a fruitful one. Briefly, the theory studies the areas in question as self-regulating systems that have mutual exchange relations with each other and the rest of society. In contrast to an action-theoretical analysis, it is not the actors' *intentions* that are supposed to coordinate events, but the *consequences* of the actions. In such an approach, the concrete actions of the agents are implicit in the analysis, rather than being the focus of it. However, Habermas finds that Parsons and Luhmann go too far when they claim that the entire society can be reconstructed in this manner. The theory of communicative action leads Habermas to conclude that society will inevitably disintegrate if we do not make room for actions oriented to reaching *understanding*, which can take care of the symbolic reproduction of society. Therefore we must, alongside the system areas, operate with a lifeworld which is communicatively integrated, and which also establishes the necessary symbolic foundation on which the system is built.

THE STRUCTURAL CONCEPT OF THE LIFEWORLD

Between the action-oriented Weber tradition (the 'Social Definition Paradigm') and the structurally oriented Durkheim tradition (the 'Social Facts Paradigm') within the social sciences, there has always been disagreement about how we should understand human agency. Should the actors be regarded as the sovereign creators of events, or are their actions only an expression of powerful supra-personal structures and traditions that wins through, so to speak, behind the actors' back? To Habermas (1987a: 135), the point is precisely that both these traditions are partly right in their claims. Agents are on the one hand initiators with a personal responsibility for their actions; on the other hand, they are themselves a product of obscurely transmitted traditions and other external, impersonal forces. The concept of the lifeworld is central in order to see both these aspects.

In Chapter 3 we wanted to describe the lifeworld from an actor perspective, i.e. as the concept has been used in the phenomenological tradition. However, Habermas thinks that we need to use an external perspective on the lifeworld as well in order to develop a concept that can to a greater extent be applied by social science. The phenomenological concept may be said to have a 'culturalistic' bias, as it is concerned with how we relate to our ballast of knowledge which is transmitted by tradition. According to Habermas, this is only part of the picture. In order to grasp all aspects of the lifeworld, we need to ask: *Which tasks or functions are taken care of by language as a medium?* Habermas sees three such functions. First, we use language in order to arrive at a mutual understanding of an issue. In this way, we pass on the stock of cultural knowledge, while at the same time we renew it. (This is the function of language that has been in focus within the phenomenological tradition.) Secondly, understanding-oriented communication is used in order to coordinate actions, and it contributes to social integration and to the establishment of relations of solidarity. Thirdly, language is the medium through which socialisation takes place. It is hence instrumental in the formation of personal identities. The three functions of language help maintain what Habermas (1987a: 137 f.) refers to as the three structural components of the lifeworld, viz. *culture*, *society*, and *personality*. We may here note a clear parallel to respectively the objective, social and subjective worlds, to which agents relate in their communicative interaction. However, there is nothing unique in the one-sidedness that we find within the Husserlian tradition in the form of a culturalistically biased perspective on the lifeworld. Correspondingly, he maintains that there is an institutionalistic bias within the Durkheimian tradition, since in that tradition everything is apparently related to the conditions for social integration and solidarity. Further, within the Meadian tradition we find a social-psychological bias that repeatedly moves the focus to the conditions that determine the socialisation of new individuals.

Thus, there are three linguistic reproduction processes – cultural reproduction, social integration, and socialisation – which maintain the three structural components of the lifeworld – viz. culture, society and personality. However, the three processes are not linked to the three components in a one-to-one relation. Instead, each of the three reproduction processes contributes to each component, as illustrated in Figure 5.1. Yet, the relations culture–cultural reproduction, society–social integration, and personality–socialisation may be regarded as the core functions. This is illustrated by the marked diagonal in the figure. The function of the cultural reproduction process is primarily to provide new knowledge which is compatible with the picture that has been created by tradition. That is, the new knowledge must be understandable in light of those interpretation schemes which we habitually use, and which make it possible to arrive at an identical understanding of a situation. However, such interpretation schemes are necessary also in order to keep society together in a normative sense. They help maintain the understanding that the institutions of society are legitimate. In addition, culturally transmitted frames of interpretation are important to the socialisation of complete personalities, as they represent the means by which individuals acquire behavioural patterns and standards, which are internalised through a formation process.

The primary function of the social integration process is to keep society together. It does this by providing for action coordination through the establishment of legitimate forms of interpersonal relations. Such relations include every form of interaction in everyday life that depends on the existence of norms, conventions and institutions that can tell us what we are expected to do or not to do in different situations. For this to be possible, however, there must, on the one hand, exist culturally institutionalised ideas about which normative obligations the members of society have. On the other hand, a social identity must be created, which gives the members the feeling of belonging to society. The main function of the process of socialisation is to make sure that the ability to act and interact is passed on to new generations. This happens when personalities are developed who have an identity which enables them to handle the situations they are faced

Structural components / Reproduction processes	Culture	Society	Personality	Dimension of evaluation
Cultural reproduction	Interpretive schemes fit for consensus ('valid knowledge')	Legitimations	Socialisation patterns Educational goals	Rationality of knowledge
Social integration	Obligations	Legitimately ordered interpersonal relations	Social membership	Solidarity of members
Socialisation	Interpretive accomplishments	Motivations for actions that conform to norms	Interactive capabilities ('personal identity')	Personal responsibility

Figure 5.1 *Contributions of reproduction processes to maintaining the structural components of the lifeworld*

Source: Habermas 1987a: 142/143.

with, and in a way which is in harmony with collective forms of life. With this goes, on the one hand, the ability to interpret the cultural impulses we are confronted with, and on the other hand, the internalisation of values which may motivate us to act in accordance with established normative expectations. The criteria of success for the three reproduction processes are respectively how rational the transmitted knowledge is, how strong the solidarity of the members gets, and how responsible the new personalities are (cf. the right-hand column of Figure 5.1).

If the reproduction processes for some reason or other are disturbed, so that they are not taking place in an adequate manner, certain pathologies will arise which are specific to the different lifeworld areas. First, there is the danger that there may be a general loss of meaning linked to the cultural reproduction (cf. Habermas 1975). According to Weber's diagnosis of his own times, this was happening to modern society, and it was a consequence of the replacement of the religious world view by the rational, scientific one. In Weber's view, (purposive) rationality was not capable of providing people with motivation and direction in life, in contrast to the traditional world views. Secondly, if the social integration process fails, society will enter into a state of *anomie*, which is the result of a breakdown of solidarity. This was the danger with which modern society was faced, according to Durkheim's diagnosis of his own times. Finally, disturbances of the socialisation process will lead to a formation of personalities with so-called psychopathologies, i.e. different forms of mental illnesses (Habermas 1987a: 140 ff.).

As we have already seen, Weber primarily wanted to show how the reproduction of the material foundation of modern societies has been rationalised and made more efficient through the spread of the purposive type of action. By contrast, Habermas's main point in this respect is to demonstrate how the symbolic, meaning sustaining foundation of society has also been rationalised through the process of modernisation, but now on the basis of the communicative type of action. He ties his claims precisely to the development of the structural components of the lifeworld. What he emphasises in particular is that the lifeworld structures have been going through a process of differentiation. The result is that culture, society and person have been clearly separated, which was not originally the case. In order to understand this, we can return to Durkheim's description of typical traditional societies given in the previous chapter. Here culture consisted in a religious world view and ritual practice, which at the same time constituted society's basis for integration, as well as the 'personal' identity of the members. What happens through the linguistification of the sacred is that this unit dissolves; the different elements become more autonomous in relation to each other. This is also related to the fact that all areas see the emergence of a stronger demand for justification of meaning content.

> [T]he further the structural components of the lifeworld and the processes that contribute to maintaining them get differentiated, the more interaction contexts come under conditions of rationally motivated mutual understanding, that is, of consensus formation that rests *in the end* on the authority of the better argument.
> (Habermas 1987a: 145)

We see that the lifeworld contributes to shaping those individuals who have it as a frame around, and a condition for, their lives. Thus, in that sense people are products of their lifeworld. However, due to the structural differentiation of the lifeworld, they are not completely determined by this background. A critical distance has been created between individual, collective and cultural tradition, which makes it possible for agents to act self-determined and autonomously. On the other hand, if the individuals had been deprived of their lifeworld context, they would have had no basis for appearing as autonomous, rational actors. It is through the lifeworld that we also receive those impulses that turn us into independently acting, unique individuals. Thus, the context of tradition represented by the lifeworld may be said to represent a potential limitation for as well as an essential condition for our human autonomy.

THE POSITION OF THE SYSTEM PERSPECTIVE

When Husserl and Schütz introduced the concept of the lifeworld, their goal was precisely to emphasise the fruitfulness – also to theoretical purposes – in taking the actors' perspectives and concepts as a starting point when we reconstruct social phenomena and relations. They claimed that this approach was superior to the method of constructing specific concepts of social science which do not have any meaning to the actors themselves, but which only form the parts of a logical structure that becomes accessible from a scientific observer perspective. On the whole, this has also been a common point of view for all action-theoretical schools; yet Habermas (1987a: 148 ff.) concludes that this approach is too narrow. The point is that there are relations within a society that the agents are not able to see from their lifeworld perspective. Such relations can only be detected if we use a specifically scientific perspective that goes beyond the actors' understanding. Approaches that equate lifeworld and society, which phenomenology and other schools within the interpretive (*verstehende*) tradition of sociology in his opinion have done, present society with a false transparency which is in reality veiling. For while the actions of the lifeworld are coordinated through the actors' understanding-oriented intentions (there is normally a clear purpose behind what happens), a system such as market economy is coordinated through the consequences of actions, and these can be quite different from the intentions that lie behind them.[1] The intentional form of coordination is referred to by Habermas as *social integration* and takes place through communication oriented to reaching understanding. By contrast, the type of coordination that works through the consequences of actions is referred to as *system integration*. It is based on non-normative premises, and there is no subjective meaning tied to the outcome.

The starting point of systems theory is that society consists of a series of self-regulating subsystems which are mutually dependent on each other, and which regard each other as their environment (society can again be regarded as a subsystem within a more comprehensive system at a higher level) (cf. Parsons 1977). The justification for the systems is that they represent an ordering structure in an otherwise chaotic world; they reduce the complexity of the action environment and thereby pave the way for success-oriented actions. The systems have survival as their superior goal. To ensure their existence, they must continuously take care of necessary tasks and adjust to the requirements they are met with. Only in this way can they maintain their borders against their environment and obtain what is referred to by systems theory as a state of equilibrium. Further, systems theory has always been based on so-called functional explanations. This means that it has been based on the presupposition that there is not necessarily correspondence between intentions and consequences of actions. Rather, the real and long-term results of actions, which help maintain the system, may be both unintentional and not acknowledged by those who execute them. The survival of the system can thus be understood as a by-product of the actors' personally motivated efforts.[2]

While Habermas criticises a one-sided interpretation of society as a lifeworld for being too idealistic, he also finds that a one-sided understanding of society as a system is an alienated understanding. If we look at society only as different subsystems which maintain their internal and external balance by exchanging resources, we will totally lose sight of the meaning aspect of social life. This is an aspect that can only be captured through a hermeneutic interpretation of the actors' own use of symbols. The reason is that social relations distinguish themselves from biological relations, from which the systems metaphor originates, in that social relations are symbolically mediated and therefore not accessible from a pure observer perspective. And the units which systems theory takes for granted must be established in advance through social integration: 'The entities that are to be subsumed under systems-theoretical concepts from the external perspectives of an observer must be identified beforehand as lifeworlds of social groups and understood in their symbolic structures,' (Habermas 1987a: 151). To Habermas the solution is therefore to combine a lifeworld perspective with a systems perspective. The combination of these two perspectives is in no way accidental, however; rather, certain aspects of social life play a far more critical role than others in furthering social integration. Other social spheres, however, seem to function – without obvious dysfunctions – in a way that can be adequately described as systemic integration. Specifically, he claims that besides market economy, it is the political-administrative apparatus that can best be understood in a systems-theoretical perspective.

THE UNCOUPLING OF THE SYSTEM FROM THE LIFEWORLD

With respect to the subject under discussion here, Habermas's main purpose is to emphasise the long-term dynamics in the relation between system and lifeworld. The situation has not always been as it is now, and Habermas prediction is that it will be different again tomorrow. He therefore uses a developmental approach in order to explain how we have arrived at the present situation. Briefly, he views the development of system and lifeworld as a result of the increased differentiation of society. As far as the original, simple tribal communities are concerned, we may rightly equate society and lifeworld, as these societies have not yet seen the emergence of what is referred to as social subsystems. However, in the course of time there is on the one hand an increased differentiation of system areas from the lifeworld, and thus purposive rational actions become detached from ethical regulations (cf. Weber 1930). On the other hand, there is increasing complexity within the systemic interconnections, and a corresponding internal rationalisation within the lifeworld (Habermas 1987a: 153).

The first question we need to ask is how such processes are triggered. In his thesis on the division of labour in society, Durkheim (1964) links social differentiation to the concept of organic solidarity. In this kind of solidarity, people are bound together in large networks because everyone is dependent on the function performed by each of the others: the shoemaker gets bread from the baker, while the baker gets shoes from the shoemaker, etc. However, life in tribal societies is rather characterised by what Durkheim called mechanical solidarity, which means that people do not keep together because they are different and carry out different tasks, but rather because they are similar, i.e. they have the same collective consciousness, identity, tasks and goals. Differentiation of roles only takes place within small kinship groups, on which the organisation of society is based. The developmental path which has brought us from this state of social integration and little division of labour, to modern societies, with their high degree of specialisation and with autonomous subsystems, is a process with several decisive stages, and where various mechanisms have played a role.

As we have already seen, the kinship-based tribal societies are on the mental level characterised by a common, religiously structured world of ideas, which permeates all aspects of the members' lives. They constitute what is frequently referred to as total institutions, and have clear borders against the surrounding world, i.e. other tribal societies. The internal interaction is based on a presupposition of mutual understanding, while the relations to the outer world are often sparse or marked by hostility. However, there are channels that contribute to expanding the contact with the surrounding world and make such societies less isolated and autonomous. First we have the widespread practice of exogamy, i.e. the traditional exchange of women by marrying them into one of the neighbouring communities. Secondly, there is another phenomenon which has been thoroughly described in anthropological literature, viz. the exchange of gifts between members of different tribal societies. As these societies are so similar, and thus possess and produce largely the same kind of objects, the exchange of gifts has very little practical, utilitarian or economic significance. However, they help establish social relations across tribal borders. A similar function is fulfilled by the exogenous marriage practice, which is a practice that has been maintained also under far more modern conditions, for example in the royal dynasties' practice of exchanging princesses in order to ensure peace and good relations.

The kind of processes just discussed lead to a segmental differentiation of society, which means that similar social units are linked together horizontally into larger segments that have the same structure (Habermas 1987a: 161). Thus, although the practical result is the establishment of a peaceful relation between potential enemies, it is evident that such customs are primarily motivated and regulated on a normative basis, and not on the basis of functional advantage or need. Neither does segmental differentiation involve any substantial degree of functional specialisation or division of labour, and it hence does not bring any real economic or political developmental dynamics into these societies. Such tendencies only result from the process referred to as vertical stratification, in which some descent groups come to stand out as more powerful and of a higher status than others. We thus get social units based on leadership and chief power, which is the first expression of formal organisation. The chief's power, which derives from the fact that he enjoys higher prestige than do the other members of the tribe, gives him the power to issue commands that are complied with by the others, as well as the authority generally to act on behalf of the collective. In some cases there is also a differentiation of specialised roles that take care of tasks such as leadership in war, the management of religious ceremonies, the treatment of illnesses, and the resolution of legal disputes. This can give rise to social structures of considerable size. It also makes possible the exchange of goods in a more real sense, i.e. in the sense that objects are exchanged because of their utility value. However, at this stage neither economy nor politics have become separate systems, as is the case in modern societies. On the contrary, social integration and systems integration are still intertwined both when it comes to the exchange of goods and social leadership. The premises for the exchange of gods are still normative rather than economic in our sense of the term, and social power is based on ideas of differences in prestige rather than on the general political means of power. All tribal societies are thus characterised by the fact that their 'economy' as well as their 'politics' remain linked to their normative lifeworld context (Habermas 1987a: 163).

Real political power only emerges with the form of organisation that we refer to as the *state*. What is new in this organisational form is that the leaders do not only rule by virtue of some inherited, prestigious authority; in addition they have judicial means of sanction at their disposal. They thus have a steering tool which is an instrument of power in itself, rather than taking its power solely from its normative legitimacy, as was the case with the authority of the chiefs in previous times. This fact provides the basis for a systemic separation from the lifeworld; the state becomes an action system with a power potential that in each case functions independently of any normative support from the lifeworld. The establishment of the state also paves the ground for a higher degree of market economic organisation, and the medium of money begins to be used extensively. In this respect it is quite typical that it is kings who imprint coins. However, even though the economy has in this way largely separated itself from the lifeworld, we cannot say that it has yet separated itself from the state. For a long time the economy to a great extent functions on political premises. It is not until the emergence of the capitalist form of market economy (which in Europe started in the early-modern period) that the economy distinguishes itself as an independent subsystem which not only functions on its own terms, but which in addition has a structure-forming effect on society in general. The money medium is not only a functional steering tool within what in a narrow sense constitutes the economy. Through institutions such as wage labour and a state organisation based on tax income, it also becomes a medium for exchange relations between the economy and adjacent action systems, such as the household and the state. It is this unique role of the money medium that constitutes the economy as a monetarily steered subsystem (Habermas 1987a: 165 ff.).

The more complex the social system becomes, the more provincial the lifeworld becomes. From the system perspective, we may say that in modern society the lifeworld has been reduced to a subsystem on a par with the other two. However, this does not mean that Habermas believes it to be of little importance to the development of the system side of the model. On the contrary, the increased system complexity is totally dependent on the process of structural differentiation that runs parallel to it within the lifeworld, and which follows the internal logic of communicative rationality (Habermas 1987a: 173). There must be created mental space for new principles, such as private ownership and the opportunity to enter into binding contracts and to pass binding laws according to prescribed procedures. The point is that each new step on the road to greater system autonomy must be institutionally anchored in the lifeworld. This must make the new order understandable and legitimate in the eyes of the members of society. It requires an increased degree of rationalisation, especially in the areas of law and morality, as illustrated by Habermas in Figure 5.2. Here he draws upon Kohlberg's distinction between the preconventional, the conventional, and the postconventional level in individual moral development (cf. Chapter 4). He now also maintains that societies can be said to go through a corresponding developmental process at the normative level: from archaic tribal societies via traditional state societies to modern bourgeois societies.

In tribal societies, law and morality have not yet been separated; all actions and events take place within the frameworks of a ritual practice and a mythical world view. The law has not yet taken on the character of compulsory law, as there is no institution that controls the necessary means of sanction. The concept of personal responsibility for a crime has not yet been developed. The purpose of the law is here to help restore a harmonious situation. On the one hand, this may involve helping individuals who have suffered some wrongdoing, for example, by ordering or convincing the one who has caused the damage to pay compensation. On the other hand, society itself may have been subjected to damage or danger because a sacred norm has been broken. In such situations, the original spiritual purity and balance can be restored by letting the offender serve a sentence. The early state societies have not developed a clear distinction between law and morality either, but a process has been initiated which is leading in that direction. However, here the law has been able to employ means of sanction that are at the disposal of political leaders. Legal understanding has reached the conventional level. Thus, violations of the law are understood as violations of intersubjectively recognised norms, and they represent an offence for which the offender can be held personally responsible. Offences are punished not only because of their negative consequences, but also because of their reprehensible character. The legal order is regarded as legitimate in itself, and the judge can exercise his power by virtue of being regarded as a protector of this legitimate order. Hence, judicial power is no longer dependent on the personal status of the official, as is the case

Stages of moral consciousness	Basic socio-cognitive concepts	Ethics*	Types of law
Preconventional	Particular expectations of behaviour	Magical ethics	Revealed law
Conventional	Norm	Ethics of the law	Traditional law
Postconventional	Principle	Ethics of conviction and responsibility	Formal law

Figure 5.2 *Stages in the development of law*

*According to the conceptual distinction that Habermas has later developed, it would probably have been more appropriate to talk about 'Morals' rather than 'Ethics' in this column (cf. Chapter 4).

Source: Habermas 1987a: 175.

in tribal societies. Even though the law in this way attains greater importance, the fact is nevertheless that informal social customs are much more important to the regulation of human co-existence than is the institutionalised exercise of the law.

The situation is different in modern societies, where the understanding of law and morality reaches a principle-guided, postconventional level. Here morality does not primarily function as an external, social control, but as an internalised behaviour control within the personality system. On the other hand, the law – which has now been clearly separated from morality – develops into an external power which functions independently of ethical justification. It has become a type of institution that functions primarily by virtue of its compulsory character, while the attitudes of the legal subjects are characterised by abstract law-abidingness. This fact is particularly evident in the area of private law, which regulates co-existence in civil society, including market economic transactions. This great field of action is morally neutralised. However, even though each legal decision or regulation does not require normative support, it is nevertheless decisive that the legal system as a whole is based on legitimate principles. In the democratic constitutional state, the law obtains such legitimacy through fundamental constitutional rights and popular sovereignty. To the extent that the principles and procedures on which the political system builds are experienced as legitimate, the legal results brought about by the system are accepted as well (Habermas 1987a: 174 ff.).

THE RATIONALISATION OF THE LIFEWORLD

As we have just seen with regard to the development of legal and moral conceptions, Habermas claims that new levels of system differentiation can only be established when the rationalisation of the lifeworld has reached a corresponding level. Generally speaking, this has to do with the fact that the lifeworld's degree of rationalisation is reflected in the way in which actions are coordinated: 'Every society has to face the basic problem of coordinating action: how does ego get alter to continue interaction in the desired way? How does he avoid conflict that interrupts the sequence of action?' (Habermas 1987a: 179). In general, we may say that it is elements such as ego's reputation and influence that determine whether alter can be motivated to act according to ego's wishes. However, what is regarded as relevant forms of reputation and influence, in a more concrete sense, varies historically and culturally, and this is where the degree of rationality comes in. According to Talcott Parsons, increased rationality in this connection involves increased value generalisation. This means that the further the process of rationalising the lifeworld has come, the more general is the character of those motives or values that can stimulate alter to act according to ego's wishes. In socially stratified tribal societies we can see, for example, that the chief's ability to make the other members follow his orders does not exclusively or primarily depend on his purely personal qualities; it is also highly dependent on the authority he has by virtue of belonging to a high-status group or family. In politically constituted state societies there is a further generalisation, from social group to office as a basis for exercising authority (although the ruler's 'royal birth' still plays a role). Finally, this authority has in modern societies been generalised into completely abstract principles: in the area of morality, to an internalised understanding of right and wrong; in the area of law, we simply follow the principle of law-abidingness.

The development we have sketched here involves that the coordination of actions to an increasing degree rests on communicative rationality. While the authority of the leader in tribal societies follows from normative principles which are based on a religiously authorised consensus, the action-coordinating premises in modern societies must be given a rational justification solely through linguistic communication.

> In this respect, value generalization is a necessary condition for releasing the rationality potential immanent in communicative action. [. . .] On the other hand, freeing communicative action from particular value orientations also forces the separation of action oriented to success from action oriented to mutual understanding.
>
> (Habermas 1987a: 180)

If we understand the laws' regulation of our actions only as an external constraint and a fact that we relate to in order to avoid the sanctions of the legal machinery, we take a success-oriented or strategic attitude towards the law. In Habermas's view, it is this type of attitude that to a considerable degree is becoming institutionalised in modern society. This is brought about through the differentiation of the before-mentioned subsystems, where action coordination takes place by means of so-called steering media and not through understanding-oriented communication. It is here that we come across what may be referred to as the paradox of rationalisation: ideas that used to be taken for granted because they sprang from a religious lifeworld context, are questioned as a result of the advance of rationalisation, and need to be justified. But as more and more aspects of life are being problematised in this way, there is growing uncertainty, which can in principle be removed only through argumentative conviction. The problem is that this way the linguistic medium becomes overloaded: it is impossible at any given time to solve argumentatively all those questions that can be asked about contingent aspects of reality. The solution is to separate certain areas of action, which become normatively neutralised and can therefore be relieved from the demands of justification which applies in the sphere of the lifeworld. The steering media take the place of the arguments.

We can think of a variety of things that could function as such steering media. We have already mentioned that reputation and influence generally have an action-coordinating function. For example, a person may be known to have great power, and this can in certain situations intimidate others into doing what she wants. Alternatively, she can generously share her wealth with those who comply with her wishes, and the use of such economic resources can, of course, buy her influence. Further, there are people who get other people to join them because they act in a way that is regarded as responsible or confidence inspiring, or because their extensive knowledge gives them influence. All these can be regarded as steering media that can be used to get others to act in particular ways. This was also Parsons's point of departure when he developed systems theory. He regarded money, power, influence, and 'value commitment' (triggered by reputation/ confidence) as general steering media in the social system. In contrast, Habermas makes a point of the fact that there is a qualitative difference between the steering media in the former two and latter two examples. Power or money can only give an empirical motivation to act; to these media we can relate in a purely success-oriented and strategic manner. It is quite a different matter when it comes to qualities such as responsible or confidence-inspiring behaviour, or a resource such as knowledge. For these to have an action-motivating effect, there must be an understanding-oriented relation between ego and alter. Ego must be able to convince alter that the behaviour in question really *is* responsible or that the relevant knowledge *is* worth emphasising. In cases of doubt, ego must be able to give good reasons that will convince alter. This paves the ground for a rational form of action motivation, as opposed to the empirical form.

Since rational action motivation – being based on an understanding-oriented attitude – cannot be separated from its lifeworld basis, it is, however, not well-suited as the foundation for steering media that are intended to coordinate the interaction within autonomous and normatively neutralised subsystems. Here only those media are functional which may motivate the actors empirically. Unlike Parsons, Habermas (1987a: 183) therefore believes that the system concept is relevant only in areas where the steering media of money and power have become institutionalised. It is only in relation to these media that the actors can take an objectifying attitude when they act.[3] In other areas of life, they must continue to assume that they can relate to a lifeworld context consisting of shared cultural knowledge, valid social norms, as well as responsible personal motivations.

According to Habermas, the driving force in the rationalisation of the lifeworld is the linguistification of the sacred, where we at one end of the scale find the ritual practice, and at the other end the argumentative practice. The development from rite to discourse follows a logic in which an increasing number of areas are taken out of the religious context and put into a profane one, in which they can be problematised. Central in this rationalisation process is a differentiation of the various aspects of actions, or different ways of relating to the environment, which is not possible within a sacred approach.

> A modern observer is struck by the extremely irrational character of ritual practices. The aspects of action that we cannot help but keep apart today are merged in one and the same act. The element of purposive activity comes out in the fact that ritual practices are supposed magically to bring about states in the world; the element of normatively regulated action is noticeable in the quality of obligation that emanates from the ritually conjured, at once attracting and terrifying, powers; the element of expressive action is especially clear in the standardized expressions of feeling in ritual ceremonies; finally an assertoric aspect is also present inasmuch as ritual practice serves to represent and reproduce exemplary events or mythically narrated original scenes.
>
> (Habermas 1987a: 191 f.)

Because these different elements are not separated within the religious-metaphysical world view, it becomes impossible to take a critical attitude within the frames of such an understanding, according to Habermas (1987a: 188 f.). Therefore we have often observed throughout history that religions have taken on an ideological[4] function. More precisely, they have been able to give a mythical explanation and justification of the great material inequalities that have generally characterised all politically constituted societies, i.e. states. Hence, religious conceptions have contributed to the social integration of such societies, in spite of the great conflict potential which is implied in these inequalities.

THE SYSTEM–LIFEWORLD MODEL

Max Weber claimed that the modern, purposive-rational action model primarily found its expression in two important areas of society, viz. in the capitalist market economy and in the hierarchical state bureaucracy. This view is shared by Habermas, who maintains that the two areas can be analysed as subsystems which have been partly detached from their lifeworld basis, and where the coordination of action takes place by means of language-independent steering media rather than by way of communication oriented to reaching understanding. In economical transactions, money has taken on a role that makes it possible for us to act without justifying our actions in terms of normative categories, in contrast to what is the case within the lifeworld context. In the market we are free to act solely with our own interests in view. Also within Weber's ideal typical bureaucracy, we may legitimately relate to our surroundings in a purely instrumental manner. Bureaucrats make decisions in accordance with established procedures, rules and instructions, without fear that anybody may hold them personally and morally responsible for the content of these decisions. The state bureaucracy is constructed as a power relation, in which the steering medium power has made it unnecessary to ask for justification. What is crucial is that bureaucrats obey orders, i.e. that they behave formally correct in accordance with the abstract principle of legality. Put briefly, this means that money allows you to pay, while power allows you to command – without anybody questioning your actions or asking for justifications.

According to Parsons's social theory, there are in principle four functions that must be taken care of. Society must be reproduced culturally and socially, it must be normatively integrated, it must be governed, and the productive functions must be carried out. In Parsons's scheme, the four functions are assigned to their separate subsystem. By contrast, Habermas maintains that it is only the latter two tasks that can be taken care of by autonomous subsystems: the public administration takes care of the governing functions, while the market economy solves the productive tasks. However, both cultural and social reproduction (socialisation) and normative integration are described as primary lifeworld tasks, as we have already seen. It is therefore obvious that his macro-model of society must be fundamentally different from that of Parsons, since Habermas's model must include both a system side and a lifeworld side. On this basis, Habermas (1987a: 318 ff.) has designed a schematic representation of how the relationship between system and lifeworld can be understood if we view everything from the system perspective, i.e. if we look at the relationship between the parts as systems relations (Figure 5.3). As indicated, the system side consists of the two subsystems economy and administration. On the lifeworld side, we find a corresponding division between a private sphere and a public sphere. Within the private sphere, the nuclear family constitutes the institutional centre, and in modern society it has primarily a socialising function. Within the public sphere, Habermas distinguishes between a cultural and a political public sphere, but he pays most attention to the political sphere. According to the conceptual apparatus of systems theory, we can talk about exchange relations or of flows of resources between system and lifeworld, and these are linked together in pairs. First, there is a flow of labour power from the private sphere to the economic system, which

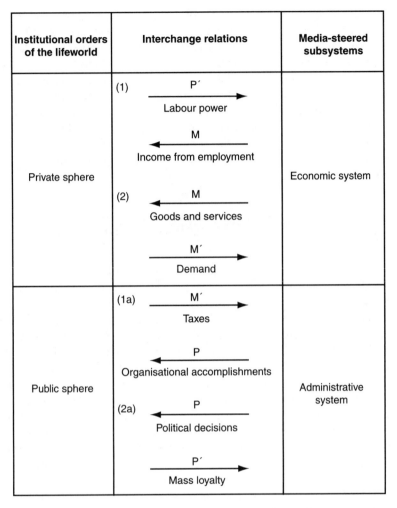

Figure 5.3 *Relations between system and lifeworld from the perspective of the system*

M = Money Medium
P = Power Medium

Source: Habermas 1987a: 320.

corresponds to a flow of income in the opposite direction. Secondly, goods and services are exchanged on demand. Between the state's administrative system and the citizens in the public sphere, there is exchange of tax money against organisational accomplishments (i.e. public services and benefits), and of political decisions against support and loyalty from the masses.

This is the situation as long as we regard the relations in question from the point of view of systems integration. However, we may also change perspective, asking what these relations look like viewed from the lifeworld, since they also presuppose social integration. With this as a starting point, the contact will be channelled through four social roles (marked with numbers and letters in Figure 5.3): (1) the role of the employee, (2) the role of the consumer, (1a) the role of the client, and (2a) the role of the citizen. Habermas (1987a: 319 ff.) maintains that there is a distinction between the role of the employee and the client (1 and 1a) on the one hand, and the role of the consumer and the citizen (2 and 2a) on the other. The former are what he refers to as organisation-dependent roles, which means that they are defined – in legal terms – from the system's point of view. The roles of employee and client have been created by the capitalist economy and the public welfare bureaucracy, respectively, and those who enter into these roles are doing it on the premises of the system side. Compared to this, the roles of consumer and citizen are in a somewhat freer position in relation to the system. They are to a greater extent defined from the perspective of the lifeworld, and they reflect preferences, values and attitudes that have been formed through the process of socialisation.

THE THESIS OF COLONISATION

However, Habermas has a wider perspective in developing this model which divides the world between system and lifeworld. He wants to critically re-evaluate the belief that the modern world inevitably moves into what Weber called an 'iron cage of rationality', which is expressed by both Weber and the early representatives of the Frankfurt School. As mentioned before, what in Weber's (1978) opinion characterised modern, Western industrial society was an increasing unfolding of the purposive-rational model of thought and action, i.e. the success-oriented attitude which had primarily been influential within economic life and bureaucracy, and which he was convinced would in time come to dominate the entire modern society. He regarded these tendencies with some ambivalence. On the one hand, this development gave us a high level of material welfare and a well-organised society in every way; however on the other hand, Weber believed that it would lead to an existence empty of meaning – a condition characterised by a lack of human relations and values.

Habermas agrees that the unrestricted dominance of purposive rationality would be a disaster to society, precisely because of the reasons mentioned by Weber. However, he does *not* agree with Weber that this is what is unavoidably happening. For as Habermas's two-track model is meant to show, there in fact exists a communicatively integrated lifeworld alongside the subsystems (which are integrated through success orientation). Further, parallel to the increase in complexity which has resulted in the separation of subsystems that are integrated through a purposive-rational attitude, the lifeworld has been going through a rationalisation based on a communicative, understanding-oriented pattern: we have developed an advanced science, we have developed moral standards which are independent of any religious context, and we have developed art and culture that have also become autonomous in relation to the religious setting it once belonged to. According to the tradition of critical Marxism to which Habermas belongs, the fact that we relate to each other in a completely impersonal manner when we use the medium of money in our market transactions may easily lead to reification and alienation. In the same vein, Weber was particularly concerned with the alienation which is expressed when the rule-abiding bureaucrat disclaims responsibility for the content and consequences of his/her decisions. However, Habermas maintains that both these warnings are mistaken. As long as the purposive-rational attitude is limited to those areas which are concerned with the material reproduction of society – i.e. areas such as economy and administration – there is no real danger. On the contrary, within these areas it is absolutely necessary to use this form of rationality for efficiency reasons.

In Habermas's view, the problem does not arise until *the purposive-rational attitude starts to penetrate the area of the lifeworld and to dominate relations here as well.*

> As our examination of Parsons' media theory made clear, only domains of action that fulfill economic and political functions can be converted over to steering media. The latter fail to work in domains of cultural reproduction, social integration, and socialization; they cannot replace the action-coordinating mechanism of mutual understanding in these functions. Unlike the material reproduction of the lifeworld, its symbolic reproduction cannot be transposed onto foundations of system integration without pathological side effects.
>
> (Habermas 1987a: 322 f.)

Habermas really sees clear tendencies of a development in modern society where purposive rationality is beginning to extend beyond its natural borders. Through this one-sidedness, the project of enlightenment has entered into a self-destructive course, in which the spread of a life form based on instrumental and success-oriented reason is about to destroy its own social and normative basis. In this connection, Habermas speaks of the *colonisation of the lifeworld by system imperatives.* The opening that these imperatives find into the lifeworld naturally follows some of the exchange relations or social roles that connect the two worlds. In particular, this concerns the roles of the consumer and of the client.

> The system imperatives gain foothold in the lifeworld by formalising interaction and networks that used to have an informal structure (legalisation), and by forcing economic-administrative utility demands onto education and the acquirement of traditions (professionalisation, success orientation). They redefine the family sphere and leisure activities as markets with an insatiable need to consume entertainment articles (monetarisation, commercialisation). They invalidate moral-normative bonds between people by putting an instrumental orientation in their place (instrumentalisation), by objectifying the individual's relation to the administration as a replaceable client (anonymisation), and finally by manipulatively obtaining support for political decisions that are made independently of a public exchange of opinions in which the voter participates with real influence, but which nevertheless needs the mock legitimacy that references to an obscure 'opinion' can give (depolitisation).
>
> If we try to gather all these features into a main tendency with which Habermas is particularly concerned, it must be the disregard of language as a medium of interaction. To Habermas, language is the primary and irreplaceable bearer of rationality.
>
> (Vetlesen 1991: 6)

Does this mean that Habermas's conclusion is that Weber was right after all, i.e. that we are heading full speed into the iron cage of (purposive) rationality? According to Habermas, it is still not as simple as that. The most important difference between his view and that of Weber is that Habermas does regard this development as inevitable. There are conflicting forces and tendencies, and the reason why we are now on a dangerous track is that the capitalist, industrial civilisation has been too one-sidedly geared to technical reason and material development. However, this is not unavoidable; it is a historically contingent tendency that can be reversed if we manage to release the potential that lies in the remaining aspects of the rationalisation of the lifeworld. This requires intervention in the form of political action, and in this respect, Habermas does not believe that anything new will come from the established political parties, which have dominated the political arena during the past century. Habermas (1987a: 391 ff.) expects future-oriented tendencies to come from the so-called 'new social movements', which have to a varying degree made themselves felt in the Western world since the 1960s. Examples are the environmental movement, the peace movement, the women's movement, religious movements, etc. Common to all these has been that they have been less concerned with the traditional problems of the welfare state, i.e. questions concerning the distribution of material goods, while focusing more on questions of value, which can only be formulated and answered on the basis of the symbolic reproduction processes of the lifeworld.

OBJECTIONS AGAINST THE SYSTEM–LIFEWORLD MODEL

In the years following the publication of the German version of *The Theory of Communicative Action* in 1981 there was a lively debate on Habermas's theory, in which some of the most prominent philosophers and social researchers participated, particularly in Germany and in the USA.[5] It is only natural that a work that to such an extent purports to construct social theory at the macro-level will contain many claims and theory-strategic choices which are debatable. And the criticism came soon. Some of the strongest objections have in fact come from some of Habermas's close co-workers and from people who share his basic theoretical approach. It seems fair to say that of the central aspects of the theory, it is Habermas's two-tier concept of modern society, in the form of the system–lifeworld model, which has been met with greatest scepticism from many quarters.

The system–lifeworld theory builds on two main presuppositions: the thesis of the system's gradual separation from the lifeworld, and the thesis of the system-imperatives' increasing colonisation of the lifeworld in modern society. Habermas's starting point is evidently that we are here faced with a real splitting of empirical reality, which must be followed up by a dual strategy also in the theoretic-analytical approach. Modern society is in reality split between areas that function as subsystems and are integrated through system integration, and other areas that function as a lifeworld and are integrated through social integration. This is not a theoretical construct, but an experience that we all must relate to in everyday life. Analytically, systems theory is the most adequate tool in the study of such objectified phenomena and instrumental relations, while a phenomenological, meaning-interpretative action theory is best suited in the study of the lifeworld.

Critics have questioned both whether society can really be split so easily into one functionally integrated system component and one communicatively integrated lifeworld component, and even if this is the case, if systems theory really is the best means in approaching the economic and administrative domains. Among theorists who share Habermas's social critical point of departure, many have problems accepting the implication of 'entering into an alliance with' systems theory, as undertaken by Habermas. Systems theory – and more generally functionalism – is regarded as anything but a critical perspective on society. On the contrary, it is known as the typical model of harmony, in which all forces and counter-forces have the same neutral normative status as balancing factors in an equilibrium game at a superior level. Further, it has been regarded as problematic that Habermas accepts and justifies the institutionalisation of the success-oriented type of action within large societal areas such as economy and administration. To Marx, the founder of the critical theory tradition that Habermas purports to continue, the aim was after all to emancipate social work from the system coercion represented by capitalism, so that production could take place in order to meet human needs and not to accumulate profit. To Habermas, this is a utopian goal that he finds it necessary to dissociate himself from. And what about parliamentary democracy in the Western world? Is it to be regarded only as an appendage to the administrative-bureaucratic machinery? Does democracy only have a self-legitimising function for the ruling elites, as claimed by elite theorists such as Weber and Schumpeter? If no dividing line can be drawn between politics and administration, does not the display of the power medium become a problem also within the borders of the subsystem, and not only when it crosses these borders, as claimed by Habermas?

In addition, it has been questioned whether the concept of system is appropriate in areas such as economy and administration, in view of their diffuse borders. Another objection is that the systems-theoretical analysis does not say anything about which internal dynamics lies behind the expansion of the two 'subsystems' (cf. Baxter 1987, McCarthy 1991b). Perhaps even worse is the fact that the purpose of the analysis – which is to demonstrate the irreparability of social integration – can be accused of being trapped in a functionalist frame of interpretation, in spite of Habermas's aspirations to the opposite. According to Habermas, system integration cannot replace social integration in the areas of the lifeworld without pathological side effects. However, if we continue to ask *why* it is important to avoid such side effects, the only answer that Habermas seems able to offer is that it would be dysfunctional in relation to the goal of social stability and order. In other words, he offers an argument which refers to functional efficiency rather than normative legitimacy. What seems to be the underlying normative motive, viz. to create a social order in which life quality is more highly valued than what has been the case in late capitalism, remains latent and implicit (Vetlesen 1991: 14 ff.).

Axel Honneth (1991, cf. p. 279 ff. in particular) is probably the one who has so far presented the most thorough critique of Habermas's dualistic social theory. The basis for the dualism seems to be the concepts of communicative and strategic action. These concepts are fruitful enough as analytical categories. According to Honneth, the problems arise when Habermas attempts to transfer this dualism to the empirical level of society, claiming that one part of society, the lifeworld, is controlled by one of the action types – viz. communicative action, while the other part of society, the system, is ruled by the other type of action – viz. strategic action. In Honneth's view, this is to simplify reality rather too much. It is a fiction that there exists an absolute correspondence between types of action and social areas, as when Habermas refers to the subsystems of economy and administration as areas of 'norm-free sociality', and to the lifeworld as if it were a sphere of 'power-free communication'. While Habermas makes a leap from the actor level to the system level, Honneth focuses on the intermediate level of social groups, where in his view the dispute concerning situation definitions as well as material interests takes place (cf. Offe 1992). According to Habermas's schema, political differences, i.e. disagreement about the direction of society, are to be understood as a type of dissent which should ideally be settled by means of argument. By contrast, in Honneth's more Marxist inspired interpretation, such disagreements are group or class conflicts which can only be solved through political struggle. This is a type of struggle that is understanding-oriented and success-oriented at the same time, and it thus fits badly into Habermas's model. It is an ideological dispute about the right conviction, while at the same time it is a struggle with strategic means.

Regarding the thesis of colonisation itself, Arne Johan Vetlesen (1991: 17 ff.) has claimed that the problem facing social integration in modern society is not necessarily the fact that the system imperatives are steadily encroaching on the area of the lifeworld, as claimed by Habermas. The problem may just as well be that understanding-oriented communication is being perverted from the *inside* and in hidden ways, in that interests with motives related to economy or power exploit the 'taken-for-granted-ness' of the lifeworld in a strategic way. One example of this is the carefully calculated attempts of lifestyle advertising to exploit our natural acceptance of certain messages and forms of presentation, to make us swallow sales tricks without critical distance. Thus, the fact that a message is communicated by way of verbal language is no guarantee for the possibility of criticism either, as is assumed by Habermas.

Habermas (1991) has also made his response to parts of this criticism. While he continues to claim that the separation of system and lifeworld is a real process, he wants to tone down the impression that there is a one-to-one relationship between types of action and areas of action. It was not his intention to indicate that the lifeworld is without power relations and thus strategic action. Further, he admits that his mentioning of the subsystems as areas of 'norm-free sociality' has been misleading:

> It is obvious that commercial enterprises and government offices, indeed economic and political contexts as a whole make use of communicative action that is embedded in a normative framework. (. . .) my thesis amounts merely to the assertion that the integration of these action systems is in the final instance not based on the potential for social integration of communicative actions and the lifeworldly background thereof – and these systems make use of both. It is not binding (bonding) forces, but rather steering media that hold the economic and the administrative action system together.
>
> (Habermas 1991: 257)

Communicative action and normative integration are also found within the subsystems; however, this is not what ultimately hold the systems together, according to Habermas. Correspondingly, it is too drastic to suggest that there are no elements of system integration in the lifeworld as well. It is only from the before-mentioned media steered subsystems that the lifeworld can be said to be disconnected. However, if there is no correspondence between action types and the social subsystems which are central to the theory, it is obvious that the status of the system–lifeworld model as a social theory is weakened. For how can we now define the categorical difference between system areas and lifeworld areas (cf. Vetlesen 1991: 27)?

What is quite clear is that several aspects of this theory *are* problematic, and that it hardly represent the best supported part of Habermas's total theoretical concept. On the other hand, such a two-level model seems to bring out important features of modern society, as indicated by the rapid spread and frequent use of this pair of concepts. When used in such a context, the systems-theoretical approach also appears to have several advantages compared to other, action-theoretical concepts. The critics can hardly be said to have pointed out better solutions in this respect. Part of the problem is that reality – as always – turns out to be more complex than what the conceptual apparatus is able to make allowance for, so that obvious discrepancies emerge when we attempt to transfer theoretical categories to empirical reality. However, this is the eternal dilemma and challenge of the social sciences, which can only be met through renewed efforts to refine the models.

FROM SYSTEM AND LIFEWORLD TO LAW AND POLITICS

In Habermas's explanation of the theory of the communicative form of action, it is fair to say that topics relating to law and politics have played a subordinate role. Moreover, we would maintain that they received a fairly one-sided and not entirely satisfying treatment in *The Theory of Communicative Action*. Politics in modern mass democracies is here perceived as practically synonymous with the bureaucratic administration of society, and the law is in this connection an instrument for the coercive realisation of power-based decisions. To be sure, some opinion-forming processes do take place in the political public sphere, but they typically result only in mass loyalty and acclamation of the solutions offered by the political power holders. In other words, popular rule is badly off according to this model, and this was probably also how Habermas viewed the situation in the bourgeois-democratic systems around 1980, at the time when he wrote this work.

In *Between Facts and Norms*, which was first published in German in 1992, what is central is precisely questions concerning the roles of law and politics in modern democracies. The problem here is more in what way communicative action must be institutionalised in order to be converted into practical results in a political context. Without such a clarification, the theory of communicative action remains a purely normative theory. It is obvious that most political questions are not decided through a general consensus in a discourse free of coercion. This is the case neither in the public sphere nor in political assemblies. Habermas nevertheless maintains that the theory of communicative action is relevant in this area as well. Communicative opinion formation is a necessary condition for being able to decide what should be done; however, communication cannot in itself realise goals or resolve conflicts. That can only happen through an institutionalised political process, in which also the media of law and power bind the participants' actions. Habermas refers to this as collective will-formation, by which he means attempts to solve coordination problems cooperatively and in a reflexive manner.

In this connection, law and power represent the ability to make decisions and implement them. As mentioned before, modern compulsory law in the hands of political authorities involves power to enforce plans because the authorities have means of sanction at their disposal. Yet in this later study, Habermas is concerned with the fact that there is an additional dimension to the law, which he barely touched in his previous work: the law is not only the tool of power; it also limits the use of power. While power represents the executive authority and is a means of organising efficient realisation of goals, the law prevents the power apparatus of the state from programming itself (cf. Habermas 1989c: 146 f.), i.e. it prevents a situation in which the power-holders define what is right. Power is institutionalised by way of law; it is only through the law that political bodies can claim authority, and it is through legal procedures that the use of power can be justified and checked. Thus, the law plays a central role in the integration of modern societies. This is a point on which many people will agree. The big question is what the force of the law is based on.

Is it, as claimed by the legal realists, only the condition that the law can be supported by sanctions which explains why its commands are obeyed? Does the law take care of its social integrative role only by threatening to punish people who break some norm, or does it have other resources at its disposal? The question is whether the law can be explained in purely functional categories (as suggested by, among others, the systems theorist Niklas Luhmann), or if it also includes an element of normative validity. This is what the title *Between Facts and Norms* refers to, namely that the factual ability of the law to stabilise expectations to behaviour depends on the condition that it is done in a way which is perceived as normatively legitimate. According to Habermas, there is a tension within the law which has to do with the fact that the law cannot function efficiently unless it is perceived as a resource of justice, i.e. as a result of a reasonable process of will-formation. The ability to enforce the law depends on legitimate legislation, i.e. on a legislative process which claims to be rational because it guarantees equal freedom to all citizens. Thus, democracy is in focus within the discourse theoretical theory of law. In modern societies it is the democratic procedures of legislation that guarantee the legitimacy of the law. This normative basis of law and politics is an aspect that Habermas himself to a great extent seems to have overlooked in *The Theory of Communicative Action*.

CONCLUSION

The lifeworld can be said to consist of three structural components: culture, society and personality. These are maintained through three linguistic reproduction processes: cultural reproduction, social integration and socialisation. However, modern reality is too complex to be intelligible from the lifeworld perspective alone. We can hence look at the action areas of economy and administration as being coordinated on the basis of system integration. This means that interaction is taken care of by the steering media of money and power, through the agents' purposive rational actions. The development in this direction was caused by two different, but related processes. On the one hand, there is a rationalisation process which has taken place within the framework of the lifeworld, and which has turned communication oriented to reaching understanding into an increasingly important means of coordination. On the other hand, the complexity of the social world has increased to such an extent that it has burst the capacity of language to function as a coordinating force within all areas. In Habermas's opinion, it is unproblematic that areas such as market economy and bureaucratic administration function through systemic integration. We only have a problem in this respect if imperatives from the system integration begin to encroach on and colonise the symbolically structured reproduction processes of the lifeworld. There are tendencies of this in modern society, but they can be averted through political action on the part of the citizens.

The social theory under discussion here has also been strongly criticised, partly because it incorporates systems theory as one of its pillars, and partly because it has been accused of oversimplifying reality. The debate has made it clear that there is no basis for drawing a sharp line between the lifeworld, social integration and communicative action on the one hand, and the systems, system integration and purposive-rational action on the other.

Notes

1. Cf. Adam Smith's postulate of the 'invisible hand': while every agent in the market acts in order to maximise his/her own interests, the consequences of all these single actions – in a way that was not intended by anyone and by ways that are not immediately transparent to human reason – becomes a system which produces and distributes goods at the lowest possible cost, and which thus maximises the interest of the *community*.
2. Functional explanatory models were up to the 1970s a central paradigm within social sciences such as social anthropology and sociology, through pioneers such as Bronislaw Malinowski and Talcott Parsons/Robert Merton, respectively. After this time, functionalism has lost ground rather drastically, partly because of the well-founded objection that the conditions for using this type of explanation (in its strong sense) are rarely met within the social sciences. The most prominent critic of the theory has been Jon Elster (1984: 28 ff.).
3. Habermas also claims that there is an important difference in degree between money and power with regard to how well they fill the function as language independent steering media. Money generally fills this function in a *better* way than does power, because money can more easily be measured, exchanged/transferred, and stored, compared to power. According to Habermas, this is because the use of power is still more directly dependent on legitimation through linguistic consensus formation than is the use of money (Habermas 1987a: 272).
4. In a Marxist sense, i.e. as false consciousness.
5. The most important collections of such critical commentary articles is the one published in 1986 (English version in 1991 with the title *Communicative Action*), edited by Habermas's co-workers Axel Honneth and Hans Joas, and the homage volume for Habermas's 60th anniversary in 1989 (English version in two volumes 1992 with the titles *Philosophical Interventions in the*

Unfinished Project of Enlightenment, and *Cultural-Political Interventions in the Unfinished Project of Enlightenment*), edited by Honneth, Thomas McCarthy, Claus Offe, and Albrecht Wellmer. In addition there is Honneth's monograph *The Critique of Power* (English version 1991; German original 1985).

PART 2

LAW AND POLITICS IN A DISCOURSE-THEORETICAL PERSPECTIVE

CHAPTER 6

Towards a deliberative model of democracy

INTRODUCTION

Over a long period of time Jürgen Habermas has greatly influenced research on democracy, even when his political theory was only available in fragments. Not until *Between Facts and Norms*, the German edition of which came out in 1992, did a more comprehensively formulated theory appear. Discourse theory has inspired several theorists to develop a more 'Habermasian' theory of democracy, with a strong emphasis on participation, i.e., the so-called *discourse democracy*. Representatives of this school of thought are John Elster (1986), Joshua Cohen (1989), and John Dryzek (1990). In discourse ethics these theorists have seen the potential for of a new theory of democracy. However, their use of the theory has given rise to an understanding of democracy which on important points collides with the view that Habermas himself is presently advocating. Before we discuss this issue in more detail, we will explain the background of the controversy.

VOTE OR DELIBERATION?

In modern democratic theory there two camps: those who emphasise votes and voting arrangements and those who emphasise participation and deliberation. The question is whether it is the vote or the preceding discussion that represents the core characteristic of democracy. In the liberal and pluralist tradition democratic legitimacy is regarded to spring from the private and secret votes of individuals. Here, the main concern of politics is to find compromises between competing, private interests by means of formal voting arrangements. It is the right to vote that shows how collective decisions are linked with the free choices of individuals. In this tradition, democracy is frequently referred to as a decision-making method based on the principle of majority rule.

In the republican tradition, however, democracy is not limited to voting and elections only; more important is participation in formal and informal forums, where citizens get the opportunity to make up their minds about collective affairs. Representatives of this tradition claim that it is the citizens themselves who collectively must pass their own laws and create their own identity through discussion. This tradition has it roots in the Greek *polis*, where democracy is understood as an end in itself. Democracy does not only contribute to conflict resolution and the realisation of common goals; it also enlightens, develops and educates its citizens. Political participation affects the character of the citizens and is a way of reaching mutual understanding on the common good. Therefore, democracy cannot be understood solely as a decision-making arrangement, through which citizens elect and dismiss their leaders.

However, it may be argued that this participatory democracy does not work properly in modern societies. The arguments against participatory democracy are related to the facts of complexity and pluralism of the societies in question. Firstly, it is problematic to guarantee individual rights within the framework of a theory that considers the 'will of the people' to be the highest authority in all situations. (This is an issue that we will take up shortly.) Secondly, it has been argued that the very idea of participation in large and complex communities is simply utopian. It is difficult to imagine that everyone should be able to participate in all decisions which may affect them (although it has been claimed that the Internet and similar technological innovations can open up new possibilities for

---

The concept of deliberative democracy

From a linguistic point of view this concept is relatively new. David M. Estlund (1993) traces it back to Joseph M. Bessette's article 'Deliberative Democracy: The Majority Principle in Republican Government' from 1980. However, the ultimate origin of the expression is John Dewey and his monograph *The Public and its Problems* from 1927. A central point here is that the majority principle can not stand alone. A majority decision is always justified with reference to its substance, and a great deal of mutual communication is required before votes can be cast. There must be agreement with respect to what the disagreement is about, what the alternative choices are, and which voting procedures are to be used. The majority rule has its limitations not only from a normative, but also from a functional perspective. Extensive communication between the decision makers is required if the voting institution is to function properly (Rawls 1971: 356 ff., Pitkin 1972: 224). According to both Edmund Burke and John Stuart Mill, it is the public debate and the commitment to the common good which determine the vote. The thesis is that public debate and criticism improve the information basis, reduce the problem of bounded rationality, increase the level of reflection as well as the decision-makers' sense of responsibility and the legitimation of political decisions. Along with periodic elections and competition between political parties, public debate and criticism are what force the leaders of society to consider social interests and values, and thus what constitute the best way of realising the principle of popular sovereignty.

There have been a series of contributions to the theory of deliberative democracy, from philosophers, legal theorists and political scientists. These have challenged the hegemony of *rational choice* and the economic model of democracy, also referred to as 'competitive elitism' (cf. Held 1996), demonstrating that the model is fraught with a number of problems, both empirical and normative ones. Central contributions in this respect come from Cohen (1989), Elster (1986, (ed.) 1998), Manin (1987), Michelman (1988), Sunstein (1985, 1988a, 1988b, 1993), Fishkin (1991), Bohman (1996), Nino (1996), Gutmann and Thompson (1996), Bohman and Rehg (eds) (1997).

political participation (cf. Budge 1993)). The division of labour and the demand for a well-functioning economy set a limit to how much time society as a whole can spend on political activity. Moreover, expert competence is needed in order to solve many of the complex tasks in technologically advanced societies. A third problem is that extensive participation in the political process is most appropriate in small societies, where there are shared values and common norms in relation to which conflicts can be resolved. In more pluralistic societies it is more difficult to find such a common identity. A fourth factor is that in modern societies there is a right to non-participation as well. Many people would like to do something other than engage in politics on a full-time basis (cf. Bobbio 1987). Thus, the degree of participation we may expect and demand of people is limited.

Discourse theory represents a third way between the liberal and republican traditions in democratic theory. Here Habermas draws parallels with the wave of what is referred to as *deliberative politics*, which emphasises the role played by mutual argumentation in the effort to reach a common view and make collective decisions. This school originated in the USA, and it is inspired by the rediscovery of pragmatism and the works of John Dewey. It is supported by several studies that demonstrate the dominance of republican ideas over liberal ones in the American political tradition (cf. Pocock 1975, Sandel 1996). The school has also received important impulses from the recent revitalisation and innovation within the field of political theory. We are here in particular thinking of the many contributions to the discussion of rationality and intersubjective criteria of justice which have followed in the wake of John Rawls's *A Theory of Justice* from 1971. This tradition has focused on the procedural aspects of political deliberations, and on the forms of community and allegiance which are required in order to establish a stable polity. However, when it comes to understanding modern democracy, a schism has arisen between community-oriented theories, represented by the so-called communitarians on the one hand, and liberal rights-based theories on the other. Habermas is critical of both, and by means of his theory of communicative action he wants to establish an alternative which he refers to as a *discourse-theoretic model of deliberative democracy*. By this he means a system within which the citizens rule themselves through participation in legally institutionalised decision-making processes, and where only outcomes which are approved by everyone in an open debate are regarded as legitimate.

THE LIBERAL MODEL

By liberalism, Habermas (1996a) means a political philosophy that conceives the freedom of the individual as the highest good. It sees the individual as a bearer of rights. The existence of the state is justified insofar as it protects the freedom of its citizens, which is negatively defined. It is therefore important to develop a system of government that neither interferes with nor violates the private sphere. Consequently, liberals emphasise the importance of control arrangements such as the division of power, bills of rights, constitutional shackles, and the democratic process as a process of aggregation. By summarising the citizens' preferences as they are expressed in free elections, legitimate collective decisions are ensured.

This is a model of democracy which looks at democracy as a decision-making method (cf. Schumpeter 1942, Downs 1957).

The basic features of this model originate in the philosophy of Hobbes (1968) and Locke (1960) and are based on the idea that people have rights and freedoms that exist prior to, and hence independently of, any political order. This notion of pre-social and pre-political human rights stems from natural law. Human beings possess certain rights that exist prior to the establishment of political institutions, i.e. in the state of nature. These pre-political rights not only limit the power of the state, they also entitle individuals to use them at their own discretion. In this paradigm there is no basis for discriminating between different interests on a normative basis. The political order is conceived to rest on a *contract* into which equal and free individuals have voluntarily entered in order to protect their respective interests.

As we can see, basic elements of natural law and contract theory are reflected in common with the modern understanding of politics, as it is expressed in the conventional explanatory paradigms of political science. Here politics is understood as a process in which the actors try to influence the authorities in order to secure as many of the available resources as they possibly can. This is often referred to as a *competitive elitism*, a system in which the parties compete to have the best offers to the voters, thereby to win the highest number of votes and thus the right to govern. The citizens are seen as passive consumers, and the political process as a struggle between competing interests (Schumpeter 1942). This is the 'realistic' political view, which is reflected in different theoretical schools within political science. From elitism and pluralism, from pressure group theory via neo-corporatism and to the economic view of democracy we learn how public policies come about in competition and cooperation between powerful groups and the authorities. The electorate demands welfare goods from the government, and it has rights, constitutions and 'checks and balances' to keep potentially corrupt rulers in check. The focus is on how the authorities can be controlled, and how the interests or preferences of individuals can be maximised through formal procedures of registration and aggregation of preferences. No widespread consensus and common view of interests and valid norms are presupposed. Bargaining, logrolling, pork-barrelling, horse-trading based on strategic interaction, rather than deliberation, explain behaviour and the outcome of decisions. Conflicts of interests are regulated by formal procedures. The validity of those procedures is quite simply presupposed; no attempt has been made to explain them.

This liberal model of democracy has also been theoretically supported by utilitarianism and modern theories of rational choice. The utilitarian philosopher Jeremy Bentham (1982) claimed that all collective and ideal entities are metaphysical. There is no such thing as natural or universal rights, since these cannot be localised in time and space. Furthermore, the common will is nothing but the sum total of everybody's will, i.e. an aggregated will. The task of the legislators is to aggregate the citizens' preferences and make adjustments when this is necessary from a utilitarian point of view. The legitimacy of the legislators stems from the outcome of elections. It is presupposed that the politicians comply with the voters' wishes out of pure self-interest, i.e. because they want to be re-elected.

AGGREGATION PROBLEMS

Through game theory and social choice theory, the theory of rational choice has contributed many valuable insights into the substantial problems related to the aggregation of preferences and strategic action, including those sub-optimality and contra-finality problems which arise when we presuppose that agents act strategically. When actors act out of pure self-interest, the outcome is not as optimal as if they coordinate their actions. The theory of rational choice has demonstrated the problems with, and the limitations of, this type of selfish behaviour. In this model, society consists of individuals who are not tied together by any mutual bonds. The model is atomistic and creates a political order which is uncertain and unstable. This is reflected in the analysis of the voting institution.

The voters have no direct influence on the decision-making process, as there is no voting rule which ensures a fair and meaningful aggregation of private preferences. The so-called 'Condorcet's paradox' shows that in situations where there are three or more alternatives, and where these are voted over in pairs, there may be a rotating majority. This means that a majority of the voters prefer alternative x to y, and alternative y to z, while at the same time another majority prefer z to x. This, in conjunction with the fact that individuals may vote strategically or tactically, makes it more difficult to ensure that a vote really reflects the will of the citizens. Democracy based on the voting procedure cannot guarantee a rational outcome, i.e. a logically consistent ranking of preferences. Hence, Arrow's impossibility theorem: there is no satisfactory way to map individual preferences onto a social decision (Arrow 1963, cf. Hardin 1968, Riker 1982).

The majority principle is normatively problematic even in cases of a clear majority. 'It cannot live up to the ideals of democratic legitimacy because outcomes can only claim to represent winners and not a common will,' (Chambers 1997: 1). According to liberalism, the majority principle represents coercion. No contract theory is able to defend the principle of majority rule without undermining the basis of individual rights (Shapiro 1996: 16 ff., cf. Ackerman 1980). However, it is an outright 'unfair' method of aggregation when we know that it is impossible to define who the 'majority' really is. It not only threatens minorities, it also *creates* a 'majority' that does not represent the opinions of the (actual) majority. This is due to cyclical majorities, strategic voting and manipulations of the voting order. The outcome of legislative processes is likely to be determined by who controls the agenda and where in the voting cycle a decision appears (Riker and Weingast 1988). It is clear that the revelations of social choice theory pose a number of challenges to the liberal aggregation model. The problems are summarised by David Miller:

> there is no rule for aggregating individual preference that is obviously fair and rational and thus superior to other possible rules; and that virtually every rule is subject to strategic manipulation, so that even if it would produce a plausible outcome for a given set of preferences if everyone voted sincerely, the actual outcome is liable to be distorted by strategic voting.
>
> (Miller 1993: 80)

The problems raised here have led some theorists to conclude that it is necessary to lower the ambitions of popular rule. It has been claimed that the influence of the voters is limited to dismissing rulers whom they distrust. William Riker (1982) maintains that democracy only can be used to prevent tyranny. Rather than being interpreted as an expression of the popular will, elections should be regarded as an opportunity for popular veto on the preferences of the legislators.

This is a model that focuses on the limitations of politics, not on its creation. The main deficiency of this model stems from the fact that they put all emphasis on the aggregation of preferences and the procedures that control it. To these theorists, this is the very essence of democracy. However, the approach turns out to be problematic for several reasons. First of all it is a point that even fair procedures can produce unfair outcomes (van Mill 1996). A mere observance of procedures cannot in itself make decisions legitimate; they must be justified in a deliberation that focuses on the content of the matter (Bohman 1996: 51). Secondly, the findings of social choice theory give us reason to expect that, due to rotating majorities, unstable patterns of cooperation would be a more dominant feature of politics than what is actually the case. Thus the theory has problems in explaining the stability we are in fact witnessing. Thirdly, a theory which regards politics as an aggregation of interests and a veto-game will have difficulty explaining the integrative aspects of political life. For example, how are political competence and identities created within such frames (Warren 1994: 16)? How can we explain consensus building processes and the formulation of a public interest? Why do people vote if they are merely rent seekers and why do they trust politicians if they are of the same kind?

In recent years many people have called attention to these and other problematic presuppositions made by the *rational choice* paradigm.[1] One has criticised the fact that popular rule is conceived of as an 'adversary democracy',[2] and one has demonstrated the importance of deliberations in constitutional contexts.[3] It has been pointed out that there are some unreasonable logical presuppositions in this understanding of democracy, as well as a lack of empirical correspondence and relevance. Last, but not least, it has been claimed that it is difficult to understand how collective decisions can legitimately be based on the citizens' private, idiosyncratic preferences or self-interests. Such decisions will be random in relation to different views of justice and the common good, and they are hence not a good foundation on which collective structures can be built. Why should the citizens feel committed by decisions which are nothing but 'arithmetic artefacts' – a mere statistical determination of whether there are more in favour than against?

THE REPUBLICAN MODEL

An alternative concept of politics stems from Aristotle and the Italian renaissance.[4] 'Republic' is an anglification of the Latin *res publica*, which was considered to be the opposite of *res privata*. The term denotes that which people have in common outside the family, as well as the institutional structure of public life. The republican model can be traced back to the Greek city-state, but also to the Rousseauian idea of the general will. Here the political process is not regarded simply as a procedure for electing and getting rid of leaders by adding up the citizens' preferences. Society does not consist of self-interested actors asserting their preferences, but of virtuous citizens who are actively engaged in collective affairs, on the basis of some shared views of the common good (cf. Sandel 1998, Walzer 1983). Here, we get a picture of citizens with virtues, rather than citizens with rights.

> For the Greek, therefore, the city was a life in common; its constitution, as Aristotle said, was a 'mode of life' rather than a legal structure; and consequently, the fundamental thought in all Greek political theory was the harmony of this community. Little distinction was made between its various aspects. To the Greek the theory of the city was at once ethics, sociology, and economics, as well as politics in a narrower, modern sense.
>
> The pervasiveness of this common life and the value the Athenians set upon it, is apparent upon the face of their institutions. Rotation in office, the filling of office by lot, and the enlargement of governing bodies even to unwieldiness were all designed to give more citizens a share in the government. The Athenian knew the arguments against all these devices as well as anyone, but he was prepared to accept the drawbacks for the sake of the advantages as he conceived them.
>
> (Sabine 1937: 13)

Michael Sandel (1996) emphasises two points on which republicans distance themselves from modern liberalism. The first point concerns the relation between 'the right' and 'the good'. Here liberals give preference to rights and justice, while republicans build on an idea of *the common good*. Liberals emphasise the use of constitution, human rights and neutral principles to settle controversies. The inviolability of the individual is protected by justice and cannot be disposed with through political compromises or social utility calculations (Rawls 1971: 4, Dworkin 1977: 194). By contrast, republicans believe that rights are political by nature, and that democracy is the ultimate good. It is in the political process that rights are shaped and it is through collective decisions that they become mandatory and committing. Therefore, what duties and rights are to apply in a society are determined by the level of reflection of its citizens. The citizens are themselves sovereign when it comes to deciding their conditions of communication in democratic forums. The result is a *politics of virtues*, where the aim is to cultivate the citizens so as to enable them to participate in discussions about the conditions for their coexistence and about the common good (Michelman 1988: 284).

The second point of difference between republicans and liberals concerns the relation to democracy. According to the liberals, individuals have a *right to freedom* that precedes the claim to political freedom. Democracy is therefore bound and limited by basic individual rights that are constitutionally protected. By contrast, the republicans see freedom as dependent on political participation. When the citizens are given the opportunity to participate in the self-governing republic, they are given freedom as well. It is not necessary to follow Aristotle all the way, and say that freedom is internally related to the development of civic virtue and political participation, so that humans are regarded as political animals which can only obtain freedom in a political community. A more moderate version is that the freedom to pursue one's own goals depends on the freedom of the political community (Sandel 1996: 26). Only in a free social community can the citizens autonomously form authentic motives and pursue their goals. Here they get the opportunity to test their points of view in an open discussion.

Republicans regard politics as a normative activity, as a continuance of ethics. They criticise the liberals for not seeing that their concept of political community is reduced merely to a community of rights and which is incapable of generating the type of obligations and those bonds upon which the stability of state institutions depend. The state is, and must be, a community of values – an ethical order to quote Hegel (1967). Politics is concerned with the choice between values, aims at resolving conflicts, and defines the goals of the community on the basis of common norms and shared sentiments of attachment. These choices are conditioned by cultural heritage, solidarity and the patriotism of civil society. In this concept of politics, the question is not what serves the interest of single actors, but what rules and policies can reasonably be made applicable to everyone. It is not power, but the common will which is the basis of the state. The focus of the republican model of democracy is not the agents' wills, but the citizens' reason and ability to agree on what is the common good (Michelman 1989: 257).

Figure 6.1 sums up some of the main differences between the liberal and republican views on democracy.

Comparable characteristics	Liberalism	Republicanism
Concept of freedom	Negative	Positive
Rights	Pre-political	Political
Procedures	Decision-making method	Also an end in themselves
Justification	'The right'	'The good'
Decision-making model	Aggregation	Deliberation

Figure 6.1 *Important differences between Liberalism and Republicanism*

THE PROBLEM OF REPUBLICANISM

According to Habermas (1994a), the general problem with the republican model of democracy is that it understands politics as a form of deliberation which takes place within groups that are already socially and culturally integrated. In this perspective, democratic legitimacy springs from the free will of the people. The popular will comes into existence when citizens gather and are allowed to deliberate freely, and when they obey only the laws passed by themselves. In the republican tradition, it is only the citizens of political communities who have rights, not human beings in general. Hence, the problem of republicanism is how to ensure human rights an inalienable status.

Parallel to the individualist-atomistic bias of the liberal democracy model, the republican model can be shown to have a collectivist-holistic bias. The main problem with the republican model is not really that it does not take sufficient notice of the many structural relations – e.g. political parties, organisations, and formal procedures – which have made modern politics rather strategic and conflictual than communicative and consensual. In a model which primarily serves normative purposes, such empirical discrepancies can, with some benevolence, be ignored. It is however, worse that republicanism disregards those aspects which are a part of modern political decision-making processes, and which also control them, in a normative sense. Republicanism fails to acknowledge the fact that political decision-making involves different types of procedures and different forms of argumentation. It does not distinguish between cultural and political integration as two different forms of social integration. Neither does it distinguish between that type of allegiance which is relevant in a political context and that type of allegiance and commitment which is relevant in a social context, where group memberships provide the individuals with a collective identity. This fact gives rise to three types of problems.

First, republicanism does not realise that the extra-parliamentary debate which takes place in the public sphere must be separated from the institutionalised decision-making procedures used in formal political bodies, such as parliaments and local councils. As will be further discussed in Chapter 9, the public sphere should be regarded as an arena outside the state which can shape opinions, initiate criticism and control the authorities through a free and open debate. This institutional distinction between the public sphere and state organs first arose in modern societies. The problem is that the republican view of politics still relies heavily on the Greek model of democracy, where it made little difference whether the citizens met and discussed as friends, brothers, and equals in the forum (*Agora*) or as formal decision-makers in the popular assembly (*Ekklesia*). However, in today's society, both the formal and the actual distance between the state power and the citizens is greater than in the democracy of Athens. In modern societies there is a type of public sphere which is more radically beyond the control of the power holders. That such a public sphere has been firmly established in Western democracies is due to the fact that the citizens have obtained political rights which they can use against the state. There is thus a distinction between state and civil society, which localises a central part of the conditions of democracy to non-state spheres.

Secondly, the republican model does not take into account the structurally differentiated forms of discussion that characterise politics today. In the republican perspective, the way political decision-making is conducted in modern states seem almost illegitimate. For example, it is difficult to see that the neo-corporate bargaining system has any legitimacy. How can we possibly justify arrangements through which resources rather than arguments impact decision-making processes (cf. Rokkan 1966)? The republican model has problems realising that under certain conditions strategic action can be both necessary and legitimate in politics. It is also difficult to explain and justify the type of deliberations and those arrangements which are necessary today in order to get an established collective will converted into a politically binding decision through administrative and legal procedures. Competition between political parties and legal control of political power are in this perspective regarded as externally imposed limitations, and not as conditions for the realisation of popular rule. All in all, the republican model seems to have problems with the procedural realities and the structural complexity of modern political systems.

Thirdly, the model is not very well adapted to political decision-making in multi-cultural societies. It understands politics as deliberation in relation to the common good, and is thus adapted to what Habermas refers to as ethical-political questions. The citizens, who share the same idea of the good life and of the common good, can agree on what has to be done with concrete conflicts and problems. In other words, political agreement depends on a community of common interests, shared world views, and thus also on standards for the good society.[5] However, the question is whether this is sufficient to understand decision-making in complex societies which are characterised by functional differentiation, social complexity and conflicting interests. In such societies it is not realistic to expect a comprehensive agreement on values and interests because such societies are also pluralistic in a moral and religious sense. As claimed by Rawls (1993), there are different doctrines in these areas. We must therefore take a different perspective on political decision-making than that which presupposes that citizens with common virtues and interests meet in the forum to find solutions to collective problems. The success of the modern states must be ascribed to their ability to make arrangements with which different groups can identify. Modern democracies are founded on the idea that it is possible to live with diversity and pluralism. No overlap between *etnos* and *demos*, i.e. between nation and state, is presupposed. We will return to this issue in the next chapter and in Chapter 11.

RIGHTS OR A COMMON WILL?

The problems of the republican model are thus not only due to its neglect of the differentiated character of politics, but also to the existence of individual rights and plural value structures. In this model, human rights can only be understood as emerging from the ethical community constituted by demos.

> contemporary republicans tend to give this public communication a communitarian reading. It is precisely this move towards an *ethical constriction* of *political discourse* that I question. Politics may not be assimilated to a hermeneutical process of self-explication of a shared form of life or collective identity. Political questions may not be reduced to the type of ethical questions where we, as members of a community, ask ourselves who we are and who we would like to be. In its communitarian interpretation the republican model is too idealistic even within the limits of a purely normative analysis.
>
> (Habermas 1994a: 4)

Republicanism raises the basic fundamental communitarian problem of respecting diversity. Its starting point is that society is normatively integrated, which means that it is bound together by shared values and common norms of solidarity (Taylor 1989: 165 ff.) This is an important (sociological) corrective to the liberal atomistic understanding of society; however, the problem is that modern societies are normally integrated around many different world views and value systems (cf. Kymlicka 1995). There are different conceptions as to what is good and desirable. These notions vary with different groups, milieus, local societies and cultures. As soon as a majority in a society share certain values, these may become a threat to individuals who are in opposition to the majority. Many sub-cultures, minorities and dissidents in modern societies are in danger of being suppressed by hegemonic values of the majority. We therefore need a concept of what is right and just, in contrast to concepts of what is good and valuable. The distinction is neatly captured by Michael Walzer, himself regarded as belonging to the communitarian camp:

Michael Sandel asks whether a community of those who put justice first can ever be more than a community of strangers. The question is a good one, but its reverse form is more immediately relevant: If we really are a community of strangers, how can we do anything else but put justice first?

(Walzer 1990: 9)

The communitarian view of society can be said to lack a concept of individual rights that must be respected, even at the cost of majority views and collective goods. Liberals claim that legal protection of individual rights is inevitable. It is only individuals who can claim unconditional respect. However, while the communitarians do not have an adequate conception of 'the right', it may be argued that the liberal political tradition does not have a satisfactory concept 'the good', and of rational, collective will formation. Liberals have problems explaining the emergence of a common will, while the republicans, on their part, have difficulties giving human rights an imperative status.

Habermas's criticism is basically concerned with the fact that there is an ethical limitation of political discourse in republicanism. Neither the Greek *polis* nor Hegel's concept of *Sittlichkeit* (ethical life) may serve as a point of reference in the understanding of modern politics. These models are designed for collective self-interpretation processes that take place within the framework of an already existing normative community, where there are shared opinions of the good life.

In contrast, a discourse-theoretical interpretation insists on the fact that democratic will-formation does not draw its legitimating force from a previous convergence of settled ethical convictions, but from both the communicative presuppositions that allow the better arguments to come into play in various forms of deliberation, and from the procedures that secure fair bargaining processes. Discourse theory breaks with a purely ethical conception of civic autonomy.

(Habermas 1994a: 4)

According to Habermas, it is therefore necessary to establish a new model of democracy, which is neither fraught with the weaknesses of liberalism, nor with those of republicanism, but which incorporates their valuable insights and unites them into a more adequate model. The point of departure is that the theory of communicative action has helped us define the concept of deliberation, as it is used in the republican tradition.

DELIBERATIVE RATIONALITY

What does deliberation really mean, and how is it possible to arrive at consensual solutions by means of mutual considerations? One of the problems with the established theories of deliberative politics is that they lack a micro-foundation, which can explain how it is possible to form a common opinion and solve collective problems in a rational manner. We are here speaking of collective will-formation, which can take place in two different contexts; either to resolve conflicts between conflicting individual choices, or to determine what are collective goals. Both cases involve a mutual and reflexive attempt to solve collective coordination problems (Habermas 1996a: 131). However, which qualities of the human ability to reason, or of the individuals' ability to judge, make it possible for them to agree that something is valid? How can agents arrive at a common result when from the outset there is disagreement and different opinions as to what should be done?

In the tradition that goes from Aristotle via Kant and to Hannah Arendt, the focus has been on the faculty of judgment – cf. 'phronesis' (Aristotle) or 'die Urteilskraft' (Kant), i.e. the particular quality of human reason which is based neither on intelligence nor moral virtue, and which makes it possible to make up one's mind about particular cases where there are no given answers as to what is correct. This manifestation of an ability to think is not knowledge in a cognitive-analytical sense, but 'the ability to tell right from wrong, beautiful from ugly' (Arendt 1971: 446). However, what this kind of deliberation involves, how it can be realised and what kind of rationality it expresses remain unclear. In politics, we refer to the kind of deliberation which takes place in an assembly that must find an answer to common problems on a free basis. Aristotle conceived this as the deliberation that takes place when cases fall under a general rule, but where there is uncertainty about what constitutes a rational decision, i.e. when it is impossible to make a decision which is optimal.[6]

> Deliberation occurs in cases which fall under a general rule, if it is uncertain what the issue will be, and in cases which do not admit of an absolute decision.
> (Aristotle 1987: 77)

What governs a deliberation process where there are no given answers, but where an answer has to be found? The problem can be rephrased into a question about the power communication possesses when it comes to changing actors' opinions in cases of conflict and disagreement, so that agreement can be established and collective action made possible. The contribution of discourse theory can be said to provide the deliberative model of politics with an action-theoretical basis, much in the same way as the concept of strategic rationality – rational choice – provides realism and the liberal model of politics (viz. the economic model of democracy) with an action-theoretical basis. Communicative rationality claims that actors are rational not only when they choose the most efficient means to obtain their goals, but also when they are able to justify their choices and defend their actions against criticism. They must be able to explain the reasons for their actions and to justify their demands in order to be held rational, and then also for having any hope of gaining acceptance and support. In such a process personal motives are not sufficient. Reference to one's own interests does not constitute a good argument in a context where it is important to motivate others to give you their support. It is only to the extent that one is able to apply a common standard that one can hope to gain support from others. Only statements that have a certain general quality are relevant in a political context. A point of view can be met with sympathy only if it appeals to values, norms or principles with which others can agree or disagree with. Hence the proposition that an actor does not get acceptance for his demands just because he actually wants something, but only to the extent that he or she is able to show that the demand is justified in relation to the common good or to a generally accepted concept of justice. This is based on the fact that 'The mere articulation of an interest simply does not speak for or against the rightness of a norm' (Heath 1995: 83). Even if I have a 'rational' preference for pursuing a particular interest, and even if everyone can agree that this is 'rational' for me, in a moral context it does not follow that this is right.

> The right-making force of a person's desires is specified by what might be called a conception of morally legitimate interests. Such a conception is a product of moral argument; it is not given, as the notion of individual well-being may be, simply by the idea of what is rational for an individual to desire.
>
> (Scanlon 1982: 119)

Norms that regulate the satisfaction of interests (and values) for the parties must be justified argumentatively – with intersubjectively valid reasons – in order to obtain legitimacy.[7] Justification is a matter of reasons of which other people can approve or disapprove. Giving reasons is to say that something counts in favour of something else (Scanlon 1998: 18). When the addressee has asked why the speaker maintains a certain point of view, and the speaker has no good reason for refusing to give an explanation, there is a request that no rational actor can withdraw from (Alexy 1989). 'We are the ones on whom reasons are binding, who are subject to the peculiar force of the better reason,' (Brandom 1994: 5). Taken together this makes it possible to characterise the deliberative practitioner: *a deliberative person* participates in a discourse where validity claims are raised; the person takes a critical stand to his own as well as others' statements and actions, and substantiates his standpoints with arguments. In other words, a deliberative person is reflective and responsible, and is prepared for and competent of self-correction (Günther 1999: 87 ff.).

According to Habermas, intersubjective justification is the rationality basis which explains the transformative capacity of discussions, i.e. their power to change the views and action plans of individuals. Hence the claim that reasons make a difference in the world. This micro-basis of a theory of democracy does not only represent an analytical alternative to strategic rationality and competitive democracy, it also make a normative contribution: only to the extent that the autonomy of the individuals is secured, and their freedom respected, can the required competence be achieved which is needed to be a rational participant in discussions. Only when the individual is free to give her opinion on an independent basis can we say that her consent to political decisions is qualified. Against the liberal and republican models Habermas presents an alternative which he finds better equipped to handle the realities of complex societies, viz. the discourse-theoretical model of the democratic constitutional state. We will come back to the particular elements in this model in the next few chapters; here we shall only touch upon some of its general characteristics.

A PROCEDURAL MODEL OF DELIBERATIVE POLITICS

Habermas maintains that both within and outside the parliamentary system there are higher-order processes which are designed to solve conflicts in a reasonable manner. In other words, it is possible to discuss principles in a rational manner. Discourse theory aims at observing both the liberal principle which gives the individual first priority, and the republican insight that legitimacy springs from the citizens' deliberations. The task is to formulate *the self-understanding of the democratic constitutional state* in a more adequate manner. This can only be done by giving it a more abstract interpretation from what both the liberals and the republicans do. To every idea corresponds an ideal. The basis of the democratic constitutional state is a collection of principles and ideas, of rights and procedural requirements, that correspond to certain ideals of human rights and popular rule. To varying degrees the ideals are reflected in the actual entrenchment of institutional procedures and practices; but these are the ideals to which reference is commonly made when particular institutional arrangements are being criticised and when new, more 'democratic' institutional forms are being advocated. It is the ideal aspect of our form of government which is in focus in discourse theory.

Democracy in the modern sense can be said to emerge because the cosmologies, i.e. the great ideologies and world views, have dissolved (Warren 1994: 3). There is no longer only one current authoritative recipe for what is valid. Different values and moral systems compete for the hegemony. The democratic constitutional state is necessary in order to create stable arrangements of conflict resolution and problem solving, so that different groups can live together under a common law, even if they disagree about many issues. Constitutional democracies can be understood as a *procedure of problem solving and conflict resolution* which is not itself based on any comprehensive agreement about world views and values. Agreement is required only when it comes to the principles which secure a fair handling of conflicts. Popularly elected bodies cannot themselves dispose with democratic procedures, as it is only through those procedures that they can justify their own decisions, according to Habermas. Similarly, it is only by means of legally institutionalised procedures that the citizens themselves can bring about legitimate solutions to normative conflicts. As we will return to, such procedures do not guarantee rational decisions. The point is rather that they ensure a process that makes rationality possible.

Consequently, the discourse-theoretical model of democracy maintains the liberal ideas that the modern state is based on, and exists because of, the individual, and that any agreement is fallible. In contrast to the liberal value scepticism, discourse theory nevertheless argues that our democratic systems rest on some points of agreement. Furthermore, these systems are claimed to have institutions and arrangements which make it possible to solve conflicts in a rational manner, and they are also able, more or less successfully, to create new and widespread consensus, i.e. *deliberative majorities*, in order to realise collective goals (cf. Bohman 1996: 180). Whilst the consensualistic beliefs of the republican tradition has been incorporated into the model, the republican concept of rights is weak and has had to be made adjustments for. Only when individuals are able to voice their opinion freely, i.e. when they are autonomous actors, and only when the communication between them is not hindered by coercion or strategic action, is it possible to say that the obtained agreement is qualified or valid. Hence, we may understand the negative freedoms that citizenship guarantees as a protection of the autonomy that is necessary if the actors are to be independent participants in the formation of a common opinion.

Discourse theory takes an intermediary position in the dispute between communitarians and liberals. It shares the latter's deontological understanding of freedom, equality, justice and that *the right* thus takes precedence over what is good. Discourse theory shares, on the one hand, the communitarian belief that the development of character is a result of socialisation and education and, on the other hand, it agrees with republicanism that political opinion and will-formation is an intersubjective, communicative process (cf. Habermas 1993e: 91). This gives rise to a model of democracy which is based on (1) a desubstantialised concept of popular sovereignty, (2) a procedural concept of legitimacy, and (3) a decentralised perspective of society.

(1) By a substantial concept of popular sovereignty is meant that the will of the people is expressed through a collective subject (the People). It expresses the concrete will of a collective as it is manifested, for example, in political decisions, laws or in certain institutional arrangements. In modern societies this will cannot be regarded as a result of people's concrete gathering at the forum or in the assembly room of the parliament. Habermas adopts an intersubjective interpretation of the principle of popular sovereignty which is developed by Ingeborg Maus (1992): it is the democratic procedures that provide those terms of communication which are required for will formation to be legitimate. The concept of sovereignty is now linked to the 'subject-less forms of communication' which exist in free public spheres, and which work together with the institutionalised discourses in popularly elected assemblies. Habermas makes a distinction between opinion-formation in public spheres and will-formation in formal political institutions. The people are still regarded as the basis of democratic legitimacy, but not in the substantive sense as in traditional models of democracy. It does not constitute a single subject which is capable of acting, it acts only in the plural; 'the People' consists of many peoples. Popular sovereignty should be regarded as anonymous and subject-less. It can only be expressed in so far as the democratic procedures and political culture allow the power of the better arguments to be expressed in such a way that the results of a public opinion and will-formation process can claim to be rational.

> Only the principles of the *guaranteed autonomy of public spheres* and *competition between different political parties*, together with the parliamentary principle, exhaust the content of the principle of popular sovereignty.
>
> (Habermas 1996a: 171)

(2) The procedures are thus given a decisive role in the discourse-theoretical model of democracy. In contrast to republicanism, discourse theory does not regard the constitution as secondary in relation to political opinion and will-formation. It should not be seen as an external limitation on collective action. It is only by means of constitutional procedures that one can speak of a formation of legitimate interests and goals. This concerns the institutionalisation of the right to an open, public debate as well as the institutionalisation of procedures for argumentation, negotiations, bargaining and elections in the parliamentary system. Habermas refers to the latter as *the parliamentary principle*; it comprises the rules that regulate representation, the establishment and composition of political agencies, procedures, hearings and decision-making. Jointly, they ensure that the deliberation between parties takes place in such a manner that the issue under discussion is sufficiently illuminated before a decision is made, and that decisions can claim to be qualified, i.e. rational.

To elaborate on this view on democratic institutions, we may follow the leading figure among the 'founding fathers' of the US constitution, James Madison. He claimed that one advantage of the representative system is that it contributes to refining and expanding on standpoints by letting them pass through the reflective treatment of elected representatives. Hence, just like Edmund Burke and

John Stuart Mill, he stresses that representation is necessary in order to bring about rational deliberations about what is for the common good. Secondly, this, in conjunction with the principle of the division of powers, makes the majority less inclined to violate the rights of the minorities. Thirdly, the isolation and detachment of the representatives weaken the possibility that politics becomes corrupted by special interests and local factions (Sunstein 1988a: 352). Modern constitutions institutionalise procedures that ensure free communication, and they legalise certain interests as a protection against the tyranny of the majority. Constitutions realise rather than limit the idea of popular rule in complex societies, because they establish a fair procedure for collective decision-making (Dahl 1989: 164). A consensus which is established without the use of correct procedures is tyrannical, and laws which are not legitimated by judicial procedures are not laws. However, Habermas is clearly against elitist interpretations of the principle of representation, which seeks to shield the institutional discourse from a populist and irrational public opinion. His formulation of the stated thesis of 'garbage in, garbage out' runs like this:

> Elitist interpretations of the principle of representation respond to this requirement by shielding organized politics from a forever-gullible popular opinion. In normative terms, however, this way of defending rationality against popular sovereignty is contradictory: if the voters' opinion is irrational, then the election of representatives is no less so.
>
> (Habermas 1996a: 485)

The constitution should not be regarded as an instrument to protect pre-established truths. It should rather be viewed as an arrangement which ensures that the social power generated in free public spheres is not automatically incorporated into the political-administrative apparatus and converted into administrative initiatives, before it has been tested and qualified through discursive processes. Modern constitutions do not only protect democracy against itself, by making it impossible for a majority to abolish it; they also foster rational and fair processes of decision-making. According to Habermas, legitimate political power arises through the interaction between legally institutionalised, discourse arrangements and culturally mobilised public spheres, where the citizens both have the freedom to participate and to refrain from it.

(3) Because of this, we have to abandon the idea of a state-centred society which is at the basis of both the republican and the liberal model. Both regard the state as the centre and the apex of society, to use Luhmann's (1993) terms. Further they are confined to the nation state which they also take for granted. According to Habermas, the popular will cannot be read out of the decisions of deliberating assemblies, but must, as already mentioned, rather be localised to *the free flow of communication* in civil society. A current concept in discourse theory is that of a decentralised or de-hierarchised society, where there are several power and authority centres, and several ways of making one's voice heard. In modern societies, there is not one but many central bodies with the authority to make decisions and exercise power. (This is also taking place internationally as we will address in Chapter 11.) As the exercise of power takes different shapes, and as authority has different sources and is localised in different institutions, the channels of participation and control have also increased. Here we are not only thinking of various political channels of influence, such as the participation of interest

organisations, NGOs and lobbies in corporatist bodies; it is also important to see that a set of other procedures and arrangements has been established, whose purpose is to further information, deliberation and negotiation, both within and outside the formal bodies of the formal decision-making apparatus, both nationally and internationally. These serve to increase the amount of input to the decision-making process, and to expand and ease the exchange of information and arguments, before a decision has to be made. Under modern conditions, society does not have any straightforward and direct influence on itself; however, the modern democratic constitutional state depends on our ability to make this connection plausible.

RULE OF LAW AND DEMOCRACY

It is not the form of the laws, i.e. the fact that they are general and decided by popularly elected assemblies, which guarantees their legitimacy, but those procedures which ensure a free and continuous discussion about which laws should prevail. In this perspective we may speak of a 'legal and permanent' revolution because the democratic rights institutionalise a general right to communication and participation (Habermas 1996a: 14 f). These rights exist as common ideas and mutual commitments in our civil political culture. We may well reason about them, problematise them and make decisions about them, but they are nevertheless the very building blocks in the political game, and they can therefore not be disposed with unless we choose to step outside of the political process itself. According to our political culture, there is no way outside the democratic constitutional state; its procedures are unavoidable. This shows that the constitutional state, which guarantees human rights, is not in opposition to democracy and the principle of popular sovereignty. In a normative perspective, it is impossible to imagine a democracy without a constitutional state. On one hand, the democratic process itself must be legally institutionalised. The principle that the people is the foundation of the state points to the existence of basic rights that give the citizens the right to participate. Without a fundamental legal protection of human rights, no valid democratic decisions can be made. Democracy presupposes the constitutional state, but, on the other hand, the constitutional state presupposes democracy. They are equally primary and equally important. In explaining this connection, Habermas goes deeper into the concept of law and what it means to regulate human relations through the legal medium. This is the subject of the next chapter.

CONCLUSION

To sum up, we may conclude that according to the liberal model of democracy, citizens are treated fairly when everybody's interests or preferences are given equal consideration through formal election and voting rules. By contrast, the deliberative model maintains that citizens are treated equally when the exercise of political power can be justified by reasons which can be approved by all. Deliberation, and not aggregation, is regarded as the most fundamental feature of democracy, normatively speaking. Argumentation is needed also in order to justify a decision. It is necessary in order to justify outcomes towards those affected by them. Hence: 'A deliberative principle of accountability ask representatives to do more than try win re-election, and more than to respect constitutional rights' (Gutmann and Thompson 1996: 129). However, in addition deliberation is a functional requirement: before one can bargain or vote, the parties have to deliberate, and they must also argue for and against the use of different methods of decision making.

A further characteristic of the discourse-theoretical view of deliberative democracy is that it has abandoned the idea of a common or general will. On this point, it contrasts with republicanism and communitarianism. Agreement cannot be presupposed under modern conditions; it has to be created through public argumentation. Moreover, individual rights play a central role in the deliberative concept of democracy. They guarantee the citizens' private freedom, which is a precondition for citizens to be able to exercise their right to participate on an independent basis. We have also seen that the model distinguishes between the public sphere, which is regarded as a power-free arena of public opinion and communication, and the formal political system, which is where alternatives are formed and specified, and decisions made. This implies recognition of representative democracy; representation is seen as a prerequisite for getting the necessary overview and rationality in the decision-making process. However, even if this model deviates from participatory-democratic ideals, Habermas nevertheless maintains that democratic legitimacy is possible only insofar as political power can be explained and justified in relation to the citizens' interests. The basis of popular rule is localised to those institutions and forums of civil society where equal citizens can discuss political issues as free individuals.

Notes

1. Cf. for example Elster 1983, Goodin 1986, Miller 1993; Green and Shapiro 1994, Shapiro 1996.
2. Mansbridge 1980; cf. Mansbridge (ed.) 1990, Petracca 1991, Monroe (ed.) 1991.
3. Sunstein 1990: 209 ff., Elkin and Soltan (eds) 1993, Miller 1993.
4. This understanding of politics was given a particular American stamp with Hannah Arendt's interpretation of the American revolution (Arendt 1990).
5. This is also Hannah Arendt's (1958) interpretation of the Greek public sphere; it presupposed a homogeneous political community (Benhabib 1992: 90 ff.).
6. Rawls (1971: 418) also uses the concept of deliberative rationality, but only in order to characterise the ability of individuals to make rational choices based on consistent goals: 'we should deliberate up to the point where the likely benefits from improving our plan are just worth the time and effort of reflecting,' but see Rawls 1993: 253 for another take on deliberation.
7. This is needed to avoid committing the so-called psychologistic fallacy which is a variant of the naturalistic fallacy and which denotes the practice of inferring from is to ought (Heath 1995).

CHAPTER 7

The legitimacy of law

Communicative cooperation is worthless as long as it is not converted into practical initiatives. Authoritative bodies are therefore required in order to facilitate the transformation of rational opinion-formation into binding political decisions. In modern societies the law functions as a translator between opinion-formation processes and political decision-making. The law authorises political power, i.e., it tells us who has the authority to make decisions, and establishes procedures to control that power. The crucial question pertains to what the legitimacy of the law consists in. Does the law itself possess normative validity, or is it just a functional means for social integration? It is important to answer this question, as it concerns the foundation of the democratic constitutional state. If the law indisputably builds on normative principles, random political majorities should not be able to set it aside. Is there, then, a way of justifying the law which makes it possible to use it to check majority decisions? If so, the paradoxical question we have to ask is whether the constitutional state, i.e. the principle that politics is subjected to law, is consistent with the principle that the people are sovereign to pass their own laws.

One approach to this problematic is to investigate why citizens obey the law. Is it because disobedience is punished, or is it because obeying the law is conceived as a (moral) duty? We have mentioned before that realists claim that the citizens obey the law because it has been decided by competent bodies. Additional legitimacy is unnecessary, because the state embodies the power to sanction non-compliance. A further justification of the law is not possible, according to legal positivists (Jellinek 1919, Kelsen 1968). The answer to the question of why the citizens are committed by the law, is that it has been passed in a constitutionally correct manner. But why, then, is the constitution binding? It may be argued that this is the main problem for the discourse-ethical theory of law, since it recognises as a fact that modern law rests on political decisions which again are possible to alter. Even constitutional norms may be changed. This is what is meant when we say that *modern law is positive*. It is made by human beings and can be enforced, but it is also revisable.

Laws can be enforced despite opposition, but strangely enough, they claim at the same time to be legitimate. This is the situation Habermas tries to capture with the inter-linked concepts of facticity and validity. Laws are factually or socially valid since they can be enforced, but according to the self-understanding of the democratic constitutional state they are also in need of legitimacy. In a democratic constitutional state, it is the law that binds the legislators to the citizens. This means that the legislators must find a way of justifying the laws in order to ensure support from the subjects, i.e. those who are going to be affected by them (cf. Dyzenhaus 1997: 132). The laws are passed on behalf of the citizens, and the legislators must therefore be able to justify them in relation to the interests and well-being of the citizens; the laws must deserve recognition. This is one aspect of the validity problem. The other aspect concerns the normative content of the procedures themselves. Democratic procedures build on the principles of equality and freedom for everyone, principles that can not be set aside. They claim to be universally valid because they protect the integrity of the citizens. We may say that the authority of the state is justified when the citizens have a moral commitment to obey its instructions.

The built-in tension between facticity and validity in the modern concept of law reflects the general tension between reality and ideal, which is an integral part of all social relations. There will always be a discrepancy between how the world is and how it ought to be. This chapter raises the question of how modern law, which is based on individual rights and the use of coercion, can have a socially integrating effect. The solution to this question must be sought in *the interaction between law and communicative action*. These are the two media that make it possible to find solutions to practical questions in democratic societies. On the one hand and as a precondition to ensure overall compliance and obedience, the purpose of the law is to sanction the violation of norms. On the other hand, laws are also in need of justification, which can only take place in a free discussion regulated by the principles of truthful communication. This sheds light on the discourse-theoretical postulate that the constitutional state and democracy

---

The democratic constitutional state

This is a type of government where the majority's opportunity to put its will through is subjected to clear bindings and limitations. The state is bound by the constitution to respect the rights of the individual, as these prototypically are formulated in the American Declaration of Independence from 1776, the French Declaration of The Rights of Man and Citizen from 1789 and the UN's Declaration of Human Rights from 1948. An important consideration here is that 'democracy' should not be able to dismiss itself, as was the case with the Nazi's seizure of power in Germany in 1933. Hitler then received support from the legal theorist Carl Schmitt, who claimed that politics is value free, and that sovereignty belongs to the person (or organisation) who is in power. The legislators cannot be subjected to legal limitations (Schmitt 1928: 81 f.). Politics is about distinguishing between friend and foe, and only the person who has the power to proclaim a state of emergency is sovereign. There is no method of checking the sovereign's 'existential' decisions in a legitimate manner (Schmitt 1988: 5).

This concerns the question whether a right to resistance exists, and if civil disobedience can be justified. In the Declaration of Human Rights, and in the legal rulings of the Nuremberg war crimes tribunal following World War II, it has been established that there indeed exists such a right to resistance, and that it is everybody's duty to try legal commands against one's own conscience. To political theory, the question is how this can be combined with the principle of popular sovereignty, which states that all power and thus all law derives from the people.

presuppose each other, and that there is an internal relation between human rights and popular rule, as mentioned in the previous chapter. Rights ensure the citizens' private autonomy, while at the same time, through the securing of political participation, they ensure their public autonomy. If the democratic constitutional state is to live up to its ideals, it must not only ensure the citizens' private freedom, but also the opportunity to participate in public law-making processes. In the light of the above, certain features characterising the legal development in modern welfare states become problematic because they limit the freedom of citizens. This will be addressed in the last part of the chapter. We shall, however, start our presentation by discussing the relation between the political-philosophical concept of *practical reason* and those conditions which necessitate a different way of thinking about morality and law in modern societies compared to pre-modern societies.

PLURALISM AND INTEGRATION

By modern societies is here meant societies which have gone through the democratic and industrial revolutions, and which subscribe to human rights and the principle of popular rule. This primarily involves Western and Western-like states. These societies are characterised not only by several centres of power and authority, but also by a high degree of specialisation and a great variety of values and opinions. They are characterised by social conflicts and profound ethical disagreements when it comes to people's views of the good life. The societies in question are complex, differentiated and pluralistic.

In classical political theory from Aristotle to Hobbes, the sources of practical reason were based on different understandings of human anthropology and social ontology. Here, it is the conception of human nature or the characteristic features of the communal setting that determine to whom or what individuals are (morally) obligated. By practical reason is meant the type of reason that is necessary in order to answer questions of whether something has to be done, and if so, what. While the aim of theoretical reason is knowledge of the empirical world, the goal of practical reason is action. Practical reason is thus concerned with the reasons that determine our will (Kant 1996a: 37 ff.). The content of these reasons and conceptions of the good has changed over time. Plato and Aristotle, who were writing from within the Greek polis, 'saw the good as objective and authoritative', while 'the eighteenth-century individualist sees the good as the expression of his feelings or the mandate of his individual reason' (MacIntyre 1967: 209). In our societies there are different perspectives as to what is good and desirable, i.e. there are many different ways of realising ones' lives in a modern context (cf. Rawls 1993). How, then, is it possible to agree on what ought to be done?

Under modern, pluralist conditions, practical reason can, according to Habermas, no longer be understood as inscribed in the individual or in the value structure of society. Given the cultural pluralism and social complexity of modern societies, the answer to the question of what should be done can not be deduced from *one* concept of what is good and desirable. A Shiite Muslim and a Protestant, an atheist and a Buddhist have different concepts of the good society. There are many conceptions of how an exemplary life should be led, and there are different values that trigger the motivation to act. This creates conflicts, of which the religious wars in Europe bear historical testimony. Religious divisions also lie behind the current conflicts in, for example, the Middle East, Northern Ireland, the Balkans and the previous Soviet republics.

In traditional or religiously integrated societies the concept of law is based on common and shared ideas, beliefs and values. Conflict-regulating mechanisms are here founded on an *ethical form of regulation*, which again reflects a collective self-understanding (Habermas 1996a: 31). In such societies the law is legitimated by a meta-social institution (for example God). It is this institution which solves the tension between validity and facticity, i.e. between what ought to be done and what is actually done. Sacred authorities such as priests, oracles, judges, and chieftains stabilise interaction by defining both what the situation is like, and what should be done about it. They may, for example, argue that: 'It is not raining because the gods are dissatisfied with our sacrifices. We must give new sacrifices.' In modern societies such strong institutions are no longer able to regulate individuals' strategic actions. The meta-social authorities of traditional societies represent a link between the empirical and the normative domains, which has dissolved in modern societies. They have lost their innocence, their validity, and their resource basis. The binding power of tradition and the imperative status of shared norms have been contested and questioned by modern criticism, pluralism and new forms of evaluation. Consequently, the room for strategic action has expanded, particularly through the institutionalisation of market economy. In contrast to the traditional, value-based form of government, there is today a conception of the constitutional state, where the regulation of conflicts is based on individual rights. The idea of the constitutional state is intimately tied to and a product of the process of modernisation.

In modern societies, where individuals have broken away from the bindings and shackles of feudal times (serfdom and adscriptions,) and from religious imperatives, new freedoms and opportunities emerge. The individual can here orient herself according to her own subjective conception of validity and may also, relatively freely, choose the action strategies that she finds worth pursuing. However, this new-won freedom threatens the integration and the collective identity of society, as it allows for a higher degree of social pluralism as well as more room for self-interest and hence more disagreement about collective goals. The tacit agreement, the background consensus ensured by the lifeworld, does no longer function as an unproblematic adjudicator of conflicts. In a de-mystified and pluralistic world, it becomes difficult to establish the kind of agreement that is needed in order for a collective command to be accepted more or less automatically. The lifeworld is subjected to potential disintegration because the agents are faced with the choice between communicative and strategic action. However, within a social order there is always interest-governed action which must be regulated by norms. In modern societies, positive law becomes a central conflict-resolving mechanism. There are two reasons for this.

Firstly, the law ascribes to individuals the rights and the freedom to decide about their own lives and coexistence. In many different areas, it is now up to the individual to find out what is to be done: where to live, whom to live with, what to work with, what to believe in, etc. (cf. Luhmann 1982: 129). This contributes not only to creating a space in which citizens solve their problems of coexistence on a private basis; it also takes certain topics off the political agenda. For example, when the right to freedom of religion was introduced, it relieved the political discourse of many intricate problems that are difficult to agree on in pluralistic societies (cf. Holmes 1988, 1995).

Secondly, the modern concept of law represents an entirely new way of deciding controversial questions. When a legal claim can be asserted in connection with a conflict, when an appeal can be made to positive law in order to solve differences, it is a different way of regulating conflicts than in traditional societies, where conflict-solving is based on conventions and customs. In modern democratic societies, where the law is secularised and positivised, conflict-resolution has been moved into the courts. It is by following legal procedures that one can find legitimate answers to the question of what should be done in a conflict situation. Consequently, the law becomes the central medium of social integration, i.e. of the way in which society can resolve conflicts and obtain and maintain its identity. This way of organising the relation between facticity and validity is connected with the individual's normative disembeddedness in modern societies. However, what does this really imply?

The traditional model for legitimising the law goes back to a norm system which was handed down from generation to generation. The law received its authority from God or from nature. In pre-modern societies the idea prevailed that authority was legitimised from above; it was religiously sanctioned. In the middle ages, for example, the idea of 'the king of God's mercy' prevailed, which saw the king as God's substitute on earth. In modern societies, by contrast, authority is legitimised from below, since the constitution binds the state's exercise of power to the rights of the individual. It is only when the modern state is conceived to be the protector of the citizens' interests that it can claim legitimacy (Habermas 1979d). In other words, the content of the legitimacy principle changed, that is, the power of the king was replaced by the power of the citizens. The idea of a sovereign political order subjected to constitutional limitations, could only assume the form of democracy when political rights were detached from property and religious authorisation, which first happened with the democratic revolutions (cf. Held 1996: 36 ff.). The law does no longer derive its legitimacy from metaphysical principles.

In modern, pluralistic societies, there is not one single dominant norm system, but many, and the law must be able to communicate with all of them in order to obtain legitimacy. With modernity, the question of the legitimacy of the law therefore arises in a qualitatively new way. In order to clarify this issue, we may here recollect the previously introduced concept of a *post-conventional level of consciousness*, where the moral systems assume a universal character, where tradition is placed under the burden of justification, and where validity must be brought about by argumentation. According to Hegel's philosophy of right, whatever claims validity in modern societies cannot be legitimised with reference to traditions, customs, or power, but only with reference to insight and good reasons (1996: 322). Habermas argues that political legitimacy under modern conditions can only be achieved through moral discourses which aim at an impartial regulation of action conflicts. It is no longer sufficient to receive instructions for action from passed-down traditions or from other 'objective' sources, such as the church, the state or a political party. Modern societies require individuals to take a personal stand on practical and moral questions, and here it is arguments in first person singular that count. We must be able to justify our standpoint on the basis of our own opinions and what we can answer for, and not on the basis of what a third party might think. It is a question of a principled-oriented moral consciousness, based on the ideas of self-determination, personal responsibility and conviction. This constitutes the modern ideas of *the self-determining individual and a just society*. The crux of the modern concept of democracy is that free and equal individuals pass their own laws.

So far it has been argued that the law must be seen as a special type of coordination and conflict-regulating mechanism. It is the democratic procedures that provide laws and collective decisions with legitimacy. How all this links together, can be better understood if we take a closer look at the kind of competence that is needed when the aim is to solve normative questions rationally.

NORMS AND VALUES

In spite of the term 'nation state', it is only in principle that modern states are based on a particular collective identity. In reality they are (usually) peopled by more than one (ethnic) group, and they build on laws that aim at making possible peaceful coexistence between groups with different world views and cultures. In modern states, there is no necessary connection between *etnos* and *demos*, between ethnic and political borders. Habermas joins the liberal tradition, which maintains that these states only need a common commitment to the protection of individuals' fundamental rights, i.e. to a just arrangement for regulating human coexistence. While Rawls (1993: 133 ff.) refers to this as an 'overlapping consensus', Habermas (1996a: 500) speaks of a 'constitutional patriotism'. There is no need for a more comprehensive, value-based agreement about the good life; it is sufficient if all citizens commit themselves to obeying the basic constitutional rules that make possible peaceful coexistence in modern states.[1]

The background for this is that the modern legal order must be understood as a norm-rational order. This in contrast to the value-based *order* of ethical communities in pre-modern times. Basic rights are not only an expression of a community's common values or conceptions of the good. Freedom, democracy, equality and rights have a deontological status in modern societies. They constitute principles with which it is our duty to comply, even if it should be at the expense of the majority's values and the collective utility. They demand absolute validity. This is why rights can function as trumps in a collective political decision-making process (Dworkin 1984). Constitutional rights may for example check majority decisions because they are given superior validity. Habermas explains the fact that one basis for the regulation of political behaviour ranks above another by introducing a *conceptual distinction between values and moral norms*, where the latter refers to higher-order principles which hence claim universal validity. By contrast, values are understood as collective conceptions of the good life that vary according to different cultural and social contexts, and which therefore are both relative and particular in character (Habermas 1996a: 259). Values compete with each other, and refer to more or less particular forms of life. Values create identification in concrete communities and forms of life. They say something about what is important and good for us as members of a particular group, and hence about which action rule should be chosen in order to reach a goal. Whether actions are governed by values or norms are reflected in the degree to which we are committed by them. When we act in accordance with moral norms, the action gives the impression of being obligatory or compulsory. By contrast, when we act in accordance with some value, it is only a question of which action is the more recommendable (Habermas 1996a: 256).[2] For example, when we say that we should not discriminate against people because of their beliefs, we give an instruction or a command which expresses a moral norm. However, when we say that someone should get more education or exercise more, we give a recommendation which is based on a particular opinion of the good life.

How can we agree on what norms are valid when we cannot refer to a shared set of values? As mentioned in the first part of this book, the theory of communicative action builds on the assumption that normative questions also have a cognitive core. This is the reason why we can speak of intersubjective criteria for the evaluation of the rightness of actions. The right thing to do is that which can be argumentatively justified if we take an impartial point of view, as when we in a given situation ask what is right or fair. Just as 'truth' is the predicate of the validity of assertive sentences, 'rightness or fairness' is the predicate of moral sentences. We say that something is true when we refer to an accurate description of the facts of a case, and that something is right when we refer to legitimate behaviour or valid norms. An action is not true or false, but it can be right in relation to a value or a goal, or it can be (un)fair in relation to other people's interests. The question of justice does not make reference to a value, but to a moral norm, because it concerns what we are obliged to do when our actions have consequences for others. It is in this Kantian sense that Habermas uses the concept of morality. Moral norms involve values and interests, but only those that are universalisable and deontological in character. These norms claim to be universally valid and committing and therefore binding on everyone.

Habermas thus contends that he has only given a purely epistemological priority of the 'right' over the 'good'. We have an objective, intersubjective basis for deciding what is right or fair, not for deciding what is good. This does not tell us anything about what is most important to the individual, i.e. what motivates her actions. Values or opinions about what is good may influence behaviour even more than moral norms, because they motivate and engage on an emotional basis. However, what they consist in and how they are to be understood and interpreted are questions that can only be determined by those who share particular, ethical opinions of the good society, i.e. those who share the same values and 'strong evaluations'. It is the community or group of which one is a member that is the frame of reference for deciding these types of questions, which Habermas refers to as ethical. In contrast, the frame of reference for moral questions is humanity as such (Habermas 1996a: 108): it is the appeal to the universal public that constitutes the basis for the higher-order principles upon which the democratic constitutional state is founded. For example, when there is a clash between the interests of ethically integrated groups, we must resort to moral considerations in order to find legitimate solutions. This is the basis for the thesis about 'the priority of the right'. However, such examples make us realise that the implications of Habermas's ranking of the right over the good is not limited to the epistemological level, but may also have significant practical and political consequences. This will becomes clear in Chapter 11 on the prospects for cosmopolitan democracy.

We have previously introduced the distinction between integration based on money and power in the system sphere, and social integration, which is based on the self-understanding of the citizens and their mutual communication about norms and values in the lifeworld. We can now make a further distinction between two forms of social integration. The first type is based on common values, and springs from particular forms of life and solidarity norms. Habermas (1993a) refers to this as an *ethical form of integration*. The other type is political, and implies that the citizens are given certain rights through their citizenship. The basis for this so-called political integration is citizens' mutual recognition of one another as persons with equal rights. This type of allegiance and commitment is more limited, because it only requires agreement about the basic principles of coexistence. According to Habermas, citizens of a modern political community do not need a more comprehensive identity in the form of shared norms and values, language and culture, in order to regulate their shared life through the means of law. Political identity develops out of a shared respect for the common laws (Habermas 1996a: 501).[3] It is only this type of loyalty that can be demanded from us as citizens. Constitutional patriotism expresses a limited consensus, and is based upon an agreement on those principles that form the foundation of the democratic constitutional state. Thus, the kind of consensus which is required in modern constitutional democracies is based on abstract principles and not on exemplary forms of life which is implied by the classical concept of practical reason.

FROM PRACTICAL TO COMMUNICATIVE REASON

In general, a common conception of what should be done in cases of conflicting interests or disagreements on collective goals, can only be established when these issues are addressed in a reciprocal discussion between all affected parties. It is only in the search for mutual understanding and when one is acting according to the rules and procedures for a fair testing of the validity of different arguments, that one can find rational – if uncertain – answers to what ought to be done. Every consensus is fallible. Moreover, a consensus may be false, and its legitimacy therefore hinges on the possibility of testing its validity discursively which is the only way to establish the required basis for mutual trust between citizens. It is not until we know how an established truth has come about, and have the possibility to scrutinise it, that we can have confidence in it. Hence, communicative reason has binding power only as long as the actors presume that the pragmatic conditions for a free process of understanding have been met. In other words, a result can be expected to be accepted only when the participants comply with the validity requirements of sincere communication (i.e. the claims that concern comprehension, truth, correctness and truthfulness). Such *idealising presuppositions* which are made by communicating individuals – that all participants have an identical understanding of meaning and concepts – do not only refer to a necessary precondition for understanding-oriented communication, but also to what applies at the empirical level. These abstractions and idealisations that communicating individuals necessarily must make, if they wish to solve problems consensually, have on the one hand a universal and context-transcending content. On the other hand, they have action-regulating power only when they are referred to by communicatively acting agents in relation to concrete problems and conflicts, i.e. when they are contextualised (Habermas 1996a: 20). Thus, according to Habermas, the tension between facticity and validity (between what applies and what ought to apply), is embedded in language itself – a tension that is only reinforced by the process of modernisation.

Increased reflection over knowledge which has been passed down, and criticism of established agreements and belief systems represent a potential for conflict and dissent. To an increasing degree it is the achievement of mutual understanding and communicative action that represent the power of integration in modern societies. It is when we give reasons for our claims, which others may accept or refuse to accept, that it is possible to reach an agreement about how conflicts of interest should be regulated. As a result, communicative rationality to a certain extent takes over the position of the classical concept of practical reason in political theory (Habermas 1996a: 9 ff.). However, communicative reason plays a more limited role than what practical reason did in traditional societies, because communicative rationality has only a limited capacity to help us determine what should be done. It does not tell us what the good society consists in, or how we should live our lives; instead, it tells us what we ought *not* do. Communicative reason does not itself generate action maxims; it only tests whether our aims are in accordance with moral insights. Communicative rationality may extend beyond purely moral questions, but it is only here that reason and normativity merge. Understanding-oriented communication may also provide answers to questions about which values we should adopt, and which strategies are best suited to reach our goals. It is, however, only when deontological morality norms or duties are involved, i.e. questions of rightness and fairness, that communicative procedures may be said to guide and motivate our actions in a direct way. When it comes to other questions, the foundation for consensus is more uncertain and preliminary. This is one of the reasons why we in multicultural communities cannot ask of citizens to be virtuous or public spirited – express loyalty and commitment to a comprehensive common good or an extensive solidarity towards collective goals – but only to be loyal to legitimate laws, i.e. constitutional patriotism.

Consequently, communicative rationality does not simply replace practical reason. Its ability to produce answers and rational motivation is weaker and the relation between knowledge and action is also uncertain, as pointed out by Habermas (1996a: 114). Moral insight does not automatically lead to correct behaviour, because morality requires freedom. Only a free actor can make moral choices. Moral action comes at a price; it requires a contribution or sacrifice from agents and faces them with a choice. Weakness of will is also a factor that cannot be ignored. Thus, a general and abstract moral consciousness is insufficient for solving integration problems, because it only tells us what is valid under ideal conditions. The cultivation and preservation of a personal consciousness on its part depends on a successful realisation of an individuated, responsible person through socialisation and education processes. However, these processes are too frail and uncertain to be able to function as general stabilisers of behaviour.

In sum, there are two conditions that give the law a central position in modern societies. First, social complexity and value pluralism give rise to conflicts. Second, moral norms alone cannot in themselves be expected to control actions in a post-traditional world. Only the law can create the necessary commitment to act, because it connects norms with sanctions. 'Law is not only a symbolic system but an action system as well,' (Habermas 1996a: 107). It is a medium for collective action.

LAW AND MORALITY

Habermas seeks to overcome the shortcomings of the hegemonic research paradigms concerning the relationship between morality and law through an argumentatively based theory of rationality which ties the question of the validity of norms to the conditions for rational agreement.[4] However, there can only be transcultural agreement about superior principles such as equality, freedom, solidarity, self-realisation and human dignity. Other types of consensus will not only be difficult to achieve, but will also have limited validity because they depend on shared, strong value-evaluations. Consequently, discourse theory, which is based on a post-traditional, principled-oriented morality, must be supplemented and stabilised by positive law. The universalistic character of morality and thus its difficulty of committing the individual to act in accordance with universally valid norms, makes the law indispensable as an action regulating mechanism. It compensates for the weak action coordinating potential of moral norms. The test to the validity of moral norms is that they can be accepted by everyone; however, no one is obliged to comply with them unless everybody else does (Habermas 1987c: 14.) Norms that have passed this test can therefore only be imposed on the individual *when everybody obeys them*, and this is what the law ensures. Moral norms can only be collectively binding if they are converted into legal norms. Morality can, in other words, only be realised by legal means. On the other hand, one can also claim that the law makes it less costly to act morally. By sanctioning non-compliance and preventing violence, the constitutional state makes it possible for its citizens to act in accordance with their own conscience, out of a sense of duty (Apel 1998: 755).

Law and morality, which both concern practical questions and claim to regulate interaction in the interest of all parties involved, refer to different contexts of cooperation and have different validity bases. Whereas the law applies to a concrete community of people which can be subjected to the same duties, i.e. a political community, morality refers to humanity as such. Law is also different from morality in that it only regulates external behaviour. According to Kant, the law says nothing about the citizens' motives for abiding by the laws; it only tells us what actions are illegal and indictable. Moral duties are thus not linked to coercion. For example, we have a moral but not a legal prohibition against suicide in many countries. Morality presupposes freedom to make one's own choices. A final distinction between legal and moral questions is that the law is also a means to realise political goals, while moral norms are ends in themselves. Legal norms apply to territorially demarcated communities and regulate behaviour that has consequences for different sets of interests. In other words, legal norms are too concrete merely to be justified on a moral basis. However, 'this does not absolve legislators and judges from the concern that the law should be in harmony with morality' (Habermas 1998f: 257). Instead of governing legal decisions directly, morality constrains the law.

> The moral universe, which is *unlimited* in social space and historical time, includes *all natural persons* and their complex of life histories; morality itself extends to the protection of the integrity of fully individuated persons (*Einzelner*). By contrast, the legal community, which is always localized in time and space, protects the integrity of its members precisely in so far as that they acquire the artificial status as *rights bearers*.
>
> (Habermas 1998f: 256)

With this claim, Habermas demonstrates that the law cannot be understood as a reflex of morality, as implied by natural law and the rational law of Kant. Nor can we understand it as a special version of moral justification discourses, as proposed by Robert Alexy (1989), among others.[5] Legal norms are premised not only on moral reasons, but also on utilitarian considerations, collective values such as the balancing of interests as well as compromises between power constellations. There are many types of legitimate considerations that must be taken into account in a legislation process. We may mention factors which concern justice and moral legitimacy, the realisation of collective goals, or the solving of material conflicts and social problems. The hierarchical conception of the relation between morality and law that we find in pre-modern societies and in natural law, where the law obtains its legitimacy from higher-order, supra-positive norms, must today be replaced by a model that understands morality and law as a relationship based on mutuality and co-originality. Morality cannot be conceived of as supra-positive norms that oversee and sanction the law; rather, it must be understood as embedded in the procedures that give the laws their legitimacy, according to Habermas. The relation between autonomous morality, that refer to humanity as such, and positive law, which regulates actions that have diverse consequences, is a complementary one; moral norms must be implemented and the law must be justified. Moral norms can only be realised if they are formulated in legal categories which allow sanctions, and the law can only obtain legitimacy to the extent that there is equality before the law. We must, however, take into consideration that the norms that have passed the test of justification have to be put into practice. In this connection Habermas introduces the concept of the *application discourse*, which throws light on the structure of legal argumentation.

THE LEGAL DISCOURSE

There is an important distinction between the type of knowledge and discourses which are required in order to justify a norm morally, and the knowledge and forms of argumentation which are involved when norms are to be applied in a normatively responsible manner. In line with a proposition from Klaus Günther, a distinction is here made between justification and application discourses, as mentioned in Chapter 4. The point is that legal argumentation is understood as a special version of moral application discourses, where the principle of universalisation (i.e. the validity criterion in justification discourses), has been replaced by the principle of *appropriateness* (Habermas 1996a: 232). While justification discourses require that all interests are considered and judged impartially, application discourses require a procedure where all relevant features of the situation are given equal treatment (Günther 1989: 155). In a legal debate where concrete matters are to be decided, the question of the universal validity of the law is put into parenthesis. This validity is simply presupposed, and one proceeds to ask which norms are relevant and fit into the particular situation.

It is the consequences which are at issue in application discourses. The point of interest here is what the effect will be if justified moral norms are implemented. In an application situation, we are faced with a choice between justified norms. The choice between norms in application discourses must be made in relation to a number of factors: empirical reality, the type and quality of the information available, actual power relations, the important values at stake as well as the balancing of non-generalisable interests. As already mentioned, legal norms have a much more complex validity basis than have moral norms. The law realises political values and ethical and moral norms by positivising them. Through this procedure, they become sanctionable and collectively binding. Morality, on its part, tests and justifies positive legal norms. Whether legal decisions are correct, ultimately depends on whether the decision process has made possible impartial judgement, which requires that certain higher-ranking conditions for argumentation have been met.

We see that this ideal is reflected in the idea of a justly organised legal process. Lawyers make up their minds about practical questions, and through justifying arguments, they arrive at presumptively correct answers, i.e. that equal cases must be treated equally. This is why the kind of reasoning carried out by lawyers can be referred to as a practical discourse, and not as logical deduction or strategic interaction. Even in a lawsuit, where lawyers struggle to obtain the best possible result on behalf of their clients and themselves, reference is made to objective legal norms and principles when they try to justify their claims. When appeal is made to impartial judges or to members of the jury, it must be made with reference to arguments on which rational actors can agree, even if the aim is not to convince the opponent. Admittedly, a legal discourse is constituted and regulated by the existing laws. But positive legal norms are too unclear to give unambiguous, correct answers to normative problems. Lawyers must therefore make use of know-how that is partly determined by the prevailing conceptions of law, and partly by how the law has been practised earlier (precedent, custom). But more importantly, legal norms must first and foremost be in accordance with the criteria for rightness that are specified by means of discourse theory (Alexy 1989: 11, 18). The rules for legal and practical argumentation penetrate each other without destroying each other's respective logics. This is because judicial procedures guarantee symmetrical conditions for communication within the legal community (Habermas 1996a: 234). According to Habermas, these procedures do not govern practical argumentation directly, but establish the institutional framework which makes possible a rational discourse on which norms are appropriate in a given case. How is this possible?

Both judicial and argumentative procedures aim at rational outcomes. However, none of them can guarantee these, as the procedural conditions are rarely met. It is difficult to get enough time in legal discourses, where a decision has to be reached within a given time limit. The problem with argumentation in a practical discourse is that only the participants can judge if a consensus is qualified; there is no procedure-independent criterion for the evaluation of a rational argumentation process. The judicial procedure compensates for this weakness, because the legal institutionalisation of argumentation is subjected to temporal, social and substantive constraints (Habermas 1996a: 178). Legal procedures regulate what topics and questions may be raised, the use of time, the participants, the distribution of roles, etc. The judge as a neutral third party controls that the norms are followed. These procedures limit the access of premises, they ensure an unambiguous and binding result, and they connect argumentation to decision making. Hence, the judicial procedures compensate for the fallibility of communicative processes and improve their incomplete or quasi-pure procedural fairness (Alexy 1989: 179). This takes place in two ways.

First, argumentation is disciplined in relation to judicially binding decisions, through the institutionalisation of an *expert discourse* that can interpret and adapt codified law in a professional manner, according to internal criteria. Judicial institutions are designed to systematise and adapt prevailing law to the matter which is to be regulated, according to specified procedures. Secondly, correct outcomes can be ensured because the discourse is tied to a *legal public sphere* characterised as an open, inclusive and transparent discussion forum. This can be referred to as the external justification of the principles that are operative in the expert discourse, and it concerns those premises which are not derived from positive law itself (Alexy 1989: 228). In addition to a wide supply of source material – preparatory works, customs, precedent – moral and political considerations are also taken into consideration, as is demonstrated in the discussion of so-called *hard cases* (i.e. fundamental, precedent-forming cases with a legal political significance). These are extra-legal factors that are used to decide which norms should have priority, on the basis of substantial conceptions of justice and freedom (Habermas 1995: 55, Dworkin 1977: 81 ff.). Whether these factors are legitimate, and whether the judges' interpretations of the situations are correct, can only be legitimately tested in the wider public sphere where competent citizens and all affected parties are present.

In application discourses, a particular decision can be regarded as correct or rational when it is presupposed that political legislation is valid. However, the point is that the judges cannot avoid evaluating the validity of approved norms, because only a uniform and consistent legal system can ensure a rational decision. This is also a prerequisite for solving conflicting norms and ethical dilemmas that arise in practical life in the court-house (Habermas 1996a: 232).[6] Legal norms must be interpreted and operationalised, and even a valid legal norm, for example a constitutional norm, must be given a legal interpretation in relation to validity criteria before its correctness and relevance can be established (Alexy 1989: 23, cf. Dworkin 1986, Hart 1961).[7] Judicial procedures exist in order to guarantee decisions which are legally correct and rationally acceptable, i.e. decisions that can be defended both in relation to legal statutes and in relation to public criticism.

THE REALITY DISCOURSE

In choosing between justified norms in an application situation, actual power relations and interests need to be taken into account, because justified norms can be abused, and the end may justify the means. We will therefore introduce a category that Habermas does not employ, namely *a reality discourse*. This category is required because, as pointed out also by Max Weber, the road to hell is paved with good intentions. Not all good actions have positive consequences. Under-specified concepts such as good will or good intentions cannot replace the duty to know. Therefore the ethics of conviction – or deontology – plays only a limited role in politics, while the ethics of responsibility plays a much more central role. In other words, the ethics that takes into consideration our human 'shortcomings and fragility. As pointed out by Fichte, and rightly so, we are not allowed to presuppose that people are good and perfect' (Weber 1919: 43). Human beings are limited and fallible, and we have to take into account negative consequences or by-products of good intentions. The good will must therefore be institutionalised and controlled by a type of reason which aims at maintaining the legal community. We do not necessarily come closer to a free society by acting as if it was already realised (Elster 1983: 42).

> No ethics in the world can dodge the fact that in numerous instances the attainment of 'good' ends is bound to the fact that one must be willing to pay the price of using morally dubious means or at least dangerous ones – and facing the possibility or even the probability of evil ramifications. From no ethics in the world can it be concluded when and to what extent the ethically good purpose 'justifies' the ethically dangerous means and ramifications.
>
> (Weber 1965: 47)

Karl-Otto Apel has discussed this as a *principle of political reality*. He maintains that the politicians can only follow moral maxims as long as they do not set aside political imperatives that are meant to protect and maintain the political community (Apel 1992b: 29 ff., cf. Apel 1988). They are accountable to their electorate, not humanity as such. Thus, it becomes clear that the constitutional state is based on norms which are not valid simply because they can be approved by everybody in a free debate; their social validity is to a large extent based on the fact that they can be enforced by the state's monopoly of violence. This is necessary because there will always be citizens who do not recognise universally valid norms (Apel 1998: 832). From international politics we also learn that since there is no superior, international authority that implements mutually binding initiatives, nation states do not have any choice but putting the interests of the state first (Oppenheim 1991: 41 ff.). A political agent is responsible for the integrity and welfare of a particular collective which again is the source from where the state is legitimised and authorised to use violence (cf. Weber 1978, Lübbe 1990):

> The individual may say for himself: '*Fiat justitia, pererat mundus*' (Let justice be done, even if the world perish), but the state has no right to say so in the name of those who are in its care.
>
> (Morgenthau 1993: 12)

'The reality discourse' is to be understood as a particular version of application discourses, where the justification of actions gets its normative power from the value conceptions, as well as from the welfare and utility considerations of a given community. It is an expression of the view that it must be possible to protect the legal community by strategic means, for example through surveillance and intelligence operations.[8] Whether strategic means are legitimate, depends on whether the principles that govern these activities can themselves be accepted in an open debate. If the regime is to live up to the ideals of the democratic constitutional state, the norms and principles that regulate the use of means which are illegitimate in a moral sense must themselves be justified with reference to universalistic premises (cf. Apel 1996: 40).

In light of 'the reality discourse', it is easier to see that if we wish to understand the normative structure of the modern state, the relationship between morality and law must be supplemented also to include a consideration of political power. The law is not effective until it is tied to power; the law derives its sanctioning power from the fact that resources have been made available by political means.

The law can only be applied when its claims are supported by power. It is not effective until there are resources that motivate people to obey. By resources in this connection is meant not only formal instruments of power, such as the right to use physical power, but also social support and loyalty. This is important because it is only when the coercive means are kept latent, i.e. when they are *not* used, that the law is in fact effective.

The law, then, is in a complementary relation not only to morality, but to political power as well. Politics, which should be regarded as a separate structural level in addition to morality and law, is linked to the realisation of collective goals by means of power. Political 'reality discourses' are designed to maintain and reinforce the political community through the activation of collective commitments (cf. Parsons 1963). However, collective will-formation does not in itself generate power. Consensus on collective goals is only effective when the goals are made binding by being incorporated into political programmes, and when resources are mobilised to realise them by way of administrative measures. It is the law that legitimises and authorises politics by giving political power a legal form. It is through legal procedures that representatives obtain power and executive organs are authorised. When political authority is formulated in legal categories – as a legal-rational authority – a *binary code of political power* is constituted. Those who have been given the right to exercise power can command, and those who are addressees must obey (Habermas 1996a: 132 ff.).

Political power on its part authorises the legal system and establishes the *legal code*. The politically generated power makes the law effective through legislation and the distribution of resources. Thus, also the law becomes capable of functioning through a binary code; judges decide what is legal/non-legal, as pointed out by Niklas Luhmann (1983), but cannot themselves give the norms. It is important to emphasise that although the law contributes to establishing a power code for the political system, it has power and authority only insofar as it does not become an instrument of political interests. The law must be autonomous, i.e. it must remain neutral and impartial, and thus stay within the constraints of morality. The law shall guarantee legal protection or equality before the law. This is what makes it trustworthy as a resource of justice. The law, which operates through rights, is the central stabiliser of behavioural expectations in modern states; it tells us what behaviour can be expected. Habermas finds no functional equivalent to it. It represents both a peaceful conflict-resolving mechanism and a medium for the realisation of moral norms on a wide scale. This is possible because it ensures predictability and eases the requirement of a personal grounding and justification of action plans. In a functional perspective, the law takes some of the burden off morality in that it reduces the cognitive demands on individuals to make up their own minds about what is right. Further, it sanctions non-compliance by making it costly for individuals to break the law. Finally, it takes care of problems that can only be solved through collective action – through political decisions and formal organisation (Habermas 1996a: 115 ff.).

> As positively valid, legitimately enacted, and actionable, the law can relieve the morally judging and acting person from the considerable cognitive, motivating, and organizational demands of a morality based entirely on individual conscience.
>
> (Habermas 1998f: 257)

However as mentioned above, Apel (1998) insists that the law has a moral content by the very fact that it sanctions violence and binds others, so that individuals can freely comply with moral orders and consensual norms. Figure 7.1 summarises some of the basic aspects of moral, law, and politics.

Structural level	Functions	Type of discourses	Court of appeal
Morality	Legitimacy/ testing of norms	Justification discourse	Humanity
Law	Positivisation of norms	Application discourse	The community of law
Politics	Collective goal achievement	'Reality discourse'	The political community

Figure 7.1 *Structural properties of morality, law and politics*

THE TENSION BETWEEN POSITIVISM AND LEGITIMACY

To modern societies, which link their understanding of the law to the rights of the individual and to objective principles, the problem that arises is from where the law gets its legitimacy. Positivised law based on individual rights disentangle individuals in a moral sense. Legal rights represent an institutionalisation of purposeful action. As long as the actors operate within the boundaries of the law, they can do what they want. To quote article 5 in The French Declaration of the Rights of Man and Citizen (1789): *Whatever is not forbidden by the law may not be prevented, and nobody can be forced to do what it does not prescribe.* Thus, civil formal law is said to be a *legally organised egoism*. The legal system ascribes the individual the right to satisfy an interest that is recognised, and provides it with legal power to realise this interest. But how is it possible to connect a concept of rights with validity? For a long time validity claims were given a moral philosophical justification based on natural law. Humans are from birth equipped with certain inviolable rights – rights of life, liberty and property (Locke 1960). With Kant's rational natural law, where the autonomy principle was regarded as the moral basis of the law, this fundament was expanded. In his *Metaphysics of Morals* Kant (1996c) claims that the only natural right is the right to freedom, defined as type of freedom that is only available in so far as at it does not encroach on other people's freedom. An action is right if the freedom of one individual does not infringe another person's equal right to the same kind of freedom in accordance with a universal law. However, it has remained an unsolved problem how individual rights could in themselves claim any legitimacy and have an integrating effect. How can citizens freely be motivated to support laws that only guarantee equal positive rights for all?

There may be many reasons why citizens obey the law, opportunistic as well as moral ones. The problem is that although the law forces people to behave in accordance with prevailing norms by sanctioning breaches, this does not in itself create legitimacy. The law can enforce compliance, but not necessarily *respect*. This follows conceptually from Kant's point that no one can be forced into wanting something: 'Only I myself can make something my end' (Kant 1996c: 513). Kant's claim that the laws must be rational or valid is also necessary in order for them to function empirically. The law can only maintain its socially integrative function, that is, it can only be effective, to the degree that it corresponds to what the citizens find normatively right, to what is fair and deserves respect and recognition. If this were not the case, the state's sanctioning power, in the form of punishment and surveillance, would have to be used continually. Such a regime demands a great deal of resources and would be highly unstable (Weber 1978: 311 ff.). In other words, positivised law cannot secure the foundation of its own legitimacy through legality.[9]

However, the tension between positivity and legitimacy is built into the medium of law itself. On the one hand, it is only by means of the law that it is possible to prioritise between values. Only in this way can shared values and moral norms obtain legal validity, and only in this way can they apply to everyone without exceptions. On the other hand, if citizens are to abide by the law out of duty, it must be able to justify the law beyond the fact that it ensures equal freedom to all. It must be of such a quality that it can demand 'unconditional' support. It is the fact that the laws are *laws of freedom* and not just coercive ones which constitute their basis of legitimacy; this is where we can find the source of their *commitment competence*. However, to clarify this issue according to Habermas, liberal theory and Kant need to be supplemented by Rousseau and the republican tradition of political theory, which gave priority to the common will formation process.

RIGHTS AND POPULAR RULE

In the previous chapter we discussed the differences between liberalism and its emphasis on rights, and the republican tradition with its emphasis on common opinion-formation and citizens' self-legislation. The cardinal problem of political theory – i.e. why a person should comply with the laws of the political community when he or she only has a moral duty to comply with self-imposed laws – is expressed in the following classical formulation by Rousseau:

> Find a form of association which will defend and protect, with the whole of its joint strength, the person and property of each associate, and under which each of them, uniting himself to all, will obey himself alone, and remains as free as before.
>
> (Rousseau 1994: 54 f.)

Rousseau replaced the autocratic monarch with the autocratic people. The people is sovereign and its power cannot be delegated or negotiated. The popular assembly is the immediate expression of the people's will and is sovereign when it comes to legislation. Consequently, the laws are an expression of the general will – La volonté générale – which is something different from and more than the sum total of individual wills. The general will is always right. Where the general will rules, there is no coercion, and vice versa; where the citizens are oriented towards their own interests only, there must be a considerable degree of coercion. The state is regarded as a legitimate expression or instrument of the popular will. The problem with Rousseau is that there are no criteria for determining what the general will is. He does not realise that it is the citizens themselves who must, through common deliberations, agree on the criteria for identifying the general will in different sets of questions, and that there may very well be fundamental disagreement about these criteria. The legitimacy of the laws is derived from their semantic form (their wording) as general. Thus all laws become just or right. With this there is no distinction between law and right. There is no basis for criticising either the law or the legislation process.

Another problem is that Rousseau's thinking was confined to the framework of the city-state (Geneva) – a small, egalitarian and homogenous society so far as values were concerned.[10] The laws were regarded as expressions of the ethical self-understanding of the community. Consequently, all deviations are regarded as failures to act in solidarity, and it becomes legitimate to suppress opposition. As maintained by Habermas, Rousseau demands too much from the citizens; they become *ethically overloaded* (Habermas 1996a: 102).

If coercion is to be avoided, and if the laws are to be regarded as expressions of what is in the equal interest of all and not only what is in the common interest of a collective, the principle of popular sovereignty must be reformulated. It cannot be modelled on a concrete unit of citizens who act on the basis of a shared conception of the common good; instead, it should be modelled on a *principle that respects the individual and its right to freedom* (Habermas 1996a: 474). The principle of popular sovereignty should not be linked to the collective values and action competence of a concrete community, but to individual rights, to the procedures for participation, and to the possibility of free opinion- and will-formation. This is what Kant attempts to do when he develops Rousseau's intention further, but on liberal premises. He realises that legislative authority can only spring from the united will of the people.

> Because all right and justice is supposed to proceed from this authority, it can do absolutely no injustice to anyone.
>
> (Kant 1996c § 46, quoted from Habermas 1996a: 472)

We cannot act unfairly towards ourselves, and if we freely consent to a law, we cannot be oppressed; it would be like oppressing ourselves. As legislators we are not subjected to others, and we can treat other human beings as ends in themselves (Habermas 1998b: 30). It is only the united and agreed will of all that has the normative power to authorise laws. The legitimacy base of the laws is linked to the participation of the individual in legislative processes. Thus, human rights are included in the legislation process itself and become a part of the principle of popular sovereignty. A common will is not valid if it is not approved by everyone. Hence, all non-generalisable interests (special interests) are excluded, because citizens can only approve of laws that guarantee equal freedom to all (Habermas 1996a: 473). It is against this background that Habermas formulates his discourse principle (D) (cf. Chapter 4):

> *(D)* Just those action norms are valid to which all possibly affected persons could agree as participants in rational discourses.
>
> (Habermas 1996a: 107)

In the exercise of popular sovereignty, the citizens pass their own laws and secure human rights at the same time. It is in the legislation process that the citizens, who are equipped with equal rights, simultaneously appear both in the role as legislators and addressees of the law. It is in this process that the citizens learn about joint commitments and the necessity of submitting to collective decisions. In short, this is where *solidarity* is generated, and it can only be brought about in a valid manner in so far as the freedom of the individual is guaranteed. Individual rights create no social integration in themselves, but in a public discussion the citizens are forced to grant each other *equal* rights. In the legislation act itself, they are forced to regard each other as equals, while at the same time they see themselves as both authors and addressees of the law (Habermas 1996a: 104). We are here speaking of *an enlightened will* which is not discovered (in the formulation of the laws, as in Rousseau), but which is established through open discussions between citizens. The question, then, is how such an autonomous common will can come about by way of the legal medium, which is based on the principle of individual rights.

PRIVATE AND PUBLIC AUTONOMY

Habermas uses Kant's term the 'system of rights' to characterise the modern form of civil law, i.e. the guarantee of an *equal right to freedom* for all citizens. This guarantee legitimates positive law in general through the principle that what is not prohibited is allowed. This is the principle that makes it possible to combine each individual's free choice with anybody else's free choice. Rights are Janus-faced. From a functional perspective, they can be seen as the institutionalisation of the market system and a means that make strategic action possible. From a normative perspective, they guarantee individual freedom. People have private autonomy to the degree that they are not responsible to anyone for their actions (Habermas 1996a: 120). Individual rights guarantee agents the liberty to do as they please; they warrant *negative freedom*. They make selfishness and irrationality possible because they exempt individuals from the burden of justification. The citizens are given rights that protect their private autonomy, i.e. they have the right to pursue their own goals as long as they operate within the limits of the law. However, how can this be explained by discourse theory, which builds on the principle that only those norms that are accepted in an open debate are valid?

In modern constitutional states, people have a right to non-participation, and thus also a right to non-explanation or non-justification. It is possible for citizens to abstain from their right to communicative freedom and to assume a purely strategic attitude towards the law. This is because freedom in modern societies is not only of a moral, but also of a legal nature. The most important difference between basic rights and human rights is that the latter type refers to humans as such, while basic rights are given to individuals in so far as they are citizens, i.e. members of a state (Höffe 1996: 51). Human rights can be justified on a purely moral basis, but they are also entrenched in positive legal norms as *legal rights* (Habermas 1996a: 105, Brunkhorst 1996: 194).

> Though human rights are for the time being only realized within the framework of a national legal order, within this sphere of validity they ground rights for all persons and not merely for citizens.
>
> (Habermas 1998e: 190)

However, this creates a problem for the thesis that the constitutional state and democracy mutually presuppose each other. The problem is that democracy only exists at the level of the nation state, i.e. it exists in particular states. By contrast, human rights are universal, and with the expansion of international law they have also gained an authority that limits the state's self-legislation (cf. Apel 1998: 833). This points to a problem in discourse theory as well as to the quest for post-national or cosmopolitan democracy that we will discuss in Chapter 11.

To Habermas it is the law, i.e. the existence of legal rights, which realises freedom. Negative freedom is made possible through the means of law. The liberal legal principle which states that what is not prohibited, is allowed, guarantees the citizens of a democratic constitutional state individual freedom to act. Kant's point is that citizens, who recognise each other as free and equal, must give each other the same and the greatest possible degree of freedom if they want to regulate their coexistence through law. In Habermas's opinion, this follows when the discourse principle is applied to the legal form as such. Only laws that can be supported by everyone in an open debate can be considered legitimate, and only laws that guarantee the highest degree of equal freedom to everyone will be able to pass such a test. Citizens can only legitimately regulate their coexistence through the means of law in so far as they also are given the opportunity to participate in the legislation process. Hence, rights warrant not only the citizens' private autonomy, but also their public autonomy.

This has the additional implication that citizens are free to consider the validity of the law. They must be free not only to choose whether they wish to comply with the law, but also whether they at all want to make up their minds about it. They can be forced neither to approve nor to participate if the law is to claim legitimacy (Habermas 1996a: 121). Everyone must have the opportunity to choose *exit* or to not have an opinion at all. The adopted discourse principle consequently operates at such an abstract level that it only takes into consideration the legal autonomy of the citizens and the legal form. It gives the citizens the right to submit only to those laws that they approve in a rational discourse.

Citizens are not only free to say yes or no to a legal norm, they are also free to decide if they want to say yes or no at all. In this perspective both the practice of capital punishment and conscription in nation states are problematic.

We have seen that legal freedom is different from communicative or moral freedom. From a moral point of view, there is no legitimate alternative to explaining and justifying our actions to our fellow beings; however, such a possibility exists when we act as legal subjects. As legal subjects, we can refer to the rights that are legally ascribed to us and we also have a right to act selfishly. The citizens' *legal* self-legislation is not the same as their *moral* self-legislation, because unlike morality the legal form provides relief from the burden of justification. However, the democratic constitutional state presupposes that people do not make wide use of their right to non-participation, for example by not taking part in elections. This right is dependent on a modern, civic political culture, where the citizens are morally and ethically motivated to make use of their rights of participation.

It should be clear by now that the democratic constitutional state on the one hand requires, in a functional sense, civic virtue and a population that values freedom. If these conditions are not met, democratic institutions will disintegrate (Habermas 1996a: 130). The liberal constitutional state is not self-sufficient. Habermas and the communitarians agree on this point. As we know from the previous chapter, the latter regard polities as communities of shared values and belonging. On the other hand, the discourse-theoretical reconstruction of democracy and law also gives us a normative concept of *civil disobedience*. In order to assess whether the law is legitimate, citizens must be able to make use of their communicative freedoms, which must again be institutionalised as civil, negative rights. In this perspective, civil disobedience must be regarded as a normal activity within a constitutional democracy – indeed, it is the very litmus-test of the soundness of the political culture, because it shows the power-holders' democratic disposition and ability to be responsive in relation to popular opinion (Habermas 1985a, Cohen and Arato 1992: 564 ff.).

Individual rights, then, are both a result of and a prerequisite for democratic legislation. Human rights are not only instrument for collective will-formation, i.e. for democracy, they also have an absolute status. They have a value in themselves. They precede and limit collective will-formation, but must at the same time be justified in an open discussion (Bal 1994: 77, Peters 1991, 1994: 114 f.) Individual rights must therefore not be seen as limitations on the actors' private autonomy or on the autonomy of the legislator. That is how they are frequently regarded in conventional political theory. There is a dialectics here. The formation of a qualified common will depends on free individuals, but the conditions for free opinion formation can only be established and realised collectively. This explains why democracy and the constitutional state are equally fundamental and co-original. Individual freedom, which is guaranteed by human rights, is both a condition for and a result of the legislation process. This is not a contradiction, as some argue (Larmore 1993), but rather the very crux of the discourse theory of law and democracy (Günther 1994: 471, Maus 1996: 838).

The political right to participation presupposes individual freedom and that the agents are capable of granting each other equal rights. Without an equal right to freedom, it cannot be expected that legal subjects are willing to regulate their coexistence through law. This is the first step in the reconstruction of how legitimacy can spring from legality, i.e. from the legal form – the right to equal freedom. The next step is that the system of rights cannot be justified unless it guarantees the citizens' public autonomy. That legitimacy springs from legality can thus be explained with reference to the rights that make private and public autonomy possible.

The solution described above, is neither based on the legal form of the law, where the formal procedures themselves ensure the legitimacy of the law, as is claimed by the legal positivists; nor is it based on the philosophy of natural law. It is not formal procedures, natural law, or other meta-principles that legitimate the law, according to Habermas. Neither legal nor extra-legal principles can legitim-ate the law, but rather the rationality that is ensured by the mutual guarantee of private and public autonomy. It is in this light that we can see the basic constitutional rights as an institutionalisation of equal conditions for communication. This claim notwithstanding, it has been argued that there is a natural-law-residual in Habermas's theory, as we will see in Chapter 11.

THE SYSTEM OF RIGHTS

Political deliberation takes place within a system of constitutional rights. Con-stitutions containing bills of inalienable rights and competence clauses for delimiting the powers of the various branches of government, distribute rights and duties, establish rules and procedures for deliberation and decision-making, give prerogatives and protect minorities from the tyranny of the majority. There are formal rules for representation and decision-making, for how laws can be amended, and there is an independent legal system to protect the rights of the individual.

The discourse-theoretical concept of law dismisses neither the liberal nor the welfare state paradigms of law (which focus on formal and material aspects respectively), but represents an attempt to reformulate the law on a different basis, so that the weaknesses of the existing paradigms can be remedied. The contributions of the civil and democratic constitutional state as well as the wel-fare state are evident in the way Habermas formulates basic rights. He operates with five categories of rights that the citizens must mutually grant each other if they wish to regulate their coexistence in a peaceful manner via the instrument of law:

(1) classical liberty rights (basic negative liberties)

(2) civil rights to protection (membership rights)

(3) legal procedural rights (due-process rights)

(4) political rights

(5) welfare rights.

What we have here is not concrete rights on a par with those we find in actual constitutions or in human rights declarations; it is a general and non-substitutable 'system of basic rights', which legal subjects must mutually grant

The tension between facticity and validity

This has various dimensions and is related to the fact that the distinction between *is* and *ought* is not mixed up, as in pre-modern societies, but singled out as two separate factors of social interaction (Habermas 1996a: 21). There is consequently an *internal relation* between facticity and validity which is operative in the language itself.

This tension is involved in the legal medium as the law positivises and enforces rights, while at the same time claims legitimacy. The application of the discourse principle to the law provides a justification for the *legal form*: individuals who wish to regulate their coexistence through law must grant each other the same right to freedom unless they want to commit a performative contradiction. This can only be done by means of the law, which ensures individuals legal freedom. However, this also implies that individuals are given a right to relate to the law in a solely strategic manner, which consequently does not explain how it can be obeyed out of respect. When the discourse principle is applied to the legal form, the *code of law* is established, and thus also the mutual freedom and protection the laws must guarantee in so far as they are to be considered legitimate. It is by virtue of these rights that citizens are ensured private autonomy which enables them to participate independently in the legislative process. Participatory rights, which are inferred from the discourse principle itself, enable citizens to take a performative attitude to the law, i.e. to use their communicative freedoms to participate in the decision about which rights should prevail. In this way one may say that the system of rights operationalises the tension between facticity and validity that we first discovered as a tension between positivism and legitimacy in the medium of law itself (Habermas 1996a: 129).

Finally, there is an *external connection* between facticity and validity. There is a clash between the democratic constitutional state's understanding of a legitimately instituted legal order, and the actual institutionalisation of rights in modern capitalist societies. The democratic constitutional state does not live up to its ideals, as it, for example, leaves many of the decisions that have consequences for the citizens' interests (such as the establishment and localisation of jobs) to private actors which are beyond democratic control. Consequently, the tension between facticity and validity repeats itself at different levels, and by both enforcing integration and ensuring legitimate processes, it manifests itself in our democratic constitutional state as two aspects of the law.

each other if they want to regulate their coexistence by means of law. They are principles to which the founders of a constitution must subscribe. The principles justify categories of rights that are prior to concrete laws and rights. This suggests a solution to the contradiction between the principle of popular sovereignty (which says that the people should govern themselves autonomously) and the constitutional state's guarantee of individual freedom. It is a solution that refers to the fact that when citizens have to regulate their differences by means of law, it can only be done through communication. It is only concrete citizens embedded in a social context, with a history and a tradition, who can develop and substantiate the content of these rights. The rights are an expression of the procedures that must be followed if the development of the legal system can be said to proceed in a legitimate manner (Habermas 1996a: 127 ff.).

Within the discourse-theoretical paradigm of law, priority is given to political participatory rights. The first three categories of rights are therefore introduced with the reservation that they can be justified in an open political debate (cf. Alexy 1994: 230). The first type of basic rights arise through the development of *equal individual liberty*. These rights must be supplemented by a set of rights which protect the membership status of the citizens of a voluntary association, and by rights that provide legal guarantees that the above-mentioned rights will be protected and realised (Habermas 1996a: 122 f.). These three sets of rights make possible legitimate law and establish the legal code; no legitimate law is possible without these rights. It is the legal code that ascribes to citizens their status as legal subjects, i.e. as individuals with a protected status. Moreover, the legal code provides individuals with rights that ensure their private autonomy, and it is also the medium facilitating the public use of reason. It is only in so far as they have the rights in question that the citizens can become independent participants of a public communication process. Negative rights thus have a derivative status. The fourth category, i.e. political rights to participation, has a special position, because they guarantee the citizens' public autonomy. They are therefore without reservations described as:

> Basic rights to equal opportunities to participate in processes of opinion- and will-formation in which citizens exercise their *political autonomy* and through which they generate legitimate law.
>
> (Habermas 1996a: 123)

What we see here is a change of perspective. The rights which are listed first can be conceived of as inferred when we attempt to understand what the legal code implies, i.e. as the rights the citizens must mutually grant one another when they wish to regulate their coexistence by means of positive law. However, the political right to participation follows naturally from the citizens' own perspective in so far as they are seen as legislators. As members of a legal community, citizens must grant one another equal rights to participate in public opinion-formation as well as in law-making processes. In their roles as fellow legislators, they are not free to choose their medium; they participate by virtue of being bearers of rights, and must therefore allow others the same freedom that they claim for themselves.

These four supreme, justified rights to freedom, equality, legal protection and participation have priority in the system of rights. They form the basic conditions that make possible an autonomous treatment of rights in general, and they represent a standard against which we can evaluate the overall substantiation and development of rights. The rights in question guarantee that decisions taken in a procedurally correct manner can be recognised as legitimate. On the other hand, civil and political rights, which ensure private and public autonomy, justify a fifth set of rights. For us to be able to exercise our status as equal and free citizens, certain material conditions must be met. We are therefore given a *right to welfare* as well:

Basic rights to the provision of living conditions that are socially, technologically, and ecologically safeguarded, insofar as the current circumstances make this necessary if citizens are to have equal opportunities to utilize the civil rights listed in (1) through (4).

(Habermas 1996a: 123)

Welfare rights thus possess a relative status. The justification of such rights is indirectly related to the fact that they make individuals capable of participating on an equal basis in the political process (Habermas 1996a: 417). Ulrich Preuss refers to these rights as rights which increase the citizens' civic competence – 'Staatsbürgerqualifikationspolitik' (Preuss 1991: 124). Habermas (1994c) offers a similar justification of *cultural rights*, because access to one's own culture can also be seen as a resource which is necessary to enable us to make use of our civil and political rights. One reason why welfare rights do not have an absolute status is that it is difficult to give exact measures as to the amount of resources that is needed to make individuals capable of realising their political rights. Welfare demands raise imperfect commitments, as no one can give more than partial assistance (O'Neill 1989: 230). Many liberalists also maintain that, in contrast to negative rights, it is costly to observe welfare rights, and they can therefore not be guaranteed in the same way. However, the categorical distinction between the right to welfare and the right to freedom is disputed. All rights cost, not only positive, social rights, but also negative rights of property and contract. They are public goods rendered possible by political decisions and through public institutions (Holmes and Sunstein 1999, cf. Plant 1993).

One problematic aspect of discourse theory – as pointed out by many commentators[11] – is that welfare rights are seen only as justified in relation to democracy, i.e., with regard to realising the public autonomy of the citizens. They are not assigned any value in themselves. Only in so far as they improve the competence of the citizens, are they justified. What then about our duty to give assistance also to those who can never become competent citizens, and what about our moral duty to fight poverty and misery irrespective of the consequences this may have for the development of the citizens' competence? The point is that these duties are of a purely moral character. They follow from our being humans, not legal subjects. According to Habermas (1996c: 1543), they cannot be rephrased into legal rights without destroying the division of labour between morality and law, and thereby weakening the principle of autonomy.

This somewhat one-sided way of justifying welfare rights is directed towards the paternalism and the expert rule that are lurching in the wake of the welfare state. In this connection it is important to notice that the procedural legal paradigm does not replace or reject the legal principle of the welfare state, but continues it at a higher level of reflection (Habermas 1996a: 410).

WELFARE STATE PATERNALISM AND LIMITS TO JURIDIFICATION

This reconstruction of modern law creates a basis for thematising the paternalism of the welfare state, which is said by Habermas to be a consequence of the attempt to use positive law to undo the unfairness of the liberal state. The liberal legal paradigm, which gives priority to formal equality and private freedom, is blind to the problem of *social justice*. The legal paradigm of the welfare state in general and the social rights in particular are meant to solve this problem. However, the competition between these legal paradigms reveals a contradiction between the state's objective and its method. The state's objective is equality and freedom; its function is simultaneously to contribute to a more just and egalitarian society, and to allow spontaneity and self-realisation to flourish. This double purpose cannot be realised by means of administrative and legal instruments (Habermas 1989b: 58 f.). Admittedly, the welfare state has a positive effect in so far as its programmes contribute to liberating its citizens from suppressive and degrading conditions; however, the state does not possess the means that are needed to realise freedom. The very idea of freedom or autonomy in the modern sense builds on the principle that the citizens pass their own laws. No external bodies have the competence to decide what is good or bad, right or wrong for me (Hegel 1967: 22). Negative freedom can never be anything but an abstract idea, and any attempt to define its content will destroy it. The right to self-determination constitutes the principle of the democratic constitutional state and this right must be indefinite and 'unlimited'. The problem of the modern welfare state is the *overprotection of interests* that takes place through the extensive codification of rights, which limits freedom. The right to health, work, education, leisure, etc. reduces the possibility of individual, as well as collective self-determination. Such rights determine once and for all what is to be considered the correct handling of equal and unequal matters. The legal paradigm of the welfare state materialises or determines the content of the law, which makes politics more technocratic and in addition has unintended side-effects such as paternalism and overprotection (Habermas 1996a: 407).

Technocracy or expert rule emerge because the parties involved do not have actual influence on decision-making in those policy areas that have consequences for their own interests. 'Expertocracy' has its roots in the welfare state paradigm, which (like the liberal legal paradigm) generates all rights from the concept of individual rights. In this way all interests that need public protection are legally guaranteed as individual rights. Both paradigms give priority to individual rights, and the welfare state runs into problems of paternalism. The welfare state must ensure the citizens' autonomy 'through publicly guaranteed entitlements for clients of welfare bureaucracies' (Habermas 1998f: 264). The problem is that rights abstractly conceive of what is for the individual's own good, and are realised via legal regulation, professions, and bureaucratic administration. This is particularly true within social politics, and Habermas uses examples from both family law and gender politics to illustrate the nature of the problem. What is at issue is the introduction of general rules regarding what serves women best with respect to pregnancy, child-care and divorce. The law has to build on general and thus 'false' classifications in order to get something done. It treats all cases alike and declares what is in the best interests of the group in question, without being able to listen to or consider individual wishes and requests. The problem is that such over-generalised classifications may lead to new damages and discriminations (Habermas 1996a: 407, 422). What is for the good of the child who is not taken properly care of, or what is in the interest of women when it comes to work and pregnancy are not simple things that can be decided once and for all. Here material rights have their limits. In these areas, we must leave open the question of which measures are adequate in concrete situations. Very often the question can only be settled through deliberations among the parties involved. Within the discourse-theoretical paradigm of law, which puts equal emphasis on private and public autonomy, the citizens' autonomy must also be secured in the implementation and not only in the legislative process (cf. Eriksen 2001a). It is only when all those affected have been allowed to participate freely and independently in the formulation and concretisation of political decisions, that it is possible to argue that the respect for individual freedom and the achievement of a legitimate process are ensured.

CONCLUSION

The above analysis shows that the way the neutrality principle is used in discourse theory differs from how the way it is used in liberalism. In discourse theory the principle in question is not in itself a morally neutral principle, as it has been implemented in accordance with the principle of equal rights for all. Consequently, it excludes only those positions that are incompatible with this principle. Moreover, it becomes clear that it does not prescribe formally equal treatment of all permissible standpoints, as in the liberal conception of neutrality where the goal is a fair aggregation of preferences, between which there is no rational way of discriminating, and where the strategy is to unload the public debate of controversial questions (cf. Ackerman 1989, Rawls 1993). The discourse-theoretical principle of neutrality only states that everyone must be treated with equal consideration and respect, so that the better arguments can prevail. The task of the state is hence to encourage a rational debate on conflicting issues. In the discourse-theoretical version, difference is not only tolerated and accepted, but regarded as a condition for a rational debate. Neutrality and impartiality have to do with ensuring mutual respect and equal conditions for communication, and not with predetermining what is to be considered as valid (Baynes 1995: 223). It is in the interplay between legal procedures assigning equal rights to all parties, and argumentation procedures that make the force of the better arguments prevail that we find the validity basis of political decisions.

With the institutionalisation of the democratic constitutional state, modern societies have established legal structures that themselves provide the standards for evaluating the rationality of political consensuses. For every idea there is a corresponding ideal. Hence, Habermas refers to the reconstruction of the normative content of the democratic constitutional state as a form of *idealisation*. This does not mean that the institutions which function to realise the idea of the democratic constitutional state in Western societies – for example presidential or parliamentary democracy – are necessarily legitimate; however, its basic principles of popular sovereignty and human rights are incontestable. It is only through the ideals of freedom, equal rights, and everyone's right to participation that a fair organisation of social life can come about, and it is only against the background of these ideals that existing forms of democracy can be criticised. It is to these – often contrafactual – standards of deliberation and collective decision making that modern societies link their identity and collective self-understanding. In this perspective, constitutional rules should be regarded as rules which, admittedly, may be discussed and problematised during the political game, but it is only their existence and the fact that the players accept them which make it possible to play the game at all.

Here we have arrived at the main point of the discourse-theoretical approach to law: *The law is merely potent and can only be justified with reference to a democratic procedure, but at the same time its legitimacy depends on the fact that people respect a system of fundamental rights.* This approach makes it possible to avoid conceptions of human rights as pre-political rights which are protected by the constitution and thus threatened by popular rule. Although formulated by humans, individual rights claim universal validity. Rights violations result in a loss of legitimacy for the sovereign. This is not only because of the moral content of rights, but also because they establish the conditions that are required if the citizens are to regulate their coexistence by means of law. Human rights facilitate the exercise of popular sovereignty through the institutionalisation of communication forms which ensure legitimate legislation by guaranteeing the protection of individual liberty, equality and participation. This understanding of the law does not only exist in the constitution and in the heads of lawyers, but also in the citizens' consciousness. The law is autonomous and has normative power only when it contains non-manipulative elements. There is consequently no autonomous law without real democracy (Habermas 1987c: 16).

In this chapter we have seen that it is only through the means of law that the state can rule legitimately in modern societies. This is not only because these societies are so heterogeneous that they have no general value base, but also because they are rights-based communities. Here Habermas introduces the important distinction between norms and values, to which he assigns different epistemological statuses. The modern state does not build on a thick value consensus, but on the moral principle of the inviolability of the individual. It can thus only obtain legitimacy by demonstrating that it deserves to be recognised by its citizens. Political power, which is constituted by positive law (which is coercive, but also instituted by people), is dependent upon the legal form in order to obtain legitimacy. In the democratic constitutional state, legislation is the result of a collective will, and not the product of a free play of forces, or of some mythical or divine authority.

In political theory there are two competing conceptual strategies that aim at explaining this state of affairs. Whereas liberals refer to human rights and maintain that the legitimacy of the state lies in the constitutional state's ability to protect the integrity of the individual, republicans find that the source of all political legitimacy is the citizens' participation in legislation processes. Habermas attempts to link the two traditions by indicating that although rights are formulated by people and approved by political bodies, the political process itself is also regulated by legal principles, including human rights. We have, however, seen that there is a need for a conception of a political 'reality discourse' to balance the constitutional norms which rank above the principle of democracy. As pointed out by Apel, this causes a greater problem to the thesis that democracy and the constitutional state mutually presuppose each other, i.e., the fact that democracy is linked to the nation state, while a great deal of the current legislation, especially in the area of human rights, is established at an international level. This is the theme of Chapter 11. In the next chapter we turn to the discourse-theoretical concept of the political process.

Notes

1. We will return to this in Chapter 11.
2. This is a distinction between axiology and deontology. 'Norms and values therefore differ, first, in their references to obligatory rule-following versus teleological action; second, in the binary versus graduated coding of their validity claims; third, in their absolute versus relative bindingness; and fourth, in the coherence criteria that systems of norms and systems of values must respectively satisfy' (Habermas 1996a: 255, cf. Habermas 1998e).
3. For a critique of this view, cf. Bader (1995).
4. Through discourse theory, an attempt is made to find a way between a purely normative theory, as we find it in contract theories, natural law and realism, (the latter as it is expressed in social scientific traditions such as elitism, group-pluralism and system functionalism). Whereas plain normative theories based on abstract and hypothetical constructions are out of touch with social realities, realism is based on objective facts without normative content, according to Habermas. Realism has nothing to say about the validity of principles; instead it supports their ability to veil power relations, in that the actors may camouflage their self-interests by referring to impartial norms in their justifications.
5. However, one may reply, as Alexy (1995: 173) does, that Habermas himself argues that the legal discourse is not closed and self-sufficient but needs support from external or morally based arguments in order to able to reach a correct decision.
6. Although the law has rules that regulate collisions between norms, for example lex superior, lex posterior, and lex specialis, these are too unspecified to solve disputes in a consequent and systematic manner.
7. This is a comprehensive process, which starts with the public legal-political debate about which laws and regulations are needed to resolve conflicts and realise collective goals, and goes via legal-dogmatic investigations and statements from lawyers, to the court discourse and its core, that is, the courts' adjudicating practice (Habermas 1995: 54).
8. 'Means that are normally illegitimate are permitted when and in so far as they are necessary in order to give institutions reasons which are suited to ensure a free and peaceful social order, in a strategic purpose-rational sense, and in accordance with pragmatic criteria.' (Lübbe, cited in Reese-Schäfer 1992: 64.)
9. It is, however, a point that positivated legal norms in themselves represent a fundamental value of the constitutional state: The legislation process is regulated by procedures that guarantee the citizens the protection of the law, which in itself is an important aspect of any justification. The right to participate, for example the right to vote, is a positive norm. Also human rights are rights in a legal sense (Habermas, 1996a: 105).
10. Of all the European states, it was only Corsica that could satisfy the requirements of popular rule, given that it adopted and implemented a correct constitution, Rousseau maintained (1994: 86).
11. See e.g., Peters (1994: 130), Skirbekk (1996), Frankenberg (1996).

CHAPTER 8

A political process model

So far we have argued that the legitimacy of the law must be sought within democracy. It is the democratic procedure that carries the burden of legitimacy. At the same time, this procedure must guarantee private and public autonomy. Rights cannot be adequately formulated and interpreted as long as the parties involved have not been heard. This normative argument has its empirical counterpart in the fact that political power cannot be mobilised to convert demands into legal obligations, unless the parties have participated in a public debate. Such debates are required in order to justify interests, to evaluate and interpret new demands and needs, and to define collective goals and prioritise resources. It is from a *public* point of view that a perspective is formed with regard to how equal and unequal matters should be treated. Normatively speaking, it is only in an open and free political debate about which demands deserve public support and which do not that it is possible to establish a concept of legitimate interests and mobilise the power that is necessary in order to convert these into effective policies.

The state is vital as a sanctioning and implementing body, because rights and collective goals must be carried out in an equally binding manner. In order to be a stable regime, the political community needs not only an organised jurisdiction, but also a collective identity (Habermas 1996a: 168). As already mentioned, it is neither the formal, legal forms, nor a given moral content that ensures the legitimacy of the law, but the legislative procedure itself. This links political power to opinion-formation processes in civil society. Constitutional arrangements that secure a thorough treatment of bills, voting rights, eligibility, regular elections, independence of the executive, balance of powers, etc. are safeguards against arbitrariness and misuse of power. Such arrangements, in addition to an open debate about common concerns in informal public spheres, and deliberation and voting within institutionalised decision-making systems, jointly constitute the basis for claiming that the democratic constitutional state is founded on the principle of popular sovereignty. Habermas maintains that it is this relation between open, non-institutionalised deliberations, competition between political parties, and institutionalised debates and negotiations which is the source of legitimate politics and the use of power. Political power can only justify itself by referring to the fact that it is in agreement with an open communication process, which makes it dependent on resources beyond its own control. It is only when the conditions for reasonable communication are met that the legitimacy of power can be tested, but the direct communication within the public sphere is also a source of legitimate power. This brings civil society (which is the topic of the next chapter) into the analysis.

In the present chapter we will concentrate on the political process itself and the concept of democracy. Before we turn to Habermas's model of the political process, we will discuss the discourse principle and its relation to the principles of morality and democracy. Subsequently we give an account of different specialised types of discourse. Finally, we address the problem of the relation between the principle of democracy and the principle of majority vote, in addition to the distinction between social, communicative and administrative power.

DISCOURSE AND DEMOCRACY

In *Between Facts and Norms*, Habermas's early theory of practical rationality is further developed and modified. Originally this was modelled on the type of argumentation that is required in order to determine the rules for peaceful co-existence, i.e. questions of justice. Hence, practical reason was assimilated with *moral* reason, and democratic decision making was taken to be analogous with the justification of moral norms in accordance with democratic ideals of participation (cf. Habermas 1975). However, the idea that normative questions can unambiguously be decided in a rational manner was disputed. The criticism was that the moral type of argumentation became a kind of meta-discourse to all types of normatively relevant argumentation (Taylor 1986, Schnädelbach 1990). The problem is a too great emphasis on the cognitive element and the consensus-generating potential of language. Especially as a political theory, this is insufficient, because of the qualitatively different questions that must be answered in a collective will-formation process. These also require other types of knowledge than moral *know-how*. It is not only the answer to the question of what is correct from a neutral and impartial point of view that has normative force in political deliberation processes, but also goal and value considerations. Teleological questions, not only deontological ones, play a role as well. Also cultural values and the realisation of collective goals should be included in a normative theory of politics. Thus, it becomes important to Habermas that his normative discourse model is able to make adjustments for other kinds of argumentation procedures than moral argumentation, so that not only opinion-formation processes, but also will-formation processes are included in a normative concept of discourse (Habermas 1996a: 152, cf. Habermas 1998b: 45 f.). Habermas's discourse theory must also be able to handle collective will-formation, which is vital to social problem solving and to the establishment of common goals and policy programmes. Finally, it must be able to handle impartial conflict regulation out of considerations of justice.

In Chapter 4 we mentioned Habermas's distinction between the *principle of universalisation* (U), which formulates a general standard against which moral norms can be tested, and the *discourse theoretical principle* (D), which is concerned with how we arrive at valid moral norms. In *Between Facts and Norms*, the relation between these two principles is somewhat different from what it has been previously. Of the two, it is (D) which is at the highest level of abstraction, and which is consequently least specified with regard to content; (D) only indicates a quite general procedure for the justification of norms. Habermas needs this in order to apply discourse theory to other kinds of action norms than just moral ones. (D) is now reformulated into a general *discourse principle* with a weak normative content and with the following slightly revised wording:

> *(D)* Just those action norms are valid to which all possibly affected persons could agree as participants in rational discourses.
>
> (Habermas 1996a:107)

While Habermas earlier one-sidedly analysed practical reason in line with Kant's moral theory, he has in recent years (as shown in Chapter 4) opened up to the idea that normative questions have more dimensions than just the formal universalisability of moral rules. This opening requires a principle like (D), which represents an impartial standard of judgement for all forms of action norms. This principle is neutral in relation to various facts and various types of norms and justifications, and it constitutes a higher-order's standard for the evaluation of different types of validity claims. It is a principle of rationality for how to justify norms in general. More concretely, the purpose of the principle is here to prevent moral validity claims from obtaining an absolute and superior status as the sole legitimating body of the law. This is the problem with Kant's rational law of reason, where the categorical imperative itself becomes the standard against which the validity of the laws is measured.[1]

In the justification of the law there are other reasons involved than just moral ones, and the autonomy of the law is not equivalent to moral autonomy, as was mentioned in the previous chapter. The discourse principle is neutral to the distinction between law and morality, but from this principle we can derive those demands that must be made on moral and legal action norms. When the discourse principle is specified with respect to moral norms and facts we get the *moral principle* (U) (which is identical with the previously mentioned universalisation principle), and when it is specified with respect to legal norms we get what Habermas refers to as the *principle of democracy*. Thus, he operates with a principle of justification which is more general than the principle of universalisation. The latter says something about which norms are valid, ideally speaking, and not which of them are actually valid to a specific group of people. To decide this, a different type of knowledge and justification is required than the strictly moral type.

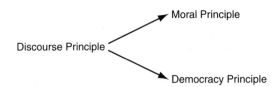

Figure 8.1 *The structure of discourse theory*

As illustrated in Figure 8.1, the discourse principle exists at a level which precedes the differentiation between law and moral, but it takes on the shape of (U) when it is specified with respect to morality norms. Simultaneously with (U), the democracy principle is introduced, which is reserved for those norms that appear in legal form. The *democracy principle* establishes a procedure for legitimate legislation, and maintains that

> Only those statutes may claim legitimacy that can meet with the assent of all citizens in a discursive process of legislation that in turn has been legally constituted.
>
> (Habermas 1996a: 110)

While the moral principle – which involves a requirement of universalisation – regulates the type of discourses where moral justifications alone are decisive, the principle of democracy governs those action norms that generally appear in legal form. Put simply, we may say that the principle of morality regulates informal and face-to-face relations, while the democracy principle regulates relations that exist between bearers of rights. However, it is important to note that the discourse principle does not function as a meta-norm from which the other principles are derived. There is no relation of superiority and subordination here; instead, we have a principle which is made concrete in relation to different types of action norms.

In a discourse-theoretical perspective, legislative functions may be distinguished from judicial and administrative functions, because each of them involves particular types of communication with appurtenant justifications (Habermas 1996a: 235). Before we discuss this issue in more detail, we will give an account of the objective-legal basis for distinguishing between different types of discourses. This has to do with the types of freedom recognised by the modern state.

LEGAL AND ETHICAL FREEDOM

The principle of democracy formulates the demands that are made on a legislation process. It is a broad principle, and it is formulated in order to capture all different types of knowledge and institutional practices that are required in order to bring about legitimate laws and valid collective decisions. In relation to the principle of democracy, the moral principle here refers to only one out of several types of arguments which are relevant and legitimate in collective decision-making and political legislation. It is particularly two other sets of considerations and procedures that are included, namely those referring to *negative freedom* and to *ethical freedom*.

The first consideration is based on the principle that individual rights relieve the individuals from moral demands of justification. It ensures the citizens' private autonomy, i.e. their negative freedom (Habermas 1996a: 120). These are rights which are judicially specified and guaranteed, and which give agents freedom to make their own free choices. They legalise selfish actions. These action principles are most evident in the modern market economy, where the individual's free choices have been generalised. The citizens' private autonomy, which is ensured by these rights, implies that the citizens need not be accountable for their action plans, let alone give publicly acceptable justifications for their choices. They are exempted from the duty to justify their actions, which is required for communicative freedom (Habermas 1996a: 119). Citizens can act strategically within legally secured domains.

As mentioned before, the modern legal system observes the principle that everything which is not prohibited is permitted. The relevant principle, in conjunction with the right to private property, which Hegel (1967) sees as a way of providing negative freedom with a real foundation, gives the individual *a right not to be rational* (Wellmer 1993: 15 ff.). There is a right to non-participation, and thus a right to be in opposition to even rationally grounded opinions. This gives rise to the thesis that even in a political process, there is legitimate leeway for preferences and interest-based actions. In this connection, Habermas introduces the concept of pragmatic discourses and bargaining in political will-formation processes, in addition to moral discourses.

The private autonomy that is ensured through individual rights does not only give rise to the above-mentioned form of *legitimate individualism*; it also protects the ethical freedom of individuals. By this is meant that existential choices which single actors or groups might face are protected. We may say that there exists a right to one's own culture, because individuals need access to common values and standards in order to develop an adequate self-consciousness (cf. Kymlicka 1989). This is also what we find in modern constitutions in the form of rights that ensure the cultural reproduction of society. In this group of rights we find freedom of opinion and speech, freedom of assembly, freedom of the press, etc. (Habermas 1989a: 83). According to John Rawls (1993), the various life projects that do not affect the interests of others are protected because the freedom of individuals is guaranteed by such things as freedom of religion and thought. With this we see the introduction of another legitimate consideration in connection with political decisions and legislation, viz. the formation of opinions about the good life. Also those discourses which concern who we are and who we want to be are an important part of the political will-formation process. They have to do with the establishment of common interests and the formation of collective goals, based on the values, solidarity and commitments that we have as members of a social and cultural community.

Modern constitutional states exhibit a complex institutional arrangement, where the individual is both free and bound, and where collective decision-making involves something different and more than that which has to do with purely moral considerations. Also pragmatic and ethical norms have their natural place. Thus, practical reason actualises the three discourse types or application forms which were in focus in Chapter 4: pragmatic, ethical and moral discourses. In political contexts these have a specific orientation, according to the nature of political issues.

First, there is the type of problems agents face that act on the basis of given goals, but who need to know which means are most rational. *Pragmatic discourses* are concerned with questions which can be answered by means of empirical knowledge, but they are also concerned with the balancing of different goals in the light of accepted values. In the first case the question is decided on the basis of pure efficiency considerations, i.e. what means are best suited to reach a given goal? This is the type of question that can be answered by various forms of expertise. In the second case we have to do with values of a *weak* character – i.e. preferences – between which we have no rational grounds to discriminate. When we decide what we want, what serves our goals, actor-relative reasons suffice (Habermas 1996a: 120). We may be faced with conflicting interests or questions regarding different wishes and goals which need no further thematisation or clarification. When different preferences clash, the conflict is normally resolved by means of simple decision rules that have been agreed in advance. Conflicts at this level do not affect the collective self-understanding, and the agents are 'free' to do as they please. Cost/benefit calculations and technical coordinating procedures may suffice to justify these types of decisions. However, it is important to note that such procedures are based on established agreement about those values and preference parameters against which action alternatives are ranked. Pragmatic discourses presuppose a value consensus.[2] Thus, the distinction between these various aspects of practical reason is mostly of an analytical character. In connection with actual political deliberation processes, the different discourse types will frequently merge into one another.

Ethical-political questions pertain to what is valued – what is the good life for a given social community. To answer such questions is at the same time to decide who we are and who we want to be, as a collective, i.e. to which values, ideals, and form of life we subscribe, and which goals we want to pursue. This is a parallel to the ethical-existential questions at the individual level that we discussed in Chapter 4, but there is a new dimension, because this concerns collective will-formation. As a consequence, each person must have regard for others – not only as relevant discussion partners who can help us define what should be done, but as independent persons with their own wills and interests. A collective consisting of several individuals will face disagreement and hence a decision-problem that an enlightened individual will not face (cf. Waldron 2001: 113). In this connection, Habermas talks about *the reality of the foreign will*, which helps decide which problems should be in focus, and how they should be solved. The collective will-formation supplements the individual one, and pertains to who and what we want to be as a part of a community of citizens. The only way to get an answer to such questions is to enter into collective self-interpretation processes, and these can be understood as a form of 'clinical deliberation'. The answers to the question of what is good for us can be found in a hermeneutic clarification of who we are and want to be. The arguments that contribute to an authentic interpretation of the historically constituted community, and of what consequences a choice of values will have for our understanding of the good life, will here be decisive (Habermas 1996a: 163).

The necessity of *moral discourses* becomes evident when we are forced to find valid answers across conflicting interests and differing ethical opinions. It is a question of what is the right thing to do when actions have consequences for other people's interests, a question of what is just or fair. Thus, a more absolute validity claim is raised than that which we find in connection with ethical questions about the good life, where the answers are relative to the cultural context. What is fair is due to everyone in the same way and to the same extent. The decisive arguments are those than can be made universal. Here a perspective is required which aims at neutrality with respect to differences in cultural context and ethnic affiliation. The superior status of moral duties is expressed in the fact that they, according to Habermas (1996a: 161), 'have the semantic form of categorical or unconditional imperatives'.

With this, discourse theory has been expanded to include three basic forms of practical reason, which relate to different types of questions that arise in political deliberation processes. Here the participants must deal with both purely utilitarian aspects (expediency and prudence), teleological aspects of value, and moral validity aspects in order to agree on what should be done. To these different problems correspond different categories of answers. Habermas regards this classification of practical discourses as only part of the more general differentiation into communication forms that takes place when culture is rationalised and made autonomous. At the same time, practical reason is distinguished from theoretical reason, morality from law, law from politics, and argumentation from bargaining. Because of this, two additional types of politically relevant discourse emerge, viz. *procedure-regulated bargaining* and *legal discourses*. We may get a clearer picture of the role of these discourses by constructing an idealised version of the political decision-making process.

THE POLITICAL PROCESS

Political will-formation can be seen as a process that starts with pragmatic discourses. As long we are dealing with more trivial value choices and only empirical facts are taken into account, this type of judgement is sufficient. Experience-based knowledge, actor-relative justifications and scientific expertise are required in order to decide what should be done. When we know what we want to achieve at this level, all we need to do is test the rationality of the means we have chosen, and possibly resolve the relevant conflicts through utility calculations. Questions involving economic or technical considerations and weak evaluations are paradigmatic for pragmatic discourses. However, as soon as conflicts arise, as soon as there is disagreement about goals, values and interests, other types of discourse must be used, viz. the *ethical-political* or the *moral*, according to which type of disagreement one has to deal with.[3] Ethical discourse regulates discussions concerning the identity and self-understanding of society. Such discussions arise primarily in connection with those areas of politics that are most seriously concerned with what values should be protected. For example, environmental matters raise the question of why nature should be protected, and the answer refers to the qualities of a good society. If environmental protection is important to us and to the life we want to live, we can only find reasons for it in our common value base. It is an issue which has to be clarified through a hermeneutic enlightenment – 'Aufklärung' – of the values that define us as a cultural group. Environmental protection refers to the ethical dimension of practical reason, because this concerns the quality and standard of the society we want.

However, as soon as we start looking at a concrete area, we see that the different aspects of practical reason are in reality intertwined. With regard to environmental protection, it is obvious that it is also a question of empirical knowledge, of clashes of interests, and of weighing means and ends. To answer the question of what really threatens the environment and what is a good strategy for creating ecological balance, we need other kinds of knowledge from those which hermeneutic discourses provide. However, when that knowledge is established, it is only the ethical-political type of discourse that can answer the question of what should be done. In other words, when the necessary empirical documentation is available and something has to be done, it is only the value-based answer we get through ethical-political discourse that can guide our actions.

On yet another level, environmental protection raises questions that cannot be solved through scientific and ethical-political discourses. Such questions arise when our answer to what a good society demands from our natural environment is at odds with the concerns of other areas. The requirements of the economy, the demands we have to welfare etc. may easily collide with environmental protection interests. It is in such cases that moral discourses are needed, because they aim to give an answer to what should be done when different interests and different opinions of the good life come into conflict. In case of conflict and disagreement institutionalised procedures for formal conflict resolution may be required. The system of institutionalised bargaining in wage settlements in Western welfare states provides an example of such conflict regulating procedures.

Moral discourses are attempts at settling conflicts neutrally and impartially. This is the main area of discourse theory. The requirement of universalisation constitutes the standard of validity, as mentioned several times. Typical political questions that refer to the need for moral discourses are those which concern the distribution of resources, and problems of justice and fairness in general. For example, the choice of a particular income policy for one group will have consequences for other people's interests. When the income level of one group is to be determined, the decision also affects other groups, directly and indirectly. Wage earners and employers have different interests, and the state also has an interest in the issue, because it attempts, among other things, to achieve a favourable price trend. It is clear that such issues may also include pragmatic discourses, which for instance aim at finding the optimal relationship between the development of wages and prices. In addition, ethical discourses may be involved, for example discourses which ask how much inequality can be tolerated in relation to the collective identity and value base of the society. It is nevertheless only through a moral discourse that we may get an authoritative answer to the question of what development is preferable when it comes to income policies. Only when we ask what is in the equal interest of all within the community, and the wage question is decided in an impartial and neutral manner, with due consideration of all parties, can we arrive at an answer which can be generally accepted as valid. However, in practice it would probably be too optimistic to believe that the income level for different groups can be decided through such moral discourses. The problem is that very often it is not possible to reach an agreement on these questions, simply because of the clash of interests. Therefore a complex arrangement has been developed in the political-administrative system in order to deal with this type of conflict. In discourse theoretical terms, we refer to this as procedurally regulated bargaining.

Bargaining is an alternative to moral discourse, and it is relevant when there are no prospects of reaching agreement when there is a conflict of interests.[4] Habermas is talking about those procedures that regulate the handling of conflicting interests and the need for reaching decision such as the voting procedures in the parliamentary system and group bargaining in the neo-corporatist channel of political influence. The concept of 'bargaining' is here linked to the reconstruction of social cooperation as strategic interaction which has been made within rational choice theory.[5] It is not the arguments in themselves that govern this cooperation, but those *threats* and *warnings* that can be realised outside the bargaining arena. What characterises bargaining, then, is the latent presence of coercion in the interaction. It is the resources that the parties possess, and how these are employed, which determine the outcome. A positive outcome of bargaining is a *compromise* and thus sub-optimal from the point of view of the parties. Ideally they would like a better outcome on their part. Hence a compromise is fundamentally different from rational consensus.

> Whereas a rationally motivated consensus (. . .) rests on reasons that convince all the parties *in the same way*, a compromise can be accepted by the different parties each for its own *different* reasons.
>
> (Habermas 1996a: 166)

Thus, an operational indicator is established which helps determine whether an interaction has a strategic or a communicative course. In the case of strategic bargaining, we will notice that the agents do not change their original attitudes and views, but are satisfied with what they possibly can get, given the interests and resources of other actors. Yet they may change standpoints for tactical reasons in order to achieve a better outcome. By contrast, if what we have is agreement that comes about through a communicative process, and which is hence the result of arguments, there will be a change of view in at least one of the parties. He or she will have learned from the process and has been convinced by a better argument. The parties will then justify their agreement by referring to the same arguments, to the same norm, or at least to mutually acceptable reasons. We will return to this in Chapter 10.

Habermas proposes to analyse the interaction in bargaining institutions by using the concept of strategic action. It is nevertheless clear that for the results to be regarded as valid, the constituting rules of the game must be neutral and ensure fair treatment of the parties. The institutional arrangements, i.e. the procedures that regulate the bargaining process, can potentially be tried in a moral discourse. Bargaining is justified when it is better to bargain than not to bargain, and because it excludes 'free riders' and ensures that nobody is exploited (Habermas 1996a: 166). These are the conditions that must be met if bargaining processes are to be regarded as fair. This discourse does not aim at consensus about the outcome, but at consensus about a procedure that ensures the balancing of interests – a procedure that ensures that all parties have the same opportunities for a breakthrough of their interests and preferences. It is in this light we must see the *parliamentary principle*, which regulates the establishment of representative bodies for deliberation and decision making. The aim is to establish conditions that ensure competition on equal terms. It is assumed that the goal can be reached through elections which are open, equal and free; and through delegation, hearings and representation; and by means of formal rules for decision making, and by guaranteeing minority rights. When parliamentary procedures have been observed, it is reasonable to expect that decision outcomes can be regarded as acceptable.

Finally the process results in decisions that that can be formulated in terms of legal categories that specify responsibilities socially, spatially and temporally. This requires consideration of everybody's interest, of what is viable and prudent in time and space, i.e. in a given historical and social context. Political decisions must also ensure equality before law and be consistent with existing laws. It is this legal protection that is tried in *judicial discourse*. Legal norms are constrained by morality, but in addition they often articulate the self-understanding of the legal community and its most profound values, as well as a fair balancing of interests and a purposive-rational search for effective solutions. Thus, in the justification of legal norms, we make use of the entire spectrum of arguments within practical reason according to Habermas. Legal discourses vary according to what types of legal norms we are talking about – material or formal law, constitutional or statutory norms – and according to what bodies are involved, i.e., courts or administrative agencies. The point of procedural law is primarily to ensure a communication process where relevant factors are taken into consideration, and where the arguments of the different parties are given proper weight, all in a process which is aimed at making legally correct and rationally acceptable decisions. Like pragmatic discourses, legal discourses also pertain to the use of expert knowledge in some form.

The various argumentative practices are embedded in five different forms of politically relevant discourses, as illustrated in Figure 8.2.

(1) *pragmatic discourses*, which are about utility calculation and collective priorities;

(2) *ethical-political discourses*, which aim to clarify collective identity and self-understanding;

(3) *procedurally-regulated bargaining*, which is initially governed by resources rather than arguments, and where the discourse pertains to the conditions for compromises between interests that cannot universalised;

(4) *moral discourses*, which relates to whether conflicts of interest and values can be decided according to universal standards; and

(5) *legal discourses*, which pertains to the consistency of judicial norms and rules.

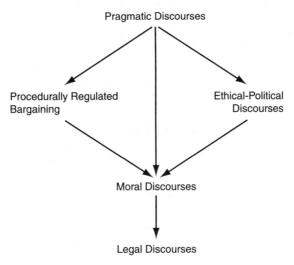

Figure 8.2 *A process model of the rational political will-formation*
Source: Habermas 1996a: 168.

167

DIMENSIONS OF COLLECTIVE WILL-FORMATION

We have just introduced a more differentiated concept of collective reason. The result of pragmatic discourses and fair bargaining processes is an *aggregated will*. It is a will that is nothing but the weighing and balancing of different interests and preferences. The aggregated will is the result of voting procedures and procedure-regulated bargaining in the political-administrative system. It should be distinguished from the authentic *common will* that emerges through hermeneutic discourses which aim at reaching a collective self-understanding, and in which the participants are free to express who they are and who they want to be. In ethical-political discourses, citizens who share a form of life discuss what are authentic expressions of this form of life, and by which goals they are committed. Such discourses arise in political forums, where the participants by means of arguments attempt to form a common will with regard to what should be done. This type of agreement will be relative to the strong evaluations which are shared by the participants. However, conditions for sovereignty are not the same as conditions for autonomy (Habermas 1995: 59). Sovereignty designates the possibility for making the common-action norms one is bound by, while autonomy refers to the conditions for reaching rational decisions. From these two forms of will we must therefore distinguish an *autonomous common will* or *a general will*, which is formed in moral justification discourses. What is important here is not only to find out what the citizens as a collective 'we' would want to do, but what can be made universal. This is truly a communicatively produced will, which makes greater demands on the redemption of validity claims.

According to Mead, an autonomous common will is the result of an argumentation process where the ideal role-taking implies everyone reciprocally. Habermas maintains that there are no realistic prospects of a general consensus of this kind in modern states. The reason is that the kind of consensus in question requires a fearless and unconstrained discourse in a non-institutionalised public sphere. This seems highly difficult to obtain in a world like ours, which to such an extent is characterised by strategic action and distorted communication processes. However, if the concept of a moral discourse does not provide the correct picture of how political solutions actually come about, why should we pay attention to it? According to Habermas, we need concepts that describe idealised states as well as the empirical states, for various reasons. First, this is because we will always recognise ideal elements in the real world. For example, we need the entire architectonic of Habermas's political process model to be able to grasp the complex procedural arrangements that exist in modern democracies, and the idealisations that are actually involved in the social practices making up these empirical realities. The different concepts of discourse may then function as analytical distinctions when we try to understand such phenomena, even though in any real deliberation process the various discourses will be intertwined and difficult to discern. Secondly, the diverse concepts of discourse may serve as normative assessments standards when we investigate whether a political decision is in line with the self-understanding of the democratic constitutional state. It is a standard that can be applied in the evaluation of political argumentation and decision-making. Furthermore, as will be discussed in Chapter 10, it can also give us some hints as to how institutions should be designed.

The distinction that has been made between the various discourses, then, strengthens the empirical adequacy of the theory, by providing the tools that are necessary to understand the political process in modern states. However, the theory also provides a normatively more adequate understanding of the complex forms of argumentation which are pertinent to a legitimate exercise of politics. Of course, with this conceptual complexity there are more types of rationality to keep track of. It implies greater uncertainty as to whether it is possible to make a rational decision when there is a collision between different sets of rules and norms (cf. Teubner 1996, Luhmann 1996). In short, it becomes more difficult to know what the result of a practical discourse will be.

However, the theory is 'de-fundamentalised' as well, in that the various discourses have the same status and are regarded as co-original (*gleichursprünglich*) from a genetic point of view. The different discourses are seen as equally important when it comes to bringing about collective deliberations. Also from a normative perspective, Habermas makes a point of the fact that ethical-political discourses are not subordinate and secondary in relation to moral ones, i.e., it is not less important to the individual or to a political community. On the contrary, the area of ethics is of the greatest importance; it is ethical discourses that enable individuals to make their choices in life, and a cultural community to agree on mutual interests and collective goals. Impartial justice only concerns the testing of norms in cases of conflict. Therefore it applies to only a limited set of cooperative situations. However, it is in moral discourse that we with the greatest certainty may expect consensus, given that the prescribed procedures are followed. Although Habermas still regards morality as the superior judge of normative questions, 'ethics' is nevertheless seen as even more important when we need to orient ourselves in practical action contexts in everyday life.

By this, a space for other reflections and concerns are opened up. Normative considerations pertaining to collective goal attainment and to value-orientations are included in the discourse-theoretical conception of the political process. However, on these questions Habermas does not say very much. This may be due to the fact that they are particular and culturally embedded and hence unfit for further theoretical formalisation.

DEMOCRACY AND MAJORITY RULE

Any political community may experience an acute need for action in a situation where there is not enough time to gather sufficient information or to discuss matters long enough to reach consensus about what should be done. Decisions must be made, and even a bad decision can be better than no decision. Often decisions must be made that are not supported by any form of legitimate consensus, and the modern, representative democracy has institutionalised mechanisms that are designed to deal with such situations.

The legal system has institutionalised certain procedures for the political system which provide relief from the requirement that agreement must be reached. The majority principle, representation, the principle of legality and rules that regulate instruction and delegation are examples of such institutions, which make action possible in a wide area. They make possible action without consensus, and they make the political system capable of acting in over-complex situations. They supplement and compensate for problems with informal action coordination. In the political world, it is not only when the participants disagree that communicative coordination of actions fails; this is also the case in all situations characterised by problems with operationalisations and interpretations of situations, or by lack of motivation, weakness of the will and limited commitment to moral norms.

Bargaining is regulated by several institutions. However, in Habermas's definition of the concept, which also includes decisions reached through voting, the majority principle becomes a particularly important institution. It is the regulating mechanism that formally mediates between the individual and the state. The majority principle represents a widely used and effective decision-making mechanism. It respects the citizens' preferences and reduces the costs of decision-making, both with the regard to the search for information and in the coordination of interests (Offe and Preuss 1991). There have been attempts to justify the majority principle in different ways, but it is still challenging from a normative point of view. As mentioned in Chapter 6, contract theories are not capable of justifying the majority principle, and it is also a challenge to discourse theory: it is the numeric majority, and not the qualified argument, that is decisive. Majority decisions do not satisfy the requirement of being accepted by all in an open debate. It is sufficient that they are accepted by the largest group. How does discourse theory explain this?

Habermas understands the majority principle as a form of *conditional agreement*. It is a principle that is internally related to truth, in that the relevant decisions claim to be correct in relation to actual circumstances and procedural norms. Here Habermas finds support in two monographs by Julius Fröbel from 1847 and 1848, which in an interesting way link the majority principle to the open discussion process within the public sphere. The majority principle reflects the need to have decisions made, but they are only accepted because the minority can work to make the 'truth' win through at a later stage. Minorities do not give up their will, but accept that what they think is right does not win out, because they have the opportunity to come back and win in a future election. Minorities give licence to the majority on behalf of their own standpoints, because they have the opportunity to work to gain support for their standpoint and thus become a majority at the next crossroads. Votes therefore represent only temporary stops in the continuous discussion about what should be done (Habermas 1996a: 179). In so far as the various groups have equal conditions for making their cause known and fight for it, they will accept 'wrong' decisions. Such a procedural interpretation of the majority principle makes it consistent with the concept of freedom, when it is not applied to irreversible decisions.

It has been claimed, however, that in most cases it is unclear what is an optimal decision, that the level of conflict is too high for there to be any prospects of consensus, and that the truth relation is therefore problematic (McCarthy 1994, 1996, cf. Warnke 1996: 75 ff.). We may also ask whether the majority principle is not in itself a respectable principle. Citizens accept majority decisions because these are made through a procedure that makes possible peaceful coexistence between parties in conflict. According to Rousseau (1994), the majority principle is conditioned by a general right to vote, which is a reason for accepting it. Democracy has a numeric dimension, because it consists of individuals that can be counted, which gives the majority's opinion a certain weight in itself. The interests of the majority must simply be preferred to those of the minority, according to Tocqueville (1969). Another point here is that the demand for unanimity in reality disturbs the principle of equality, because it pays undue attention to special interests and idiosyncratic arguments. Majority decisions are regarded as more legitimate, because they treat everyone in the same way (Ingram 1993: 302). The majority principle respects the formal equality that exists between citizens, and thus it has a certain independent moral value, we contend.

However this may be, discourse theory has difficulty protecting the minority and justifying negative freedom. How can majority tyranny be avoided? How can discourse theory give the individual a right not to submit to laws that are passed in a rational way (Larmore 1993, Höffe 1994)? On the one hand, the democratic principle guarantees the citizens autonomy in a very powerful manner. Those laws that the citizens cannot accept in a rational debate are illegitimate. Unfortunately, this weakens the realism of the theory, as most laws do not satisfy such a criterion. On the other hand, the majority principle adds more realism to the theory; it is brought closer to the way that laws are made in modern democracies. However, if the majority principle can be justified in itself, i.e. it is found to have legitimising power, the freedom of the individual is threatened. In that case, the right to have a say is no guarantee against unjust encroachments on the freedom sphere of the citizens (Engländer 1995: 494). This is one of the most difficult problems of discourse theory, and one that has not been solved so far, i.e., how human rights can ultimately be justified, as will be explored in the last chapter.

One answer concerning the status of the majority principle can be linked to its limited normative validity. It is simply not fit to decide all types of conflicts. It is only well-suited to regulate strategic interests when voting results are compromises which reflect the distribution of resources, i.e. when pragmatic issues and non-generalisable interests are involved (Habermas 1996a: 177). Conflicts about principles are not appropriately settled by means of majority decisions. Institutions based on political power are simply not suited to determine such questions; they can neither deny nor confirm the validity of a moral argument (Preuss 1996: 109).

Secondly, majority decisions are restricted by fundamental rights that protect minorities. Majority decisions which limit future possibilities of will-formation or decision making are in this perspective illegitimate because they violate the rights that make autonomy possible (Habermas 1996a: 180). Majority decisions therefore do not suffice as a legitimising body for decisions that have irreversible consequences (cf. Offe 1982, Guggenberger and Offe 1984).

Thirdly, democratic procedures are designed to ensure that negotiations take place in a way which guarantees a thorough discussion of the relevant issue; in specific, all parties must be given the necessary information, all parties must be heard, and relevant factors must be taken into account before decisions are made. It is a point that majority decisions in themselves are normally justified further; they are justified on account of their substance and claim to be qualified and rational. At least they are supported by someone's good grounds. The way in which the majority principle is used involves a certain reflection on its status as a conflict-solving mechanism. For example, a qualified majority is sometimes required in debates about whether a referendum is needed. In the debate that took place in Norway in 1994 about whether the country should join the European Union, some political parties beforehand had reservations against following the vote of a narrow yes majority. Majority rule only has power and legitimacy in so far as the discussion about voting procedures makes the participants agree about what is the correct procedure. Hence, majority decisions can only be justified indirectly, and they are secondary to the democracy principle.

To sum up, in Chapter 6 we learned that voting does not guarantee rational decisions, but is nevertheless necessary for decisions to be made. Because of those democratic procedures that ensure a continuance of the discussion, the voting result may be granted legitimacy. The minority do not give up their will; they only postpone its implementation until they have succeeded in finding arguments that will convince more people. The democratic procedure itself represents a barrier against the threat of majority tyranny that the liberals see in democracy. The opposition between democracy and the constitutional state, which is characteristically made in classical liberalism from Tocqueville and J. S. Mill, is therefore false, Habermas maintains. And one can add that historically, increased democracy goes hand in glove with an increased respect for human rights (Dahl 1989: 311 ff.) The majority principle is important because it allows us to make decisions even in highly complex situations. This institution, together with other formal procedures, is the very reason why we can speak of legal and administrative power as different from social and communicative power in a modern political context.

SOCIAL, COMMUNICATIVE AND ADMINISTRATIVE POWER

Habermas distinguishes between *social power* that arises on the basis of resources and interests in civil society, and the discursive testing of the extent to which interests can be made universal, which results in legitimate power. By social power is meant the factual ability to carry out one's goals against opposition. This is the conventional definition of power by Max Weber (1978) and Robert A. Dahl (1957) and which was earlier used by Habermas, i.e. power defined 'as the ability to prevent other individuals or groups from pursuing their interests. Usually power is asymmetrically distributed. In that case, one party can interfere with the other's (strategically effective) pursuit of interests, or one of the parties can force his own interest on the other' (Habermas 1971c: 254). This concept of power refers to the resource basis that is needed for the actors to realise their goals. However, the problem is that social power is not normatively evaluated, and it may therefore both allow and prevent the formation of legitimate power (Habermas 1996a: 175).[6] The democratic constitutional state institutionalises distinctions that are meant to remedy this problem. The principle of a separation between state and society implies institutions and a political culture separated from economic and class interests, so that the unequal distribution of social power can be neutralised. This should make it possible to test the legitimacy of social power (Habermas 1996a: 216). The democratic constitutional state can be regarded as an institutionalisation of those procedures that are necessary to ensure that the factual, resource-based power which exists in civil society is not converted into collective decisions until it has been tried by norm-testing reason. In order to talk of real popular rule, three conditions must therefore be met:

(1) a principle of *individual protection of rights*, which is guaranteed by an independent judicial system;

(2) the institutionalisation of the *legality principle*, which secures political as well as legal control of the administration;

(3) a principal *distinction between state and society*, which ensures that social power in civil society is not converted into administrative power unfiltered, i.e., without being tested communicatively (Habermas 1996a: 169).

It is these distinctions that make it possible to talk about the formation of *communicative power*. By communicative power is meant the kind of power that emerges when the citizens come together in public forums and come to an agreement about the rules for social coexistence and about which collective goals should be realised. Here Habermas builds on Hannah Arendt's distinction between *power* and *coercion*. That the individuals give up their natural rights is not the basis for legitimate power. The former is claimed by the liberal, contract-theoretical tradition from Hobbes and Locke, where the state emerges as a coercive power – a Leviathan. Instead, power is seen by Habermas as an expression of the cooperation of united citizens (1996a: 149). It is the open and unrestricted use of the freedom of communication that generates power. Political power arises in the communication between citizens when they gather. Power is collective and intersubjective by nature; it is created in the interaction between agents, and it is only in operation and is only strong as long as the people are assembled and agree. This gives rise to the communicative concept of legitimacy, which says that to the extent that the actual policies spring from extensive deliberation processes and can be tested through free communication, there is a basis for speaking of legitimate power.

It is the consensus-forming processes that take place in the public sphere that generate and authorise power. The source of power is to be found in free communication. However, as will be further discussed in the next chapter, the public sphere does not act; rather deliberation takes place in it. The common opinions that emerge in the free spaces of civil society are converted into binding decisions via the law. Thus, political power is again differentiated, this time in *communicative* and *administrative power*. The differentiated concept of power is illustrated in Figure 8.3. Communicative power, which derives from the free opinion-formation in the public sphere, is held by Habermas to guarantee control with the legislative, judiciary and executive powers through legal freedom. Administrative institutions, which realise collective goals, are separated from the judiciary power by law. This separation is necessary if the distinction between state and society is to be maintained. The use of already constituted power, represented by the political-administrative system, must be distinguished from the generating of power in free communication in public assemblies. However, this does not tell us anything about the use of political power, or about the competition for positions and offices, which is regulated by the parliamentary principle of representative bodies and quorums.

On the one hand, the administration has at its disposal competence and means of power which can only be used by bodies which are under legal control.

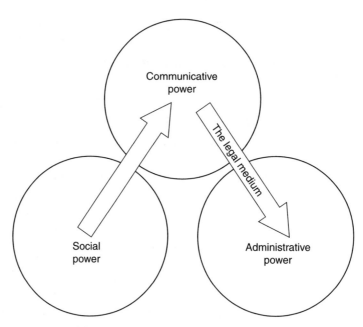

Figure 8.3 *The three-fold model of political power*

Political and judicial bodies possess their own resources. These can only be employed in connection with particular political and judicial tasks, and must be separated from the legislative power (Habermas 1996a: 212). On the other hand, the legality principle ensures the citizens' rights in that only a new law can change the prevailing law. The law does not control institutions of political power, but it is the medium whereby communicative power is converted into administrative power. Such divisions of competence are important in order to ensure the interests and rights of the citizens and the legitimacy of political power. Power and legitimacy are linked together in complex ways. The problem is that in modern welfare states, courts of justice exercise a great deal of legislative power; they create law. In the same way, the administration and the professions to a large extent use their own discretion when they make decisions; the shaping of new policies is often based on delegation, frameworks, and authorisation. This fact creates problems for the old distinction between legislative, judiciary and executive branches of government. Some even claim that these distinctions are no longer important (for example Luhmann 1995, Wilke 1992). Nevertheless, Habermas wants to maintain them, and he maintains that the decisions of executive-administrative bodies of power are binding and legitimate only insofar as they can be justified on a legal-rational basis. It is the communicative power and the factors that condition its formation which ensure the legitimacy of the law. This is not solely a normative point, as it is only the politicians, in their capacity of legislators, that have unlimited access to making decisions with a normative justification, and who are consequently free to use normative judgement. Administrators cannot make unlimited use of their own discretion in this manner, just as lawyers cannot apply the law in an arbitrary or personal way. The administration implements political decisions and thus makes use of norms, but these are externally given, and it is presupposed that civil servants comply with them in a

Branches of government	Functions	Institutions	Types of discourse
Legislative power	Setting of norms	Parliament	Pragmatic, ethical, moral
Judiciary power	Application of norms	Court	Legal
Executive power	Implementation of norms and goals	Cabinet/ Administration	Pragmatic

Figure 8.4 *Division of powers in a discourse-theoretical perspective*

predictable and purposive-rational manner, i.e., that they do not follow their own interests (Habermas 1996a: 192).[7] In Figure 8.4, we have summarised the distinctions under discussion.

These distinctions between the estates help ensure that the realisation of the administration's goals is in proportion to a communicatively generated will, so that it is not an expression of brute power, i.e. factual social power relations or arbitrary administrative power (Habermas 1996a: 231).

CONCLUSION

It is the procedures that are the unifying institutions in pluralistic societies, according to Habermas. It is the procedures which make possible collective action and a peaceful resolution to conflicts. Therefore it is not only civic virtue and personal conscience which make possible the ability to act in solidarity and distribute resources fairly; it is also those procedures which have been instituted in modern constitutional states to secure democratic opinion and will-formation.

This has to do with the fact that the modern legal system ensures the individuals' political interests by formalising them as *individual rights*. In this way, actors are guaranteed a free space in society, where all they need to relate to is the law's explicit demand of obedience. In order to be law-abiding citizens, they only need to stick to the letter of the law. The positivism and formalism of the law is the reason why citizens can take a purely strategic attitude to it, i.e. consider it as a framework for pursuing their own goals, without having to get the recognition and approval of others. However, positive law also claims to be legitimate law, which makes it liable to assessment with regard to it being justifiable from the citizens point of view. This, then requires that citizens be able to take another attitude to their political rights as well. They must see them as communicative freedom rights which make possible participation in political opinion and will-formation processes. By this is meant that agents must be able to change from a result-oriented to an understanding-oriented attitude, and they must try to agree about how their coexistence should be regulated through the establishment of common laws.

In this chapter we have seen that there exists a complex set of procedures in modern constitutions, which corresponds to analytical distinctions in everyday language. We can distinguish between 'ought' and 'is', between what is good and what is just, between morality and law, politics and administration, etc. Different types of questions require that we follow a particular logic of argumentation in order to come up with reasonable answers. Thus, the constitutional state has institutionalised possibilities of entering into pragmatic, ethical-political, and moral discourses, as well as strategic bargaining and discourses which concern the legal rights of the citizens. These analytical distinctions are entrenched in the differentiation of political power into social, communicative and administrative power, and they are institutionalised in the division between legislative, executive and judiciary powers. Together this justifies, according to Habermas, the presumption of rational and legitimate law-making.

Whether and how democratic policy-making comes about is not only a question of rational procedures as it also involves certain democratic 'virtues'. This is so to the extent it depends on a modern liberal culture, in which individual freedom, tolerance, political participation and an argumentative solution to conflicts are valued. Deliberative politics hinges on a rationalised lifeworld, which meets it 'halfway' according to Habermas. It rests on a background consensus that makes it possible, through mutual reflexive efforts, to deal with that disagreement and potential instability which exist in such societies. In other words, the political culture must be so 'enlightened' that the actors know what counts as rational reasons, that they are able to distinguish between case and persons, and perhaps especially that they are motivated by reasonable arguments in carrying out their voting rights. The quality of political decisions is conditioned by the level of education, refinement and enlightenment in the relevant society. Thus, the democratic constitutional state is also an expression of a culture and a way of life, and not only of abstract legal and moral principles. Democracy demands, as an functional requirement, an active and vital, and not least a rational civil society in order to live up to its ambitions of peaceful conflict resolution, and of catering for different needs in the equal interest of all the citizens. On the other hand, this raises the question of what means there are in civil society – i.e. in the public sphere – for generating collective action and for testing the legitimacy of the power holders in a way that prevents social power from being converted into administrative power, unhindered and unfiltered. This is the topic of the next chapter.

Notes

1. However, Ingeborg Maus maintains that Kant is here misinterpreted by Habermas, and that the similarities between Kant and discourse theory is greater than what Habermas wants to admit (Maus 1992, 1996). Karl-Otto Apel (1998) on his part, criticises Habermas for not realising that the discourse principle itself is normatively charged, and that morality must necessarily be superior to the law, as argued by Kant.
2. This is informed by McCarthy's insight that values is a way for actors to rank their needs and interests and that different kinds of values can provide incompatible frameworks for this ranking or assessment (McCarthy 1991a: 191).

3. For a critical analysis of these distinctions from a rational choice perspective, see Heath 2001: 219 ff.

4. According to Thomas C. Schelling 'most conflict situations are bargaining situations. They are situations in which the ability of one participant to gain his ends is dependent to an important degree on the choices or decisions that the other participant will make. The bargaining may be explicit, as when one offers a concession; or it may be by tacit manoeuvre, as when one occupies or evacuates strategic territory,' (1980: 5)

5. Or rather game theory that is based on strategic rationality and that analyses bargaining as a non-cooperative game. Non-strategic bargaining models, including the 'integrative bargaining' associated with Nash and Raiffa claim to avoid suboptimal solutions. Regarding this it is an observation that regular cooperation builds levels of trust and goodwill and reduces the inclination to act strategically (Heath 2001: 248 f.)

6. In a text from 1971, Habermas makes a distinction between the manifest exercise of power, which is based on actual use of violence, or threats to use it, and legitimate exercise of power, which is based on approved norms. Further, 'Herrschaft' is understood as a special instance of normative exercise of power: 'Power is always built into prevailing norms (. . .) when our mutual expectations to behaviour permit us to cater for different needs only on the condition that *other* postulated needs are renounced, when permission is linked to prohibition' (Habermas 1971c: 254, our translation). See further Honneth (1991: 279 ff.) for an analysis of Habermas's conception of power.

7. This will be discussed in more detail in the next chapter.

CHAPTER 9

Public opinion formation and rational politics

INTRODUCTION

Modern societies are characterised by conflicts of interest and a plurality of values. Conflicts and disagreements are not only caused by a clash of interests and the widespread use of strategic action in differentiated capitalist societies, they are also caused by profound ethical conflicts, and in modern societies these have surfaced because individuals have acquired *the right to disagree*. Through the institutionalisation of different types of freedom within the liberal constitutional state, principles were adopted which said what the state should do and how it should do it. The aim was to protect individuals and societal institutions against encroachments and injustice. The democratic constitutional state is both bound and limited. Its power is curbed in that its authority is limited, and also because it is obliged to respect the highest priority of liberal society, i.e., the freedom of the individual, which is in principle indeterminate as human beings are their own legislators. In the discourse-theoretical reconstruction of the democratic constitutional state we have seen that the freedom of the individual – its private autonomy – can only be ensured to the extent it also has public autonomy. The liberal principle of freedom must therefore be combined with the republican principle of popular sovereignty by making room for common opinion and will-formation. In the democratic constitutional state, there are three overlapping constitutional arrangements that can be seen as designed to achieve this:

(1) The *principle of the division of power*, which splits the power of the state into separate, but mutually dependent and limited decision-making bodies.

(2) The institutionalisation of *the public sphere*, which is a power-free space outside of the state, where society itself mandates the exercise of power and also criticises the way in which power is used.

(3) The *legality principle*, which connects the state to the law and makes it use its power in a way that is predictable, neutral and fair (Poggi 1978: 135).

From a normative perspective, the public sphere holds a unique position, because this is where everyone has the opportunity to participate in the discussion about how common affairs should be ruled. In the widest sense, the public sphere is merely that social room which is created when individuals act communicatively (Habermas 1996a: 360).

In this chapter we will take a closer look at some aspects of Habermas's early and recent discussions of the public sphere. First we will see that the category public sphere is a critical concept, which has implications for the legitimacy of political authority. Then we will discuss the thesis about the decline of the public sphere and its normative and empirical status. In doing this, we will focus on the public sphere as an analytical category. How can it be identified, and what criterion can we use to determine if it functions? Finally, we will explain in what sense the public communication process is a condition for solidarity politics to be carried out in a parliamentary democracy.

THE PUBLIC SPHERE – WITH NO HISTORICAL PRECEDENTS

Habermas's *Strukturwandel der Öffentlichkeit* (1962) or *The Structural Transformation of the Public Sphere* (1989a) has for several decades represented a standard work when it comes to the concept of the public sphere. Here the public sphere was seen as the arena where civil society was linked to the state as a power structure:

> The bourgeois public sphere may be conceived above all as the sphere of private people come together as a public; they soon claimed the public sphere regulated from above against the public authorities themselves, to engage them in a debate over the general rules governing relations in the basically privatized but publicly relevant sphere of commodity exchange and social labor. The medium of this political confrontation was peculiar and without historical precedent: people's public use of their reason (*öffentliches Rässonnnement*).
>
> (Habermas 1989a: 27)

The public spheres that developed in English coffee-houses from 1680 to 1730, as well as in drawing-rooms and clubs in France, were at first literary, then political, public spheres.[1] The term public sphere signifies that equal citizens assemble into a public and set their own agenda through open communication. What characterises this public sphere is that it is power free, secular and rational. The modern, civil public sphere, which is localised in civil society as a 'state-free' room, is without historical parallels. In the ancient Athens, the citizens gathered at the marketplace (*Agora*) to talk about what should be done, before they appeared in the popular assembly (*Ecclesia*) as decision makers. There was no essential distinction between deliberation and decision making. The Athenian Assembly was not a free public sphere but the government. Informal discussions were not separated and did not have a distinct status outside the power apparatuses. That the modern public sphere is *secular* means that it does not originate in a particular world view or a particular societal system. Hence, the modern public sphere is quite different from, for example, that of the stoics or the Christian Church. The pre-modern public spheres were formed around ethical communities. They were an expression of a particular discourse that was limited with respect to content and linked to the undisputed authority of certain ways of life. The modern idea of a public sphere broke with the notion of a society based on harmonised forms of life and hegemonical values. The ideal of a conflict-free order was replaced by the ideal that conflicts should be resolved through debate (Warner 1990: 41).

The essence of the modern public sphere is the rational debate. There are no elevated dogmas to be protected and to which we may appeal in conflict situations. In this type of public sphere, actors have to seek support on a broad basis and across established religions and status hierarchies. The public sphere under discussion is greater and wider than that which is formed around a particular ethical basis, i.e. around the state or the Church and their institutions of power. The modern concept of a public sphere spread to all of civilised Europe (Taylor 1995: 266). It became possible to appeal to a public that was greater than the nation state. This idea of a public sphere adopted the principle of universalistic argumentation, and it not only makes possible, but presupposes impartiality and rational argumentation. In principle, there are no limitations with regard to topics, participants, questions, time or resources. The discussion can go on indefinitely, and the participants can address an indefinite circle of interlocutors, who are scattered in time and space. This is the basis for speaking of a modern public sphere that is *critical* of power. We are here concerned with the political public sphere, but it is important to note that in the most different social areas – e.g. science, economy, art, education, religion – we witness an increase in communication and in the formation of public forums.

The idea of public spheres, which signifies the room for free exchange of opinions in society, has no limits or bodies of authority besides the free discussion. The public sphere is reflective. Through it society thematises itself; its members write and read about themselves. However, the public sphere has not come about merely because the people has taken the law into their own hands and organised anti-power bodies in civil society. The modern state itself has instituted it by establishing civil rights which allow citizens to gather in order to discuss politics. It is not until after the creation of the modern state that negative rights take the form of rights that protect citizens against the state, according to Habermas (1996a: 250). It is not until human rights are positivised and can be sanctioned through independent courts that they protect the citizens' integrity and give them a potential of power. The public sphere is a critical institution, which gives citizens an opportunity to assemble in order to hold the power holders accountable for their actions.

> The public sphere ... is ... the informally mobilized body of nongovernmental discursive opinion that can serve as a counterweight to the state.
>
> (Fraser 1992: 134)

With reference to England Habermas writes that 'by the turn for the nineteenth century, the public's involvement in the critical debate of political issues, had become organized to such an extent that it had definitively broken the exclusiveness of Parliament and evolved into the officially designated discussion partner of the delegate,' (Habermas 1989a: 66). With the establishment of such a public sphere, the power holders' basis of legitimacy is changed. Now they must enter the public arena in order to justify their decisions and gain support. The power holders can no longer count on institutional, traditional or religious authority, and they can no longer confine themselves to posing for the masses in a representative public sphere, as did the Roman emperor. There are no external bodies that guarantee the legitimacy of power, neither divine law nor traditional authority. Its authority can be found in the public 'reasonable' debate. Thus, legitimacy is not only precarious, but also a critical resource – something which is 'outside the reach of individuals'. We see a transition from the speech of power to the *power of speech* (Lefort 1988: 38). Neither given institutions nor concrete persons guarantee the legitimacy of the law. Only the public debate in itself has norm-giving power.

In the public sphere there is no other authority than that which springs from the spoken word. According to Kant, enlightenment involves that all authoritative statements can be tested by means of an open, public use of reason.[2] Indeed, the very existence of reason is conditioned by this freedom. Only those claims which free individuals can support in an open debate are rational. We may now reformulate Hobbes' principle of absolute monarchy – *'auctoritas facit legem'* ('authority makes the law') – into *'veritas non auctoritas facit legem'* ('the truth, not authority makes the law') (Habermas 1989a: 53). Reason will tame power:

> All actions relating to the rights of others are wrong if their maxim is incompatible with publicity.
>
> (Kant 1996b: 347)

Publicity both places state actions under the public eye and subjects these actions to the public reason. 'Legitimacy is pursued through public accountability. Public and rational scrutiny of state actions keeps the state honest' (Cambers 2000: 202). But the public sphere also contributes to educating and refining the citizens and to teaching them what is in the interest of the general public (Hegel 1964: 482). In his monograph *On Liberty* from 1859, John Stuart Mill maintains that the freedom of thought and speech plays a decisive role in the realisation of the citizens' potential and in the development of prevailing ideas.[3] Mill's point is that it is not only when one is hampered by external circumstances that one is unfree, but that there are internal barriers to freedom as well (Taylor 1985b). The individual may be subjected to self-deceit, delusions, and ignorance. The realisation of freedom must also involve the possibility of developing and refining our own goals and purposes, which is only possible to the extent that one is met by counter-arguments and fresh views. The freedom of thought and speech is the basic condition for personal opinion-formation. We do not know if we are right until we have heard the counter-arguments. Habermas speaks of a *communicative freedom*, which is based on the right to speak our mind. However, in the next instance this right involves a moral duty to justify our standpoints. Anything else would be to claim infallibility: *One thing is to assume that the opinion I have is true; it is something quite different to claim that it cannot be wrong, and that it should not be tested or be allowed to be rejected.* The absence of freedom of speech involves a loss both to those who gag, and to those who are gagged. Those who are gagged lose the opportunity to change their minds in case they should be wrong. The absence of such freedom also involves that those who prohibit competing opinions will degenerate, because they do not get the opportunity to prove that they may be right. Their conviction becomes a dogma. Jon Hellesnes has reconstructed John Stuart Mill's argument for freedom of speech into four steps:

(1) If an opinion is suppressed, there is a danger that a truth is suppressed. To deny this would mean to claim infallibility.

(2) If the opinion which is suppressed is mainly wrong, and perhaps also irrational, it may still contain an element of truth. If the deviating opinion was no longer suppressed, it could be used to correct, or supplement, the prevailing view through discussion.

(3) Even if the prevailing opinion were the whole truth (which is of course

unlikely), it would still need to be challenged. If the challenge failed to appear (for example because of a prohibition against opposition), people would forget *why* the prevailing view is the true or right one. For only in a free and argumentative intersubjective debate can the pro arguments be asserted.

(4) Without challenge, the essence of the prevailing opinion would gradually be lost. It would only remain in the form of a dead dogma which is celebrated from time to time through empty formulas. It would no longer be able to influence human character and behaviour (Hellesnes 1992: 192 f.).

The freedom of the individual is conditioned by the freedom of others, because some individual's opinion is neither the only possible one, nor is it the final and complete truth. In the public sphere, it is possible to bring about an argumentative process about how society should be. This is a prerequisite for a rational opinion and will-formation process to take place.

THE DECLINE OF THE PUBLIC SPHERE

Free opinion-formation is made possible through the various types of freedom, viz. of religion and thought, of opinion and speech, of the press and media, and of assembly and organisation. The modern state is only legitimate if it guarantees these rights, because this is the only way to test the validity of its commands. The original capitalist state model built on the idea of a self-sustaining economic sphere, constituted by small producers. Through the neutral market mechanism these were expected to compete on equal terms. The market was regarded as autonomous and self-regulating. It had the ability to convert selfish preferences (private vices) into public benefits in an efficient manner – 'as by the intervention of an invisible hand', according to Adam Smith. However, the belief in automatic, non-political society rapidly disintegrated when it became obvious that it was impossible to realise the idea of a self-regulating economic system which was based on the exchange of commodities between small producers. More precisely, the belief in the idea began to disintegrate when wealth concentrated in a few hands, and when structural poverty, injustice and inequality emerged as distinct features of the system. These factors challenged the legitimacy of the model, and new institutional arrangements were inevitable. These, on their part, undermined the idea of government through public reasoning. The general right to vote, the organisation of the Labour movement, and the formation of political parties, these factors in reality rendered impossible the idea of politics as a discourse between equals.

After 1830 the public sphere degenerated and with it the practice it instituted all over Western Europe. The concept was discredited in political theory.[4] Habermas spoke in 1962 of a *re-feudalisation of the public sphere*. By this he meant that the economic relations in society, which were out-differentiated as a private realm of action through the civil-democratic revolutions, reappear on the public agenda. This causes the public debate to break down under the pressure of contending groups that are fighting for power and economic compensation from the political system. Also the reading public degenerates. With the emergence of a modern journalism linked to commercial interests, the reading public is transformed into a minority of specialists, who present their message for mass consumption and the entertainment of an uncritical audience.

Rather than being decided after a free and open debate, political questions were now decided in closed assemblies and through institutionalised bargaining. There was competition between political parties, a propagandistic press, and the neo-corporate channel of influence, which channelled social power directly into the political-administrative decision system. There was no question of a general public testing the validity of the relevant interests. What characterised the public sphere was no longer principle-oriented debates, but rather the noise from the competition between political parties, efficiently sponsored by sensation-oriented and commercialised media. Power was realised in cloakroom talks, in committees, boards, and councils, and the people in charge were left alone by a servile press which was loyal to political parties.

The autonomy of civil society – its self-supporting capacity – and the self-regulation of the economy thus turned out to be a mere fiction. This had consequences for the way public authority was exercised. The state could no longer act solely as the constitutional state's surety for the political public sphere. Its limited role as a guarantor of the relation between law and public opinion could not be maintained. The state had to regulate the (self)destructive business of private agents through legislation. It also had to supplement the market with publicly produced goods and services, when the market mechanism failed, and it had to compensate for the negative consequences of the market economy through social and welfare state measures (cf. Habermas 1975, Offe 1984). The state became a producer of welfare, and the public sphere became more an arena for propaganda and strife between clashing interests than for rational deliberation.

Normative theories about the public sphere seem slightly idealistic in modern societies, where economic relations can be regarded as an out-differentiated self-regulating system, and where also the state machinery itself can be said to operate according to functional imperatives (cf. Chapter 5). Money, ballots, and instructions partly replace human communication. The construction of an administrative machinery, as well as the instrumentalisation of politics through party-competition have undermined the possibilities of democratic will-formation through public reasoning. Politics can not be seen as a reflection of public opinion. It is not the rational debate that explains political action, as was presupposed by the classical model of the public sphere. The nature of society has changed in the sense that it is not only the economy which has taken the form of a functionally independent system. The state machinery has, through new channels and contributions, become divorced from democratic will-formation. We therefore have to give up the ambition of 'total democracy', as well as the idea of the public sphere as the superior forum of reflection for the public will. Democracy can not govern the entire society, simply because society has become too complex (Habermas 1996a: 370). The presumption of political integration of all parts of the society through law and politics, and hence the conception of society as a macro-subject, has to be replaced by a more pluralistic approach. In opposition to his earlier thoughts about how radical democracy can do away with the distortions of communication that had hollowed out the bourgeois public sphere, Habermas now relinquishes seeing society as an association writ large, i.e., where 'associated individuals participate like the members of an encompassing organisation' (Habermas 1992d: 443). He now claims that the task is rather to

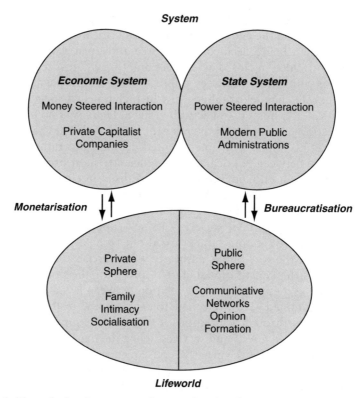

Figure 9.1 *The relation between spheres of action from a system's perspective*
(Cf. Sales 1991: 306).

establish a democratic barrier against the colonisation of civil society by money and bureaucracy (Habermas 1992d: 444). Figure 9.1 illustrates this relation.

In this perspective, the only function of the public sphere is to protect central social areas against the threats of commercialisation, bureaucratisation and clientisation. In the public sphere, we can thematise private experiences, demand new initiatives, call attention to faults and defects, criticise injustice, etc., and in this way help keep the 'systems' in check. There is a potential for revision and critique, but it is not possible – nor desirable – to abolish the system of market economy or the political-administrative machinery. The out-differentiated systems make for a more efficient administration of the common resources, and also has positive consequences for individual freedom. The welfare state and social rights ensure a certain degree of fairness, and the market economy generates more efficiency than do competing principles of organisation, according to Habermas.

The fact that society has acquired the character of a system and has become increasingly complex hence frustrates the classical hopes of government by public deliberation. In this perspective, the public sphere has acquired only a defensive role (cf. Cohen and Arato 1992: 408). Nevertheless, this seems to be a too pessimistic diagnosis, and it gives too great concessions to the functionalist and realist positions in political analysis. On the basis of *Between Facts and Norms*, we may justifiably speak of a *restoration of the public sphere*.

A COMPLEX PUBLIC SPHERE

The public sphere is a common room in society, but it is a room which is presently divided into different types and categories. It consists of different assemblies, forums, arenas, scenes and meeting-places where the citizens can gather. Today the public sphere is a highly complex network of various public sphere segments, which stretches across different levels, rooms and scales. These are subaltern public spheres, municipal, regional, national and international public spheres. There are different arenas, where elite and mass, professionals and lay-people, prophets and critics can meet and cooperate with various degrees of intensity and enthusiasm. The public sphere extends from episodic café and street gatherings, via organised professional, cultural and artistic public spheres, to abstract public spheres, where listeners, readers and viewers are isolated and spread in time and space. There are strictly situated public spheres, where the participants meet face to face; there are written public spheres, and there are anonymous, faceless public spheres made possible by the new electronic technologies (Habermas 1996a: 373 ff.).

With this Habermas makes adjustments for the critique that his early 'bourgeois' concept of a public sphere involved a fixed, ontological distinction between the public and the private spheres – between the common good and special interests. 'We must distinguish *procedural constraints* from a constraint or limitation on the *range of topics* open to public discourse' (Habermas 1996a: 313). We return to this. Further, the criticism has been that the original use of the concept involved *one* uniform and national public sphere, and that the increasing division and duplication of the public sphere which followed in the twentieth century (for example represented by the labour and feminist movements) must inevitably be regarded as a decline and not as a contribution to the democratisation of society.[5]

In line with a proposal from Nancy Fraser, Habermas now also distinguishes between *weak* and *strong* public spheres. The latter concept alludes to parliamentary assemblies and discursive bodies in formally organised institutions, while the concept of weak public spheres signifies deliberations outside the political system (Fraser 1992). It is in the latter sense that Habermas primarily uses the concept, and it is the weak public spheres that he links to opinion-formation processes. Will-formation and decision making are reserved for institutionalised discourses in the political system in for example The Parliament, which is conceived of as a strong public.

The free public debate has the ability to both identify and interpret social problems; this is where we find the attention shaping and innovative opinion-formation processes. Here we have to do with a *context of discovery* for the perception and thematisation of problems. By contrast, parliamentary, institutionalised discussions help us filter out and make priorities between claims on the basis of the more immediate demands of justification which arise when resources are limited and decisions must be made. Habermas refers to this as a *context of justification* (Habermas 1996a: 307). It is in this interplay between institutionalised and non-institutionalised discourses that a collective process of self-understanding can take shape, and this is where deliberative politics has its place. The principle of popular sovereignty can only be realised under the guarantee of a free public sphere and competition between political parties, together with representative bodies for deliberation and decision making (Habermas 1996a: 171). Gutmann and Thompson add that continuous and repeated deliberation, punctured by periodic elections give the best hopes of democratic responsibility (1996: 144).

The public sphere is a communication structure localised in *civil society*: 'a communication structure rooted in the lifeworld through the associational network of civil society' (Habermas 1996a: 359). With this, Habermas emphasises the connection with a social sphere that is distinctively different from the economic sub-system and its instrumental orientation and contract-based behaviour. In sociological terms, civil society can be identified as a sphere outside the state and the market, which is private and potentially public, and which constitutes the social basis of the public sphere. It is characterised by forms of activity which are not only means to reach other ends, but which are also ends in themselves. It contains an *intimate sphere* based on personal emotional bonds within primary group relations (relations of love, friendship and kinship), a *voluntary sphere*, which is an area for activity and experience based on membership in secondary groups, and finally a *cultural sphere* for the interpretation and formation of opinions. Within civil society, the voluntary groups or associations are the central institutions for the handling of collective problems (Habermas 1996a: 367). Although the public sphere first of all represents a normative category, a connection is here made to the sociological term of associations. In this way, Habermas is able to express the connection with the element of unconditional solidarity, patriotism and collective action in civil society on which the public sphere thrives. He also makes a distinction between the concepts of 'organisation' and 'association'. Organisations are groups which are formed in order to realise given, pre-political interests. They are normally referred to as interest organisations. By contrast, associations are the kind of free groups or social movements which are formed without any pre-defined goal, but where the purpose is developed through the cooperative process itself.

PUBLICITY AND RATIONALITY

The public sphere is constituted by freedom of communication, which makes possible the public use of reason. It is not a concrete institution, but rather a communication network. This network of 'subject-less interaction' is not given special, restricted functions that aim to realise particular results. The public sphere is that social space, which is created by communicatively acting operators which are bearers of opinions and interests. The public sphere is not characterised by a type of interaction, which is designed to bring about immediate results; rather, it is a forum where what happens is determined by what can be made generally understandable, interesting, believable, relevant and acceptable, through the use of everyday language. A public sphere not only consists of a *speaker* attempting to convince an *addressee* that he is right; there is also a neutral third party present – a *listener*. When we have such a triadic relation between a speaker, an addressee and a listener, the speakers feel obliged to argue primarily with a view to obtain the support of the listeners. The general public functions as a judge or referee in relation to the contending parties. It is then the neutral observers that have to be convinced.

It is the spectators that must be convinced, but their approval can neither be bought nor enforced. This is a consequence of the logic of a public argumentation process, where the resources that an actor has at his disposal must remain hidden. When we argue publicly in favour of a particular solution to a practical problem, it is useless to threaten or pressure our opponents to accept our standpoint. That would be the same as admitting to neutral listeners that our arguments are insufficient. One practical consequence of this is that if somebody is able to demonstrate that the spokesperson for some cause is a resourceful person, or that she has a personal interest over a specific outcome, her motives are immediately rendered suspect and her arguments lose much of their force.[6] Those who manage to demonstrate that their own arguments are both unselfish and correct, have the greatest chance of winning in an open, public debate. Thus we may say that such public testing of views contributes to eliminating bad and selfish arguments, so that only the generally acceptable ones are left. Since it is the existence of a public that constitutes the public sphere, it is the public that possess the authority to decide what rules should apply. When an outcome is accepted even though it is different from what each of the participants originally intended, it may have to do with the actors' ability to learn and to change their opinions through the exchange of arguments.

The result of a public debate is hence unpredictable, in a strictly, mono-causal scientific sense. It is the quality of the interaction that becomes the explanatory category. The outcome of a discussion is determined by the arguments as well as the agents' ability autonomously to form an opinion, communicate it and make others accept it. When the public sphere is functioning properly, opinion and will-formation can neither be explained solely with reference to the actors' qualities, resources, status and power; nor can it be explained in terms of socio-economic, cultural and ecological variables. It can only be explained with reference to arguments and justifications and the manner in which the communication between the actors took place. In a non-deformed public sphere it is the rules for rational communication that govern the formation of opinions. Prototypically, it is the interaction process itself that generates results. Deliberation explains politics when the public sphere is functioning.

Whether the public sphere is functioning and whether it is of importance to political decision-making, are hence questions which do not only depend on whether it can be proved that actors through public argumentation have managed to obtain a breakthrough in relation to the political system; it depends even more on whether, and to what extent, it can be demonstrated that rational, impartial arguments have won out. To test if the public sphere has had any influence, we must demonstrate that political decisions are not only a result of the influence of powerful groups, or the dispositions of strategic actors, or the politicians' attempts to please voters, but rather that they are based on qualified and generalisable reasons. Do we have any examples of this?

ANTENNA AND SLUICE

If we look at the development of public policy in a wider historical perspective, we find that the great reforms have been inspired by extra-parliamentary actions. Norwegian examples are the organisation of the Labour movement and the pressure to get an alternative economic policy and greater social equality. This social mobilisation was instrumental in the creation of the modern welfare state. Many lay movements may be interpreted as the result of an active and powerful use of public reasoning. We may mention low-church pietism, the temperance movement and the Norwegian language disputes, but in particular recent social movements such as the workers', women's, students', and green and antinuclear movements. For a long time they have had a decisive influence on public policies. These were policies which were implemented although they were against the established interests of the political system. Admittedly, some movements used the party system and formed interest organisations that also had resources (threats) that were used to enforce their demands. However, from the beginning they were *social movements* which used the public sphere in order to mobilise support for their cause. They used the weapon of demonstration, campaign and appeals, and made use of the press and media for all they were worth.

Such social movements have added dynamism to modern politics. They have forcefully advocated new causes, come up with new arguments, and put matters in a new light. Popular protest movements develop and help realise new collective goals and new forms of rule by making modern norms and values acceptable to wider social strata in modern societies (Eisenstadt *et al.* 1984).They have not taken over the established parties or the established interest organisations, but have forced them to relate to new problems. Gradually, this pressure, these demonstrations and campaigns and argumentation have exerted influence and have changed the political agenda and the programmes of the political parties considerably (cf. Olsen 1983). The new social movements represent a form of intellectual mobilisation, which has its source in international relations. They constitute an independent explanation of social change (Bendix 1978: 266). With reference to Danish conditions, Jørn Loftager maintains that the development has shown

> that the existing political parties and organizations have *not* had a monopoly on defining the content of politics. Various popular initiatives and new social movements have to a great extent contributed to defining the political agenda.
>
> Why is it that gender and equality problems have made themselves felt to such an extent? Why is there no nuclear power in Denmark? Why have environmental questions come to the front in the political debate? Why was an 'alternative majority' formed within the Danish parliament in the discussion of foreign and security policy in the 1980s? Why have new so-called 'post-material' values come to compete with material ones? The series of such questions could be continued, and in all cases the answer could not be ascribed primarily to activity within the established political parties.
>
> (Loftager 1994: 179)

It is not the actors' self-interests or the strategies of powerful groups that explain the opinion-formation processes of which the new social movements are exponents, but the universalistic character of the topics. The opinion-formation processes which are used by the new social movements must be explained in terms of their general character, and not with reference to agents' self-interests or the strategies of powerful groups. The relevant causes win through not because they represent the interests of a particular group, but rather because they express something general, which motivate other groups to act in solidarity. If we look at the public sphere in a wider time perspective, we are struck by its positive role as a sensitive sensor or *antenna vis-à-vis* new questions and problems. Neither détente politics, nor minority rights or third-world problems were taken up by the established system; instead they were advocated through extra-parliamentary actions (cf. Dalton and Kuechler (eds) 1990, Offe 1990). To explain this ability to influence politics, we must see the public sphere not only as a 'warning system' with sensors, but also as a 'system of influence' (Habermas 1996a: 359).

Core and Periphery

Today the public sphere does not primarily consist in the gathering of citizens in the forum or in a café to discuss political questions. As already mentioned, there are many public spheres, and they are constituted by different kinds of discourses, not only the strictly moral discourse, or the pragmatic or professional types, but also aesthetic, expressive and ethical kinds. These discourses thematise an increasing number of relations, and they reach deep into questions which were previously kept away from the public debate, for example private, intimate and religious questions. The borderline between the public and the private spheres has been moved considerably during the last few decades, because of the novel form of unrestrained communication and criticism.

A possible interpretation is that that new forms of communication which originated with the Enlightenment in particular were stimulated as a result of the educational revolution of the 1960s and the subsequent criticism of hierarchical authority, self-appointed authority, stiltedness, technocracy and guardianship. Late-modern *society* is characterised by dominant discourses, world views and forms of understanding which are put under pressure, and new, more unconstrained patterns of communication emerge. New forms of communication develop, new discourses emerge and are in constant competition. The public sphere has become anarchistic. Today it forms *'einen wilden Komplex'*, which is vulnerable to perversions and communication disturbances. On the other hand, this open public sphere is a medium for unlimited communication, and it is hence much more sensitive to social pathologies (Habermas 1996a: 374).[7]

The public sphere 'sluices' new problems into the political system. *It besieges the parliamentary system without conquering it*, according to Habermas (who here sounds like the Italian Marxist Antonio Gramsci). Habermas makes use a model developed by Bernard Peters (1993: 327 ff.), in which the circulation of political power is modelled according to a centre-periphery scheme. The parliamentary complex consists of formal political institutions or strong publics, such as the parliament, political parties and different types of bodies that influence choices and decision making – such as expert committees, boards and councils, which commonly include members of interest organisations. This complex constitutes the centre, because it has the authority to make binding collective decisions (Peters 1993: 331). This centre, which is the focus of attention and enjoys the highest legitimacy, is connected to the periphery though a set of channels of political influence (ibid.: 340 ff.). The periphery is civil society, which consists of pressure groups, clients, organised interests, NGOs, etc. For this system to be regarded as legitimate, it must be demonstrated that its decisions started with a communication process which originates in the periphery, but which has been introduced into the formal power apparatus in a procedurally correct manner (Habermas 1996a: 356).

> In the proceduralist paradigm, the public sphere is not conceived simply as the back room of the parliamentary complex, but as the impulse-generating periphery that *surrounds* the political centre. In cultivating normative reasons, it affects all parts of the political system without intending to conquer it. Passing through the channels of general elections and various forms of participation, public opinions are converted into a communicative power that authorizes the legislature and legitimates regulatory agencies, while a publicly mobilized critique of judicial decisions imposes more intense justificatory obligations on a judiciary engaged in further developing the law.
>
> (Habermas 1996a: 442)

While the centre possesses instruments of power and decision-making competence, the public sphere is the only possible channel of influence for the periphery. The public sphere lacks formal instruments of power, it does not make decisions, and it does not discuss all aspects of a problem. This may be regarded as a weakness; however, it is also a resource, as the participants may give full attention to the general and principal aspects of a matter. Given that it is no obligation to act, it is easy to understand the public sphere's sensitivity to all types of problems. Actors need not take a stand on all practical difficulties, trivialities and considerations with regard to available resources, customs and precedence that formal decision-makers must take into account. The public sphere is not responsible for the practical consequences of its opinion formation. It may therefore on a free basis relate to all types of injustice, imbalances, suppression and threats against people and the environment. Here the moral perspective takes precedence, or more precisely, the moral perspective in politics is formed when matters are viewed from a public perspective. It is only from a neutral and impartial point of view, when taking into account all relevant considerations and interests, that authoritative decisions can be made with regard to justice and what principles should guide public decision making. When matters are tried in relation to moral standards, all ungrounded deviations and injustices become problematic. It is social injustices and what is *not* done or *not* given any attention which are challenging and which have a mobilising effect. They are the very ammunition of the public debate.

This aspect of the public sphere may also explain why particular groups with particular (human) needs can quite easily get through to political bodies by means of the public media. This results in problematic and often obviously 'wrong' decisions. Many see this as an unfortunate aspect of the public debate, and not only as a result of pressure-group activity in a media-ruled society. One standard criticism is that the public sphere is unable to handle the problems of individuals – of concrete others – with the respect which is required in order to protect privacy and human dignity. If that is really the case, it is not due to a defect of the public sphere, but rather of the politically institutionalised justification discourse, according to Habermas. 'Problems voiced in the public sphere first become visible when they are mirrored in personal experiences,' (Habermas 1996a: 365). What is public and what is private – which interests are universal and which are special interests – are not given. There are no objective criteria which tell us that a topic rightfully belongs in one specific sphere; over time there have been vast changes with respect to which problems are regarded as private and which public. The point is rather that the rules of communication are different. The public sphere deals with problems that arise in the private sphere, in so far as they become publicly relevant. In contrast, the private sphere is regulated by those rules of communication that must be followed if we wish to establish intimacy and emotional ties (Habermas 1996a: 366). We can now specify the deliberative model of power and the political process model it implies.

THE CIRCUIT OF POLITICAL POWER

In the public sphere ideas and standpoints are launched; here individuals and groups claim support for their demands; here the prevailing collective mentality is challenged, and here the politicians must defend their solutions against the opposition. In the public sphere, actors can form common opinions with respect to what should be done, as well as about what is valid and what is required from a moral point of view. In the public sphere, problems are discovered and pressure is exercised against public agencies. Here decision-makers are controlled and constitutions are monitored. In this perspective, public norm-forming processes are also given independent significance; they influence the self-understanding of the citizens. They shape common opinions, and they also create standards for how equality/inequality should be approached, and of what are authentic expressions of our collective self-understanding and identity. The public debate thus has an important integrative role in society, even if it should not result in concrete political decisions. It *shapes identities and generates solidarity*. This is the first step in the reconstruction of the political circuit.

From this complex repertory of opinions and wills, which exists in various public forums, some opinions crystallise which gain so much support that it is possible to demand that they should be translated into practical policies. To put it differently, the political-administrative system is continuously bombarded with demands and expectations from different bodies in civil society. Normatively, only those wills are justified which are 'laundered' – i.e., purified and tested – through a public debate about which are legitimate interests, what is for the common good, and what is in the equal interest of all. As mentioned in the previous chapter, the *social power* in civil society, viz. the factual, non-authorised power of actors and groups, must therefore be converted into normative valid power – *communicative power* – through a public debate. This happens in accordance with a standard of justice, i.e. on the basis of which considerations and demands deserve public attention, and which deserve it to a lesser degree or not at all. The open discourse that deals with the justification of needs and interests constitutes the second step in the reconstruction of the political circuit. In a liberal public sphere 'actors can acquire only influence, not political power ... public influence is transformed into communicative power only after it passes through the filters of the institutionalised *procedures* of democratic opinion- and will-formation and enters through parliamentary debates into legitimate lawmaking' (Habermas 1996a: 371).

When social power has been subjected to such a test, the political-administrative machinery comes into effect. In this third step of the political circuit model, we not only ask which demands deserve public support, but also which resources are available to support legitimate demands. We ask how demands fit into established political programmes, and into administrative and legal categories. Demands must be justified in relation to a wider set of considerations. In the political system, the arenas for deliberation and bargaining are institutionalised. In representative assemblies and in corporative and administrative bodies, one must take account of political programmes, established rights, prerogatives, precedence, resources, etc. before demands can eventually be converted into decisions or bills that can be sanctioned and implemented. Thus, it is a rather cumbersome process from the point where a common opinion is formed and until it is converted into a common will and developed into collective goals that can again be translated into binding decisions, i.e. into administrative power. These procedures are meant to filter out poorly grounded, unjustified, politically impossible and legally untenable demands. On the other hand, an integration of different standpoints is taking place, as well as a reinforcement of relevant arguments to the extent that relevant cases satisfy normative requirements. This transformation of power is outlined in Figure 9.2.

In the discourse-theoretical model of politics, the filtering and integration processes are related to the logic of argumentation. However, the point is also to demonstrate that politics is something more than simply making concrete decisions about the distribution of resources. All the communication and opinion-formation, debate and argumentation which is continuously taking place in the public sphere is conducive to solidarity in civil society. In lucky moments, these processes create increased understanding and insight as well as a we-feeling that is sensitive to inequality and injustice in the population. They shake the citizens together into a community, but they also contribute to clarifying relevant distinctions. It is necessary that some things are excluded for actors to see that they have something in common. Identities are based on exclusion. Citizenship rights, for example, are by their very nature reserved for the members of a state – the inhabitants of a community that share some common opinions, commitments and evaluations.

A rational open public debate does not only establish more qualified agreements; it also discloses mock agreements and ritual consensus and creates an understanding of relevant distinctions, nuances and limits. Communication not only creates identity, but frequently also differences; not only agreement, but also more conflict and disagreement, because increased communicative freedom also leads to increased individuation (Habermas 1992c: 140). A free public exchange of views makes for more well-founded convictions and rational standpoints required for the political system to function legitimately and efficiently. The right to vote can only become effective if there is an effective use of communicative freedom in society. Only after extensive communication is it possible to establish

Figure 9.2 *The transformation of power*

common understandings and enlightened opinions, which enables citizens to vote according to their own convictions, without the danger of a completely random or irrational result. In this perspective, political parties take on the role of mediator between public opinion-formation and political decision making. Even though they have specialised in winning elections and function as a recruiting system for political leaders, they are also catalysts for public opinion and hence participants in political opinion-formation processes (Habermas 1996a: 443). We may add that also interest organisations, which are represented in the neo-corporative channel of influence, take on such a mediating role. Figure 9.3 illustrates this model of the political process.

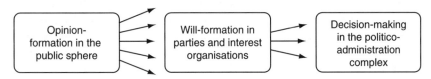

Figure 9.3 *The political circuit*

One question is whether administrative power is really controlled by communicative power in complex welfare states, where so much of the authority to make decisions is delegated to the professions and administrative agencies through frameworks and enabling legislation. These not only make decisions which are based on discretion; they also contribute to new legal developments by using their authority in new areas. To a considerable extent, they create new law. The same can be said about the legal system, because it has made itself independent in relation to input from legislative power. Administrative bodies as well as courts make law. The law has become an autonomous and self-referring (auto-poetic) system (Luhmann 1983, 1995). It has been claimed that the public is too far away from the bureaucracy to exercise any control, and that administrative procedures rather contribute to making the bureaucracy independent of the support of relevant parties (Luhmann 1983: 121). Luhmann speaks of an *unofficial counter-circuit* of power. He claims that the administration dominates politics, while politics, through the political parties, 'suggestionise' the public opinion. Furthermore, due to societal complexity, it is impossible for the public to gain sufficient insight, overview and control (Luhmann 1981: 164). The administration functions according to its own logic of implementation, and normative justifications often appear to have been formed in retrospect. The justifications that are necessary to make an appropriate decision are provided by the administration itself. In that case, we are witnessing a process of justification which is based on an exchange between mass loyalty and welfare-state contributions; hence, legislation and political decision-making follow the logic of social power and that of the experts rather than the logic of democratic public opinion formation.

However, although the administration treats political decisions and legal regulations instrumentally, it must nevertheless continue to plead normative grounds in order to achieve legitimacy. We have previously pointed out that administrative bodies must refer to a rational basis for their dispositions. For the sake of legitimacy, they must emerge as a resource to justice. Habermas's point (1996a: 484) is that such normative reasons constitute the resources that are needed for communicative power to be implemented. He further claims that the communicatively shaped power in the public sphere can have indirect influence by gaining control over those justifications which are available to the administrative system. 'Communicative generated legitimate power can have an effect on the political system insofar as it assumes responsibility for the pool of reasons from which administrative decisions must draw their rationalisations,' (Habermas 1996a: 484). The extensive extra-legal (as well as extra-professional and extra-administrative) debate that surrounds administrative agencies makes it possible in principle to test the worth of this form of independent power. This happens when the administration's use of normative arguments is criticised and declared invalid in a public debate. It is an empirical question whether the public sphere merely creates mass loyalty, i.e., is reduced to an acclamation forum for the power holders, or if it is a real source of popular power. To answer this, we need, among other things, a closer investigation of the effects of some relatively novel principles relating to general transparency and openness in the administration (cf. the 'Freedom of Information Act'), the special right to information and hearing for affected parties, as well as the ombudsman institution.

In addition to bureaucracy and expert power in the administration, the new media situation represents a challenge to democracy understood as government through public deliberation. However, it does not only represent new possibilities of manipulation, but also new possibilities of argumentation.

LIMITS TO MANIPULATION

The criticism of the mass media is substantial in Western societies. The strong position of expertise, the mix of entertainment and information, the fragmentation of connections, simplification, stereotyping, interruptions, disturbances, etc. contribute to de-politicise the public sphere (Chomsky 1989). Political debates often take on the form of a circus and have the entertainment character of mass-culture (Edelman 1964). The new communication media function as catalysts for this development. The possibilities for propaganda and for influencing public opinion are growing, and they provide economically strong actors with new ways of articulating their interests and realising their goals (Abramson 1990). This makes the conditions for political discourse less favourable, and it provides more room for symbol politics. There is a lot of one-way communication and mutual understanding is blocked. Because of the new communication media, the public sphere is today non-dialogical in an entirely new way (Thompson 1990).

The development of modern computer technology and the Internet have opened up new channels of influence and manipulation. New information spaces are established – viz. so-called Cyberspaces – which can be used for manipulative and propagandistic purposes. Here PR-agencies and consultant businesses can prepare information for special interests. Net actors can influence the public opinion by directing people's attention in a certain direction. Leakage, blackening of opponents and presentation of 'objective' information, which in fact serves special interests are some of the forms of influence that have been demonstrated. The consultant business has discovered a new lobbying market in presenting PR-material to clients. New media make it possible for powerful institutions with special interests to buy themselves space in the news picture, and they provide the power holders with an effective instrument for influencing the public opinion in the direction they want. Experiences from the USA indicate that the net will become an important tactical instrument in the struggle to obtain the favour of the voters. The net also gives small activist groups new possibilities of making themselves felt (Rash 1997: 87 ff.). However, the effects are unclear, and there are contradictory tendencies and contradictory courses of development.

The new communication media reinforce linguistic expressions, but they also increase the possibilities of communication, and they build bridges in time and space.[8] Hence, the level of information increases as well, along with the possibilities of criticism. It is not least because of the media development that the new social movements and civil initiatives, NGOs, have been able to obtain a political breakthrough to such an extent. New issues have been put on the agenda and have received support *against* the interests of capitalists and the established political parties. As mentioned before, this has for example happened with regard to security politics, minority politics and environmental protection. The limits to manipulation and mass hypnosis lie in the fact that propaganda and advertising inevitably depends on the categories of human language, according to Habermas. It is not only the case that communicators have the language in their power; language can also be used against them. Also manipulators are bound by the rules of truthful communication, because only when at least someone believes in the spoken word can cheaters succeed. These rules can of course be manipulated, they can be stretched and made the subject of irony, but they severely recoil on those who are caught sinning against them. Linguistic manipulations thus have their absolute limit in the intelligibility and credibility of the linguistic expressions. Rhetoric is Janus-faced (Habermas 1990h: 10), i.e. it involves speech and justification requirements that punish pure sophistry. In open, democratic societies this represents constraints on legitimation strategies. The possibilities of sincere communication reduce the scope of manipulation. It may also be argued that the decline which has been taking place within the media, and which is frequently seen in association with the media's increasing tabloidisation and market orientation, has been described in terms that are too one-sidedly negative.

This description does not take into account the vital role played by publicly owned media in most Western countries – i.e. their reputation, size and status, and the importance of this in attracting talents and producing programmes of high quality (Keane 1993: 235). Neither does the description take into consideration (a) the fact that technological advances provide novel conditions for opposing and critical voices, and (b) the possibilities this gives for protecting oneself from the appeals of the mass media.

(Keane 1984, 1989, Perrow 1984)

The increased level of education and reflection makes new demands on 'the mediators' and makes it easier to reveal attempts at manipulation. A sharpened critical ability, alternative channels of information and new attitudes towards the media make it easier to unmask the tabloidisation of the media, as well as purely commercial interests. Many studies show that citizens are aware of the distinction between propaganda and enlightenment, between entertainment and information, between report and comment.

(Keane 1991, cf. Chambers and Costain (eds) 2000)

The description does not take into account the new possibilities of the Internet to create dialogic public spheres by establishing discussion groups where two-ways communication is made possible.

(cf. Buchstein 1997: 250)

The homogenising effects of the media are limited, according to this analysis. Public opinion can not be subsumed under one single concept or one hegemonic discourse. There is not *one* public opinion, but many. Public opinion-formation is characterised by fragmented attitudes and standpoints, by dissent and value conflicts. It reflects different experiences, traditions, interests, and social affiliations rather than a fabricated will, as claimed by Schumpeter (1942, cf. Thompson 1984). In addition, there is a normative aspect of public sphere that cannot be brushed aside by empirical arguments. The idea of a free and open debate counterfactually takes care of the idea of a legally governed popular sovereignty. Only by using their public autonomy can legal subjects legitimately establish the rules for their coexistence. The very concept of a public sphere refers to a condition where the public sphere has developed into a structure that stands on its own feet. It refers to a reflective form of self-understanding. The more it is criticised, the more it is accused of being on the decline, the clearer it gets that it is actually functioning. When we criticise the quality of the public debate, we at the same time confirm its existence. Before anyone can make strategic use of the public sphere – before anyone can act manipulatively and bargain about public opinions – it must have become sufficiently developed to possess general standards and an audience to which reference can be made. Only with the existence of an audience can we speak of a public sphere. We can only complain about faults and wants of popular rule by investigating how communication has been disturbed in relation to the idea of undisturbed communication. The awareness of the potential of the public sphere is probably most often latent in Western democracies, but it takes shape and demonstrates its power when it is mobilised by groups in order to realise common interests (Habermas 1996a: 364).

CONCLUSION

The public sphere is the place where civil society is linked to the power structure of the state. The public sphere is the basis for deliberative politics because it is here that the power must find its justification. Here binding decisions must be justified *vis-à-vis* the citizens who are bound by them. The public sphere, which is based on communicative freedom, gives citizens the right to discuss the general conditions for the common weal. Here they can make the politicians responsible. It is only through public deliberations that citizens can find out if political decisions are *correct* because only then are counter-arguments voiced. Although this idea exists as an essential part of the self-understanding of the democratic constitutional state, we have seen that the increasing societal complexity has made it necessary to renounce the idea of rule through public reasoning. Nevertheless, Habermas's view of the role of the public sphere from the 1990s is more positive than the view expressed in his book on the public sphere from 1962. This is not only due to the fact that Habermas now employs different basic concepts in his political analysis; it is also related to some changes in his views on democracy.

In the 1960s and 1970s, Habermas's views were more radical and closer to a substantive understanding of democracy based on real popular participation in political will-formation than are the views which he advocates today (cf. Habermas 1975: 36). Now that system-theoretical elements have been introduced, and he distinguishes between the opinion-formation processes that take place in the weak public sphere and the will-formation processes of the political system, we find that the distance to radical, participatory democratic ideals has increased. The insistence on the fundamental position of the law in a democratic society points in the same direction. Political discourse is regulated by procedures that cannot be ignored. Because of the pluralism and complexity, and because the constitutional state is unavoidable, democratic decisions cannot govern the whole society. The implication is lower ambitions on behalf of popular rule.

The question is, however, if Habermas is not going too far in reducing the possibilities of political government via public opinion and democratic will-formation. Due to the sharp distinction between deliberative practice in the weak public sphere and will-formation and decision making in parliamentary assemblies, it becomes difficult to explain in what sense public deliberation and political decision-making are connected. Thus, the very idea of popular sovereignty is at stake. As pointed out by James Bohman (1996: 180 ff.), it is difficult to determine who is the political subject, and how communicative rationality intervenes in the formation of a majority will. We seem to need a concept of *deliberative majorities*. Also majority decisions must be based on good reasons in order to claim legitimacy. A reason is only convincing as long as it is *somebody's reason*. A disintegrated and decentralised concept of popular sovereignty such as that advocated by Habermas can not govern. It is not fit to establish that foundation of common convictions which is necessary in order to formulate a collective will. It becomes difficult to derive authoritative instructions for what should be done, if no connections are established to social interests and needs articulated by real actors.

In the previous chapter, we imparted nuances to Habermas's analysis of majority decisions by referring to the fact that these are always justified with reference to their substance. We further argued that they are at least in someone's interest and can hence be supported by 'good reasons'. In this chapter, we have problematised Habermas's distinction between opinion and will-formation processes by referring to the powerful role played by social movements in determining public policies in several areas of our society. Neither are deliberations restricted to the public sphere; they also take place internally in the political-administrative system. Here also opinion-formation frequently takes place, not only decision making on the basis of established views; here also there is a need for communicative rationality. Habermas is open to this fact to some extent, since he endorses the idea of parliamentary deliberations as an institutionalised discourse – a *strong public sphere*. However, this is first of all limited to parliamentary, political assemblies, and secondly, he does not say much about how the frames for such interaction can be designed in order to ensure rational outcomes. We will therefore in the next chapter take a closer look at the possibility of institutional design in a discourse-theoretical perspective, with the emphasis on the professional, collegial form of organisation which is so central in modern welfare states.

Notes

1. At the beginning of the 18th century, London had approximately 3,000 coffee houses, and towards the end of the century, Germany had 270 literary societies (Habermas 1989a). Cf. also Michael Warner (1990) for an analysis of the public sphere of colonial America, based on correspondence.
2. It is thus claimed in the *Critique of Pure Reason* that 'The touchstone whereby we decide whether our holding a thing to be true is conviction or mere persuasion is therefore external, namely the possibility to communicate it and of finding it to be valid for all human reason,' (cited from Habermas 1989a: 108).
3. John Stuart Mill is here greatly indebted to Wilhelm von Humbolt's *Ideen zu einem Versuch, die Grenzen der Wirksamheit des Staates zu Bestimen* from 1791 (Humbolt 1954).
4. Habermas found it flawed because the fictitious identity of the roles of property owner (bourgeous) and of human beeings pure and simple (homme) (Habermas 1989a: 56, 87).
5. For more information on this debate, cf. especially Negt and Kluge 1994, Calhoun (ed.) 1992, Fraser 1992, Habermas 1992d.
6. However, we are not saying that a standpoint and the arguments behind it *should* automatically be rejected if it is possible to prove a connection to the spokesperson's self-interests. In addition to self-interest, the relevant view may well be supported by general, morally valid arguments. Thus, it need not be illegitimate to advocate one's own interests; however, there may be reason to investigate the argumentation more thoroughly if someone refers to general interests in order to justify a standpoint which at the same time serves their own interest (see Eriksen and Weigård 1997).
7. However, the question is whether this variety of public spheres, which creates different identities, does not also fragment the political community: 'Identity politics' has become a prominent feature of American politics (cf. Gutmann 1993).
8. Cf. also Habermas 1984: 372.

CHAPTER 10

Communicative design

INTRODUCTION

We have seen that discourse theory is the source of a particular political theory and a particular conception of democracy. To be sure, the relevance of this perspective in political analysis is controversial, and in many areas operationalisations and concrete analysis are missing. In particular, we need concepts at a lower level of abstraction, and with a more distinct practical affinity. However, these must be developed through a closer confrontation with empirical realities; they cannot be established solely through principle-oriented theorising. Context and situation make distinct normative demands. In concrete situations we have to take into account empirical considerations as to what may happen when principles of justice are put into practice (Phillips 1995: 38). We dealt with this in Chapter 7 when we discussed application discourses and the principle of *realpolitik*. Not only is coercion often necessary in order to realise a democracy; in addition, rational discussions must be institutionalised. Even in a free society, these discussions will be fragile; they will be exposed to disruptions, and they will be vulnerable to deceit and self-deception of various kinds (Elster 1983: 42). The discourse-theoretical interpretation of modern constitutions explains the rational content of the procedures of the democratic constitutional state, the structures required to ensure legitimate deliberation and decision-making processes. The question is whether practical instructions can be derived from discourse theory when it comes to institutional design, i.e. procedures and criteria for legitimate solutions to normative, political questions. Is it – from a discourse-theoretical perspective – possible to prescribe guidelines for how institutions, norms and procedures for problem- and conflict regulation should be established?

Discourse theory provides criteria for rational decision making and for evaluating the validity of norms based on the conception of a justly organised process. A deliberation and decision-making process is fair to the extent that all parties involved are heard and can voice their opinion on equal terms, and when the discussion has lasted long enough for a mutually acceptable agreement to be reached between the members of society. The very point of a theory that aims to be practical on democratic premises is that it is the citizens themselves who must determine the rules. They are the competent ones when it comes to deciding what is a good outcome. In a process of enlightenment there can only be participants (Habermas 1994b: 101). The theory does not only function as a critical standard in the evaluation of existing social and political power structures; it also has a liberating purpose as it refers to the conditions that must be met for a society to be free. Unconstrained communication is not the quintessence of the good society; it is rather what enables citizens to decide its content.

Another important aim is to contribute to a conception of institutional design which is different from that expressed in conventional constitutional theory, as we know it from classical liberalism and modern economic institutional theory. Departing from alternative conceptions of rationality, it is possible to establish a design concept that may at the very least supplement the traditional ones. Instead of starting with some idea that human nature gives rise to actions that must be controlled, or that there is a particular function which is to be maximised through the institutional design, the starting point of discourse theory is what it means to bring about a rational solution to problems and conflicts through argumentation. In discourse theory law is not only seen as needed for constraining non-compliers but also for facilitating the trust and stabilisation of behaviour expectations required for actors to act morally or communicatively rational. Further, discourse theory is based on an assumption that only needs which can be articulated, and only interests which can be presented in public, can claim validity. Only when they can be verbalised and made public is it possible to test their creditability (Benhabib 1986: 338, cf. Eriksen 1996). From this theory, we may deduce criteria which can be used to judge if a consensus has come about in a valid manner, and if the outcomes can be considered legitimate.

There is, however, no rule without exceptions. In the real world it is impossible for everybody to be heard. In practice, any 'just' procedure will be incomplete and thereby unjust. Any actual attempt at sketching out the guidelines for a discourse-theoretical institutional design, will necessarily imply the exclusion of certain interests. It is therefore important to implement procedures that will block irreversible decisions, and which ensure that outcomes are re-evaluated. However, we will not adopt a utopian view of institutional design. Criteria for evaluating existing institutions and for turning them into democratic institutions will be developed, but these should not be seen as an ideal or blueprint of democratic design. The aim is rather to use discourse theory to establish institutional principles that can bring *relatively more* communicative reasoning into decision-making situations. Thus, the point of departure is that institutions and practices may be constructed in a manner which increases the scope for either the communicative or instrumental rationality. In the next section we set out the analytical frame of reference.

The Analysis

In the present context, communicative design pertains to institutions with decision-making competence, and encompasses all public and civil agencies and problem-solving organisations in general. Institutions possess rules that frame and limit actors' behaviour, by stating what is to be done and how. Institutions impose duties on the individual, establish rights and introduce prohibitions through authorised roles and action prescriptions. On the one hand they exempt individuals from the demand to justify their actions and to make their own evaluations by laying down the premises for and by sanctioning action choices. This can be referred to as *institutionally bound speech acts*. The role prescriptions state what is expected from the actors. On the other hand, institutions also depend on support from individuals in order to survive, and they therefore have norms based on a common value basis, which commit their members. The norms in question say something about the institution's constitutive foundation, about its identity, function and status. It is important in any situation that such constitutive rules do not become objects of utility calculations. With Durkheim (1964) we refer to this as *the non-contractual element of the contract* (cf. Chapter 4), i.e. that which makes choice possible, but which is not itself an object of decision. However, this value basis is not given once and for all. It has to be interpreted and reinterpreted, and this can only be done in a legitimate manner to the extent that there is room for institutionally unbound speech acts. It is the possibility of communicative, illocutionary action, unrestrained by conventions and power politics, which may test and develop the institution's identity in a creditable manner, i.e. in such a way that members may be motivated rationally – out of a sense of duty – to act in conformity with norms.

Thus, the rules are both cognitive and moral in nature, which reflect the fact that institutions face a double requirement; they have to provide both meaning and results. By meaning is meant that the rules must be of such quality that they are able to mobilise support and loyalty from the members. This requires that they have a certain ethical or moral substance so that they will be obeyed out of respect. The rules of the institutions state what is proper and correct behaviour, and they sanction breaches of norms. On the other hand, institutions are social constructions designed to solve common problems and prevent or resolve conflicts (cf. Ostrom 1992). Therefore, they also need rules which say something about how results should be obtained. A logic of appropriateness must be supplemented by a logic of consequence (March and Olsen 1989: 160). Institutions represent choice frameworks within which instrumental orientation is constrained by moral and ethical norms. Hence, institutions have rules that tell the members both what is proper or correct, and how they should proceed to achieve results. The latter points to the institution's organisational level, which means that an institution also has to be instrumental in the realisation of collective goals. The difference between institutions and organisations may be expressed as follows: while an organisation depends on its ability to obtain results, an institution does not necessarily cease to exist even if it does not produce the expected results (Offe 1996a: 206). How to apply discourse theory to institutional design?

Discourse theory can only be used for this purpose if we make a distinction between purely normative principles, which apply under ideal conditions, and principles that apply under non-ideal conditions. We have previously developed the reality discourse based on the ethics of responsibility, which take into account the significance of strategic action, and which may be seen as a supplement to discourse theory.[1] We will now proceed to ask how discourse theory can handle those requirements that agents are faced with in a practical decision-making situation, i.e. a situation where time and resources are limited, and where communication may be disrupted by power and strategic action. How can discourse theory contribute to improve the possibilities for communication under non-ideal conditions, in a way that heightens the quality of the decision-making?

We begin with the argumentation rules that apply to the ideal discourse situation – institutionally unbound speech acts – through which we arrive at the discourse principle. By applying the discourse principle to the concept of institutions described above, we arrive at the ideal principles that apply to democratic organisations. This is the second step in the derivation, and it concerns the procedural requirements argumentation must meet for the final agreement to be regarded as valid. Such principles are of a quite abstract and general character, and they must be seen in relation to the structural limitations within which the communication process takes place. In this manner, we are able to establish more specific institutional principles, and this constitutes step three in the deduction. When we at the fourth level apply these principles to the requirements for efficient decision making, we can derive organisational principles, i.e. norms for argumentation and for group composition.

The organisation of the chapter follows this logic, but first we will briefly comment on the conventional design perspective, as we know it from economics. In the following part, we introduce the discourse-theoretical *ideal requirements for democratic design*, their basis and status. From these ideal requirements for rational communication, we deduce *principles for institutional design*. The third part of the chapter discusses the *organisational principles* that emerge when the institutional principles are applied to the requirements for efficient decision making. Here we establish concrete norms for group composition and deliberation, which will enforce a change of roles, and which aim at generating rational decisions. These are eventually supplemented by agreement-promoting measures, so-called *mechanisms*. Finally, we discuss some modifications and limitations. The point in this connection is that we must lower our ambitions concerning the rationality of the final decision, and thus design institutions for second-best solutions and for the re-evaluation of outcomes.

INSTRUMENTAL DESIGN

Institutional design, which may be perceived as a wider concept than constitutional design, has received a great deal of attention lately. This is due to the constitution-building processes in the EU, South Africa, Eastern Europe and Canada, but also because it has been used in connection with the handling of environmental problems, the designing of resource management regimes and the resolving of civil conflicts in general. Within the social sciences, such processes have been discussed particularly from the point of view of economic theories.[2] The question here is how institutions can be designed in order to obtain optimal solutions to collective problems.

Worst Case Scenarios

The theory of rational choice is in its original form modelled as a utilitarian calculation process. In a purely aggregative decision-making procedure, actors choose by signalling their preferences. The sum total of these preferences becomes the collective choice. This theory is based on several assumptions: There is a given set of actors (who the affected parties are is not problematised), who are faced with a given set of non-manipulative choices, and who have exogenous and fixed (non-adaptive) preferences against which the choices are evaluated. The arrangement that emerges when all preferences are summed is complete (transitive) and rational, which means that the collective result respects the individuals' preferences in one way or the other (Elster 1983: 30 f.). This variant of utilitarianism and welfare economy assumes that 'a society is just when its institutions maximise the net balance of satisfaction' (Rawls 1971: 24).

The criticism against this form of institutional design is that it does not take seriously the differences between preferences, and thus also between persons.

Utilitarianism does not respect distinctions between individuals, and possible qualitative differences between various individual goals. This represents a moral problem as one individual's misfortune may not be discounted to other people's happiness account: 'there is no moral outweighing of one of our lives by others so as to lead to a greater overall *social* good' (Nozick 1974: 33, cf. Rawls 1971). Not only does utilitarianism fail when it comes to recognising that welfare cannot legitimately be maximised as an average value for a group of individuals (and that the level of welfare hardly can be compared interpersonally). In addition, the utilitarian institutional perspective does not take into consideration the fact that some measures and values are superior and thus more worthy of recognition than others. Consequently, it is not possible to assess the validity of goals or values, only the common welfare. Institutions are designed and evaluated according to its efficiency potential, i.e. according to how good they are at maximising the collective welfare. In a utilitarian calculation process, the standard of rationality is the utility or effect the use of resources has on the total welfare. However, this does not give us an adequate measure of justice. It does not tell us how we can protect the people's integrity, their particular needs and their demand for respect. The freedom of the individual is not given an inviolable position.

Another variant of economic design is represented by the *public choice-theory*, which claims that procedures are legitimate when they respect the actors' preferences on an equal basis (Buchanan 1991, Ferejohn 1993). This can only be achieved when there is unanimity, which can only be expected in the case of Pareto-optimal solutions, i.e. when an improvement in some people's situation does not aggravate other people's situation. Hence, the parties have a veto right. Anything short of unanimity will threaten the rights of the minorities (Brennan and Buchanan 1985: 22, cf. Buchanan and Tullock 1962). Within this tradition, many hypotheses have been developed about how different constitutional arrangements representing different sets of incentive structures will influence behavioural patterns and collective choices. These hypotheses are based on the assumption that agents act strategically. One has modelled the effects of asymmetric information in cases of conflicting interests, misrepresentation of interests (manipulation), and how various sanctioning mechanisms can relieve those problems.

Although their approaches are different, none of these two alternatives of institutional design suffice from a normative perspective. Traditional utilitarianism does not give sufficient protection to the individual when his/her interests clashes with the regard for the collective good. By contrast, the *public choice* version of utilitarianism 'solves' the dilemma by giving the individual absolute precedence. However, this may also result in morally reprehensible situations, because individuals who profit from unreasonable privileges are given the right of veto against attempts to abolish them (Sen 1970: 22). In short, it is very difficult to reach collective decisions when unanimity is required. What none of these schools have adjusted for is that we need a normative understanding of when it is possible and correct to make a majority decision. When is it legitimate to take a vote and set aside minority interests, and when is this not legitimate? The requirement of unanimity may prevent 'rational' decisions from being made, because it also gives the right of veto to 'quarrellers'. Secondly, this is related to another weakness of the economic approach, i.e. that no adjustments are made for the fact that actors' preferences are of differing quality, and must be tested in relation to this fact in order to be entitled to respect. Election results based on the aggregation of preferences are arithmetic artefacts, devoid of any moral quality. The outcome might just as well have been the opposite, and in that case just as valid (as mentioned in Chapter 6). Preferences must be justified in order to be considered valid. Unreasonable or inconsistent requests can not be regarded as rational reasons for action. Neither is it possible to avoid evaluating the consistency and validity of preferences when we identify them. The concept of rationality must also include the quality and consistency of preferences, in those desires that govern our actions (Elster 1983, cf. Davidson 1980). It is problematic to call an agent rational, even if he or she chooses the best means to obtain a goal, if the goals or preferences themselves are inconsistent or morally reprehensible. Habermas may add that since needs and wants are interpreted in light of intersubjectively shared cultural values 'the descriptive terms in which each individual perceives his interests must be open to criticism of others,' (Habermas 1993e: 67).

The liberal concept of constitution as well as the microeconomic concept of institution are based on worst-case scenarios, which means that institutions are designed to prevent the worst prospects from being realised. It is presupposed that agents act in their own interest, and that they are potentially corrupt. It is therefore important to design sanctioning systems that prevent negative effects of asymmetric information, of strategic voting, etc. First of all it is important to keep greedy and powerful actors in check. The success and merit of liberalism has to do with exactly this ability to build defence mechanisms against power abuse. Constitutions give the citizens rights *vis-à-vis* the state, and function as negative sanctioning mechanisms that prevent majority tyranny as well as monopoly of special interests. In the American context, the focus has been on the division of power – i.e. on what is referred to as 'checks and balances' between state powers (bicameral system, right of veto, a powerful Supreme Court, and federalism) and on ensuring a balance between public interests ('*countervailing forces*' and pluralistic representation of interests) etc. (Moe 1990). One of the problems with this type of design is that it treats everybody as 'devils', as claimed by Kant in *Perpetual Peace*, and thus runs the risk of creating devils even out of 'angels'.[3] Constitutions do not only limit arbitrary use of force, nor do they only make possible rational problem solving; they also influence the identity and character of the citizens (Elkin 1993: 124). This way of thinking about constitutions is based on a fixed perspective on human nature – a rather pessimistic anthropology. Designs are made on the basis of a presupposition of egotism, which in turn legitimates egocentric action. This type of design can have atomistic consequences. It may undermine the norm structures and solidarity in civil society because it expands the area of utility maximisation.

Constitutional design, like any other institutional design, is neutral neither in relation to social norms, nor in relation to interests, since some lose and others profit under an institutional arrangement. Thus, some types of action motivation are favoured at the expense of others. In the liberal tradition it is possible to prevent injustice, but it is not possible *to find out what justice consists in*, according to Wolin (1989). It is impossible to say anything about what positively must be done, which collective goals should be realised, and which social problems should have priority. In contrast to conventional theories of institutional design, which presuppose that agents are instrumentally and strategically motivated, discourse theory presupposes the ability to submit to better arguments. This is a precondition for being able to agree on which norms are valid and which collective goals are legitimate. It is therefore important to design institutions in a way that enhances the actors' chances and abilities of expressing themselves and of questioning established arrangements and assertions. A prerequisite for legitimate decision-making is that the validity of norms is tested and the legitimacy of goals is evaluated in an open debate. Only then is it possible to establish common standards and perceptions of justice, as well as those legitimate collective goals that constitute the basis for the evaluation of consequences and for cost-/benefit calculations. Instrumental design presupposes communicative design, because there is a need for normative discussion of the common parameters that are required in order to decide, for example, which are Pareto-optimal solutions in an organisation. In such cases, actors' activities are coordinated on the basis of their universal or trans-subjective interests, and not on the basis of convergent coinciding interests. Thus, what we have here is reciprocal (that is, mutually oriented) actions.

Constitution and Critical Evaluation

Constitutions not only allocate competences, positions and powers; they also establish a framework for government without any specific goal, but with an infinite number of possibilities (Elkin 1993: 125). Constitutions specify fundamental procedural conditions for democratic legislation, and must therefore be interpreted as *abstract structures of legal principles*, which may be specified in various ways according to empirical circumstances. The discourse-theoretical interpretation of the democratic constitutional state understands it as a set of ideals that can be used in order to evaluate the actual institutionalisation of political power. With the help of these, one may ask if established institutions represent a good way of realising democratic ideals. It is further possible to test whether legal norms and political majority decisions are in accordance with moral requirements. However, the legitimacy of political legislation does not only depend on the fact that the laws are in harmony with morality; they must also be in harmony with a broader set of action justifications. The discourse-theoretical interpretation of democratic legislation procedures also allows a pragmatic examination of relevance, accessibility and the selection of information. Further, there is room for an ethical interpretation of the situation where one asks if the values and strong evaluations that inform the choices are authentic expressions of a collective identity. Finally, we may ask if the bargaining about non-generalising interests has been carried out in a correct manner, if the correct voting procedure has been chosen, if the result of the election is legitimate, and if compromises have been reached in a fair way (Habermas 1996a: 233). Thus, important normative lines of demarcation have been developed within the model. In this perspective, the constitution establishes procedures for the exercise of the right to self-government. The law is not only justified because it is in accordance with constitutional procedures; it must also reflect the opinion and will-formation process that precedes the legislation. It is not legitimised exclusively by clauses carried out by the legislator (Maus 1989: 208).

In modern democracies, constitutions are a way of ensuring the citizens' private and public autonomy through institutional design. Constitutions guarantee civil and political rights, they regulate the activity of political bodies by stating rules for elections, representation, and decision making, and they generally establish areas of competence, terms and qualifications. Such arrangements are sensitive to the power of factions and to the representation of self-interest in political bodies (Sunstein 1988a: 352). They are intended to secure the popular control of the state powers, and to isolate representatives from pressure groups, so that the political discourse is given a degree of autonomy in relation to material interests and force (Sunstein 1985: 41). The purpose of several regulations within modern law is to increase political equality and secure the conditions for deliberative decision-making, or 'to promote deliberation in government, to furnish surrogates for it when absent, to limit factionalism and self-interested representation, and help bring about political equality' (Sunstein 1990: 171). The democratic constitutional state is hence not a fixed idea. It is at least halfway institutionalised, as shown by some existing principles for representation. Since the seventeenth century, we have seen the introduction of the following principles:

1. Those who govern are appointed by election at regular intervals.
2. The decision-making of those who govern retains a degree of independence from the wishes of the electorate.
3. Those who are governed may give expressions to their opinions and political wishes without these being subject to the control of those who govern.
4. Public decisions undergo the trial of debate.

(Manin 1997: 6)

The prevalence of such principles makes the communicative design into a realistic and not merely a normative project. The conditions for democratic legitimacy are not only counterfactually present in our ideas about self-governance. They are also, at least partly, institutionalised and entrenched in the democratic constitutional state. These ideas and conditions are what we appeal to when from a discourse-theoretical perspective we embark on the project of designing institutions in such way that communicative rationality increases.

THE PRINCIPLES OF DESIGN

Discourse theory establishes an ideal standard for institutional design. It relates to the rules that regulate the relation between free and equal individuals who cooperatively want to solve problems. More precisely, the standard pertains to those norms that regulate behaviour in social relationships where interaction is based on free and open communication. The discourse-theoretical concept of institution is derived from the conditions for a legitimate consensus. The discourse principle as applied to institutions gives procedural criteria for conflict and problem-solving, and for the derivation of concrete organisational principles. All this will be discussed step by step, and we start out with the ideal standard of discourse theory.

Process Rules

The normative knowledge of discourse theory is based on a multi-step argumentation, which can be sketched in the following formalised and simplified manner:

1. To justify a normative assertion in a rational manner means that those involved in the discussion try to agree about what is the right thing to do, i.e. about what norms are valid when a concrete answer is required to a morally relevant problem. We may then come up with norms such as 'it is unjust to discriminate against someone because of their skin colour'.

2. Such agreement can only be obtained by following the rules for an open and fair discussion. The rules for an open discussion can be formulated as 'formal-pragmatic' prerequisites for rational argumentation. These may be called *process rules* for argumentation, and are formulated as follows:

   (2.1)[4] Everyone who can speak may take part in the discourse.
   (2.2)a Everyone may problematize any assertion.
         Everyone may introduce any assertion into the discourse
         Everyone may express his or her attitudes, wishes, and needs.
   (2.3) No speaker may be prevented from exercising the rights laid down in (2.1) and (2.2) by any kind of coercion internal or external to the discourse.

   (Alexy 1989: 193)

3. These rules reflect the respect for the inviolability of the individual, as well as the norm that the viewpoints of different individuals should be respected in an equal and neutral way. Thus, the rules have a certain moral substance.

4. From this follows the moral norm that actors should be given the opportunity to express their opinion in a free and equal manner (Benhabib 1992: 31).

This standard regarding the assessment of just procedures refers to a situation where all force and all limitations of time and resources are set aside. Everyone should have an effective opportunity to participate, to express their opinion as well as their interpretation of interests and needs. This demands fear- and power-free bodies and a high information level. In practice this requires

- equal access to discussions

- no limitations on the discussion

- equal opportunities to oppose an assertion, and

- equal opportunities to put forward arguments (Kemp 1985: 186).

This meta-norm for justification of norms constitutes the ultimate court of appeal in order to criticise established institutional arrangements, and it represents a fundamental standard for the evaluation of democratic legitimacy. It may be used to settle the question whether the outcome of a collective decision-making process deserves the members' recognition. When there is dissatisfaction with the outcome, and conflicts and problems arise in connection with an institutional arrangement, one may look into who has not been heard – or how they have been heard and taken into consideration. When, for example, differences in resources gives different terms of admission, when discussions are limited because the members have deep rooted commitments and loyalties, and when participants retain information regarding interests and standpoints, or misrepresent their interests, the deliberations will not be of such a character that they lead to a qualified consensus or to mutually acceptable results.

In discourse theory the interests and values of each party is ensured by the provision that only those norms that are accepted by those affected in a free debate are legitimate. This implies that no one is privileged and that each is able to present his own reasoned judgement. Here it is a problem that the principles in question are not arranged lexically, i.e. in preferential order. Instead they are given equal weight. Because we are not told which principles are most important, the theory becomes under-specified and unable to discriminate between different democratic arrangements (Blaug 1997: 109). We will therefore add one requirement, viz. that there must be *a qualitatively good discussion*. The formal requirements cannot in themselves answer the question of how the needs and views of the various actors may influence the final decision. It is not enough that there are equal opportunities to participate and discuss; we must also make sure that arguments are heard and taken into consideration, i.e. that the debate is good. This follows from the discourse-theoretical concept of procedure. A decision can be justified neither solely by the formal qualities of the procedures followed, nor solely by substantial reasons. What is important is that the process has paid sufficient attention to objections and counter-arguments, so that the decision can be defended against public criticism.

> legitimation through procedure does not result from the structure of procedure itself, which guarantees the right of participation, but rather from the quality of discursive processes which they make possible.
>
> (Maus 1996: 880 f.)

By procedure is hence also meant procedures of argumentation, and not only legally organised processes, i.e. formal or judicial procedures. Any substantial standpoint raises a demand for justification and for knowledge that can only be met by argumentation. On the one hand, it is a fact that only substantial viewpoints may justify an outcome. We cannot know if a case has been treated correctly until we know the parties' grounds. On the other hand, the validity of the reasons can only be tried in an open argumentation process; consequently it is the process that ultimately justifies outcomes (Habermas 1996c: 1508). But how can we know the quality of the reasons in non-ideal situations?

Design and Rationality

Habermas is himself cautious when it comes to the question of institutional design. To design practical institutions is outside the theory's area of competence. Because of the level of abstraction the discourse theory is unfit for deriving actions' prescriptions.[5] The regulation of any conflict situation involves concrete individuals with a unique biography and life story that deserve respect. Situational insight and practical judgement (*phronesis*) are required, as mentioned in connection with the application discourses discussed in Chapters 4 and 7. Designing institutions *ex ante* may therefore easily be at odds with the moral requirement that we should protect vulnerable individuals. The danger is that a particular institutional set-up may be selective, exclusive, or characterised by asymmetrical argumentation, meaning that some dominate others because of an unequal distribution of resources. Thus, there is a danger of paternalism and new forms of technocracy under cover of 'just' procedural principles. The liberation of the suppressed must be their own responsibility; it should not be put into the hands of theoreticians. They will easily take on the role of master thinkers or moral experts. The most this theory can do is therefore to prescribe autonomous public spheres which can function as safety nets and courts of appeal for problematic decisions.

This is why we have to give up the utopian presupposition of a completely just procedure, i.e. a procedure which guarantees rational and legitimate decisions. However, even if we lower our ambitions, the theory may be used in a constructive manner. The idea is that we may come a few steps closer to a rational debate, even under non-ideal conditions. The theory must be supplemented with some realistic elements, and its status must be relative. We thus postulate that this way of reaching a decision – *ceteris paribus* – is more in accordance with a normative rationality requirement than are other forms of decision making, such as instruction, voting and strategic bargaining.[6]

Relativisation also implies that the design principle is not applied at the level of society, but at the level of social organisation – groups and associations – where the participants themselves may choose the framework of their interaction. Here we build on a proposal by David Sciulli (1992, 1996), who links Talcott Parson's concept of the *collegial organisation* of the professions to legal procedural requirements.[7] In this connection, we will point to the variety of organisation forms – outside as well as within public administration – where interaction is not necessarily authoritarian and governed by legal regulations or strategic action. We are here referring to all the committees, councils and panels, teams and cooperative bodies, which are engaged by public authorities to solve problems and conflicts without a blueprint, and which therefore make communicative action both possible and necessary (cf. Eriksen 1999). The relevance of communicative design can be seen also in these bodies as they often amount to mini-populous or strong publics, and not only in voluntary organisations or in the general public sphere. The discourse principle requires that the procedures which regulate the discussion, its mandate, the selection of participants, issues and problems must be approved in an open and rational debate.[8]

In everyday speech, the concept of design calls forth associations of manipulation. It has to do with controlling behaviour in order to obtain particular goals. Actors try to achieve something by designing institutions in specific ways. All those who are trying to improve current conditions by prescribing rules of action, are performing design (Simon 1969: 55). If one design institutions with the purpose of changing patterns of action, this is an act of will where one manipulates choice situations in order to obtain goals. In its simple form, the design principle thus breaks with Kant's third formulation of the categorical imperative, viz. that human beings should also be treated as an end in themselves. On the other hand, the design concept is essential because although practical decision-making involves free and equal participation, resources scarcity affects choices and efficient goal attainment, and thus there are restrictions on participation, time and subjects. Social organisations are, as is reflected in their structure of communication, command and control, means to realise collective goods, and the parties participate for instrumental reasons. It is therefore important to establish a concept of design, which meets the requirements of effective decision making, while at the same time respecting the integrity and autonomy of the individual. However, it should be emphasised that not all collective questions can be decided in this manner. We must build on worst-case scenarios when we try to maximise security or prevent corruption and free-riding. Also, when the aim is to ensure predictability and legal protection, or to realise super-ordinate political objectives in an equal and standardised manner in relation to different groups, we must build on instrumental and bureaucratic principles of organisation.

Organisation and Efficiency

Social and political organisations are established in order to realise goals and distribute goods and burdens efficiently. Their *raison d'être* is not primarily the protection of everybody's interests, but the attainment of collective goals. Their purpose is instrumental. Thus in practice, we have to consider design within an organisational order which is interest- and power-based, or which has arisen on a conventional basis, and for that reason does not respect everybody in a neutral and equal manner. Hierarchy, division of labour, technical mechanisms of coordination, and formal communication and information channels are all required in order to get something done which would otherwise not have been done. The organisation principle reduces transaction costs and is justified by its efficiency. This often licenses asymmetric relations between the members, and it is the source of conflicts, disagreements, and struggle for power and influence. For example, there may be conflicts about the distribution of resources within organisations, about rights and duties within companies, and about influence within political decision-making bodies. Thus, the question is how to handle the relationship between efficiency and legitimacy, which basically are intertwined: even an optimal decision may be opposed if it has not been made in a procedurally correct manner, and, similarly and simultaneously, even good procedures are worthless unless they also produce good and timely decisions.

Discourse theory proposes the rational resolution of conflicts, based on the conception of a justly organised decision-making process. It suggests a method that is allegedly superior to other conflict-regulating mechanisms. It is superior because it respects the actors' autonomy by adopting the principle that only those norms are valid which are approved by the parties in an open debate. When someone has not been heard, or when someone does not get the opportunity to – or does not dare – voice their opinion, it is impossible to know whether the norm in question is valid. Consequently, the discourse theoretical requirement of qualified agreement guarantees the individual a strong position, just like *public choice* theory. It grants the participants equal status, on paper and in reality.[9] On the other hand, the requirement of a rational justification of standpoints may lead to a shift in blocking standpoints, so that we avoid the inertia which often results when unanimity is required.

However, this easily gives rise to the thesis that everybody must participate in the decision-making process if we are to know which decisions are rational. In other words, the more people participate, the more optimal the results will be.[10] There are several problems with this. First, we run into a delimitation problem when it comes to deciding who are in fact parties in a case. Many people are directly or indirectly affected by decisions, but it is practically impossible to give them all participatory rights. The state of affairs in modern societies is increasingly determined by decisions made at an earlier time, and by current decisions that are not under democratic control. It has been maintained that within the modern so-called *risk society*, the gap which exists between decisions made by authorised decision makers, and the potential negative consequences these may

have for the parties, is increasing and is becoming more difficult to bridge politically (Beck 1992, Luhmann 1993).

Secondly, as already demonstrated by Plato, it is a simple observation that
there is no connection between increased participation and increased rationality.
On the contrary, it turns out that the higher the number of participants, the more
difficult it is to reach agreement, and the more sub-optimal are the decisions (cf.
Barber 1983, 1984). This can be explained by the simple fact that the more
people are involved, the more questions have to be answered, and the more views
and positions have to be clarified. Inclusive procedures not only increase the use
of time and resources; they also increase the possibilities that the debate may
involve demagogy, dramaturgy and seduction. Extensive participation can lead
to a situation where special interests are given priority at the expense of common
interests, because the situation becomes over-complex and turbulent. Free
riders get an easy way to success. In what way can discourse theory handle the
requirements of efficiency in decision making?

The fact that the legitimacy of decisions is the result of an open debate does not
exclude claims of efficiency. In any practical context, the actors are faced with
pressure to make decisions with limits on time and resources, and decisions must
be made even when there is no agreement. It is impossible to discuss all aspects of
a case. We cannot wait to make a decision until everyone has been heard, and
often even a sub-optimal decision is better than no decision at all. There are
several types of disruption of communication. First, there are structural disruptions, as when economic, legal and political imperatives demand that some goal is
reached instantly, no matter what communicative rationality tells us. Secondly,
there are time limitations. Reaching agreement is costly, and we need to act even
when there is disagreement. Thirdly, there may be motivational limitations, as
when someone has an interest in a particular outcome, or when the will to do the
right thing is weak, i.e. when we act against our better judgement. Finally, there
are cognitive limitations, as when actors have limited horizons of understanding
or a limited ability to process information and to view things from others' perspective. Majority vote and bureaucratic instruction are therefore a prerequisite
for pressing decisions to be made.

In such situations, it is necessary to lower one's ambitions with respect to the
procedural requirement that everybody should have equal opportunities to voice
their opinions. The view of discourse theory in this respect is that such concessions to efficiency considerations may be perceived as a 'trade-off' between procedural justice and efficient decision making. However, such a trade-off must
itself be tried in an open debate. It is the possibility of a discursive qualification of
such concessions to effectiveness that decides whether or not this is legitimate.
Thus, exceptions to the principle of open, rational debate must itself be justified
in an open debate (Baynes 1991: 1, Blaug 1996: 67).

There are several problems pertaining to the contingency of the communication, i.e. the fact that outcomes are determined by factors beyond the control of
the discourse participants. Among other things, a number of facts must be clarified before the discussion can start and some facts and participants are given prior
to the discussion; and path dependency, time and coincidence determine the
course of events, rather than rational arguments.[11] However, the *contingency*
problem, which has been pointed out by Luhmann (1971), has changed since the
introduction of the distinction between justification and application discourses.

In justification discourses, problems relating to time and knowledge are put into parentheses, and we ask what is right or just from an impartial and neutral perspective. By approaching the question from a general point of view, or from the ideal perspective of humanity as a whole, we may arrive at a presumptively rational answer to what is a justified norm, i.e. what is valid for everybody, with no exceptions. In this way, deontologically valid norms are established, i.e. norms which it is everyone's duty to follow. However, it is impossible in this kind of discourse to predict all possible combinations of empirical facts or changes in objectives and value structures. It is these kinds of problems that must be dealt with when norms are applied to concrete situations, and in such cases a different procedure must be used if we wish to arrive at the correct result (as mentioned in Chapters 4 and 7). As we know, in practice justified norms may collide, and in order to find out which norm is appropriate in a specific situation, we need to take into consideration all relevant information be it of empirical or normative nature. This conceptual strategy makes it clear that the rationality presuppositions which must be met in order to obtain a rational justification of norms are not totally unattainable after all (Günther 1993).

Another difficulty is that in discourse theory, the validity of the outcome depends not only on the fact that the different parties are heard on an equal basis. The problem is not only the existence of demagogues and sophists who may manipulate the audience, but also the fact that a procedure which includes the parties, and which takes into account strategic action and unequal distribution of resources, does not in itself guarantee a reasonable outcome. If the process itself is not good, if the debate is dull and the arguments are not tested, the decisions will not be good. A good – correct or right – result presupposes a good discussion. Therefore, the procedures that ensure participatory rights cannot guarantee rationality, as already mentioned. Also those demands that must be made on the structure of normative argumentation must be met for rational results to be expected with some certainty. We may speak of a discourse, which has the power to change the agents' preferences and justify interest-regulating decisions only if certain conditions are met. Specifically, actors must relate to each other's statements and reasons in a sincere manner, evaluate each other's views in a critical manner, and be prepared to justify their own claims and succumb to the force of the better argument. Thus, in addition to the requirements that there must be equal access to discussions, no limitations on discussions, and equal opportunities to discuss, there is the requirement of *qualification*. This requirement implies that actors must not only approve a solution; rather, they must do so on the basis of rational reasons, of mutually acceptable grounds. This is why we have to involve means of organisation that may compel role-taking and rational communication. Different organisational initiatives and social mechanisms may be used to ensure a qualitatively good debate, not only a democratic and efficient decision-making process. However, before we discuss this in more detail, we will derive some more concrete institutional principles, which follow when the discourse principle is applied to actual institutions under realistic circumstances.

Principles for Institutional Design

The concept of communicative design relates to the fact that groups may be composed in a more or less legitimate manner. Our point of departure is an already existing formally organised order where both patterns of participation and communication are pre-structured. If institutions exhibit a minimum of democratic features, discourse theory may be applied. Groups may use that power which is invested in institutions in order to make more democratic bodies. It is also possible to create new public spheres for open discussions (Bohman 1996: 133, 197 ff.), and we may institute new and more deliberative bodies to include previously excluded groups (Gutmann and Thompson 1996: 42). When it comes to the composition of groups, we can use David Sciulli's proposition of a *collegial form of organisation*, which is found in various types of civil and public institutions. Here it is the members themselves who decide their mutual terms of cooperation, as they have equal rights and similar formal competences. Sciulli uses a modified version of communicative rationality as a characteristic of the collegial organisation, and in his opinion it can be used to evaluate the degree of democracy in social and political associations. In this connection, he specifies some procedural norms that are meant to function as a threshold, which a group must cross in order to become a collegial type of collaboration. Individuals are competent to understand and accept mutual commitments when the following fundamental procedural norms are met:

1. The rules that constitute the group are general and comprehensible to all parties.

2. The rules are consistent, and they give all parties the opportunity to participate.

3. The rules may be revised by the parties.[12]

These superior principles ensure everybody equal rights to participation within an order that is self-statutory but are too general to give directions for practical organisation. It is therefore important to derive more concrete instructions for how common problems should be solved. However, different types of questions require different procedures.

In all situations where conflicts and problems need to be solved, it is vital to define goals and collective commitments, and this has consequences for the interests of individuals. Hence, unavoidable normative validity claims are raised. We need to ask what is the *right* thing to do, in relation to the affected parties. Further, we must ask what kind of problem-solving strategy should be used to achieve different collective goals. It is mainly when ethical and moral problems are involved that democratic procedures are required. Thus, questions that are obviously of a technical or pragmatic nature may be solved without extensive participation. Although it is difficult to specify the borderline between the two types of problems in a neutral manner, there is fairly wide agreement in our culture as to which types of tasks can be solved with the help of technical and scientific expertise, and which can not. This has to do with the fact that there is a categorical distinction between *is* and *ought* in our culture, which again constitutes the distinction between science and politics, and between politics and administration. To the extent that we can isolate questions where the answers depend only on what *is* actually the case in the world, and not on what we think *ought* be the case, we may rightfully claim that solutions may be chosen without the participation of the parties involved. Scientific evidence and empirical knowledge are often sufficient when we wish to find out what is actually the case, and when we have to do with means-end and cost-benefit considerations.

According to discourse theory, there are no objective criteria for what is the correct answer to normative questions. We can only know if the answer is satisfactory if certain procedural requirements have been met. The outcome must be based on insight and good reasons. It must not be contingent or accidental. In the final instance, the answer has to stand public exposure. It must be rational to such a degree that it can be defended against criticism. We therefore need practical institutional principles that can satisfy several requirements:

- they must be so inclusive that outcomes can be accepted by the parties;
- they must be so exclusive that it is possible to reach a decision within a reasonable time frame;
- they must be able to sanction strategic actions;
- they must be able to prevent paternalistic argumentation;
- they must be able to compel role exchange (Kettner 1993).

These less abstract principles of institutional design still have the character of being assessment standards. They show what is required for outcomes of communication processes to be regarded as legitimate. These principles say nothing about why actors should solve problems communicatively, or what makes them act communicatively rather than strategically. In order for the group to get together, to function and be able to discuss problems rationally, these principles must be made concrete and embedded in practical organisation principles.

ORGANISATION DESIGN

Several types of practical means may be used when it comes to stimulating rational deliberation and decision making. This concerns both (I) conditions related to the composition of the group and the type of tasks involved, and (II) conditions related to how communication between the participants is regulated.

Organisation Principles[13]

(I) First, it is important to establish representative and competent groups, and it is also vital to neutralise differences in resources and power. Important measures in this respect are rules that include relevant parties, the distribution of competence, the abolishment of force, and resource compensation for deprived groups including advocates for weak or incompetent actors. Such initiatives are necessary in order to establish equal possibilities for everybody to promote their cause and voice their opinion. In the bodies we are discussing here, what is at issue are the conditions for an *application discourse*, which requires an adequate description of the situation in order to make it possible to choose the appropriate norms for the regulation of interests. It is therefore important to include all normatively relevant aspects of the context in question.

However, it is not enough to be able to justify the outcome of a decision. It is also important to establish bodies which can motivate actors to participate, and which are able to make decisions without using too many resources. Thus, problems that require discussion are of a special nature; they must be of importance to the participants. We propose the following practical principles for the design of deliberative and decision-making bodies:

There must exist:

1. A problem which requires *practical judgement* or *normative discussion*. The problem in question should not be of such nature that it may be answered through scientific procedures or through the aggregation of preferences. It should not be of a theoretical or pragmatic nature only, but must require normative considerations. If the answers can be computed this type of participation is redundant.

2. A *documented problem* which motivates the persons involved to participate. The participation must be related to a subject that is genuinely interesting to those invited. Participation it should not just be an end in itself. Participation which takes place exclusively on the basis of expressive or learning-related functions – participation may develop human capacities and enhance the we-feeling – will not be sufficient motivation, and may also potentially disturb the debate between those who are genuinely affected by the problems at the agenda.

3. A willing, competent, and trustworthy mediator, who can lead and throw light on the discussion. This should be a neutral *third party*, who, due to oversight and analytical abilities, can help eliminate non-essential factors and attempts at manipulation and trickery, thereby enabling the parties to think through their actual disagreements and differences in a reasonable manner. The mediator should not be a head of negotiations, examiner, expert, judge or arbitrator, but rather a person who makes sure that the conditions for communicative rationality are met to the highest possible extent. The neutral third party is a person who is familiar with the rules for unbiased argumentation, and who can thus lead the debate by pointing out inconsistencies in the speakers' argumentation and force them to view the matter from each other's perspective. According to the literature on the neutral third party, the person in question makes a diagnosis and functions as a catalyst, bringing about solutions that would otherwise not have been realised (Fisher 1972). The third party contributes to analysing the conflict, 'but also facilitates the group discussion by providing the appropriate situation, norms and interventions' (Fisher 1983: 323). A chairperson who acts according to these criteria may be fit to function as a third party.

4. Participants with approximately the *same capacity*. This means that the participants must be able to acknowledge each potential participant as an equal party. Any disparity may be relieved by advocatory communication, which means that the weak parties may get appointed a more efficient spokesman for their interests. Asymmetric competence may also be relieved by limiting the possibilities that strong agents have to pursue their own interests. For example, there may be limitations on speaking time.

215

The above principles represent some minimum requirements for legitimate organisation; however, they do not by any means guarantee rational decisions. They are necessary, but not sufficient conditions for such decisions to come about. It may be difficult to list further conditions independently of a particular context, but normally the following additional conditions must be met:

5. No party with great influence must be excluded, since these may easily sabotage any agreement. When powerful parties are included, they are also made responsible. However, their strong position should be balanced in the deliberation process by giving the weaker parties assistance in presenting their arguments.

6. If we include too many in the process, it becomes impossible to view the others as single actors, rather than an undifferentiated crowd. In such situations, free riders will be able to operate efficiently. The number of participants must be kept at a manageable level. One line of reasoning here is that while small groups will reach decisions more efficiently, larger groups will increase the possibility that more generalisable interests will win out. Hence, larger assemblies will potentially produce more legitimate decisions.

7. There must be a *contract zone*, i.e. a set of decisions which can be supported by all parties if agreement is *not* obtained. If there is no such contract zone, it may be created with the help of a third party, or through a preliminary clarification of the principles and limits for the discussion (Dryzek 1990: 100, cf. Young 1972, 1979).

The concept of a contract zone needs to be defined more precisely. It may be seen as a decision, which is made prior to the actual proceedings concerning the actors' intentions. Here the parties make it clear, to themselves and to the others, what they are not willing to risk in the interaction. They ask questions such as how do matters stand now, what is the situation, what should be discussed, what do we agree on even if we should continue to disagree on the actual case. The participants agree to observe procedures and rules, and to continue to cooperate even if they fail to agree on this particular issue. Such a contract zone helps reduce the number of relevant questions in the decision-making process, and it helps cool down differences and enhance trust, while at the same time a common definition of the situation is established, which will make further discussion easier. In general, it is important that procedural questions take precedence over substantial ones, i.e. that the parties make it clear which procedural rules they can accept and which eventualities they cannot accept. If we follow this strategy, there will be no disagreement about procedures when substantial questions are discussed (cf. Preuss 1996).

Principles of Argumentation

(II) There are several norms for how the discussion should proceed. For example, there are norms of cooperation which say that participants must reveal their real opinions, and that they must consider the opponent's arguments. In addition, the discussion must last long enough for the issues to have been thoroughly examined, i.e. all positions must have been clarified, and all relevant information presented. Such rules will have to vary according to the nature of the case and the specific language games and the argumentation types that accompanies it. Robert Alexy has formulated four rules which he claims are conditions that must be met for linguistic communication to produce *valid* results.

(1.1) No speaker may contradict him- or herself.

(1.2) Every speaker may only assert what he or she actually believes.

(1.3) Every speaker who applies a predicate F to an object *a* must be prepared to apply F to every other object which is like *a* in all relevant respects.

(1.4) Different speakers may not use the same expression with different meanings.

(Alexy 1989: 188)

We have already (p. 207) given an account of the *process rules* of discourse theory. In addition to these validity rules, we need some principles for allocating the burden of argumentation. Concerning the requirement that agents must justify their claims, it is obvious that it must also include the right to explain why they are perhaps *not* willing to provide such justifications (Alexy 1989: 192). We can distinguish between four sets of *justification rules*, which all rest on the principle of the burden of proof or argumentation:

(3.1) Whoever proposes to treat a person A differently from a person B is obliged to provide justification for so doing.

(3.2) Whoever attacks a statement or norm which is not the subject of the discussion must state a reason for so doing.

(3.3) Whoever has put forward an argument is only obliged to produce further arguments in the event of counterarguments.

(3.4) Whoever introduces an assertion or an utterance about his or her attitudes, wishes, or needs into a discourse, which does not stand as an argumentation in relation to a prior utterance, must justify this interjection when required to do so.

(Alexy 1989: 196 f)

In any concrete discussion, such demands can only be met to a certain extent, and they must be adapted by the participants themselves. However, they must be supplemented by rules of a more ethical and moral nature, for if the parties are not treated with the necessary concern and respect – if they feel disrespectfully treated or offended in the discourse situation – they will not come forward with their opinions. It is a common observation that there are a great deal of fear and informal power relations present in discourse situations, and that this prevents formally equal parties from behaving in an equal manner. Competence-based arrogance and condescending attitudes flourish. It is therefore essential to have a set of rules that ensures the moral autonomy of the participants, so that they will not feel like instruments in the search for the truth. Also intellectual instrumentalisation is instrumentalisation, and it may potentially destroy social communities (Hösle 1990: 151, cf. Hösle 1997). Finally, we need norms for politeness, friendliness and decency, i.e. so-called *solidarity rules*, which may ensure mutual confidence and respect during the discussion. The chairperson may be of help here, bringing in a greater degree of security and safety. By means of these argumentation rules, we may define more precisely what is required of the chairperson. He or she must make sure that the rules are followed to a greater extent. This means that he or she should preside over the debate, aiming to make all arguments heard, reveal inconsistencies and misunderstandings, clarify the governing idea of the debate, make the issues more concrete, and seek to reach a result by adhering to formal proceedings.[14]

There is a limit to how far we can go with institutional design without relating the principles to the cases that are to be regulated, and which raises particular normative claims. The principles we have explained here are probably general enough to be used in most cases but additional moves may be necessary in order to make actors take each other's arguments seriously. The organisation principles laid down will therefore be supplemented with some institutional mechanisms that will influence the actors to move in the direction of agreement in decision-making contexts. Note that we are here speaking of a type of agreement that cannot necessarily be regarded as qualified.

How to Achieve Agreement?

There are many suggestions and 'recipes' telling us how to negotiate better. There are explanations for why communication fails, and for why collaborating bodies succeed or fail. There is a great deal of practical wisdom in this area. We will point at various types of arrangements at the social micro- and macro-level that may apply. In addition to practical instructions for how we can create a real communicative process between group members (b), there are a number of institutions at the macro-level, which may force participants into understanding-oriented communication (a). On the latter category we will briefly discuss five such types of institutions: publicity, the use of closed doors, blocking, vetoes and sounding out.

(a) Macro-level mechanisms

Publicity is of course a central institution in bringing about rational communication (cf. Luban 1996). As we have seen, it is fundamental to discourse theory. Its particular coordinating function lies in the fact that it, in contrast to institutionalised bargaining, does not only bring together parties that have interests in certain outcomes. When the political debate is carried out in public, we are not only dealing with position and opposition that 'fight' each other as best they can; included in the process are people who may potentially be affected by the decision, as well as an unspecified number of listeners. These function as referees in the exchange of arguments. Hence, rulers must justify their actions not only towards political opponents, but also to a broadly composed public. What we have is a *triadic relation* between senders, receivers and listeners. In order to have their actions approved, the parties must appeal to the public as a neutral third party. It is this third party which has the ultimate authority, and which must be convinced, as mentioned in the previous chapter. Here the quality of the arguments are essential, because threats and warnings that people use to force their views through in closed forums, are useless in relation to the general public. Here there is no one to threaten. On the contrary, the situation involves people who are competent judges of how compliant, competent and reasonable agents are who act in public. However, publicity may also ruin a serious discussion, strangely enough.

The use of closed doors is therefore another important mechanism, which is necessary in certain situations in order to bring about a rational exchange of views. Within a deliberative model of politics, we are faced with the paradox that we can only know if decisions are correct if they are tried in an open, public debate, because only then is it possible to know which voices have not been heard in the proceedings. However, it is often in closed forums – far away from the noise of the media and special interests – that debates can be carried out which are not disturbed by strategic action. It can therefore be important to arrange closed meetings, i.e. institutionalised discourses, which are separated from social interests and power structures, and where representatives can deliberate undisturbed. If the communicative process is interrupted frequently, it is not always the case that many heads are better than few (cf. Elster 1983: 39). On the other hand, the use of closed doors may lead to the exclusion of many considerations, view points and interests. Powerful social actors have the means to assert their interests efficiently. They may sabotage any arrangement, no matter its quality, if they have not been allowed to participate in designing it. The use of closed doors must therefore be combined with publicity.[15] There must be public hearings and debates, where the concrete results from deliberations in closed meetings are discussed. Taken together three goals are secured. First, everyone gets the opportunity to participate. Different points of view can be aired, and this is decisive for the legitimacy of a decision. When everyone has been heard or has had their chance to voice their opinion, it is more difficult to raise objections. Secondly, different interests are forced to come forth with their arguments, and the strength and credibility of those arguments can be tested. Special interests have to argue their case, and are thereby forced to see their interests in a broader perspective. Weak groups may receive legal assistance in order to make their arguments heard. Thirdly, the strategy under discussion also creates publicity around political decisions, which increases understanding and accountability, and eases implementation.

Another mechanism has to do with the slowness and *blockages* involved in modern procedure-regulated deliberation and bargaining arrangements. Under organised capitalism, many groups have obtained the right to participate, and there are rules which regulate conflict situations. These are rights which are used by the parties in a dispute, not only to get their standpoints through, but also to slow down the process, so that it will take longer before decisions are made and implemented. Thus, the parties are forced to take some time to think, which increases the possibility that new points of view may be taken into account. Even strikes are frequently used not primarily to force through a demand efficiently; instead, the main purpose behind them may be to pave the way for new ideas and to make possible the testing of decisions not through institutionalised bargaining, but through appeals to other, more superior procedures for conflict resolution. Such blocking of a decision-making process may be understood as temporary checkpoint, which provide an opportunity for discussion and reflection (Beck 1997: 104 ff.). The formal procedures represent a way of ordering the line of political questions, which gives the participants some breathing space, and thus greater possibilities for self-reflection and for recovering their senses.

The right of veto functions as a trump in decision-making situations. It ensures minority rights by blocking majority decisions. The right of veto can prevent legislation based on self-interest, and it protects against majority tyranny (Elster 1995: 16 ff.). It also gives the weak parties a chance of protecting themselves against the lobbying of organised groups and professional negotiators (Preuss 1996: 108). On the other hand, it is a problem that such a right may prevent effective solutions. Single individuals are given a means to obstruct even 'rational' decisions. The right of veto has the weakness that it gives 'quarrellers' an unreasonably strong position.[16] However, the right of veto is more than a check on the majority. It may itself become an important mechanism to bring about a rational discussion. When people can veto a decision they dislike, it gives the parties an incentive to try to convince everybody that their view is the right one. Hence, an actor who wants to promote an interest cannot be content with getting a majority vote (simple or qualified) in favour of his standpoint by creating a strategic alliance; he must have everybody's approval. This forces the parties to act in a much more understanding-oriented way than they would otherwise have done. Those who have an interest in a certain result must argue and show that their view is in agreement with everybody's interest. This principle reduces the tendency for agents to act tactically or strategically, which is common when all that is required is a majority decision.

If we wish to reach agreement in situations where an optimal solution is not obvious, and where the criteria of relevance are ambiguous, we may use another central mechanism, viz. informal consultation or *sounding out*. In such cases, a decision-making situation is redefined into a deliberation situation, where the important point is to prevent the participants from being tied up in pre-defined solutions, and to make them enter into a dialogue.

> In situations where it is difficult to obtain agreement, and where there is no clear, mutual understanding, the participants will avoid clearly defined, common arenas of decision making. [. . .] One way of avoiding clearly defined arenas is to institutionalise the use of *ad hoc* committees. By sending the decision out of the decision unit, one makes possible informal consultation, give potential participants a chance to document their interest by showing a high degree of activity, and provoke reactions by using indirect means, such as rumours, gossip, jokes, hints, etc.
> (Olsen 1988: 286 f., cf. Thompson and McEwan 1958)

Hence, sounding out is a mechanism which can be used to create agreement.

(b) Micro-level mechanisms

Based on the study of negotiations, conflict resolution and problem solving in general, a series of assumptions have been developed concerning what disturbs communication and what prevents actors from reaching agreement at the micro-level. A large part of the literature in question is about phenomena such as psychological and cognitive disturbances, idiosyncratic frames of interpretation, the problems of strategically operating actors, masculine dominance, the rationalisation of motives for action, risk aversion and irrationality within complex systems.[17] What is important from a discourse-theoretical perspective is to come up with directions for how a real exchange of arguments can be enforced, not only to ensure that all information, views and interests are made known, but also to compel the parties to view the problem from different angles. Only in this way can a normative claim be put into force, i.e. by making sure that only those proposals can claim validity which are for the common good, or which treat everybody in the same way.

Roger Fisher and William Ury have introduced the following method for principle-oriented or case-oriented negotiations, which they claim can be used in almost any context:

People: Separate the people from the problem.
Interests: Focus on interests, not positions.
Options: Invent options for mutual gain.

Criteria: Insist on using objective criteria.

(Fisher and Ury 1991: 15)

These are practical remedies that may increase the rationality of the negotiations, but which must be modified and adjusted to the various types of material that need to be regulated. As mentioned earlier, one procedural requirement in this connection is that when concrete groups are put together in order to solve problems, both the mandate of the group, its members and its methods should be discussed in advance. The purpose of such discussions is to establish some common definitions of the situation, as well as some norms for how the deliberation process should proceed. The constitutional rules must be clear, and there must be agreement about the purpose of the discourse, so that the reliability and relevance of utterances may be checked. When disagreement arises after an exchange of opinions, and there is no shift in views, one solution may be to compel the parties to speak in favour of the opponent. This is a means that can be used both to improve understanding and to reduce the effect of rhetorical power. Another method is an active use of voting arrangements. Trial votes are often used, and votes where you are not allowed to vote in favour of your own proposal is another mechanism. Yet another technique is role-play, which is particularly useful in emotionally charged contexts. The techniques mentioned here are not substitutes for a mutual exchange of arguments; rather, they are means to create movement in deadlocked interaction processes, so that the discussion can continue on a different and sometimes on a more enlightened basis.

The theory of *group think* introduces several guidelines that are seen to enhance the quality of the decision-making process:

a) Each member must be a critical evaluator of the group's course of actions; an open climate for giving and accepting criticism should be encouraged by the leader.

b) The leaders should be impartial and refrain from stating their personal preferences at the outset of group discussion; they should limit themselves initially to fostering open inquiry.

c) Set up parallel groups working on the same policy question under different leaders.

d) When policy options are evaluated the group should split up in two or more subgroups, eventually coming together to compare and resolve their different assessments.

e) Each member of the group should privately discuss current issues and options with trusted associates outside the group and report back their reactions.

f) Different outside experts should be brought in from time to time in order to challenge the views of the core members.

g) There should be one or more of the devil's advocates during every group meeting.

h) In conflict situations, extra time should be devoted to interpreting warning signals from rivals and to constructing alternative scenarios of their intentions.

i) Second-chance meetings should be held to reconsider the decision once it has been reached and before it is made public. (Janis 1982: 262 f.)

TYPES OF AGREEMENT

What is the discourse-theoretical criterion for rational decisions, then, and what alternatives are there to rational consensus, which is so difficult to obtain in real life situations? It is also necessary to say something about the *limitations* of the theory, since no procedure can guarantee rational decisions, no matter how good it is.

Rationality Criteria

The principles of institutional design were derived from the ideals of discourse theory, which are deduced from the pragmatic presuppositions of the discourse situation, and which are of a counterfactual nature. The principles in question, which give equal access to and equal opportunities in the communicative process, form a basis for the establishment of more specific organisation principles. Finally, these were supplemented by institutions and mechanisms that favour a communicative and understanding-oriented attitude, rather than a strategic attitude based on self-interest.

These institutions, organisation principles and mechanisms promote communicatively rational decisions. But how do we know that the communication has not been strategic or paternalistic after all? What are the criteria which tell us that it has been a communicative process, in which the power of the arguments has been decisive? According to aggregative approaches, the influence of the various agents is measured in terms of their influence on the election result. By contrast, deliberative theories have no such criterion of influence. Here the point is rather that some preferences must be changed, but there is no external standard which tells us which preferences would be good candidates. Is it still possible to say something about criteria of communicative rational decisions?

The sign of a qualitatively good, democratic process is that the actors learn something new when there is a disagreement, and that at least some of them will change their minds during the process. Only then is it possible to reach a collective decision through open discussion. Consensus rests on mutual convictions (Habermas 1984: 287). Before we discuss criteria of different types of consensual solutions, we will problematise the assumption of discourse theory that all types of disagreements can be solved by means of arguments. John Rawls maintains that rational actors may remain at odds with each other even after a rational deliberation. There are unavoidable limits to a qualified agreement. These are the result of what Rawls refers to as the 'burden of judgement', and they relate to those sources of disagreement that may arise even if the actors reason as rationally as they can (Rawls 1993: 54 ff.). The potential causes of disagreements are many. For example, the relevant data may be contradictory, or agents may weigh different views differently, Further, many concepts are discretionary and value-based, and hence dependent on the interpretative frames in use. Finally, experience, history and personal biography necessarily influence the perception of what

is regarded as normatively correct or good, and that sometimes different normative arguments may be of equal weight. Such limits of judgement tell us that there
may be understandable and rational reasons to disagree, and hence that a rational
discussion does not necessarily result in qualified consensus. Rational actors may
disagree even after a rational discussion. There are various degrees of agreement
and different rules for deliberation, and moral standards are complex.[18]

However, as mentioned when we discussed the problem of contingency, the
distinction between justification and application discourses implies that the conditions for rationality may nevertheless be met in a justification process. Thus, the
thesis of the limitations of judgement should rather be taken to imply that the
social sciences need a less demanding concept of consensus for analysing communicatively achieved agreements rather than relinquish discourse theory as such
for descriptive purposes. We propose a preliminary or provisional consensus, or
what we call a *working agreement*. This is different from the qualified consensus
which arises under power-free conditions, and which is based on a strong form of
idealisation. Such a shift to a higher abstraction level, where the participants take
a disinterested perspective and try to determine what is in everybody's interest, is
not always necessary in order to reach binding agreement in cases of norm collisions. In concrete deliberation and decision-making situations, it is obvious that it
is the good argument which mobilises most support, and not the argument which
is able to convince all parties (Manin 1987: 367). Hence, we suggest a category
for a weaker form of agreement than the type of agreement which is referred to as
rational or qualified agreement. However, just like the latter type, working
agreement is created through the use of arguments instead of threats or power. It
does not merely represent a convergence of interests. It is a under-theorised and
under-justified agreement (Sunstein 1995), but it can be supported by arguments,
and thus it has a certain normative quality. This type of agreement does not rest
on identical arguments, but rather on mutually acceptable arguments. The arguments in question express values that are not incompatible with the principle of
equal freedom for all, and which are accepted in the name of pluralism and
tolerance (cf. Gutmann and Thompson 1996: 65).

We make a distinction between rational consensus and a working agreement
(cf. Figure 10.1), where the latter refers to a type of agreement that has come
about argumentatively, but where the actors may have different, but mutually
acceptable reasons for their support. It expresses the successful solution to conflicts on the basis of the preceding clarification of the value-basis of the choice
situation. Such working agreement may again be separated into two categories,
viz. mini- and quasi-consensus. By *mini-consensus* is meant the kind of agreement
that is created when the actors simply exclude fundamental points of disagreement from the agenda, and only discuss issues on which they may possibly agree.
The institutional background for this is the fact that certain rights, such as the
right to privacy, to freedom of religion etc. relieve the political agenda of many
controversial issues (Ackerman 1989, Holmes 1988). Rights, especially constitutional ones, function as trumps in a deliberation process, and make it possible
to obtain agreement on a minimal basis.[19]

The term *quasi-consensus* refers to a type of agreement which emerges when
agents have analysed the conflicts and been able to find out why they disagree,
thereby establishing a platform for further cooperation. The participants have
understood what they disagree on, but since decisions must be made, they may

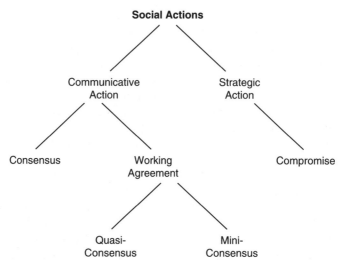

Figure 10.1 *Categories of agreement*

agree to follow certain procedures for conflict solving. For example, they may decide to follow certain voting procedures, which means that they agree about what questions should be put to the vote, about how the vote will be conducted, and that the result should be respected. As mentioned in Chapter 8, Habermas sees this as a conditional kind of agreement. It is a provisional type of consensus, which reflects the need for making decisions, and which involves that it will be possible to make a different choice later on.

Rational Conflict Resolution

The question that remains to be answered is what are the discourse-theoretical criteria for a rational solution to problems and conflicts? How can we know that deliberation has been going on and that a rational solution to conflicts has been obtained? Disagreement or conflicts in a case are typically due to such facts that (a) someone is wrong, or (b) the parties have preferences over the outcome, i.e., there is a clash of interests.

In the former case, the criterion for a rational collective choice is that some argument has caused someone to change their opinion. According to the discourse-theoretical perspective, the conflict may (a_1) be due to the fact that agents simply disagree about the facts, and about how realities should be described. In discussions of action-related conflicts, an amazingly great amount of time is spent clarifying this type of disagreement. This is done in so-called *theoretical discourses*. If everybody ends up with the same definition of the problem, the disagreement can be settled through rational consensus. The entire scientific methodology has been developed in order to settle such disagreement. However, theoretical discourses are concerned with how the world is, not about how we should act in it. Given that there is agreement about goals, and more or less complete agreement about the state of things, there may (a_2) nevertheless be doubts about how we should act – i.e. what means should be chosen – in order to realise our goals. This issue may be clarified through a *pragmatic discourse*, as when doctors decide what treatment a patient should have, or when engineers discuss the construction of a bridge on the basis of concrete considerations of facts. Consensus is obtained in such cases, because the questions are decided with reference to established preferences and professional methods, and hence are relative to the value-basis at hand.

However, it is also possible (a_3) that the disagreement is due to a real conflict of values, a conflict about what should be the collective goal of a group or a society. In such cases, a solution must be reached through an *ethical-political discourse*, which takes the form of a hermeneutic clarification process. The actors reason their disagreement through. This gives them a clearer picture of, and enables them to define, the common interests of the group. Some interests or standpoints are not compatible with the defined common interests. We thus have a criterion for what interests and standpoints must yield, viz. those that are in opposition to the defined common interests. We are here talking about interests that cannot be generalised within the group, and with this term we mean interests that cannot be articulated in public within a given community of values without facing qualified opposition with regard to the common normative basis of the community. Within ethical-political discourses, the criterion is that those who share a common interest or have the same values, agree about the result. Their agreement rests on mutually comprehensible and mutually acceptable arguments, and such cases hence belong to the category of working agreement. Habermas refers to this as *Konzens*, which is in contrast to the compromise-based *agreement* and the rational *consensus*.

> The consensus issuing from a successful search for collective self-understanding neither expresses a merely negotiated agreement (*Vereinbarung*), as in compromises, nor is it rationally motivated consensus (*Einverständnis*), like the consensus on facts or questions of justice. It expresses two things at once: self-reflection and resolve on a form of life.
>
> (Habermas 1996a: 182)

(a_4) Another way of resolving conflicts is through a *moral discourse*, where the parties admit that there may in fact be different common interests and different perceptions of the good life, but where they nevertheless try to seek a solution which is in everybody's equal interest. Here it is important to describe the situation in such a way that a justified norm can be applied to settle the conflict. The criterion in this respect is that the decisions can be universalised.

In general, a consensus is legitimate only insofar as the actors can justify the result by using arguments in the first person singular. Further, it is only rational when the participants have the same reasons for supporting it. Regarding moral discourses, we have to do with a universalistic justification, where the actors support the result because of a fair treatment, in which everybody's interests and values have been considered.

(b) In situations where interests or values clash, and where there is no acknowledged common interest on which resolution can be based, the parties may proceed to bargaining regulated by procedural norms, as mentioned in Chapter 8. The procedures in question must themselves pass a normative test in a moral discourse if the result is to make claims on legitimacy. Specifically, the procedural norms must give everyone the same opportunities, prevent free riders, and generally make sure that the negotiated result is better than no result. With this the moral discourse is given normative priority, which is reflected in the quality of the agreement that can be achieved. As mentioned before, the interaction between strategically operating agents prototypically results in a compromise.

> Whereas a rationally motivated consensus (*Einverständnis*) rests on reasons that convince all the parties *in the same way*, a compromise can be accepted by the different parties each for its own *different* reasons.
>
> (Habermas 1996a: 166)

In strategic bargaining, the criterion is not that the actors should be able to support the result by identical arguments, neither by mutually defendable arguments. What is important is rather that they have the same understanding and acceptance of the procedures, and that they accept the result because it is the best possible outcome achievable under present conditions. As an example we may mention wage bargaining situations in which workers and employers typically reach a result which is acceptable to both parties. The result is nevertheless a compromise, as both parties would have preferred a different and 'better' result, seen from their respective perspectives. Thus they have different grounds for accepting the result; the employers accept it because it does not cost the company too much, the workers because it does not cost the company too little. Figure 10.2 shows some main features of the varies forms of rational conflict resolution.

Thus, the criterion of communicatively rational decisions is that someone has learned something and changed their original standpoint, they may be presented in public and be defended against criticism, that the parties can justify them in the first person singular and that they have mutually acceptable or identical reasons for supporting them. However, we generally have the problem that even though the procedure has been followed, and even though there is agreement about the result, the consensus can be false. Consensuses are fallible because people also in a cognitive respect are finite, limited beings, i.e. individuals who are aware neither of all the alternative choice opportunities, nor of the complex relation between values and goals. Moreover, there will always be pressure to reach a result with minimal use of resources. We therefore need institutional mechanisms which prevent the discussion of important questions from ending when consensus is obtained.

Types of discourse	Type of will	Type of agreement
Theoretical	—	Rational consensus
Pragmatic	Enlightened common will	Consensus
Ethical-political	Authentic common will	Working agreement
Moral	Autonomous common will	Rational consensus
Procedurally regulated bargaining	Aggregated will	Compromise

Figure 10.2 *The relationship between discourse, will and agreement*

Reservations

The procedure recommended here has the ability to produce results with a high degree of legitimacy. It is relevant in all situations where interest-regulating decisions are to be made, and when important principles and goals are at issue. It is relevant in questions relating to policy choices and the distribution of goods and burdens and it is particularly relevant when it comes to establish *procedures* for problem solving and conflict resolution. However, as already mentioned, this involves a new danger, viz. that the consensus that has been obtained may be perceived as more valid than it really is. There will always be preferences over outcomes. Some results will be in the interests of particular actors, and when these actors can demonstrate that the 'correct' procedure has been followed, they have a legitimacy basis. They may now with emphasis declare that the result is 'just'. This makes possible technocratic abuse of the theory.

There are exceptions even to valid rules, and a consensus may be fallible even under ideal conditions. This also concerns theoretical discourses in the natural sciences; thus rationality cannot be equated with absolute certainty. Any procedure aimed at decision making will be limited in regard to time, participation and information, and will hence be potentially unjust:

- some voices will necessarily be excluded (Moon 1993: 96);
- discussions may be distorted even under optimal conditions (Peters 1994: 113);
- even a fair process may produce an unjust result (Dahl 1989: 161);
- a procedure that guarantees certainty is not yet in sight (Alexy 1989: 293);
- perfect procedural justice is impossible (Rawls 1971: 198).

A procedure which is designed to obtain rational results cannot *guarantee* such. There will always be new perspectives to consider, and the existing normative evaluation schemas are too manifold for lasting consensus to be expected. This makes it necessary to take the following precaution: *The institutional application of discourse theory does not guarantee correct decisions.* Instead, the relevant procedure gives hope of relatively 'more valid' and fair decisions than what could be expected if we had followed a different procedure. However, additional procedures are necessary. First, we need procedures that ensure a periodic *re-evaluation* of the results. Communicative design involves the institutionalisation of a process which makes it possible to evaluate the obtained consensus at a later time. The guarantee that the discussion of problematic claims will continue after a decision has been made is in itself appealing and creates a climate favourable for communicative interaction.

Secondly, there is a need for *second-best arrangements* that we can fall back upon if discussions should fail, or if for other reasons rational consensus is not reached. One possibility here is to lower the requirements for what is rational, and be content with the fact that the parties have changed their views somewhat compared to the original disagreement or conflict. Here there is a possibility of a *working agreement,* which is nevertheless qualitatively different from a compromise, because it has come about communicatively and hence has a certain normative validity. It has been stabilised by mutually acceptable arguments. To achieve this, we need a procedure that allows a more selective selection of participants, and a mandate which both limits the formulations of the questions, and allows the use of the majority mechanism when certain requirements are met. Specifically, the discussions must have lasted long enough for the participants to have agreed on certain questions, such as what questions should be put to the vote, what the voting alternatives are, and that the outcomes must be respected.

CONCLUSION

Democracy is a prerequisite for determining what is just and what are the correct solutions to collective questions. However, democracy involves government according to particular procedures, but with uncertain results (Offe 1996b: 254 ff). Even good procedures may lead to bad solutions, and only the participants themselves can decide what is valid. The participants must decide both the form of the cooperation and the content of the discussion. Form influences content and vice versa, so that not any kind of content is compatible with any form. By means of discourse theory, the procedural requirements of a democratic deliberation process have been formulated more precisely. The thesis is that when the procedural requirements of discourse theory are met, the outcome will be both legitimate and rational.

This procedure is widely relevant. It may be applied to several problem- and conflict-solving situations where there is no recipe for a correct solution. Many have realised that only solutions which are based on the participation and acceptance of the parties are robust solutions. This is evident in situations of civil conflicts. Here legal norms which are normally straightforward cannot be used because there are collisions between different legitimate norms. This is frequently the case within healthcare and social policy. Deliberative conflict resolution is also required in resource and environmental policy areas, where the efficiency of the regulations are to a great extent conditioned by their legitimacy. We also see it in all ethnic-political conflicts, where different collective identities collide, and where only public discussion can bring about development and mutual understanding. Problem solving by means of majority vote often appears authoritative; material legal regulations are often unfamiliar, and using political force in situations of ethical and moral schism does not change the fundamental differences, i.e., the sources of conflicts. Over time certain learning processes have taken place within civil law, regulatory law-making and political conflict resolution. Thus, the theory is not only normative in that it prescribes an ideal procedure. It is also practically relevant, since it is only when such normative requirements have been met (fully or partly) that we may get effective, robust solutions.

The problem with the deliberative democratic procedure is that it presupposes a fairly high degree of *equality* between the participants of the discussion. If that is not the case, the free discussion will probably favour those who have more information and are generally resourceful. However, if it requires approximately the same resource level, how can this form of democracy be realised? It is well known that modern societies – and in particular the US – are based on an economic system that breeds inequality, and consequently there are vast differences between the resource basis of different social groups and classes. This has caused many people to regard deliberative democracy more as an attractive normative ideal than as a practical system. Others have discussed basic capacities and resources, as well as various forms of inequality that must be dealt with for a deliberative process to be possible (Bohman 1996, Knight and Johnson 1997). However, certain forms of inequality may in fact be a resource (Young 1997). It is problematic to state, on purely theoretical terms, what degree of equality is required in order to say that citizens possess acceptable opportunities to partake in the discussion of those decisions that affect themselves.

By analysing how institutions can be designed in a way that makes communicative interaction possible, we have pointed to another strategy for realising deliberative democracy. This has been done in the context of the European/Scandinavian welfare state. Here social rights are institutionalised, the general welfare is relatively high, and the collegial organisation is well established. By applying the discourse principle to the concept of institutions, we came up with some ideal requirements for democratic design. Subsequently, we developed some principles for institutional design. When these were in the next instance applied to the requirements for efficient decision-making, we were finally able to derive some organisation principles. These are based on the 'trade-off' between legitimacy and efficiency that any form of organisation must strike. Furthermore, they were supplemented by some agreement-promoting mechanisms. In this way, we arrive at a strategy for realising deliberative democracy which builds on some realistic assumptions about how we, by means of organisation variables, can compel agents into a communicative mode of interaction. However, it is important to emphasise that this may again create possibilities of abuse, and that it is only in the general public political debate that such principles can be justified and the results of institutionalised discourses can be tested. Here we are at the core of the deliberative concept of democracy, because justification in relation to those who are concerned is part of what is required for getting the results right. Moreover, this is not merely a normative requirement because those who are bound, must also accept, for in a democracy those who have the power to force others may themselves be forced – in the last instance through elections.

Notes

1. This was discussed in Chapter 7, and is inspired by Apel's distinction between part A and part B of discourse theory – i.e. the element that controls for power politics – and Rawl's distinction between 'ideal and non-ideal theory' (Apel 1992b, Rawls 1993).
2. Cf. Goodin (ed.) 1996 for an overview of the literature on institutional design within the different disciplines.
3. 'But by 'designing institutions for knaves' such mechanical solutions risk making knaves of potentially more honorable actors' (Goodin (ed.) 1996: 41). On the other hand, Kant in *Perpetual Peace* sees the possibility of 'making devils into good citizens when only they possess Vernunft'.
4. The numbering here refers to the wider context of these process rules, being part of the argumentation rules of discourse theory. We will discuss two other types of argumentation rules later in the chapter.
5. It hence cannot replace social scientific research programmes, but rather

establishes a context for evaluating their contribution (Habermas 1987a: 375).

6. Thus, to determine which decision-making procedure is most appropriate in a particular case, we must take into account the context and the premises for the decision. For example, if decisions are made through voting in popularly elected assemblies and subsequently implemented by the bureaucracy, on the basis of instruction, this would often be more in line with the normative rationality requirement which is deeply rooted in our democratic system than would be the case if bureaucrats made the decisions through deliberation and on the basis of their own discretion.

7. Sciully makes a point of the fact that Habermas does not give professions a more important role in the civilisation process. He maintains that this and the implied collegial principle are the 'the missing link' in the theory, which may explain why modern democracy survived in spite of the fact that the public sphere was 'refeudalized' after 1830. On the other hand, Sciully criticises Parsons for attaching too much importance to the norm-internalisation of the professions and their moral integrity compared to importance of the collegial principle (Sciully 1992: 251 ff).

8. It should be emphasised that communicative design is intended not as a substitute for a free debate in autonomous general public spheres, but rather as a way of making institutions more democratic by increasing their ability to make communicatively rational decisions.

9. In this way we avoid the problem of adaptive – or context-dependent – preferences, i.e. the circumstance that actors do not signal their real opinions, but adapt their preferences according to what they think is expected from them, or what they think may possibly be achieved.

10. The points made here are inspired by Offe and Preuss 1991.

11. 'Time is the reason for the compulsion to select in complex systems, for if there were an infinite amount of time available, everything could be coordinated with everything else,' (Luhmann 1984: 15, cited from Günther 1993: 8).

12. This is a modified version of the eight principles which Sciulli (1996) discusses, and which are based on Lon Fuller's 'Threshold of Procedural Norms' from *The Morality of Law (1969)*.

13. This sequence builds on Dryzek 1990: 97 ff and Eriksen 1999: 63 ff.

14. Cf. Horster 1989: 151; Alexy 1981. Cf. also Apel 1989: 55 ff. and Pröpper 1993.

15. This is for example built into the working methods of the Norwegian Parliament. Here there are first preparatory discussions in closed committees, whereupon the same cases are debated in open plenary meetings. The discussion in the committees gives the representatives the opportunity to sound out their proposals and arguments without paying attention to party lines and the prestige which publicity automatically involves. The succeeding public debate ensures that solutions are not chosen which do not stand up to public scrutiny.

16. Under certain conditions, the right of veto may cause actors to be more selfish than they would otherwise have been (cf. Goodin 1996: 339 f.).

17. Cf. for example Bovens and 't Hart 1996, Schön and Rein 1994.

18. For this see e.g., Larmore 1987, McCarthy 1994; Bohman 1995, Gutmann

and Thompson 1996, Heath 2001, Waldron 2001, Rehg and Bohman (eds) 2001.

19. A decision to forbid the circumcision of girls or forced marriage in Western societies can in this perspective be justified on the grounds that such practices violate the principle of individual autonomy. This is a principle to which even 'outlandish' religious and cultural groups must submit in a modern democratic constitutional state.

CHAPTER 11

A world domestic policy

INTRODUCTION

The purpose of this book is to present and discuss the main aspects of Habermas's social and political theory as it has developed since 1981 with the publication of the German edition of *The Theory of Communicative Action*. In the aftermath of the original publication of *Between Facts and Norms* (1992) Habermas has commented upon international political events and written on a world domestic policy ('Weltinnenpolitik') in such a way that we see the contours of a discourse-theoretical conception of the cosmopolitan order. In this chapter we will outline the basic structure of this order while drawing on categories established in the preceding chapters, in particular Chapters 6 and 7. It should be pointed out from the outset that Habermas's contribution is multi-faceted, has many targets and that there are tensions between different parts of it. In working out this outline we have drawn upon our own application of discourse theory to international relations.[1] We hope the outline may help readjust the impression from his *Theory of Communicative Action*, namely that this work, as Habermas himself acknowledges, conveyed the impression that the nation state was the model for society in general (Arnason 2000).

The democratic *Rechtsstaat* exhibits universalistic traits, and the discourse theory of law and politics postulates co-originality between constitution and democracy, between human rights and popular sovereignty. Without a fundamental legal protection of rights, no valid democratic decisions can be made. And without democratic procedures there is no guarantee that human rights will be upheld. The co-originality of rule of law and democracy appears in Habermas's conception of order in modern, complex and pluralist societies. He maintains that the political orders of modern societies are not necessarily founded on comprehensive agreements based on shared values but rather on the rights-based, democratic procedures the observance of which commands respect.

But so far the principle of popular sovereignty has only been made applicable to the rule of particular societies; as yet it is at this level that democracy is institutionalised. Democracy is in other words limited to the nation state, as 'a national community of fate' that governs itself autonomously, and which is primarily geared towards self-maintenance. Hence the propensity of conflict between sovereign states: observing the borders and upholding state autonomy have priority over global concerns. Even though there are trends towards a post-Hobbesian world order, i.e., the domestication of the anarchical international order, further democratisation is needed for this order to achieve functional stability and normative legitimacy.

Human rights on their part are universal and refer to humanity as such. There is a tension between international law's recognition of sovereign states and the regulative idea of equal rights for all, which is reflected in an actual opposition between democracy and law, and between foreign and domestic politics. However, one may say that the autonomy of the state is being undermined by international human rights politics, due to the taming of the willpower of the nation state, and that the principle of popular sovereignty is about to be transformed into a law for the citizens of the world.

In this chapter we will address the contribution of discourse theory to international relations. First we will do so in relation to human rights politics, then in relation to globalisation or *denationalisation*. Currently, there are global structures of finance, production, trade and communication that evaporate the boundaries of the nation state. Citizens' interests are affected in ways and by bodies difficult to hold responsible via the ballot box. The sovereign state is being challenged by a vast array of international institutions, organisations and regimes. Globalisation creates growing interdependence and escalation of risks that require transnational and supranational cooperation and new forms of governance. To catch up with globalisation and human rights violations *a cosmopolitan law of the people* as well as *a world domestic policy* are, according to Habermas, needed. What are the prospects for institutionalising democracy beyond the nation state?

In section two we start with the tension between democracy and rights which points to a cosmopolitan order for its solution. Only in such an order can the rights of human beings be reconciled with the principle of democracy. Even though the parameters of power politics have changed due to the growth of international law, human rights enforcement is still arbitrary. Human rights, which are supra-positive, claim universal validity, as we saw in Chapter 7, but how can they be defended? The normative dimension of human rights, or *the rights to have rights*, should be clarified. In the third section we address the need for cosmopolitan democracy in order to protect human rights and prevent war, and we outline Habermas's position as one between proponents of a world state and Kant's plea for a mere confederation at the world level. According to Habermas, the shared values of a global order are too thin to generate obligations necessary for state-like integration. Rights have to be rooted in practical, socio-cultural contexts. However, allegiance is not merely given with historical descent but can be fostered through democratic procedures. The positive functions of the nation state have to be protected, but a distinction between cultural and political integration should be made. In the fourth section the deliberative perspective is applied to new forms of transnational governance and the reconfiguration of political power we are witnessing in Europe. Habermas vacillates between stressing the function of the law to supranational integration and that of the epistemic value of transnational network governance in reconstructing the *post-national constellation*. Law needs to be laid down authoritatively and made equally binding on every part for integration to come about. We apply this perspective to the European Union which Habermas holds to be the prime example of a world domestic policy able to control the negative consequences of globalisation. This is the theme of section five in which we analyse the potential for post-national democracy and also the need for a European constitution. The last section contains the conclusion and some synthesising remarks.

DOMESTICATING INTERNATIONAL RELATIONS

The state is a war-making system; it has the monopoly of violence (Weber 1978) and collectivises *the right to kill*, to quote Carl Schmitt (1996: 32 f.). Moreover there is no binding law above the nation state as laid down in the *Westphalian order:* nation states are sovereign with fixed territorial boundaries and entitled to conduct their internal and external affairs autonomously. What is at stake in the current process of legalisation of international relations is the sovereignty of the modern state. In a post-Westphalian constellation there is law above the state to sanction the use of violence by the states.

The Tension between Human Rights and Popular Sovereignty

From the very beginning there was a basic normative dualism in the constitution of modern societies:

> [Yet] international law (jus gentium), since its origins at the beginning of modern times, has been characterised by a dualism of its normative focus: on the one hand, the concern for human rights, which was first grounded theologically and meta-physically on natural right; and on the other hand, especially since the end of the Thirty Years' War in 1648; the principle of inviolability of the sovereignty of the particular states, which was primarily oriented towards the preservation of peace.
>
> (Apel 2001: 32)

In the Westphalian order prohibition of violence against sovereign states is priori-tised over the protection of human rights, thus this order safeguards the rulers' *external sovereignty.* Interstate relations are generally conceived of as being in a state of anarchy. International order is founded on the principles of co-existence and non-interference among sovereign states.[2] The latter principle, however, cannot prohibit genocide and cannot be sustained.

The principle of state sovereignty which international law after the Treaty of Westphalia 1648 warranted, is a principle that has protected the most odious regimes – and it should be recalled that it was only when Nazi Germany attacked Poland that World War II broke out, not when the persecution of Jews started. This demonstrates the limitations of nationally founded and confined democracy that autonomously governs itself.[3] While human rights are universal and appeal to humanity as such, democracy refers to a particular community of consociates who come together to make binding collective decisions. The validity of the laws is derived from the decision-making processes of a sovereign community. The propensity to adopt rights, then, depends on the quality of the political process in a particular community.

When peoples' basic rights are violated, and especially when murder and ethnic cleansing (ethnocide) are taking place something has to be done, our moral con-sciousness tells us. The growth in international law ever since its inception and in particular the system of rights embedded in the UN represent the transformation of this consciousness into political and legal measures. The purpose of these institutions was first to constrain the willpower of the nation states in their external relations to other states. The politics of human rights by means of sys-tematic legalisation of international relations implies the domestication of the existing state of nature between countries. Institutions above the nation state are needed to constrain the internal willpower of the state, i.e., the power exerted over its citizens. Article 28 of *The United Nations Universal Declaration of Human Rights* (1948) made it clear that there is a right to a lawful international order: 'Everyone is entitled to a social and international order in which rights and freedoms set forth in this Declaration can be fully realised.' In the last decades we have witnessed a significant development of rights and law enforcement beyond the nation state. Human rights are institutionalised in international courts, in tribunals and increasingly also in politico-judicial bodies over and above the nation state that control resources for enforcing norm compliance. Examples are the international criminal tribunals for Rwanda and the former Yugoslavia, The International Criminal Court, the UN and the EU. In addition, European states have incorporated 'The European Convention for the Protection of Human Rights and Fundamental Freedoms' and a good deal of its protocols into their domestic legal systems. These developments are constrained by the limitations of the international law regime as it is based on the principle of unanimity and as it lacks executive power. The Charter of the United Nations prohibits violence but forbids intervention in the internal affairs of a state. However, this is not the only difficulty of an international human rights regime.

The problem with human rights politics is due to their non-institutionalised form. Human rights exhibit a categorical structure – they have a strong moral content: 'Human dignity shall be respected at whatever costs!' Borders of states or collectives do not make the same strong claim – 'they do not feel pain'. In cases of violations of basic human rights, our human reason is roused to indignation and urge for action. When conceived abstractly human rights do not pay attention to the context – e.g. to the specific situation and ethical-cultural values – and may violate other important concerns. As human rights do not respect borders or collectives, as they appeal to universality as such, they may threaten local communities, innate loyalties and value-based relationships. When you know what is *right*, you are obliged to act whatever the consequences. Imperialism in more than a moral sense, is among the problems of actual human rights politics performed by states. This cosmopolitan universalist idea of doing good set the European nation states on missions for human rights across the globe, a mission that the USA overtook in the twentieth century (Eder and Giesen 2001: 265). Habermas maintains that the Europeans have learnt from past failures and that they today pursue a different strategy regarding human rights.

> The USA conceives the global enforcement of human rights as the national mission of a world power which pursues this goal according to the premises of power politics. Most of the EU governments see the politics of human rights as a project committed to systematic legislation of international relations, a project already altering the parameters of power politics.
>
> (Habermas 1999b: 269)

Cosmopolitan Law

The general problem comes down to the following: in concrete situations there will be collisions of human rights as more than one justified norm may be called upon. To choose the correct norm requires interpretation of situations and the balancing and weightening of norms in application discourses. Another problem with the politics of human rights is its arbitrariness at this stage of institutionalisation. They are enforced at random. Some states are being punished for their violations of human rights while others are not. Today, there are sanctions against Iran and Iraq, but not against Israel or China. Some states violate international law with impunity. The politics of human rights is criticised for being based on the will power of the US and its allies, not on universal principles applied equally to all. Human rights talk may well only be window-dressing, covering up for the real motives of big states. Recall the rhetoric 'of the free world' in the Vietnam War by the US, a country that was accused also of intervening in the Gulf War because of its interest in oil resources. All too often ideals are a sham – they are open to manipulation and interest-politics and new imperialism. Human rights politics is often power politics in disguise. Carl Schmitt, who is the prominent adversary in Habermas's writings, sees this as endemic to international relations as such because there can be no supranational law:

> When a state fights its political enemy in the name of humanity, it is not war for the sake of humanity, but a war wherein a particular state seeks to usurp a universal concept against its military opponent.
>
> (Schmitt 1996: 54)

The solution to the twin problems of the politics of human rights – the problems of norm collisions and of arbitrariness – is positivisation or constitutionalisation, which confers upon everybody the same obligations and connects enactment to democratic procedures. Disregarding the ideological function of human rights serving as they often do to actual exclusion and unequal treatment and hence shielding a false universality, Schmitt is wrong because there in fact is an international law that claims normative validity. This is so because human rights 'are juridical *by their very nature*', (Habermas 1998e: 190). They are not merely moral norms that can be enforced in the name of humanity, but legal rights depending for their legitimate enforcement on democratic procedures. The coercive power of the state has to be regulated both externally and internally by legitimate law. It is democratic legitimacy that warrants the claim that law can be 'in harmony with recognised moral principles. Cosmopolitan law is a logical consequence of the idea of the constitutive rule of law. It establishes for the first time a symmetry between the juridification of social and political relations both within and beyond the state's borders,' (Habermas 1998e: 199).

There are corresponding empirical developments as human rights now are incorporated both into international law and into the constitutions of the nation states. The UN was primarily founded to prevent the recurrence of war. Democracy was not a condition for membership. Increasingly, the UN has taken up human rights and democratic questions and has been supporting women's and children's rights, the protection of the environment, the promotion of development, participation, etc. in many ways.[4] The UN helps facilitate transitions to constitutional democracy at the state level. Increasingly human rights are positivised as *legal rights* and made binding through the sanctioning power of the administrative apparatus of the states. This has changed the very concept of sovereignty. Today, for (some) states to be sovereign they have to respect basic civil and political rights. In principle, then, only a democratic state is a sovereign state and in such a state the majority cannot (openly) suppress minorities (Frank 1992).

Human rights are important because they directly point to the constitutional principle of modern states, whilst also constituting a critical point of reference for their justification. While basic rights are given to individuals in so far as they are citizens – members of a state – human rights have a moral content that is not absolvable in positive law, as we discussed in Chapter 7. The democratic *Recthsstaat* is founded on the rights of the individual, her autonomy and dignity. It claims to derive legitimacy from the protection of the individual – her freedom and welfare. Human rights are thus part of what it takes to validate a procedure for legitimate decision making. This is also seen in all liberation movements and claims for secession: they are first recognised by international society when they can show that basic rights are violated by the power holders.

About 95 per cent of all wars are within states and not between them. This among other things has brought human rights to the fore in international politics and changed their political status. There was a remarkable shift in the discourse of how and when to intervene during the 1990s.

> Interventions once aroused the condemnation of international moralists. Now failures to intervene or to intervene adequately in places such as Rwanda or Sierra Leone do.
>
> (Doyle 2001: 212)

The position of human rights is, as we have seen, strengthened internationally. However, this is not an unproblematic development. Human rights are universal, and with their expansion within international law they have also gained an authority that limits the state's self-determination (cf. Apel 1998: 833). But human rights no longer follow from democratic states' self-legislation only, as is the case with the declarations that came about under the French and the American revolutions. They now also follow from international legislation under the direction of, among others, the UN and enforced by special human rights courts or the US and their allies. 'With the criminalization of wars of aggression and crimes against humanity, nations, as the subjects of international law, have forfeited a general presumption of innocence'; and even though the UN has got neither judicial nor military power 'it can impose sanctions, and grant mandates for humanitarian interventions', (Habermas 2001d: 106). We may therefore speak of a law of peoples that places individual human beings at the centre for the legitimacy and accountability of power (Held 2002, Rawls 1999). Hence, there is *a cosmopolitan law* in addition to state law and international law, i.e., a legal order that bypasses international and state authorities and grants individual subjects unmediated membership in a world organisation (Habermas 1998e: 181).

Before we proceed we will examine how human rights can be defended, because if this is the shared normative basis of a world order one needs to know whether they really are universal and in what sense they possibly are so. Further, if human rights are not completely absolvable in positive law, what is then the accurate discourse-theoretical conception of such rights? An answer is required as one may ask if Habermas's conceptual strategy fully grasps the normative dimension of human rights.

Is there a Right to Human Rights?

To discourse theory human rights are not ungrounded axioms or self-evident facts. They are not merely posited. Rather they are made by man and can be justified and are in need of legitimation. However, can human rights be defended in their own right, and not only as an 'instrument' for democracy? Our moral intuition tells us that human rights need protection regardless of their contribution to democracy. Here we follow a proposal made by Rainer Forst.[5] As we have seen, Habermas conceives the core content of human rights as being moral but there is no justification of their intrinsic value. They are derived from what is required for citizens to be proper participants in public deliberation. In simplified terms Habermas's conception of *private autonomy* is framed on the right not to communicate, or on a right to be left alone. Legal rights relieve the actors of the obligation to provide moral justifications.

Why do we need human rights and to what extent can we claim to be protected by them? A wider justification than the one referring to democracy is needed, partly because positive laws can be unfair and because meta-legal perspectives are called upon to change and rectify legal orders and make new laws. This pertains to the larger philosophical problem of discourse theory, whether its alleged proceduralism can be sustained or if it has to reckon with substantive, normative elements. Regarding this one may ask how it is possible to argue for everyone's right to participate in a debate without going back to some substantive normative and non-procedural argument, for example, peoples' freedom, equality and dignity as postulated by natural law. After all, procedural and substantive conceptions of justice interchange in a justification process in so far as the claims of equal access and participation, inclusiveness and openness rest on the principles of tolerance, personal integrity, guaranteed private life, etc. (Alexy 2002, cf. Günther 1994, 1999). Surely, infinite regress or circular argumentation arises here, because rights that are to ensure the process must be justified procedurally, something that in turn rests on substantial elements, which in turn again are to be justified procedurally, etc. (Michelman 1997: 162 f.).[6]

A wider justification for human rights is also required because we need to know more specifically why human rights should be respected unconditionally. A normative foundation is required in order to refute the accusation that human rights are particularistic and 'Western' values. There is need for a culturally neutral but at the same time culturally sensitive defence of human rights. Demands for human rights are moral demands as they are put forward to secure some vital interests. They are always concretely justified with regard to someone's frustrated need or unsatisfied interest and they are articulated when people are maltreated or humiliated. Human rights do not merely exist or not, they are not given by God(s) and they are not merely discovered. Rather they are created and recognised by people in certain situations and are enacted by political and judicial decision-making bodies (Köhler 1999). They arise in difficult and dire situations and are responses to normatively demanding hardships.

> The conception of natural rights, sacred and inherent in man, was written into the constitutions of the eighteenth, nineteenth, and twentieth centuries, not because men had agreed on a philosophy, but because they had agreed, despite philosophic

differences, on the formulation of a solution to a series of moral and political problems.

(McKeon 1948: 181)

Experiences of injustice which are common to all human beings give rise to demands for change and rectification – reiteration – and beneath claims to particular undertakings, to social and political remedial actions, there is a need for understanding and explanation. Why is this happening to me, and why do I have to obey rules and norms detrimental to my own interest? Claimants may have no abstract or philosophical idea of what it means to be a 'human being', but by protesting they demonstrate that there is at least one fundamental human-moral demand which no culture or society may reject: the unconditional claim to be respected as someone who deserves to be given justifying reasons for actions, rules, or structures to which s/he is subject (Forst 1999b: 40).

At the heart of human rights demands is the need of every human being for meaning and reasons – as a universal feature of human kind.[7] Religions may be seen as responses to this need as they are representations of meaning: they explain man's place in the world and provide justification of evil or injustice – i.e., teodicé. This need is also, so to speak, built into the very structure of the employment of the human language. In every social relationship, the demand for justification and explanation is present; and every human being expresses this demand from the earliest years. In modern societies this demand also takes the secular form of reason giving in first person singular and translates into the justification of political authority. Accordingly, every social order must be prepared to give reasons for their existence if they are to be recognised by their members. It is from this basis, recognising *the right to justification*, that other rights may be justified. This can be seen as the language theoretical basis for the talk of a cosmopolitan right in line with Kant, and it is an insight that is basic to the deliberative concept of democracy stating that only norms and statutes that are justified to those affected and that are accepted by all in a free debate can claim to be truly legitimate.[8] Especially it is reflected in the more strict moral principle of validation: 'A law is valid in the moral sense when it could be accepted by everybody from the perspective of each individual', (Habermas 1998b: 31).

However, in practical terms there is a tension between human rights and democracy since the latter only exists at the level of the nation state, i.e., in particular states, while human rights are propounded by non-democratic bodies such as courts and tribunals or, what is more often the case, enforced by the US and its allies. Hence, there is a need for entrenchment of rights in democratic and law enforcement bodies above the nation state and international relations.

THE NATION STATE AND COSMOPOLITANISM

When addressing cosmopolitan rights we may well remind ourselves of the words of Hannah Arendt (1986: 295 f.): 'We became aware of the existence of a right to have rights ... and a right to belong to some kind of organised community, only when millions of people emerged who had lost and could not regain these rights ...'

Cosmopolitan Democracy?

According to cosmopolitans, the urgent task is to domesticate the existing state of nature between countries by means of human rights, i.e., the transformation of international law into a law of global citizens.[9] The parameters of power politics have already changed, as we have seen. Nevertheless, the problem of arbitrariness in the enforcement of norms in the international order is not resolved. For a true republic to be realised it must be possible for citizens to appeal to bodies above the nation state when their rights are threatened. Thus there are reasons for institutions beyond a particular state in which individuals have obtained membership and which protect the basic rights of the citizen. Such a state can fail to respect a 'correct' understanding of human rights and can also fail to respect individuals with no membership rights and other states' legitimate interests.

> Since human beings are both moral persons and citizens of a state, they have certain duties in an international context. As a moral person, a member of the community of all human beings, one is a 'world citizen' insofar as one has not only the duty to respect the human rights of others, but also a duty to help them when their rights are violated, as when the basic rights of human beings are systematically disregarded in another state.
>
> (Forst 1999b: 53)

Yet the principle of popular sovereignty points to a particular society, while human rights point to an ideal republic, and only with a cosmopolitan order – democracy at a supranational world level – can this opposition finally find its solution. For the rights of the *world citizen – kosmou politês* – to be respected, human rights need to be institutionalised in bodies above the nation states that actually bind individual governments and international actors.[10] Such bodies must be provided with the resources that make sanctions credible. This is needed for ensuring norm compliance and consistent and impartial norm-enforcement. The UN needs to be made into an organisation equipped with executive power for law enforcement because law should be made equally binding on each of the member states.

> The Security Council could be transformed into an executive branch capable of implementing policies on the model of the Council of Ministers of the European Union. Moreover, states will be willing to adapt their traditional foreign policy to the imperatives of a world domestic policy only if the world organization can deploy military force under its own command and exercise police functions.
>
> (Habermas 1998e: 187 f.)

Regarding democratisation, one option is to supplement the existing order with territorial representation: a World Parliament based on a transformation of the General Assembly into an upper house sharing its competencies with a second chamber and the introduction of qualified majority rule.[11]

However, the institutionalisation of rights and decision-making bodies on lower levels is required by the cosmopolitan model. Intermediate institutions in a global world order – regional bodies capable of collective action between the UN and the nation state – are needed in order to establish democratically controlled institutions to cope with trans-border problems. That is why regional unions such as the EU are normatively attractive. Habermas, however, is not in full agreement with the proponents of cosmopolitan democracy like for example David Held and his colleagues.

We have established that there is a need for political institutions that are capable of non-arbitrary and consistent norm enforcement, but while cosmopolitans put their trust in a democratised and empowered UN, Habermas sees the role for such an order as rather limited. The cosmopolitan community of world citizens, with the UN as a government executing a common will, should be a rather constrained entity confined to maintaining order, i.e., security and human rights politics and risk prevention. Here Habermas is in line with Kant in seeing the *world state* merely as a *security state*, but he goes beyond Kant's idea of a pacific federation of independent states – a confederation. In 'Toward Perpetual Peace' Kant feared that a world government would become a global despotism or else be a fragile and impotent empire. On the other hand, *a permanent congress of states* without a constitution, as Kant opts for, is futile because a world organisation requires a procedure for authoritative decision making and adjudication: 'Just how the permanence of this union, on which "civilised" resolution of international conflict depends, can be guaranteed without the legally binding character of an institution analogous to a state constitution Kant never explains,' (Habermas 1998e: 169). According to Held, a world state is necessary to protect seven clusters of rights: health, social, cultural, civic, economic, pacific and political rights (1995: 192 ff.).[12] Habermas objects to such a universalistic cosmopolitanism. The UN cannot be a polity with the ordinary functions of a state equipped with executive and enforcement power on a whole range of areas because the sources of solidarity are lacking. The basis for common will-formation in an ethical-political sense is not available at this level. Why is that so?

The Janus Face of the Nation State

Habermas explains this lack of solidarity at the global level by pointing to the preconditions of the modern nation state regarding its capacity for integration. Only the nation state could uphold the diverse functions of the sovereign territorial state in a democratic fashion, i.e., the functions of the administrative and tax based state, on the one hand, and those of the constitutional and modern welfare state on the other hand. The modern nation state contributed to solve problems concerning both *social integration* and *democratic legitimation* because it managed to keep together 'the idea of a community of fate' based on a common language and history and the idea of a voluntary union based on citizenship rights. This type of political integration is held to be the achievement of the nation, because the latter undertakes two separate functions at once. It has two faces:

> The nation state is Janus-faced. Whereas the voluntary nation of citizens is the source of democratic legitimation, it is the inherited or ascribed nation founded on ethnic membership (*die geborene Nation der Volkgsgenossen*) that secures social integration.
>
> (Habermas 1998c: 115)

The idea of a nation has been fused with the idea of a republic. Since the French revolution the willingness to sacrifice even one's life for the fatherland has been combined with equal rights. The notion of a common history and of 'a

241

community of fate' have effectively stimulated patriotic feelings. The nation state symbolises the spirit of the people and the force of the 'conscience collective' (to quote Durkheim). Over a long period of time the language of primordial values has been used to foster allegiance, 'the language of nationalism was forged in late eighteenth-century Europe to defend or reinforce the cultural, linguistic, and ethnic oneness and homogeneity of a people . . .' (Viroli 1995: 1). The nation state created a solidarity union between individuals that originally were strangers to one another: through general conscription, education, (hi)story-telling, mass communication and mass mobilisation heterogeneous peoples were 'homogenised'. Due to changed loyalties and identities collective action on a whole range of fields was made possible. The state could act on the basis of a strong sense of common vision and mission because of the successful symbolic construction of a people. It made *trust* possible and a new form of larger *solidarity* which constitutes the social substrate of democracy. The symbolic construction of a demos or a people founded on a sense of common belonging and sentiment, is a precondition for both the nation and the welfare state.

On the other hand, the nation state made a new form of legitimation possible in that the principle of popular sovereignty replaced earlier forms of hierarchical legitimation, i.e., that of kings and princes based on 'divine right' or on traditional bases of authority. This kind of legitimation based on royal sovereignty was supplanted with the idea of popular sovereignty. Support was drummed up through the mobilisation of enfranchised voters, democratic elections and public debate. The nation state has had the main catalytic function for the democratisation of state power.[13] It contributed to the fostering of love of the political institutions – love of the republic – and the way of life that sustains the freedom of a people.

In sum, the nation state contributed to stability in two ways: it provided for solidarity and for legitimation. A new identity based on a more abstract form of social integration was created. The nation state through its naturalistic notion of a pre-political community provided a cultural-ethical substance that appeals to the hearts and minds of the people. Especially with regard to the German tradition it is held that the mythic character of nationalistic ideas established the cultural substrate necessary for people to regard each other as neighbours and fellow countrymen, as brothers and sisters. The nation, due to its deeper ties of belonging and allegiance, makes possible the transformation of a collection of disjunct individuals and groups into a collective capable of common action, the communitarians may say. Majority rule can only function when trust and solidarity prevail. A sense of solidarity and a common identification make for *patriotism* or 'love of country' and constitute the 'non-majoritarian' sources of legitimacy.

Habermas maintains that it is not only such 'a community of fate' that has the potential of explaining imposed duties. It explains sacrifice-based duties such as conscription, military duty, capital punishment. However, other duties can be explained from a rights-based perspective. For example, the duty to pay taxes and to education do not rely on such a pre-political basis of confidence. Rather they can be explained as resulting from a process of legislation where the citizens mutually give themselves rights and hence infer corresponding duties required to realise the rights. Sacrifice as a moral category belongs to the pre-modern era and is not in line with the egalitarianism of modern democratic states. The idea here is that the procedural properties of modern democracies themselves can bear the burden of legitimation and integration. Discursively structured opinion and will formation processes have themselves the capacity of generating social rights and bringing about the corresponding duties. In this regard a pre-political, cultural homogeneity, which may, historically, have been a necessary catalysing condition for democracy can be replaced by the democratic procedure itself. This is so because it includes the citizens in a process of mutual recognition where they see themselves as addressees of the same laws that they make. As we discussed in Chapters 7 and 8 this requires a radical form of liberty. Hence, only when capital punishment and conscription have been abolished, when the state gives up the right to decide over life and death, and exit is possible – i.e., emigration – the true idea of a republic can be realised. However, while Habermas objects to the republican model in its communitarian-nationalistic reading, he is also critical of the liberal universalist model of cosmopolitan democracy.

Patriotism or Love of Humanity?

The nation state model of democracy reveals a dogmatic understanding of modernity, Habermas maintains. The emancipatory force of the enlightenment is not confined to the making of a nation state because with this a new principle of legitimation emerged. The nation state form of government does not exhaust the principle of self-governance because its procedural properties refer to more profound principles of democratic legitimation, i.e., legitimation from below through public debate and individual rights. Democracy should then be conceived of at a more abstract level and not be seen merely as an *organisation principle* – e.g., the nation state form of parliamentary democracy. Rather it is a *legitimation principle* which ensures the conditions necessary for justification of political action. In other words, it is not identical with a particular organisational form, but is rather a principle which sets down the conditions that are necessary for getting things right in politics. Modern democracy is thus not one among several alternative principles of associated life that may be chosen at will but entails the very idea of civilised life itself.

While the communitarians run the risk of seeing the nation state as the only form possible for a peoples' union based on a collective identity and thus of conceiving of the nation state as an end in itself, the cosmopolitans run the opposite danger of glossing over all distinctions and differences. Habermas points to the problem of creating a political order based on universality – on the status of world citizens who are represented in a world government through direct elections. A cosmopolitan order is based on complete inclusion – it can not exclude anyone – but a community and especially a democratic one is based on a *distinction between members and non-members*. He sees the tension between universal principles – human rights – and particularistic identities based on a common culture and descent as constitutive for democratic legitimacy. The 'Janus face' of the modern nation state points exactly to this fact, i.e., it is a union based on universalistic principles, but that these principles are also embedded in specific communities and shape a collective identity that is historically and territorially situated. The citizens conceive and appropriate universalistic principles in light of their own history and tradition. They are realised in a particular context – in a particular form of ethical life founded on shared traditions and collective memories and commitments.

It is this cultural and ethical dimension that is lacking at the world level. There is no particular context of values and obligations that make rights shrewd. We have special obligations to fellow members of our society and to the specific persons that are close to us. They stem from the fact of belonging to a society and are socially ascribed and substantively underpinned. On the other hand, special obligations to strangers usually do not arise from membership in a community but from legal obligations underscored by human values (Habermas 1996a: 510 f.). Universalistic cosmopolitanism does not recognise special obligations, i.e., obligations that arise out of membership in a concrete community; the sympathy and we-feeling that engender patriotism. In liberal cosmopolitanism borders only have a derived status, and thus have no independent value: assignment of responsibilities follows from the institutional division of labour. In this perspective the freedom and welfare of human beings will best be secured by organising the human population into different societies each with their own political institutions specialised for taking care of the interests and rights of the citizens. Borders have no intrinsic value. Other cosmopolitans second this position: patriotism does not trump *the love of humanity* (Nussbaum 1996: 17). However, several objections can be raised to unlimited cosmopolitanism.

First, there is the argument that rights must 'find their home' – they must be embedded in a culture and in concrete relationships in order to be meaningful and able to protect interests (Habermas 1999b: 270). Rights have to be rooted in practical social relationships where they can be interpreted and operationalised in relation to concrete needs and interests of human beings in order to have bearing on actual problems and conflicts. It is with regard to experiences of injustice, disrespect and humiliation that claims to rectification and compensation can be made legitimately. This requires contextualisation.[14]

Second, there is the problem of *legal protection*. The principle of the rule of law – the *Rechtsstaat* – requires the state to act on legal norms that are general, clear, public, prospective and stable in order to safeguard against states' infringement of individual liberties and rights. However, rights are always contested and require argumentation and interpretation with regard to concrete interests and values and they need to be firmly institutionalised. They also require legal regulation and constraint. Individuals' rights are limited by others' rights and concerns, and the abstract law enforcement by a world state runs the danger of glossing over relevant distinctions and differences. The idea of the constitutional state is not only to protect against encroachment but also to make sure that the regulation of interests can be rendered acceptable from a normative point of view by taking stock of a whole range of norms, interests and values, as has earlier been discussed in connection with the application discourse. Correct implementation of common action norms requires concrete institutions and procedures. Hence, proponents of a world state with far-reaching competencies – with an executive government – are facing severe theoretical and practical challenges.

Third, the shared values of the global culture are too weak to provide stability and motivation for collective action and solidarity in general. This is the sphere of *universalistic claims* and responsibilities that arise from general duties. Here human rights can be defended. They are moral rights and they can only be justified with reference to duties that bind the will of autonomous persons. Human rights designate what is universally valid but not what is valid for a particular group of people. They do not generate obligations of the kind required for solidarity and common will-formation in a strong sense, i.e. the kind of solidarity that makes possible collective action in general and redistributive and welfare state measures in particular.

> [A] world wide consensus on human rights could not serve as the basis for a strong equivalent to the civic solidarity that emerged in the framework of the nation-state. Civic solidarity is rooted in particular collective identities; cosmopolitan solidarity has to support itself on the moral universalism of human rights alone.
>
> (Habermas 2001d: 108)

While welfare state measures require a kind of civic solidarity where the members actively take responsibility for each other, the solidarity of world citizens is *reactive*, Habermas maintains. It is based on reactions to violations and humiliations of individuals in their capacity as human beings. Such a solidarity is not based on a collective identity which on its part requires distinctions. To have things in common requires that other things are excluded. What is basic to us, what we share with one another and not all the others, is what makes us special; something that arouses feelings and emotions, that we are committed to and that can motivate us to collective action and solidarity.[15] The latter stems from membership in a community of compatriots while the former from the rather weak form of an all-inclusive society. World citizens do not have much in common apart from shared 'humanity'. The world order lacks the ethical-political component necessary for common will-formation and cannot be the basis for a world government. The plea for cosmopolitan democracy has to take another route, that of 'a global domestic policy . . . without world government' according to Habermas (2001d: 104).

Hence, there are different kinds of political allegiances and communities – thick and thin – corresponding to different levels of governance and their adjacent allocation of responsibilities. In a system of multilevel governance the rights and duties vary and so do the requirements for allegiance conducive to the generation of obligations. There is an institutional division of labour for the assignments of rights and duties. The requirements for political integration vary on national, regional and global levels. Habermas's analysis is quite complex, as he addresses not only different levels of integration but also relies on different conceptual strategies. He partly relies on *contingent arguments* about genealogy and historic facts, partly on normative and *conceptual arguments* about the validity of constitutional principles, and partly on *functional requirements* of what is needed for the integration of political orders. Historic, normative and functional arguments are all used in his reconstruction of the post-Westphalian political order.

Before we proceed by applying this perspective on catching up strategies regarding economic globalisation, we will sum up the implications of these findings with regard to social integration. Analysing how multicultural societies hang together can give us a clue to comprehending how post-national integration can come about.

Constitutional Patriotism

Even if many modern states are stable and well functioning, they are highly differentiated, pluralistic and contain multi-level structures of governance. There are many sorts of identities and belongings. Pluralistic societies display a heterogeneous value basis. Why these societies hang together may be explained, not by recourse to shared values and sentiments of cultural attachment but by means of a more complex model of how allegiances are formed. To do so it is necessary to distinguish between two kinds of social integration – ethical or *cultural* and *political*. The first denotes the kind of integration that is needed for individuals and groups who seek to find out who they are or would like to be. By this we think of the values and affiliations, language and history that make up the glue of society – cohesion in general and trust and solidarity in particular – and that transform a collection of people into a group with a distinct identity, i.e., the cultural substrate of the nation.

A distinction is required between the cultural or *value basis* of a political order, which is dependent upon a particular identity that prevails in the groups and nations that people are members of, and the *constitutional properties* of such an order. The latter does not rest upon a particular set of values but on trans-cultural norms and universal principles. The constitutional order claims to be binding on all subjects and to be approved by the various groups within society, each with its particular and distinctive identity(ies) and value(s). Nation states are not merely 'nation states', i.e., the state of one particular nation: as a rule they consist of many groups – social, ethnic, religious, etc. – with different identities, values and loyalties. Often, they are multicultural societies and as such require a second level of integration – political integration – which makes it possible to cope with difference and collective decision making without relapse into 'ethnocentric politics'. Hence, respect for difference, pluralism, human rights, vulnerable identities, is required. The basic structure of constitutional democracies, then, does not only express certain values or conceptions of the good society, but in addition a conception of a rights-based society. Different groups continue to live together and resolve conflicts because they agree on the basic rules and procedures that claim to secure fair treatment of the parties. 'Law is the only medium through which a 'solidarity with strangers' can be secured in complex societies,' (Habermas 1996c: 1544). In this way law not only complements morality but in a sense also constitutes it. This is even more the case in international affairs where a collective identity is missing because only with legal standards can we know what to do, what rights and duties should apply. There is no functional equivalent to law as a coordinating means in complex and non-ideal situations.

At the level of social interaction, the explanation of political integration is to be found in the way in which freedom, democracy, autonomy, equality, – in short, due process and equal respect for all – have obtained a deontological standing in our societies. They are *principles*, with which it is *a duty* to comply even though they could interfere with the values of the majority, particularly conceptions of the good, roles, identities or utility calculations. That is why constitutional rights can function like *trumps* in collective decision making (Dworkin 1984). Some norms claim categorical validity because they are derived from the inherent dignity of the person – they are so to say 'equal and inalienable rights of all the members of the human family . . .'.[16] There is, then, not a conceptual link between ethnos and democracy, although there may be an empirical one.

The ethical-political self-understanding of citizens in a democratic community must not be taken as a historical a priori that makes democratic will-formation possible, but rather as the fluid content of a circulatory process that is generated through the legal institutionalization of citizen's communication.

(Habermas 1998d: 161)

Hence, trust and solidarity required for a collective identity is made, not found as a pre-political, primordial and essentialist category. In the creation of the nation-state 'ethnos' and 'demos' were only connected for a brief period of time and citizenship is a rights based category not internally linked to a national identity, according to Habermas. He is, however, somewhat ambivalent in the way he treats the nation state as revealed in the above analysis. It is a large container of democracy and trust but it is based on shared sentiments of attachment.[17] His conception combines elements of substance – the socio-cultural substrate necessary for democracy – with the universalism of legal principles. These principles must be embedded in a specific, historically contingent political culture through a kind of *constitutional patriotism* (Habermas 1994c). Surely one has to go beyond Thomas Hobbes's idea that everybody in a post-traditional society has an interest in a legally powerful order – a state. Habermas maintains that such an order has to be supported by substantive ethical motives – a culture of a certain quality – and by rationally acceptable principles. The constitutional state is culturally or ethically patterned at the same time as it protects the equal co-existence of the citizens. Habermas's ambivalence is reflected in the way he seems to mediate between values and rational principles in the conception of the political order. On the one hand Habermas comes close to a communitarian reading, underscoring the sharing of sentiments of attachment to a culturally integrated society. On the other hand these principles themselves are based on a rational reconstruction of 'the unavoidable conditions of impartial judgement':

> If there is no authority for relations of moral recognition higher than the good will and insight of those who come to a shared agreement concerning the rules that are to govern their living together, then the standard for judging these rules must be derived exclusively from the situation in which participants seek to *convince* one another of their beliefs and proposals.
>
> (Habermas 1998b: 24)

In this manner Habermas conceives of democracy and human rights, not solely as representative of cultural traditions and shared meanings, but as manifestations of cognitive-moral principles that command respect in and of themselves. But how the balance between ethical values and rational principles should be struck is not clear. Which is the most important? For example, how can we explain that countries with the same legal basis rule differently in similar cases? If one country bans smoking and another one does not, is this difference due to different constitutional identities or to impartial judgement? However, it is clear that the latter has priority in discourse theory and that the 'communitarian strand' in Habermas's theory has more to do with *genealogy* – how things have been brought about – than with *validity* ('Geltung'), i.e., with what can be rationally defended. It is clear that Habermas sees the cognitive-liberal principles as essential prerequisites for self-governance and the cornerstone of modern constitutional arrangements. Constitutions protect the citizens' freedom by entrenching a host of individual rights. Basic civil rights cannot be altered by simple majority vote. Constitutionally entrenched rights clauses, in addition to the principle of a written constitution, the principle of separation of powers, and judicial review, etc. impose restrictions on 'the will of the people' and are meant to guarantee the freedom of the individual. They may be seen to protect the *private autonomy* of the citizens and are necessary for the formation of authentic private opinions.

Constitutional arrangements not only enable but also require and warrant popular participation in the political process. That is, they enable and warrant *government by the people*. The democratic principle entrenched in modern constitutions refers to the manner in which citizens are involved in public deliberations, collective decision making and law making through a set of rights and procedures that range from freedom of speech and assembly to eligibility and voting rights. These political rights, and their attendant institutions and procedures, are to secure the *public autonomy* of the individual. They ensure that the addressees of the law can also participate in the making of the law. The alleged problem of the so-called infinite regress – between rights and democracy – disappears, according to Habermas, once the constitution is conceived in generational terms: even though the people are constrained by the constitution authored by their forefathers, the present understanding and the full use of the constitution depend on the agency of the present generation. As a self-correcting learning process '[T]he allegedly paradoxical relation between democracy and the rule of law resolves itself in the dimension of historical time, provided one conceives of the constitution as a project that makes the founding act into an ongoing process of constitution-making that continues across generations' (Habermas 2001e: 768).

However, in practical terms there is a tension between popular sovereignty based on collective or national identities and human rights claims, because only the former is conducive to democratic legitimacy. This is the background for Habermas's scepticism about a world state and this is also why he does not see the American constitution as a prototype for European reform. European constitutional patriotism has to take seriously the differences between countries. There are different national trajectories that have shaped the collective consciousness of the people and different interpretations of the universalistic principles. However, the nation state model of democratic governance is challenged by globalisation.

GLOBALISATION AND DEMOCRACY

The modern nation state designates a governmental structure of political authority based on supreme jurisdiction over a demarcated territory, underpinned by the monopoly of the use of force and dependent on the loyalty of the ruled. Legitimacy is conferred by so-called liberal democratic institutions through which citizens elect their representatives, form common opinions and voice criticism. This model has been challenged due to several causes captured by the term globalisation that have all served to undermine and transform the liberal model of democracy.

Denationalisation and Deliberation

The world is steadily becoming one through capital and information being available everywhere. Especially in the economic area this process is picking up pace as world financial and banking centres merge into one integrated network. The concept of globalisation denotes a spatial phenomenon on a continuum between the local and the global, involving the widening and deepening of social relations across space and time and the interdependence and vulnerabilities of day-to-day activities – in short, the compression of time and space (Giddens 1991, Held 1998). Currently, there are global structures of finance, production, trade and communication that threaten to undermine the boundaries of the nation state. Citizens' interests are affected in ways and by bodies which are difficult to hold responsible through the ballot box. In democratic terms globalisation means that those who can be kept accountable have little control over the factors affecting peoples' lives, and those who have the decisive decision-making power are beyond democratic reach. David Held, in several of his works, argues that nation states lose some of their sovereignty due to globalisation and that this is wearing away the capacity for citizenship at the domestic level. Increasingly, the nation states have become 'decision takers' and not only 'decision makers'. Their *sovereignty* is eroded to the degree that the common action norms are decided by other forms of authority; their *autonomy* is reduced when their capability 'to articulate and achieve policy goals independently' is abridged (Held *et al.* 1999: 52).

Habermas on his part often uses the word *denationalisation* to depict how national politics loses control because of deregulation and new interdependencies in the world financial markets as well as in the industrial production itself. This process may reduce the tax revenues and the ability to make efficient employment and fiscal policies, redistribution and macro-economic steering. In so far as there is the emergence of a *world society*, it is a stratified one, because globalisation divides the world in two but at the same time 'forces it to act cooperatively as a community of shared risks,' (Habermas 1998e: 183). These changes, however, not only signify the spread of market economy world wide but the possible emergence of a new international political order as well. We are witnessing *a reconfiguration of political power*, which does not denote defeat of democracy but challenges the presupposition of its confinement to a bounded territory.

What is unique today compared to earlier forms of internationalisation and globalisation is that it unfolds in a situation where most of the states claim to be democratic. Globalism is connected to the end of the Cold War and the assertion of democracy as the sole legitimate system of governance:

> Globalization today thus raises an entirely novel set of political and normative dilemmas which have no real equivalent in previous epochs, namely, how to combine a system of territorially rooted democratic governance with the transnational and global organization of social and economic life.
>
> (Held *et al.* 1999: 431)

Thus if real citizenship is to be realised today, democratisation of transnational institutions that are affecting security, economic, health and environmental conditions are required. At the international level we actually see the establishment of new governance structures. The UN, OSCE, WTO, the World Bank, IMF are important and so are NGOs, social movements and transnational communication. Globalisation processes are multi-dimensional in character encompassing different domains of cooperation and do not only designate unfettered capitalism. International legislative and policy making bodies and transnational policy networks have emerged, and have added to the existing complex of local, regional and national centres of authority. There is a growing interconnectedness of states and of societies, because of multiple and rapidly growing networks of communication internationally and also because of transgovernmental regimes, diplomacy and even transnational civil society (Bohman and Lutz-Bachmann 1997: 8). Democracy is, however, only rarely brought to bear on international organisations and multilateral forms of regulation.

Government or Governance?

Traditionally, international affairs are conducted through diplomacy and intergovernmental bargaining between executive branches of national governments. Today there are new forms of political governance emerging beyond the nation state. Here one sees the impact of indirect steering mechanisms and influence where 'soft power' may force 'hard power' aside (Habermas 1998e: 175).

Cosmopolitans are faced with two options (Bohman 1999: 499 ff.): one is to create hierarchical powers analogous to the nation state, i.e., authoritative organisations making up a world order buttressed by international law. This amounts to *government*. The other represents a less supranational solution as it puts the trust in decentralisation, networks and transnational agreements – *governance* – which designates steering beyond public law. Governance is due to different steering mechanisms that are brought about by several channels of influence, and these exist on different levels, some sponsored by state and some not. Such mechanisms range from NGOs and social movements to the Internet, cities and micro regions and may be regarded as series of experiments in democracy as they amount to control mechanisms beyond governments (Rosenau 1997, 1998). New regimes are emerging based on various decentralised and cooperative solutions, and contribute to a remarkable expansion of collective power to handle new forms of risks and vulnerabilities.

This activity sometimes takes the form of a transnational public sphere and a discursive structure of opinion formation. Cross-cutting and transnational movements indicate that the world now is 'a world of overlapping communities of fate' and testify to the thesis of new forms of global governance (Held 1998). Civil society organisations, (I)NGO's, and social movements operate at this level as well and exert *communicative pressure* on power holders. Through protests, demonstrations, campaigns, Internet and media interventions they influence decision making processes. No one possesses absolute power within these structures, and for some analysts they represent functional equivalents to democracy. Pluralism and disaggregation are seen as conducive to democracy in a multi-centred world of diverse non-governmental actors.

> These regimes cannot directly control the effects of globalisation: they attempt to enable the normative constraints consistent with equality of effective freedom rather than with equal access to agency freedom over the levers of economic process.
>
> (Bohman 1999: 509)

In short, governance denotes a method for dealing with political controversies in which actors, political and non-political, arrive at mutually acceptable decisions by deliberating and negotiating with each other. It is based on a variety of processes with different authority bases, and highlights the role of voluntary and non-profit organisations in joint decision making and implementation and the semi-public character of modern political enterprise.

However, network governance actually means cooperation among representatives of the executive branch. This system amounts, in our opinion, merely to *governance without democracy*, because there is little chance of equal access and public accountability. The citizens lack the instruments of power to force decision-makers to look after their interests. The people are merely the subjects (or subordinates – *Untertanen*) of power, not the holders of power themselves – they are not empowered to authorise or instruct their rulers. The ultimate instruments of control do not rest with the people but with the decision-makers. Hence, transnational or network governance may enhance the problem solving capacity and rationality and as such have epistemic value – they improve the quality of the decisions; but it does not amount to popular rule. It compensates for lack of influence, but does not substitute for it.

Habermas, on his part, however, sees intergovernmental bargaining complemented with new governance structures and deliberation in a transnational civil society as a model for world governance, i.e., as an alternative to a *world government*. Deliberative and decision-making bodies emerge transnationally – in between societies and beyond the state. Agreements are reached via deliberation in epistemic communities and communicative spaces are created that put decision-makers to a test. This may, in his view, be sufficient for legitimating decisions in international organisations not only because of the ability of soft power to push hard power in a media society, but also because transnational decision making can be made transparent for national public spheres.

Although these structures cannot replace established democratic procedures, they exert a certain pressure and 'tip the balance, from the concrete embodiments of sovereign will in persons, votes and collectives to the procedural demands of communicative and decision-making processes,' (Habermas 2001d: 111). Transnational deliberative bodies also raise the information level and contribute to rational problem solving because they include different parties and often adhere to arguing as a decision-making procedure and not voting and bargaining. To various degrees such bodies inject the logic of impartial justification and reason giving into transnational bodies of governance. They have epistemic value even if ideal communication requirements have not been met, because deliberation forces the participants to justify their standpoints and decisions in an impartial and neutral manner. Deliberation contributes to a more rational way of solving problems and of improving the epistemic quality of the reasons in a justification process (cf. Bohman 1996: 26 f.).[18] Here, deliberation is seen primarily as a cooperative activity for intelligent problem solving in relation to a cognitive standard and not as an argument about what is correct because it can be approved by everyone. Publicity, then, is to be understood as a democratic *experimental society* for detecting and solving social problems – including identifying unintended side-effects – and not as a political principle of legitimacy.[19] Under such conditions one can make assessments and agree on certain things that must be done, without agreeing on the conditions that form the basis of the decision, i.e., they do not have to agree for the same reasons.[20] The premises for agreement may be different. This is the area for *working agreements* that we discussed in the preceding chapter.

Transnational bodies of governance and deliberation may be able to tackle normative and politically salient questions in a qualitatively good manner. 'The public use of reason' enhances problem solving capacity and political rationality at the transnational level also. This development corresponds to Habermas's *de-substantialised concept of popular sovereignty* that we discussed in Chapter 6. Popular sovereignty resides in the dispersed process of informal communication and not in a demos substantively defined. It is the autonomy of public spheres and party competition in addition to the parliamentary principle that provide the basis for democratic legitimacy. Habermas's assessment here draws on the epistemic value of deliberative democracy, which underscores the rationality presupposition and not merely the institutional or participatory presuppositions in conceiving of democratic legitimacy.

> [T]he democratic procedure no longer draws it is legitimizing force only, indeed not even predominantly, from political participation and the expression of political will, but rather from the general accessibility of a deliberative process whose structure grounds an expectation of rationally acceptable results.
>
> (Habermas 2001d: 110)

The basic problem with this solution is the lack of commitment that follows when law is not laid down authoritatively and made equally binding on every part. The role of law is to complement morality as discussed in Chapter 7. When non-compliance is sanctioned, actors may act in a moral manner without facing the danger of losing out. The incentives for strategic action are taken away. Actors comply more easily with interest-regulating norms when they are subjected to a higher authority that legislates and sanctions non-compliance unilaterally. But law is also, as mentioned earlier, constituting morality in international affairs, as in such uncharted terrains only with the help of legal standards can complex coordination of action take place. Thus, law is not only needed to pacify the state of nature between the sovereign states, it is a precondition for the establishment of a civil society based on deliberation. This is in line with Habermas's criticism of Kant who was reluctant regarding 'a *constitutionally organized* community of nations' and who had to 'rely exclusively on each government's own *moral* self-obligation,' (Habermas 1998e: 170, 169). Habermas argues for cosmopolitan law and for a democratised world order limited to security functions. He does not opt for a polity with a government, i.e., a world state. The critical point regarding the viability of this option, which we cannot pursue here, pertains to the role and functions of the constitution-based supranational order of the deliberative model of post-national politics, i.e.: how strong and competent a world organisation? In any regard, such a world organisation is not capable of constraining global capitalism.

POST-NATIONAL DEMOCRACY

Habermas is pointing to a different strategy for catching up with the negative effects of economic globalisation than the cosmopolitan plea for a world state. He puts his trust in the development of regions between the nation state and the world order, i.e., post-national federations of member states.

A Global Domestic Policy

Due to denationalisation there may be a hollowing out of the autonomy of the nation state, i.e., a declining capacity to take action on collective problems and conduct redistributive policies. If the welfare state is presently being undermined at the state level, supranational orders are needed to regain control over the vital factors affecting people's freedom and welfare. Capabilities on the supranational level are required.[21] For Habermas the EU is a candidate for rescuing the welfare state. On several occasions he has argued the case for European integration as a means to combat globalisation, ensure peace and to further some of the civilisational aspects of European culture. While Habermas finds a world state neither necessary nor desirable or feasible, the EU is a different matter: it is the prime example of a global domestic polity at the regional level. In order to combat the negative effects of economic globalisation it is necessary to expand national forms of solidarity and welfare state measures to a post-national federation at the regional level:

> Continent-wide regimes of this sort can establish unified currency zones that help reduce the risk of fluctuating exchange rates, but, more significantly, they can also create larger political entities with a hierarchical organization of competencies.
>
> (Habermas 2001c: 53)

Habermas envisages a *republican Europe* that can overcome the problematic aspects of nationalism and particularism of the prevailing nation state system of Europe, and that can solve common, trans-border problems. A republican Europe can rescue the collective self-determination threatened by globalisation. Traditionally war is the state-building impetus. What is interesting with regard to European integration is that it is a voluntary project and one that has to rely on other sources than those that established the nation states. The integration process can draw on different kinds of so-called 'non-majoritarian' sources of integration. For one, the politico-legal, socio-economic institutions are quite similar, as the representative (and mostly parliamentary) democratic system and a market economy tamed by social concerns have contributed to stabilise Western welfare states for quite a long time now. The establishment of comprehensive social security systems and domestication of capitalist economies through Keynesianism are major European achievements, according to Habermas, and may be seen as representing an attractive European common denominator.

Further, common grounds that can ease the transition to post-national democracy range from experiences dating back to the Middle Ages about how to cope with conflicts of the most diverse kind – between church and secular power, between faith and knowledge, between centre and periphery, etc. – to modern collective learning processes stemming from two world wars, devastating economic crisis, holocaust, and large social movements. Key words are *learning from catastrophe* and *reconciliation through the public use of reason*. This has led to a new sensitivity for difference and the decentring of perspectives conducive to the principles of equal protection and mutual recognition of diversity. A conflict-ridden continent has managed to cope with difference through the institutionalisation of peaceful mechanisms of conflict resolution.

> These experiences of successful forms of social integration have shaped the normative self-understanding of European modernity into an egalitarian universalism that

can ease the transition to postnational democracy's demanding contexts of mutual recognition for all of us – we, the sons, daughters, and grandchildren of barbaric nationalism.

(Habermas 2001d: 103)[22]

Lastly, European integration is possible on democratic premises, according to Habermas. Post-national democracy is a viable option because, as we have seen, the democratic constitutional states are not conceived of as reflecting merely a particular nation or *Sittlichkeit* – i.e., *Kulturnationen*. Rather, they are founded on the norms and principles underlying the French revolution – the Enlightenment era – and which nowadays are spread well beyond the Western hemisphere. These entities still constitute the most essential aspects of what may be termed 'the European identity'. This is a genuine political identity that is based upon the principle of self-rule via the medium of law, and which entails equal rights for all. Habermas's distinction between cultural/ethical integration and political integration is attuned to the phenomena of European integration, as it enables him to distinguish between national attitudes based on particularistic values and beliefs one the one hand, and the legal-political attitude of civic rights and participation that is common to all Europeans. This legal-normative basis is procedural rather than substantive, moral and judicial rather than ethical and cultural but will have effects on the latter. Transformation of attitudes and identities and collective learning processes conducive to solidarity can come about in inclusive and deliberative settings.

> *Citizens' solidarity*, hitherto limited to the nation-state, must be expanded to the citizens of the Union in such a way that, for example, Swedes and Portuguese, Germans and Greeks are willing to stand up for one another, as it is the case now with citizens from former West and East Germany.
>
> (Habermas 2000: 34)

By delineating the EU in democratic terms its boundaries can be justified within a cosmopolitan framework, we may add. The borders of the EU are in this perspective to be drawn both with regard to what is required for the Union itself in order to be a self-sustainable and well-functioning democratic entity and with regard to the support and further development of similar regional associations in the rest of the world. The borders of the EU are thus drawn also with regard to functional requirements both for itself and for other regions all within the constraints of a democratised and rights-enforcing UN. The EU is the most promising example of a post-national powerful organisation. Europe is the cradle of the so-called Westphalian order but it is also in Europe that the process of transforming or even dismantling it has progressed the furthest. That this is taking place in Europe is remarkable in itself. Even more remarkable, given Europe's violent past, is the peaceful nature of this transformation. The EU has emerged into an entity with supranational traits – as part of a rapid and profound transformation of political power in Europe. It has moved beyond an international organisation and also beyond the limitations of the Charter of the United Nations, which prohibits violence but forbids the intervention in the internal affairs of a state.

However, the EU in its present form suffers from a *democratic deficit* due to a weak parliament, the absence of European-wide parties and the absence of a European public sphere based on a symbolically constructed people. The EU, therefore, needs democratic reform and a formal constitution. This is even more urgent as the EU has become more than an intergovernmental, free trade union. 'The Maastricht Treaty establishes a basis for the development of the European Union beyond the status of a functional economic community' (Habermas 2001b: 17), but as it still is an intergovernmental agreement it 'lacks that symbolic depth which political constitutive moments alone possess,' (Habermas 2001: 4 f.).

A Post-National Federation?

Intergovernmentalists argue that the EU is a type of international organisation. It is in the hands of the member states, and as long as they are democratic there is no need for the EU to be developed into a democratic polity. In this perspective the EU regulates trade and harmonises laws and solves problems common to all. This amounts in practical terms to negative integration – i.e., liberalisation and deregulation policies – and for this neither democracy nor a common identity is required. National democracy ensures the necessary source of legitimacy. This view is strongly opposed by others who see the EU as a supranational entity that does not leave the member states untouched.

The EU's impact on the weal and woe of ordinary people of Europe is profound. Integration is both widened and deepened through measures aimed at redistribution, through regulation of social, environmental and health policies, and through police and judicial cooperation. Recent developments include three treaty revisions, the Economic and Monetary Union, the creation of the Euro and the European Central bank. The latter is of utmost interest for macro-economic steering. The EU has taken important steps towards a common security and defence policy, and towards a common justice and home affairs policy. Taken together this indicates that the Union has come a long way to taking on state-like functions.

The EU's broadened and deepened scope of action and closer and more direct links to the citizens of the member states contribute to a massive transformation of the member states. The indirect or derivative model of legitimacy which is premised on the member state as a legitimate site of authority is thus insufficient. The democratic legitimacy of the member states cannot be established independently of the EU, because the EU and the individual states have become so deeply enmeshed that the pattern of legitimate authority in the states is also transformed. The member states can therefore no longer serve as the source of their own legitimacy, independently of the EU (Eriksen and Fossum 2000).

What is needed, then, is the establishment of a formal basis for legitimacy – the development of a rights-based democratic order. The EU itself has subscribed to the principles of democracy and human rights in *The Charter on Fundamental Human Rights* proclaimed at the Nice summit in 2000, which, as Habermas notes, designates 'what Europeans have in common'.[23] The proposed charter can be read as one of – if not the most – explicit statement on the EU's commitment to *direct legitimacy* that has ever been produced in the EU, in the sense that the institutions and rights provided to the citizens by the EU in themselves shall provide the necessary basis for legitimate governance. The Charter of Fundamental Human Rights in the EU is an important step in the process of the institutionalisation of a framework of a cosmopolitan order where violations of human rights can be prosecuted as criminal offences according to legal procedures.

The system of representation and accountability already in place in the EU gives the citizens at least a minimal input in to the process of framing and concretising the rights. What is required, then, are rights that are specified with regard to the explicit duties of power-wielding bodies. The charter observes this right in securing a right to vote and to political accountability. However, the EU is in need of a more fundamental democratic reform. According to democratic standards this has, in addition to the charter of inalienable rights, to include a *competence catalogue* delimiting the powers of the various branches and levels of government. This implies further abolishing the pillar structure of the EU, altering the allocation of competencies of the decision-making bodies, empowering the European Parliament, making the Council into a second chamber and the Commission into a government headed by an (EP) elected president. Compared to the presidential regime of the USA, a European Union of Nation States would according to Habermas have to display the following general features:

(a) A Parliament that would resemble Congress in *some* respects (a similar division of powers and, compared with the European parliamentary systems, relatively weak political parties).

(b) A legislative 'chamber of nations' that would have more competencies than the American Senate, and a Commission that would be much less powerful than the White House (thus splitting the classical functions of a strong Presidency between the two).

(c) A European Court that would be as influential as the Supreme Court for similar reasons (the regulatory complexity of an enlarged and socially diversified Union would require detailed interpretation of a principled constitution, cutting short the jungle of existing treaties) (Habermas 2001f: 11 f.).

Habermas does not foresee a European Nation based on a collective identity symbolised by an empowered parliament, because of the position and legitimacy of the member states. The second chamber of government – 'the chamber of nations' – must have a stronger position than the directly elected parliament in order to secure equal protection and recognition of diversity.[24]

The problem with this model pertains to the role it allocates to 'the chamber of nations' to the detriment of a directly elected parliament. It may be a realistic model given present constraints but it is weak in democratic terms. A directly elected parliament in addition to a vibrant set of public spheres is the prime source of popular sovereignty. The disadvantage of the proposed model is that the vital concerns of the European citizens are still to be handled through a system of inter-state negotiations. The tension between constitution and democracy cannot be solved until the people or their representatives are making the same laws that they have to abide by, as Habermas generally claims. Only when the citizens can address the same questions in a free public sphere and their representatives can legislate in popular elected bodies – parliaments – can democratic legitimacy be obtained. Habermas's proposal is a modest one, and it seems also to be slightly at odds with his belief in and plea for a collective identity and for a constitution-making process to be the catalyst of such.

> Only the transformed consciousness of citizens, as it imposes itself in areas of domestic policy, can pressure global actors to change their own self-understanding sufficiently to begin to see themselves as members of an international community who are compelled to cooperate with one another, and hence to take one another's interest into account.
>
> (Habermas 2001c: 55)

For a constitution-making process to be conducted in a proper way a democratic process of legitimation is required. This takes a European civil society as well as European-wide public spheres and the shaping of a political culture. It is difficult for representatives of member states to enter into binding agreements internationally as long as they are dependent on a local electorate to be re-elected. Hence, opinion formation European-wide is necessary and can be created through a communicative context of criss-crossing national and transnational public spheres. Some of the elements needed for a democratic identity formation are to a certain degree in place such as a parliament, while others like European-wide parties are lacking. This is a major obstacle because as long as representatives have to report only to domestic constituencies, a European *bonum commune* will not be established. Habermas sees the need for a European party system which can contribute to the development of opinion and will-formation nationally, and that are also connected to and 'find a resonance in a pan-European political public sphere' (Habermas 2001d: 103).

Against the accusation that this is a futile endeavour given the present mentalities and power structures, Habermas would assert that trust and an *obligatory cosmopolitan solidarity* can be fostered, and that

> there is no call for defeatism, if one bears in mind that, in the nineteenth-century European states, national consciousness and social solidarity were only gradually produced, with the help of national historiography, mass communications, and universal conscription. If that artificial form of 'solidarity amongst strangers' came about thanks to a historically momentous effort of abstraction from local, dynastic consciousness to a consciousness that was national democratic, then why should it be impossible to extend this learning process beyond national borders?
>
> (Habermas 1999c: 58)

CONCLUSION

We are today in the midst of a transformation process where nation state based democracy is being challenged by supra-national forms of governance. The establishment of viable democratic orders above the nation state depend on successful abstraction processes. To be able to progress from nation state forms of allegiance and solidarity to supranational ones requires enlarged mentalities and inclusive forms of communication. Cosmopolitan democracy is the horizon and aim of such processes but not the inevitable outcome. History is man made, but as man is frail, so are political processes, hence their fallibility.

In Figure 11.1 the dimensions of integration from nation state to world level that we have established in this chapter are summarised in a very simplified and schematic way. In this reconstruction of the post-Westphalian order the nation state and the world order are conceived of as options on the thick/thin continuum

Levels of integration	Function	Type of rule	Forms of allegiance
Nation state	Collective goal attainment	Representative government	Shared attachment and we-feeling
Federation of states	Regulation and 'redistribution'	Post-national democratic government	Rights-based collective identity
Trans-national governance	Joint problem-solving	Networks and soft law coordination	Epistemic founded identity
A world organisation	Security and human rights protection	A law based policy without a government	Respect for cosmopolitan law

Figure 11.1 *Levels of integration and the corresponding requirements of the post-national order*

with regard to identity. While the nation state form of allegiance is based on a shared sentiment of attachment the governmental structure of the state also exhibits cognitive-universalist features. Hence, there are connections to post-national forms of governance. The universalist core of the constitutional state is similar to the normative infrastructure making up the EU as a federation of member states. However, other kinds of transnational forms of governance are also necessary to tackle problems beyond the state and cope with the negative consequences of globalisation. Some of these problems may be solved adequately by intergovernmental bargaining complemented by new governance structures such as epistemic communities and a transnational civil society. However, other kinds of problems and conflicts require firmer forms of coordination in order to be resolved properly. At the global level a world organisation without a government in the shape of a democratised UN is needed for handling risk protection, for sanctioning human rights abuses consistently, and for establishing security measures in general.

Notes

1. Especially Eriksen 2001b, Eriksen and Fossum (eds) 2000, Eriksen *et al.* (eds) 2001.
2. '[O]f course not every independent state is free, but the recognition of sovereignty is the only way we have of establishing an arena within which freedom can be fought for and (sometimes) won. It is this arena and the activities that go on within it that we want to protect, and we protect them, much as we protect individual integrity, by marking out boundaries that cannot be crossed, rights that cannot be violated. As with individuals, so with sovereign states: there are things that we cannot do to them, even for their own ostensible good.' (Walzer 1977:89) see also Walzer 1985, and Beitz 1988 for critique and overview.
3. As mentioned in Chapter 7: 'The individual may say for himself: "Fiat justitia, pererat mundus" (Let justice be done, even if the world perish), but the

state has no right to say so in the name of those who are in its care,' (Morgenthau 1993: 12, cf. Kant 1996b: 345) However, to secure the global state of peace can itself be seen to be 'a human right of prime importance', according to Apel (2001: 33). For Hobbes, the right to life was the prime natural right, but as civil wars make clear the case of freedom of religion contradicts this: freedom of belief is valued over one's own life (Cf. Höffe 1999: 62.).

4. The UN has been innovative and rather controversial. Cf. Falk 1998.

5. Forst 1999a and b. To this subject see also the articles in Brunkhorst *et al.* (eds) 1999; Brunkhorst and Niesen 1999; Brunkhorst (ed.) 1998.

6. However, one may also say that the problem of infinite regress is only a problem for foundationalists – it is the 'product of an old providential model of authority that leads us to look for authorization prior to action rather than the other way round' (Honig 2001: 796). Cf. the discussion in Chapter 7 and Habermas 2001d for a reply. We will return to this.

7. Cf. Alexy (1996) on the place of reason-giving: raising claims to correctness is the most universal human experience.

8. For less strict claims, see Gutmann and Thompson 1996: 101; Rawls 1993: 253.

9. Cf. Apel 1997, Brunkhorst *et al.* (eds) 1999.

10. 'Cosmopolitan law must be institutionalized in such a way that it is binding on individual governments,' Habermas 1998e: 179).

11. 'And equipping the world organization with the right to demand that member states carry out referendums on important issues at any time is also an interesting suggestion under discourse-theoretical premises,' (Habermas 2001d: 111).

12. In addition one may include compulsory jurisdiction before the International Court, new coordination of economic agencies and the establishment of an effective accountable, international military force in the short-term objectives of cosmopolitan democracy. Cf. Held 1995: 279.

13. 'Democratic participation, as it slowly became established, generated a new level of legally mediated *solidarity* via the status of citizenship while providing the state with a secular source of *legitimation*,' (Habermas 1998c: 112).

14. These concerns are often informed by Hegel's criticism of Kant's idea of a cosmopolitan right, see Kant 1996b. However, Hegel's critique was not of cosmopolitanism as such but of the propensity of turning it into a fixed order: 'It is defective only when it is crystallized, e.g. as a cosmopolitanism in opposition to the concrete life of the state,' (Hegel 1967: 134).

15. 'Cosmopolitanism misunderstands people's local affiliations – that is, attachments to various communities that are typically experienced as imposing responsibilities different in kind and degree from those imposed on us by our common humanity,' (Beitz 1999: 290 f.).

16. Cited from the Preamble of the United Nations International Covenant on Civil and Political Rights 1966, (Laqueur and Rubin (eds) 1990: 215.).

17. This is a hot theme in the discussion of the EU, where Habermas is opposed to the positions of Claus Offe and Dieter Grimm, who both hold the nation state as the largest possible container of democracy and trust.

18. The epistemic interpretation of deliberative democracy holds that deliberation is a cognitive process for the assessment of reasons in order to reach just decisions and establish conceptions of the common good.

19. Cf. Dewey 1927, Honneth 1999, Kettner 1998, Brunkhorst 2002.
20. See also Gutmann and Thompson 1996 and the debate in Macedo (ed.) 1999.
21. 'Welfare-state functions, obviously, can only be maintained on the previous scale if they are transferred from the nation-state to larger political units growing to catch up, so to speak, with a transnationalized economy,' (Habermas 2000: 33).
22. Cf. Habermas 2001c. At some points Habermas also argues along the lines of the old Frankfurt School, as when he hints to a European republicanism levelled against the instrumentalism and 'commodified, homogeneous culture' of the USA as a common normative basis for Europe (Habermas 2001d: 75).
23. 'This new awareness of what Europeans have in common has found an admirable expression in the EU Charter of Basic Rights. . . . articulating a social vision of the European project. It also shows what Europeans link together normatively. Responding to recent developments in biotechnology, Article 3 specifies each person's right to his or her physical and mental integrity, and prohibits any practice of positive eugenics or the reproductive cloning of human organisms,' (Habermas 2001f: 11).
24. 'because the elements of negotiations and multilateral agreements between member states that are decisive today cannot disappear without a trace even for a union under a political constitution,' (Habermas 2001d: 99).

SYNTHESISING REMARKS

The post-national constellation is torn between national and cosmopolitan concerns, between particularistic and universalistic claims, because human rights are among the constitutive elements of the legitimate procedure. The democratic *Rechtsstaat* points beyond the confinements of a particular demos. Only in a democratic world order can human rights and popular sovereignty eventually be reconciled. Genuine democracy, hence, is not possible in one country. Interestingly, globalisation brings together democracy and human rights. Globalisation makes the inhabitants of the world aware of the growing interdependence, risk escalation and common problems that require transnational and supranational cooperation. The problem is unfettered capitalism and the uncoupling of market decisions from governmental control where 'money replaces power'. However, only 'power can be democratised; money cannot' (Habermas 2001d: 78). To catch up with economic globalisation and human rights violations a cosmopolitan law of the people as well as a world domestic policy are needed. This analysis hinges on the achievements of discourse theory, which yet in its micro elements reflects the tension between particular and universal concerns.

Even though the rational principles of liberalism are prioritised in discourse theory, in practical terms it strikes a balance between rights and values, between universalism and particularism. The theory has been developed and expanded in such a way that it both captures the special duties and particular obligations arising from membership in a community of fellow compatriots as well as the individual rights and obligations stemming from belonging to the universal community of humans. It is sensitive to difference and otherness – to the inherent dignity of the person – at the same time as the requirements for social integration and collective action are fleshed out. The political order of multicultural societies is explained with the help of a refined conceptual strategy based on distinctions between norms and values, between political and cultural integration, on the one hand, and with the help of a set of discourses and their embedding in social and political institutions, on the other.

This complex and far-reaching theoretical system originates from the theory of communicative action that Habermas conceives of having the properties necessary for being able to abstract from the local and particularistic to universalistic settings. The fundamental human capacity to speak to one another, to understand each other and to reach binding agreements via speech acts, is the basic building block of the theory. This was addressed in the first part of the book, where the concept of communicative action and the basic structure of discourse ethics were spelled out. It is from the fine capillary structures of the human language that Habermas can reconstruct the limited but important universalist basis of our political order such as individual rights, popular sovereignty, democracy, the public sphere, etc., as we have seen in Part 2 of the book.

Habermas sees the theory as cognitivistic, formalistic and universalistic. The discourse principle (D) is to be understood as a formal principle of rationality of how to justify norms. However, certain substantial elements are involved. The procedure itself involves substantive categories and the concept of the person is not empty and purely formal. Even at the foundational level of discourse theory certain substantive elements are involved, reflecting modernity.

The attention to substance is even more evident in his recent work, *The Future of Human Nature*, which deals with the dispute over the ethical self-understanding of the species in light of developments of gene manipulative technology. Here he goes a long way in establishing a substantial concept of what it takes to be human. Habermas makes use of a concept of human nature to oppose cloning of human beings: 'for the person to feel one with her body, it seems that this body has to be experienced as something natural – as a continuation of the organic, self-regenerative life from which the person was born,' (Habermas 2003).

But in general the scope for substantive values and material interests is rather large in the discourse theory of politics. *The circumstances of politics* – the prevalence of conflict and disagreement – are always present in the work of Habermas. He might even subscribe to Hegel's words that the fabric of political life is made up of the 'maelstrom of external contingency and the inner particularity of passions, private interests and selfish ends, abilities and virtues, vices, force, and wrong' (1967: 215). The potential dangers emanating from this *ceaseless turmoil* in the form of war and human rights violations, require safeguards. In discourse theory morality should be seen as constituting the basic rationale behind constitutional guards. It draws the boundaries that are not to be crossed. The domain for morality in the strict Kantian sense is limited. However, it is given much attention because of its importance and suitability for theoretical formulation. Its importance derives from its ability to conceive of the basic aspects of human worth and dignity that should not be traded for whatever value or interest. Morality functions as a constraint – a negative arbiter – on value and interest based actions and hence subjects political courses of action to a test; it draws the boundaries and sets the basic conditions for civilised life, but it does not constitute social and political life as such.

Also when dealing with aspects of globalisation, such as governance beyond the nation state, we have seen that Habermas is not unconditionally subscribing to the rational principles of a universalistic cosmopolitan world order. His caution stems from recognising the fragility of the modern political order and its reliance on a concrete ethical substance with a culturalist imprint. The nation state based on a symbolically constructed people is not obsolete. It is still a context of solidarity. The furthering of European integration can only be conducted in a legitimate and successful way by respecting the collective identities of the member states. It can only be accomplished by protecting diversity and ensuring solidarity.

However, further democratisation is needed for the post-Westphalian order to achieve functional stability and normative legitimacy. This is so as there is a tension between international law's recognition of sovereign states and the regulative idea of equal rights and freedom for all which is reflected in an actual opposition between democracy and law, and between domestic and foreign policy. The growth in international law limits the principle of popular sovereignty. On the other hand, legal orders are orders of peace, and one may say that the principle of popular sovereignty is actually being undermined by international human rights politics as well. The principle of popular sovereignty is about to be transformed into a law for the citizens of the world.

REFERENCES

(Numbers in brackets [. . .] indicate year of original publication.)

Abramson, J. 1990: 'Four Criticisms of Press Ethics.' In J. Litchtenberg (ed.): *Democracy and the Mass Media*. Cambridge: Cambridge University Press.

Ackerman, B. 1980: *Social Justice in the Liberal State*. New Haven: Yale University Press.

Ackerman, B. 1989: 'Why Dialog.' *Journal of Philosophy* 86:5–22.

Adorno, T. W. 1976 [1969]: 'Introduction.' In T. W. Adorno *et al.*: *The Positivist Dispute in German Sociology*. New York: Harper & Row.

Albert, H. 1985 [1968]: *Treatise on Critical Reason*. Princeton: Princeton University Press.

Alexy, R. 1981: 'Die Idee einer prozeduralen Theorie der juristischen Argumentation.' In A. Aarnio *et al.* (eds): *Methodologie und Erkenntnistheorie der juristischen Argumentation*. Berlin: Duncker & Humbolt.

Alexy, R. 1989 [1978]: *A Theory of Legal Argumentation. The Theory of Rational Discourse as Theory of Legal Justification*. Oxford: Clarendon Press.

Alexy, R. 1994: 'Basic Rights and Democracy in Jürgen Habermas's Procedural Paradigm of the Law.' *Ratio Juris* 7:227–38.

Alexy, R. 1995: *Recht, Vernunft, Diskurs*. Frankfurt: Suhrkamp.

Alexy, R. 1996: 'Discourse Theory and Human Rights.' *Ratio Juris*. 9:209–35.

Alexy, R. 2002 [1994]: *A Theory of Constitutional Rights*. Oxford: Oxford University Press.

Almond, G. A. 1990: *A Discipline Divided: Schools and Sects in Political Science*. Beverly Hills: Sage.

Apel, K.-O. 1980 [1973]: 'The A Priori of the Communication Community and the Foundations of Ethics.' In K.-O. Apel: *Towards a Transformation of Philosophy*. London: Routledge & Kegan Paul.

Apel, K.-O. 1988: *Diskurs und Verantwortung*. Frankfurt: Suhrkamp.

Apel, K.-O. 1989: 'Das Sokratische Gespräch und die gegenwärtigen Transformation der Philosophie.' In D. Krohn *et al.* (eds): *Das Sokratische Gespräch – ein Symposion*. Hamburg: Junius.

Apel, K.-O. 1992a [1989]: 'Normatively Grounding 'Critical Theory' through Recourse to the Lifeworld? A Transcendental-Pragmatic Attempt to Think with Habermas against Habermas.' In A. Honneth *et al.* (eds): *Philosophical Interventions in the Unfinished Project of Enlightenment*. Cambridge, Mass.: MIT Press.

Apel, K.-O. 1992b: 'Diskursethik vor der Problematik von Recht und Politik: Können die Rationalitätsdifferenzen zwischen Moralität, Recht und Politik selbst noch durch die Diskursethik normativ-rational gerechtfertigt werden?' In K.-O. Apel and M. Kettner (eds): *Zur Anwendung der Diskursethik in Politik, Recht und Wissenschaft*. Frankfurt: Suhrkamp.

Apel, K.-O. 1996: 'Die Vernunftfunktion der kommunikativen Rationalität.' In K.-O. Apel and M. Kettner (eds): *Die eine Vernunft und die vielen Rationalitäten*. Frankfurt: Suhrkamp.

Apel, K.-O. 1997: 'Kant's 'Toward Perpetual Peace' as Historical Prognosis from the point of view of Moral Duty.' In J. Bohman and M. Lutz-Bachmann (eds):

Perpetual Peace. Essays on Kant's Cosmoplitan Ideal. Cambridge, Mass.: MIT Press.

Apel, K.-O. 1998: *Auseinandersetzungen in Erprobung des transzendental-pragmatischen Ansatzes.* Frankfurt: Suhrkamp.

Apel, K.-O. 2001: 'On the Relationship Between Ethics, International Law and the Politico-Military Strategy in Our Time.' *European Journal of Social Theory* 4:29–39.

Arendt, H. 1958: *The Human Condition.* Chicago: University of Chicago Press.

Arendt, H. 1971: 'Thinking and Moral Considerations: A Lecture.' *Social Research* 38:417–46.

Arendt, H. 1986 [1951]: *The Origins of Totalitarianism.* New York: Meridian Books.

Arendt, H. 1990 [1963]: *On Revolution.* Harmondsworth: Penguin.

Aristotle 1957: *The Politics.* London: Penguin.

Aristotle 1987: *The Nicomachean Ethics.* New York: Prometheus Books.

Arnason, Johann P. 2000: 'Globalism, Ideology and Traditions.' Interview with Jürgen Habermas. *Thesis Eleven* 63:1–10.

Arrow, K. 1963 [1951]: *Social Choice and Individual Values.* 2nd edn. New Haven: Yale University Press.

Austin, J. L. 1962: *How to Do Things with Words.* Oxford: Clarendon Press.

Bader, V. 1995: 'Citizenship and Exclusion. Radical Democracy, Community, and Justice. Or, What Is Wrong with Communitarianism?' *Political Theory* 23:211–52.

Bal, P. 1994: 'Discourse Ethics and Human Rights in Criminal Procedure.' *Philosophy & Social Criticism* 20/4:71–100.

Barber, B. 1983: 'Unconstrained Conversations: A Play on Words, Neutral and Otherwise.' *Ethics* 93:330–48.

Barber, B. 1984: *Strong Democracy.* Berkeley: University of California Press.

Baynes, K. 1991: *The Normative Grounds of Social Criticisms: Kant, Rawls and Habermas.* Albany, NY: State University of New York Press.

Baynes, K. 1995: 'Democracy and the *Rechtsstaat*: Habermas' *Faktizität und Geltung.*' In S. White (ed.): *The Cambridge Companion to Habermas.* Cambridge: Cambridge University Press.

Baxter, H. 1987: 'System and Life-World in Habermas's Theory of Communicative Action.' *Theory and Society* 16:39–86.

Beck, U. 1992 [1986]: *Risk Society. Towards a New Modernity.* London: Sage.

Beck, U. 1997 [1993]: *The Reinvention of Politics: Rethinking Modernity in the Global Social Order.* Cambridge: Polity Press.

Beitz, C. R. 1988: 'Recent International Thought.' *International Journal* 43:183–204.

Beitz, C. R. 1999: 'International Liberalism and Distributive Justice.' *World Politics* 51:269–96.

Bell, D. 1993: *Communitarianism and Its Critics.* Oxford: Clarendon Press.

Bellah, R. N. *et al.* 1986: *Habits of the Heart.* Berkeley: University of California Press.

Bellah, R. N. *et al.* 1991: *The Good Society.* New York: Alfred Knopf.

Bendix, R. 1978: *Kings or People: Power and the Mandate to Rule.* Berkeley: University of California Press.

Benhabib, S. 1986: *Critique, Norm, and Utopia*. New York: Columbia University Press.

Benhabib, S. 1987: 'The Generalized and the Concrete other.' In S. Benhabib and P. Cornell (eds): *Feminism as Critique*. Minneapolis: University of Minnesota Press.

Benhabib, S. 1992: *Situating the Self. Gender, Community and Postmodernism in Contemporary Ethics*. New York: Routledge.

Bentham, J. 1982 [1789]: *An Introduction to the Principles of Morals and Legislation*. London: Methuen.

Bernstein, J. M. 1995: *Recovering Ethical Life. Jürgen Habermas and the Future of Critical Theory*. London: Routledge.

Bessette, J. M. 1980: 'Deliberative Democracy: The Majority Principle in Republican Government.' In R. A. Goldwin and W. A. Schambra (eds): *How Democratic is the Constitution?* Washington: American Enterprise Institute.

Black, D. 1958. *The Theory of Committees and Elections*. Cambridge: Cambridge University Press.

Blau, P. M. 1964. *Exchange and Power in Social Life*. New York: Wiley.

Blaug, R. 1996: 'New Theories of Discursive Democracy: a User's Guide.' *Philosophy & Social Criticism* 22/1:49–80.

Blaug, R. 1997: 'Between Fear and Disappointment: Critical, Empirical and Political Uses of Habermas.' *Political Studies* 45:100–17.

Bobbio, N. 1987: *The Future of Democracy: A Defence of the Rules of the Game*. Cambridge: Cambridge University Press.

Bohman, J. 1995: 'Public Reason and Cultural Pluralism: Political Liberalism and the Problem of Moral Conflict.' *Political Theory* 23:253–79.

Bohman, J. 1996: *Public Deliberation. Pluralism, Complexity, and Democracy*. Cambridge, Mass.: MIT Press.

Bohman, J. 1999: 'International Regimes and Democratic Governance: Political Equality and Influence in Global Institutions.' *International Affairs*, 75:499–514.

Bohman, J. and M. Lutz-Bachmann 1997: 'Introduction.' In J. Bohman and M. Lutz-Bachmann (eds): *Perpetual Peace. Essays on Kant's Cosmoplitan Ideal*. Cambridge, Mass.: MIT Press.

Bohman, J. and W. Rehg (eds) 1997: *Deliberative Democracy*. Cambridge, Mass.: MIT Press.

Bovens, M. and P. 't Hart 1996: *Understanding Policy Fiascoes*. New Brunswick: Transaction Publishers.

Brandom, R. B. 1994: *Making it Explicit*. Cambridge, Mass: Cambridge University Press.

Brennan, G. and J. M. Buchanan 1985: *The Reason of Rules. Constitutional Political Economy*. Cambridge: Cambridge University Press.

Brunkhorst, H. 1996: 'Are Human Rights Self-Contradictory? Critical Remarks on a Hypothesis by Hannah Arendt.' *Constellations* 3:190–99.

Brunkhorst, H. 2002: *Solidarität. Von der Bürgerfreundschaft zur globalen Rechtagenossenschaft*. Frankfurt: Suhrkamp.

Brunkhorst, H. and P. Niesen 1999: 'Vorwort.' In H. Brunkhorst and P. Niesen (eds): *Das Recht der Republik*. Frankfurt: Suhrkamp.

Brunkhorst, H. (ed.) 1998: *Einmischung erwünscht?* Frankfurt: Fischer.

Brunkhorst, H., *et al.* (eds) 1999: *Recht auf Menschrechte*. Frankfurt: Suhrkamp.

Buchanan, J. M. 1991: *The Economics and the Ethics of the Constitutional Order*. Ann Arbor: University of Michigan Press.

Buchanan, J. M. and R. D. Tollison (eds) 1984: *The Theory of Public Choice – II*. Ann Arbor: University of Michigan Press.

Buchanan, J. M. and G. Tullock 1962: *The Calculus of Consent. Logical Foundations of Constitutional Democracy*. Ann Arbor: University of Michigan Press.

Buchstein, H. 1997: 'Bytes that Bite: The Internet and Deliberative Democracy.' *Constellations* 4:248–63.

Budge, I. 1993. 'Direct Democracy: Setting Appropriate Terms of Debate.' In D. Held (ed.): *Prospects for Democracy*. Cambridge: Polity Press.

Calhoun, C. (ed.) 1992: *Habermas and the Public Sphere*. Cambridge, Mass.: MIT Press.

Chambers, S. 1997: 'Talking versus Voting. Democratic Trade-Offs and Tensions.' Boulder, Co.: University of Colorado. (Preliminary draft.)

Chambers, S. 2000: 'A Culture of Publicity.' In S. Chambers and A. Costain (eds): *Deliberation, Democracy and the Media*. Lanham: Roman & Littlefield.

Chambers, S. and A. Costain (eds) 2000: *Deliberation, Democracy and the Media*. Lanham: Roman & Littlefield.

Chomsky, N. 1989: *Necessary Illusions. Thought Control in Democratic Societies*. London: Pluto Press.

Cohen, J. 1989: 'Deliberation and Democratic Legitimacy.' In A. Hamlin and P. Pettit (eds): *The Good Polity*. Oxford: Basil Blackwell.

Cohen, J. L. and A. Arato 1992: *Civil Society and Political Theory*. Cambridge, Mass.: MIT Press.

Coleman, J. S. 1974: *Power and the Structure of Society*. New York: Norton.

Dahl, R. A. 1957: 'The Concept of Power.' *Behavioral Science* 2:201–15.

Dahl, R. A. 1971: *Polyarchy: Participation and Opposition*. New Haven: Yale University Press.

Dahl, R. A. 1989: *Democracy and its Critics*. New Haven: Yale University Press.

Dalton, R. J. and M. Kuechler (eds) 1990: *Challenging the Political Order. New Social and Political Movements in Western Democracies*. Cambridge: Polity Press.

Davidson, D. 1980: *Actions & Events*. Oxford: Oxford University Press.

Dewey, J. 1927: *The Public and its Problems*. Chicago: Gateways Books.

Downs, A. 1957: *An Economic Theory of Democracy*. New York: Harper & Row.

Doyle, M. 2001: 'The New Interventionism.' *Metaphilosophy* 32:212–35.

Dryzek, J. S. 1990: *Discursive Democracy. Politics, Policy, and Political Science*. Cambridge: Cambridge University Press.

Durkheim, E. 1964 [1893]: *The Division of Labor in Society*. New York: The Free Press.

Durkheim, E. 1976 [1912]: *The Elementary Forms of the Religious Life*. London: George Allen & Unwin.

Dworkin, R. 1977: *Taking Rights Seriously*. London: Duckworth.

Dworkin, R. 1984: 'Rights as Trumps.' In J. Waldron (ed.): *Theories of Rights*. Oxford: Oxford University Press.

Dworkin, R. 1986: *Laws Empire*. Cambridge, Mass.: Harvard University Press.

Dyzenhaus, D. 1997: 'Legal Theory in the Collapse of Weimar: Contemporary Lessons?' *American Political Science Review* 91:121–34.

Edelman, M. 1964: *The Symbolic Uses of Politics*. Urbana: University of Illinois Press.

Eder, K. and B. Giesen 2001: 'Citizenship and the Making of a European Society.' In K. Eder and B. Giesen (eds): *European Citizenship between National Legacies and Postnational Projects*. Oxford: Oxford University Press.

Eisenstadt, S. N. *et al.* 1984: *Centre Formation, Protest Movements, and Class Structure in Europe and the United States*. New York: New York University Press.

Elkin, S. L. 1993: 'Constitutionalism's Successor.' In S. L. Elkin and K. E. Soltan (eds): *A New Constitutionalism*. Chicago: Chicago University Press.

Elkin, S. L. and K. E. Soltan (eds) 1993: *A New Constitutionalism*. Chicago: Chicago University Press.

Elster, J. 1983: *Sour Grapes. Studies in the Subversion of Rationality*. Cambridge: Cambridge University Press.

Elster, J. 1984 [1979]: *Ulysses and the Sirens*. Rev. edn. Cambridge: Cambridge University Press.

Elster, J. 1986: 'The Market and the Forum: Three Varieties of Political Theory.' In J. Elster and Aa. Hylland (eds): *Foundations of Social Choice Theory*. Cambridge/Oslo: Cambridge University Press/Norwegian University Press.

Elster, J. 1992: 'Arguing and Bargaining in the Federal Convention and the Assemblée Constituante.' In R. Malnes and A. Underdal (eds): *Rationality and Institutions*. Oslo: Universitetsforlaget.

Elster, J. 1995: 'Limiting Majority Rule: Alternatives to Judicial Review in the Revolutionary Epoch.' In E. Smith (ed.): *Constitutional Justice under Old Constitutions*. The Hague: Kluwer.

Elster, J. (ed.) 1998: *Deliberative Democracy*. Cambridge: Cambridge University Press.

Engländer, A. 1995: 'Grundrechte als Kompensation diskursethischer Defizite?' *ARSP Sonderdruck* 81:482–95.

Eriksen, E. O. 1996: 'Justification of Needs in the Welfare State.' In E. O. Eriksen and J. Loftager (eds): *The Rationality of the Welfare State*. Oslo: Scandinavian University Press.

Eriksen, E. O. 1999: *Kommunikativ ledelse*. Bergen: Fagbokforlaget.

Eriksen, E. O. 2001a: *Demokratiets sorte hull*. Oslo: Abstrakt Forlag.

Eriksen. E. O. 2001b: 'Why a Charter of Human Rights in the EU?' In E. O. Eriksen *et al.* (eds): *The Chartering of Europe*. Oslo: Arena Report No. 8. (Forthcoming on Nomos, Baden-Baden.)

Eriksen, E. O. and J. E. Fossum 2000: 'Post-national integration.' In E. O. Eriksen and J. E. Fossum (eds) *Democracy in the European Union – Integration through Deliberation?* London: Routledge.

Eriksen, E. O. and J. Weigård 1997: 'Conceptualizing Politics: Strategic or Communicative Action?' *Scandinavian Political Studies* 20:219–41.

Eriksen, E. O. and J. E. Fossum (eds) 2000: *Democracy in the European Union – Integration through Deliberation?* London: Routledge.

Eriksen, E. O. *et al.* (eds) 2001: *The Chartering of Europe*. Oslo: Arena Report No. 8. (Forthcoming on Nomos, Baden-Baden.)

Estlund, D. M. 1993. 'Who's Afraid of Deliberative Democracy? On the Strategic/Deliberative Dichotomy in Recent Constitutional Jurisprudence.' *Texas Law Review* 71:1437–77.

Falk, R. 1998: 'The United Nations and Cosmopolitan Democracy: Bad Dream, Utopian Fantasy, Political Project.' In D. Archibugi *et al.* (eds): *Re-imagining Political Community*. Cambridge: Polity Press.

Ferejohn, J. 1993: 'The Spatial Model and Elections.' In B. Grofman (ed.): *Information, Participation and Choice*. Ann Arbor: University of Michigan Press.

Fisher, R. J. 1972: 'The Problem-Solving Workshop in Conflict Resolution.' In R. L. Merritt (ed.): *Communication in International Politics*. Urbana: University of Illinois Press.

Fisher, R. J. 1983: 'Third Party Consultation as a Method of Intergroup Conflict Resolution.' *Journal of Conflict Resolution* 27:301–34.

Fisher, R. and W. Ury 1991 [1981]: *Getting to Yes: Negotiating an Agreement without Giving in*. 2nd edn. London: Random House/Business Books.

Fishkin, J. S. 1991: *Democracy and Deliberation. New Directions for Democratic Reform*. New Haven: Yale University Press.

Forst, R. 1999a: 'Die Rechtfertigung der Gerechtigkeit. Rawls' Politischer Liberalismus und Habermas' Diskurstheorie in der Diskussion.' In H. Brunkhorst and P. Niesen (eds) *Das Recht der Republik*. Frankfurt: Suhrkamp.

Forst, R. 1999b: 'The Basic Right to Justification: Toward a Constructivist Conception of Human Rights.' *Constellations* 6:35–60.

Forst, R. 2002 [1994]: *Contexts of Justice. Political Philosophy beyond Liberalism and Communitarianism*. Berkeley: University of California Press.

Frank, T. 1992: 'The Emerging Right to Democratic Governance.' *American Journal of International Law* 86:46–91.

Frankenberg, G. 1996: 'Why Care? – The Trouble with Social Rights.' *Cardozo Law Review* 17:1365–90.

Frankfurt, H. 1971: 'Freedom of the Will and the Concept of the Person.' *Journal of Philosophy* 68:5–20.

Fraser, N. 1992: 'Rethinking the Public Sphere: A Contribution to the Critique of Actually Existing Democracy.' In C. Calhoun (ed.): *Habermas and the Public Sphere*. Cambridge, Mass.: MIT Press.

Fuller, L. L. 1969 [1965]: *The Morality of Law*. Rev. edn. New Haven: Yale University Press.

Giddens, A. 1991: *Modernity and Self-Identity*. Cambridge: Polity Press.

Gilligan, C. 1982: *In a Different Voice. Psychological Theory and Women's Development*. Cambridge, Mass.: Harvard University Press.

Goffman, E. 1959: *The Presentation of Self in Everyday Life*. New York: Doubleday Anchor Books.

Goodin, R. E. 1986: 'Laundering Preferences.' In J. Elster and Aa. Hylland (eds): *Foundations of Social Choice Theory*. Cambridge: Cambridge University Press/Oslo: Universitetsforlaget.

Goodin, R. E. 1996: 'Institutionalizing the Public Interest: The Defense of Deadlock and Beyond.' *American Political Science Review* 90:331–43.

Goodin, R. E. (ed.) 1996: *The Theory of Institutional Design*. Cambridge: Cambridge University Press.

Gosepath, S. 1995: 'The Place of Equality in Habermas' and Dworkin's Theories of Justice.' *European Journal of Philosophy* 3:21–35.

Green, D. P. and I. Shapiro 1994: *Pathologies of Rational Choice Theory. A Critique of Applications in Political Science*. New Haven: Yale University Press.

Guggenberger, B. and C. Offe 1984: *An den Grenzen der Mehrheitsdemokratie: Politik und Soziologie der Mehrheitsregel*. Opladen: Westdeutscher Verlag.

Gullvåg, I. 1972: 'Innledning.' In I. Gullvåg (ed.): *Charles Sanders Peirce*. Oslo: Pax.

Günther, K. 1989: 'A Normative Conception of Coherence for a Discursive Theory of Legal Justification.' *Ratio Juris* 2:155–66.

Günther, K. 1990: *Hero-Politics in Modern Legal Times*. Institute for Legal Studies, University of Wisconsin at Madison, Series 4.

Günther, K. 1993 [1988]: *The Sense of Appropriateness*. Albany: State University of New York Press.

Günther, K. 1994: 'Diskurstheorie des Rechts oder Naturrecht in diskurstheoretischem Gewand.' *Kritische Justiz* 27:470–87.

Günther, K. 1999: 'Welchen Personenbegriff brauch die Diskurstheorie des Rechts?' In H. Brunkhorst and P. Niesen (eds): *Das Recht der Republik*. Frankfurt: Suhrkamp.

Gutmann, A. 1993: 'The Disharmony of Democracy.' In J. W. Shapman and I. Shapiro (eds): *Democratic Community*. Nomos **xxxv**:126–62.

Gutmann, A. and D. Thompson 1996: *Democracy and Disagreement*. Cambridge, Mass.: Belknap Press of Harvard University Press.

Habermas, J. 1968: *Technik und Wissenschaft als 'Ideologie'*. Frankfurt: Suhrkamp.

Habermas, J. 1971a [1968]: *Toward a Rational Society*. London: Heinemann.

Habermas, J. 1971b [1968]: *Knowledge and Human Interest*. Boston: Beacon Press.

Habermas, J. 1971c: 'Theorie der Gesellschaft oder Sozialtechnologie?' In J. Habermas and N. Luhmann: *Theorie der Gesellschaft oder Sozialtechnologie – Was Leistet die Systemforschung*. Frankfurt: Suhrkamp.

Habermas, J. 1973 [1963]: *Theory and Practice*. Boston: Beacon Press.

Habermas, J. 1975 [1973]: *Legitimation Crisis*. Boston: Beacon Press.

Habermas, J. 1976: *Zur Rekonstruktion des Historischen Materialismus*. Frankfurt: Suhrkamp.

Habermas, J. 1979a [1976]: *Communication and the Evolution of Society*. Boston: Beacon Press.

Habermas, J. 1979b: 'Toward a Reconstruction of Historical Materialism.' In J. Habermas: *Communication and the Evolution of Society*. Boston: Beacon Press.

Habermas, J. 1979c: 'Moral Development and Ego Identity.' In J. Habermas: *Communication and the Evolution of Society*. Boston: Beacon Press.

Habermas, J. 1979d: 'Legitimation Problems in the Modern State.' In J. Habermas: *Communication and the Evolution of Society*. Boston: Beacon Press.

Habermas, J. 1984 [1981]: *The Theory of Communicative Action*. Vol. 1. Boston: Beacon Press.

Habermas, J. 1985a: 'Civil Disobedience: Litmus Test for the Democratic Constitutional State.' *Berkeley Journal of Sociology* 30:96–116.

Habermas, J. 1985b: 'Reply to Skjei.' *Inquiry* 28:105–13.

Habermas, J. 1987a [1981]: *The Theory of Communicative Action*. Vol. 2. Boston: Beacon Press.

Habermas, J. 1987b [1985]: *The Philosophical Discourse of Modernity*. Cambridge: Polity Press.

Habermas, J. 1987c: 'Wie ist Legitimität durch Legalität möglich?' *Kritische Justiz* 20:1–16.

Habermas, J. 1988 [1967]: *On the Logic of the Social Sciences.* Cambridge, Mass.: MIT Press.

Habermas, J. 1989a [1962]: *The Structural Transformation of the Public Sphere.* Cambridge, Mass.: MIT Press.

Habermas, J. 1989b [1985]: *The New Conservatism.* Cambridge, Mass.: MIT Press.

Habermas, J. 1989c: 'Towards a Communication-Concept of Rational Collective Will-Formation. A Thought-Experiment.' *Ratio Juris* 2:144–54.

Habermas, J. 1990a [1983]: *Moral Consciousness and Communicative Action.* Cambridge: Polity Press.

Habermas, J. 1990b: 'Moral Consciousness and Communicative Action.' In J. Habermas: *Moral Consciousness and Communicative Action.* Cambridge: Polity Press.

Habermas, J. 1990c: 'Discourse Ethics: Notes on a Program of Philosophical Justification.' In J. Habermas: *Moral Consciousness and Communicative Action.* Cambridge: Polity Press.

Habermas, J. 1990d: 'Morality and Ethical Life: Does Hegel's Critique of Kant Apply to Discourse Ethics?' In J. Habermas: *Moral Consciousness and Communicative Action.* Cambridge: Polity Press.

Habermas, J. 1990e. 'Reconstruction and Interpretation in the Social Sciences.' In J. Habermas: *Moral Consciousness and Communicative Action.* Cambridge: Polity Press.

Habermas, J. 1990f: 'Justice and Solidarity: On the Discussion Concerning Stage 6.' In T. E. Wren (ed.): *The Moral Domain.* Cambridge, Mass.: MIT Press.

Habermas, J. 1990g: *Die nachholende Revolution.* Frankfurt: Suhrkamp.

Habermas, J. 1990h: 'Die neue Intimität zwischen Kultur und Politik.' In J. Habermas: *Die nachholende Revolution.* Frankfurt: Suhrkamp.

Habermas, J. 1991 [1986]: 'A Reply.' In A. Honneth and H. Joas (eds): *Communicative Action.* Cambridge: Polity Press.

Habermas, J. 1992a [1988]: *Postmetaphysical Thinking.* Cambridge: Polity Press.

Habermas, J. 1992b. 'Individuation through Socialization: On George Herbert Mead's Theory of Subjectivity.' In J. Habermas: *Postmetaphysical Thinking.* Cambridge: Polity Press.

Habermas, J. 1992c: 'The Unity of Reason in the Diversity of Its Voices.' In J. Habermas: *Postmetaphysical Thinking.* Cambridge: Polity Press.

Habermas, J. 1992d: 'Further Reflections on the Public Sphere.' In C. Calhoun (ed.): *Habermas and the Public Sphere.* Cambridge, Mass.: MIT Press.

Habermas, J. 1993a [1991]: *Justification and Application.* Cambridge: Polity Press.

Habermas, J. 1993b: 'Preface.' In J. Habermas: *Justification and Application.* Cambridge: Polity Press.

Habermas, J. 1993c: 'On the Pragmatic, the Ethical, and the Moral Employments of Practical Reason.' In J. Habermas: *Justification and Application.* Cambridge: Polity Press.

Habermas, J. 1993d: 'Lawrence Kohlberg and Neo-Aristotelianism.' In J. Habermas: *Justification and Application.* Cambridge: Polity Press.

Habermas, J. 1993e. 'Remarks on Discourse Ethics.' In J. Habermas: *Justification and Application*. Cambridge: Polity Press.

Habermas, J. 1994a: 'Three Normative Models of Democracy.' *Constellations* 1:1–10.

Habermas, J. 1994b [1993]: *The Past as Future*. Cambridge: Polity Press.

Habermas, J. 1994c [1993]: 'Struggles for Recognition in the Democratic Constitutional State.' In C. Taylor *et al.*: *Multiculturalism: Examining the Politics of Recognition*. Princeton: Princeton University Press.

Habermas, J. 1995: 'Om förhållandet mellan politik, rätt och moral.' In J. Habermas: *Diskurs, rätt och demokrati*. Gothenburg: Daidalos.

Habermas, J. 1996a [1992]: *Between Facts and Norms*. Cambridge, Mass.: MIT Press.

Habermas, J. 1996b [1981]: 'Modernity: An Unfinished Project.' In M. P. d'Entrèves and S. Benhabib (eds): *Habermas and the Unfinished Project of Modernity*. Cambridge: Polity Press.

Habermas, J. 1996c: 'Reply to Symposium Participants, Benjamin N. Cardozo School of Law.' *Cardozo Law Review* 17:1477–558.

Habermas, J. 1997a [1995]: *A Berlin Republic: Writings on Germany*. Lincoln: University of Nebraska Press.

Habermas, J. 1998a [1996]: *The Inclusion of the Other: Studies in Political Theory*. Cambridge, Mass.: MIT Press.

Habermas, J. 1998b: 'A Genealogical Analysis of the Cognitive Content of Morality.' In J. Habermas: *The Inclusion of the Other: Studies in Political Theory*. Cambridge, Mass.: MIT Press.

Habermas, J. 1998c: 'The European Nation-State: On the Past and Future of Sovereignty and Citizenship.' In J. Habermas: *The Inclusion of the Other: Studies in Political Theory*. Cambridge, Mass.: MIT Press.

Habermas, J. 1998d: 'Does Europe Need a Constitution? Response to Dieter Grimm.' In J. Habermas: *The Inclusion of the Other: Studies in Political Theory*. Cambridge, Mass.: MIT Press.

Habermas, J. 1998e: 'Kant's Idea of Perpetual Peace: At Two Hundred Years' Historical Remove.' In J. Habermas: *The Inclusion of the Other: Studies in Political Theory*. Cambridge, Mass.: MIT Press.

Habermas, J. 1998f: 'On the Internal Relation between the Rule of Law and Democracy.' In J. Habermas: *The Inclusion of the Other: Studies in Political Theory*. Cambridge, Mass.: MIT Press.

Habermas, J. 1998g [1996]: 'Some Further Clarifications of the Concept of Communicative Rationality.' In J. Habermas: *On the Pragmatics of Communication*. Cambridge, Mass.: MIT Press.

Habermas, J. 1999a: *Wahrheit und Rechtfertigung*. Frankfurt: Suhrkamp. (English edition: *Truth and Justification*. Cambridge: Polity Press, 2003, forthcoming.)

Habermas, J. 1999b: 'Bestiality and Humanity: A War on the Border between Legality and Morality.' *Constellations* 6:263–72.

Habermas, J. 1999c. 'The European Nation-State and the Pressures of Globalization.' *New Left Review* 235:46–59.

Habermas, J. 2000: 'Beyond the Nation-state? On some Consequences of Economic Globalization.' In E. O. Eriksen and J. E. Fossum (eds): *Democracy in the European Union – Integration through Deliberation?* London: Routledge.

Habermas, J. 2001a [1998]: *The Postnational Constellation. Political Essays.* Cambridge: Polity Press.

Habermas, J. 2001b: 'What is a People? The Frankfurt 'Germanists' Assembly' of 1846 and the Self-Understanding of the Humanities in the *Vormärz*.' In J. Habermas: *The Postnational Constellation. Political Essays.* Cambridge: Polity Press.

Habermas, J. 2001c: 'Learning from Catastrophe? A Look Back at the Short Twentieth Century.' In J. Habermas: *The Postnational Constellation. Political Essays.* Cambridge: Polity Press.

Habermas, J. 2001d: 'The Postnational Constellation and the Future of Democracy.' In J. Habermas: *The Postnational Constellation. Political Essays.* Cambridge: Polity Press.

Habermas, J. 2001e: 'Constitutional Democracy.' *Political Theory* 29:766–81.

Habermas, J. 2001f: 'Why Europe Needs a Constitution.' *New Left Review* 11:1–16.

Habermas, J. 2001g: *Zeit der Übergänge.* Frankfurt: Suhrkamp.

Habermas, J.: 2003 [2001]: *The Future of Human Nature.* Cambridge: Polity Press.

Hardin, G. 1968: 'The Tragedy of the Commons.' *Science* **162**:1243–8.

Hart, H. L. A. 1961: *The Concept of Law.* Oxford: Clarendon Press.

Heath, J. 1995: 'The Problem of Foundationalism in Habermas's Discourse Ethics.' *Philosophy and Social Criticism* **21**:77–100.

Heath, J. 2001: *Communicative Action and Rational Choice.* Cambridge, Mass.: MIT Press.

Hegel, G. W. F. 1967 [1821]: *Hegel's Philosophy of Right.* Oxford: Oxford University Press.

Hegel, G. W. F. 1996 [1821]: *Philosophy of Right.* Amherst: Prometheus Books.

Hegel, G. W. F. 1964: *Political Writings.* Oxford: Clarendon Press.

Held, D. 1980: *Introduction to Critical Theory.* Cambridge: Polity Press.

Held, D. 1995: *Democracy and the Global Order. From the Modern State to Cosmopolitan Governance.* Cambridge: Polity Press.

Held, D. 1996 [1987]: *Models of Democracy.* 2nd edn. Cambridge: Polity Press.

Held, D. 1998: 'Democracy and Globalization.' In D. Archibugi *et al.* (eds): *Re-imagining Political Community.* Oxford: Polity Press.

Held, D. 2002: 'Law of States, Law of Peoples: Three Models of Sovereignty.' *Legal Theory* 8:1–44.

Held, D. *et al.* 1999: *Global Transformations. Politics, Economics and Culture.* Oxford: Polity Press.

Hellesnes, J. 1992: 'Toleranz und Dissens. Diskurstheoretische Bemerkungen über Mill und Rorty.' In K.-O. Apel and M. Kettner (eds): *Zur Anwendung der Diskursethik in Politik, Recht und Wissenshaft.* Frankfurt: Suhrkamp.

Hobbes, T. 1968 [1651]: *Leviathan.* Harmondsworth: Penguin.

Höffe, O. 1994 [1987]: *Political Justice: Foundations for a Critical Philosophy of Law and the State.* Cambridge: Polity Press.

Höffe, O. 1996: *Vernunft und Recht. Bausteine zu einem interkulturellen Rechtsdiskurs.* Frankfurt: Suhrkamp.

Höffe, O. 1999: *Demokratie im Zeitalter der Globalisierung.* Munich: C. H. Beck.

Hohengarten, W. M. 1992: 'Translator's Introduction.' In J. Habermas: *Postmetaphysical Thinking.* Cambridge: Polity Press.

Holmes, S. 1988: 'Gag Rules or the Politics of Omission.' In J. Elster and R. Slagstad (eds): *Constitutionalism and Democracy*. Cambridge/Oslo: Cambridge University Press/Norwegian University Press.

Holmes, S. 1995: *Passions and Constraints. On the Theory of Liberal Democracy*. Chicago: University of Chicago Press.

Holmes, S. and C. Sunstein 1999: *The Costs of Rights. Why Liberty Depends on Taxes*. New York: Norton.

Honig, B. 2001: 'Dead Rights, Live Futures. A reply to Habermas's 'Constitutional Democracy'.' *Political Theory* 29:792–805.

Honneth, A. 1991 [1985]: *The Critique of Power*. Cambridge, Mass.: MIT Press.

Honneth, A. 1995 [1992]: *The Struggle for Recognition. The Moral Grammar of Social Conflicts*. Cambridge: Polity Press.

Honneth, A. 1999: 'Demokratie als reflexive Kooperation: John Dewey und die Demokratietheorie der Gegenwart.' In H. Brunkhorst and P. Niesen (eds): *Das Recht der Republik*. Frankfurt: Suhrkamp.

Honneth, A. and H. Joas (eds) 1991 [1986]: *Communicative Action*. Cambridge: Polity Press.

Honneth, A. *et al*. (eds) 1992a [1989]: *Philosophical Interventions in the Unfinished Project of Enlightenment*. Cambridge, Mass.: MIT Press.

Honneth, A. *et al*. (eds) 1992b [1989]: *Cultural-Political Interventions in the Unfinished Project of Enlightenment*. Cambridge, Mass.: MIT Press.

Horkheimer, M. 1947: *Eclipse of Reason*. New York: Oxford University Press.

Horkheimer, M. 1972 [1937]: 'Traditional and Critical Theory.' In M. Horkheimer: *Critical Theory*. New York: Herder & Herder.

Horkheimer, M. and T. W. Adorno 1972 [1947]: *Dialectic of Enlightenment*. New York: Herder & Herder.

Horster, D. 1989: 'Sokratische Gespräche in der Erwachsenentbildung.' In D. Krohn *et al*. (eds): *Das Sokratische Gespräch – Ein Symposion*. Hamburg: Junius.

Hösle, V. 1990: 'The Greatness and Limits of Kant's Practical Philosophy.' *Graduate Faculty Philosophy Journal* 13:133–57.

Hösle, V. 1997: *Moral und Politik: Grundlagen einer Politischen Ethik für das 21. Jahrhundert*. Munich: Verlag C. H. Beck.

Humboldt, W. v. 1954 [1791]: *The Limits of State Action*. Indianapolis: Liberty Fund.

Ingram, D. 1993: 'The Limits and Possibilities of Communicative Ethics for Democratic Theory.' *Political Theory* 21:294–321.

Janis, I. L. 1982: *Groupthink*. Boston: Houghton Mifflin.

Jellinek, G. 1919: *Allgemeine Staatslehre*. Berlin: O. Häring.

Johnson, J. 1993: 'Is Talk Really Cheap? Prompting Conversation Between Critical Theory and Rational Choice.' *American Political Science Review* 87:74–86.

Kant, I. 1996a [1785]: 'Groundwork of The Metaphysics of Morals.' In I. Kant: *Practical Philosophy*. Cambridge: Cambridge University Press.

Kant, I. 1996b [1795]: 'Toward Perpetual Peace.' In I. Kant: *Practical Philosophy*. Cambridge: Cambridge University Press.

Kant, I. 1996c [1797]: 'The Metaphysics of Morals.' In I. Kant: *Practical Philosophy*. Cambridge: Cambridge University Press.

Keane, J. 1984: *Public Life in Late Capitalism*. Cambridge: Cambridge University Press.

Keane, J. 1989: 'Liberty of the Press in the 1990's.' *New Formations* 8:34–52.

Keane, J. 1991: *The Media and Democracy*. Oxford: Polity Press.

Keane, J. 1993: 'Democracy and the Media – without Foundations.' In D. Held (ed.): *Prospects for Democracy*. Oxford: Polity Press.

Kelsen, H. 1968 [1925]: *Allgemeine Staatslehre*. Berlin: Julius Springer.

Kemp, R. 1985: 'Planning, Public Hearings, and the Politics of Discourse.' In J. Forester (ed.): *Critical Theory and Public Life*. Cambridge, Mass.: MIT Press.

Kettner, M. 1993: 'Scientific Knowledge, Discourse Ethics, and Consensus Formation on Public Policy Issues.' In R. v. Schomberg (ed.): *Science, Politics and Morality*. Dordrecht: Kluwer Academic Publishers.

Kettner, M. 1998: 'John Deweys demokratische Experimentiergemeinschaft.' In H. Brunkhorst (ed.): *Demokratischer Experimentalismus*. Frankfurt: Suhrkamp.

Knight, J. and J. Johnson 1997: 'What Sort of Political Equality Does Democratic Deliberation Require?' In J. Bohman and W. Rehg (eds): *Deliberative Democracy. Essays on Reason and Politics*. Cambridge, Mass.: MIT Press.

Kohlberg, L. 1981: *The Philosophy of Moral Development. Essays on Moral Development*, Vol. 1. San Francisco: Harper & Row.

Köhler, W. R. 1999: 'Das Recht auf Menschenrechte.' In H. Brunkhorst *et al.* (eds): *Recht auf Menschenrechte*. Frankfurt: Suhrkamp.

Kymlicka, W. 1989: *Liberalism, Community and Culture*. Oxford: Clarendon Press.

Kymlicka, W. 1995: *Multicultural Citizenship*. Oxford: Clarendon Press.

Laqueur, W. and B. Rubin (eds) 1990: *The Human Rights Reader*. New York: Meridian Books.

Larmore, C. 1987: *Patterns of Moral Complexity*. Cambridge: Cambridge University Press.

Larmore, C. 1993: 'Die Wurzeln radikaler Demokratie.' *Deutsche Zeitschrift für Philosophie* 41:321–27.

Lefort, C. 1988: *Democracy and Political Theory*. Cambridge: Polity Press.

Lévinas, E. 1969 [1961]: *Totality and Infinity. An Essay on Exteriority*. The Hague: Nijhoff.

Locke, J. 1960 [1690]: *Two Treaties of Government*. Cambridge: Cambridge University Press.

Loftager, J. 1994: 'Den politiske offentlighed i teori og i praksis.' In E. O. Eriksen (ed.): *Den politiske orden*. Oslo: Tano.

Luban, D. 1996: 'The Publicity Principle.' In R. E. Goodin (ed.): *The Theory of Institutional Design*. Cambridge: Cambridge University Press.

Lübbe, H. 1990: 'Are Norms Methodically Justifiable? A Reconstruction of Max Weber's Reply.' In S. Benhabib and F. Dallmayr (eds): *The Communicative Ethics Controversy*. Cambridge, Mass.: MIT Press.

Luhmann, N. 1971: 'Systemtheoretische Argumentation.' In J. Habermas and N. Luhmann: *Theorie der Gesellschaft oder Sozialtechnologie – Was Leistet die Systemforschung*. Frankfurt: Suhrkamp.

Luhmann, N. 1981: 'Machtkreislauf und Recht in Demokratien.' *Zeitschrift für Rechtssoziologie* 2:158–67.

Luhmann, N. 1982 [1972]: *The Differentiation of Society*. New York: Columbia University Press.

Luhmann, N. 1983 [1969]: *Legitimation durch Verfahren*. Frankfurt: Suhrkamp.

Luhmann, N. 1984: *Soziale Systeme: Grundriss einer allgemeinen Theorie*. Frankfurt: Suhrkamp.

Luhmann, N. 1993 [1991]: *Risk: A Sociological Theory*. Berlin: deGruyter.

Luhmann, N. 1995: *Das Recht der Gesellschaft*. Frankfurt: Suhrkamp.

Luhmann, N. 1996: 'Quod Omnes Tangit: Remarks on Jürgen Habermas's Legal Theory.' *Cardozo Law Review* 17:883–900.

Macedo, S. (ed.) 1999: *Deliberative Politics: Essays on Democracy and Disagreement*. Oxford: Oxford University Press.

MacIntyre, A. 1967 [1966]: *A Short History of Ethics*. London: Routledge & Kegan Paul.

MacIntyre, A. 1985 [1981]: *After Virtue – A Study in Moral Theory*. 2nd edn. London: Duckworth.

Manin, B. 1987: 'On Legitimacy and Deliberation.' *Political Theory* 15:338–68.

Manin, B. 1997 [1995]: *The Principles of Representative Government*. Cambridge: Cambridge University Press.

Mansbridge, J. J. 1980: *Beyond Adversary Democracy*. Chicago: University of Chicago Press.

Mansbridge, J. J. (ed.) 1990: *Beyond Self-Interest*. Chicago: University of Chicago Press.

March, J. G. and J. P. Olsen 1989: *Rediscovering Institutions. The Organizational Basis of Politics*. New York: The Free Press.

Maus, I. 1989: 'Die Trennung von Recht und Moral als Begrenzung des Rechts.' *Rechtstheorie* 20:191–210.

Maus, I. 1992: *Zur Aufklärung der Demokratietheorie: Rechts- und demokratietheoretische Überlegungen im Anschluß an Kant*. Frankfurt: Suhrkamp.

Maus, I. 1996: 'Liberties and Popular Sovereignty: On Jürgen Habermas's Reconstruction of the System of Rights.' *Cardozo Law Review* 17:825–82.

McCarthy, T. 1991a: *Ideals and Illusions*. Cambridge: MIT Press.

McCarthy, T. 1991b [1986]: 'Complexity and Democracy: or the Seducements of Systems Theory.' In A. Honneth and H. Joas (eds): *Communicative Action*. Cambridge: Polity Press.

McCarthy, T. 1994: 'Kantian Constructivism and Reconstructivism: Rawls and Habermas in Dialogue.' *Ethics* 105:44–63.

McCarthy, T. 1996: 'Legitimacy and Diversity: Dialectical Reflections on Analytical Distinctions.' *Cardozo Law Review* 17:1083–126.

McKeon, R. 1948: 'The Philosophic Bases and Material Circumstances of the Rights of Man.' *Ethics* 58:180–7.

Mead, G. H. 1962 [1934]: *Mind, Self, and Society*. Chicago: University of Chicago Press.

Michelman, F. I. 1988: 'Political Truth and the Rule of Law.' *Tel Aviv University Studies in Law* 8:281–91.

Michelman, F. I. 1989: 'Bringing the Law to Life: A Plea for Disenchantment.' *Cornell Law Review* 74:256–69.

Michelman, F. I. 1997: 'How Can the People Ever Make the Laws? A Critique of Deliberative Democracy.' In J. Bohman and W. Rehg (eds): *Deliberative Democracy*. Cambridge, Mass.: MIT Press.

Mill, J. S. 1975 [1859]: 'On Liberty.' In J. S. Mill: *Three Essays*. Oxford: Oxford University Press.

Miller, D. 1993: 'Deliberative Democracy and Social Choice.' In D. Held (ed.): *Prospects for Democracy*. Cambridge: Polity Press.

Moe, T. 1990: 'Political Institutions: The Neglected Side of the Story.' *Journal of Law, Economics, and Organizations* 6:213–53.

Monroe, K. R. (ed.) 1991: *The Economic Approach to Politics: A Critical Reassessment of the Theory of Rational Choice*. New York: Harper Collins.

Moon, J. D. 1993: *Constructing Community. Moral, Pluralism and Tragic Conflicts*. Princeton: Princeton University Press.

Morgenthau, H. J. 1993: *Politics among Nations. The Struggle for Power and Peace*. New York: McGraw Hill.

Mulhall, S. and A. Swift 1996 [1992]: *Liberals and Communitarians*. 2nd edn. Oxford: Blackwell.

Negt, O. and A. Kluge 1994 [1972]: *Public Sphere and Experience*. Minneapolis: University of Minnesota Press.

Neumann, J. v. and O. Morgenstern 1944: *The Theory of Games and Economic Behavior*. Princeton: Princeton University Press.

Nino, C. S. 1996: *The Constitution of Deliberative Democracy*. New Haven: Yale University Press.

Nozick, R. 1974: *Anarchy, State, and Utopia*. New York: Basic Books.

Nussbaum, M. 1996: 'Patriotism and Cosmopolitanism.' In J. Cohen (ed.): *For Love of Country. Debating the Limits of Patriotism*. Boston: Beacon Press.

Offe, C. 1982: 'Politische Legitimation durch Mehrheitsentscheidung?' *Journal für Sozialforschung* 22:311–35.

Offe, C. 1984: *Contradictions of the Welfare State*. London: Hutchinson.

Offe, C. 1990: 'Reflections on the Institutional Self-transformation of Movement Politics: A Tentative Stage Model.' In R. J. Dalton and M. Kuechler (eds): *Challenging the Political Order*. Cambridge: Polity Press.

Offe, C. 1992 [1989]: 'Bindings, Shackles, Brakes: On Self-Limitation Strategies.' In A. Honneth *et al.* (eds): *Cultural-Political Interventions in the Unfinished Project of Enlightenment*. Cambridge, Mass.: MIT Press.

Offe, C. 1996a: 'Designing Institutions in East European Transitions.' In R. E. Goodin (ed.): *The Theory of Institutional Design*. Cambridge: Cambridge University Press.

Offe, C. 1996b: *Modernity and the State – East, West*. London: Polity Press.

Offe, C. and U. K. Preuss 1991: 'Democratic Institutions and Moral Resources.' In D. Held (ed.): *Political Theory Today*. Cambridge: Polity Press.

Olsen, J. P. 1983: 'Citizens' Initiatives and the Organization of Representation.' In J. P. Olsen: *Organized Democracy*. Bergen: Universitetsforlaget.

Olsen, J. P. 1988: 'Alternative beslutningsprosedyrer i organisasjoner.' In J. P. Olsen: *Statsstyre og institusjonsutforming*. Oslo: Universitetsforlaget.

Olson, M. 1965: *The Logic of Collective Action*. Cambridge, Mass.: Harvard University Press.

O'Neill, O. 1989: *Constructions of Reason: Explorations of Kant's Practical Philosophy*. Cambridge: Cambridge University Press.

Oppenheim, F. E. 1991: *The Place of Morality in Foreign Policy*. Lexington: Lexington Books.

Ostrom, E. 1992: *Crafting Institutions for Self-Governing Irrigation Systems*. San Francisco: CS-Press.

Parsons, T. 1963: 'On the Concept of Political Power.' *Proceedings of the American Philosophical Society* 107:232–62.

Parsons, T. 1977: *Social Systems and the Evolution of Action Theory*. New York: The Free Press.

Perrow, C. 1984: *Normal Accidents: Living with High-Risk Technologies*. New York: Basic Books.

Peters, B. 1991: *Rationalität, Recht Und Gesellschaft*. Frankfurt: Suhrkamp.

Peters, B. 1993: *Die Integration moderner Gesellschaften*. Frankfurt: Suhrkamp.

Peters, B. 1994: 'On Reconstructive Legal and Political Theory.' *Philosophy & Social Criticism* 20/4:101–34.

Petracca, M. P. 1991: 'The Rational Actor Approach to Politics: Science, Self-Interest, and Normative Democratic Theory.' In K. R. Monroe (ed.): *The Economic Approach to Politics*. New York: Harper Collins.

Phillips, A. 1995: *The Politics of Presence*. Oxford: Clarendon Press.

Pitkin, H. F. 1972: *The Concept of Representation*. Berkeley: University of California Press.

Plant, R. 1993: 'Free Lunches Don't Nourish: Reflections on Entitlements and Citizenship.' In G. Drover and P. Kerans (eds): *New Approaches to Welfare Theory*. Cambridge: Edward Elgar.

Pocock, J. G. A. 1975: *The Machiavellian Moment: Florentine Political Thought and the Atlantic Republican Tradition*. Princeton: Princeton University Press.

Poggi, G. 1978: *The Development of the Modern State*. Stanford: Stanford University Press.

Preuss, U. 1991: 'Verfassungstheoretische Überlegungen zur normativen Begründung des Wohlfahrtsstaates.' In C. Sachsse and H. Tristram Engelhardt: *Sicherheit und Freiheit*. Frankfurt: Suhrkamp.

Preuss, U. 1996: 'The Roundtable Talks in the German Democratic Republic.' In J. Elster (ed.): *The Roundtable Talks and the Breakdown of Communism*. Chicago: University of Chicago Press.

Pröpper, I. M. A. M. 1993: 'Argumentation and Power in Evaluation-Research and in its Utilization in the Policy Making Process.' In R. v. Schomberg (ed.): *Science, Politics and Morality. Scientific Uncertainty and Decision Making*. Dordrecht: Kluwer Academic Publishers.

Rash Jr., W. 1997: *Politics on the Nets. Wiring the Political Process*. New York: Freeman.

Rawls, J. 1971: *A Theory of Justice*. Oxford: Oxford University Press.

Rawls, J. 1993: *Political Liberalism*. New York: Columbia University Press.

Rawls, J. 1999: *The Law of Peoples*. Cambridge, Mass.: Harvard University Press.

Reese-Schäfer, W. 1992: *Karl-Otto Apel. En introduktion*. Gothenburg: Daidalos.

Rehg, W. 1994: *Insight & Solidarity. The Discourse Ethics of Jürgen Habermas*. Berkeley: University of California Press.

Rehg, W. and J. Bohman (eds) 2001: *Pluralism and the Pragmatic Turn. The Transformation of Critical Theory. Essays in Honor of Thomas McCarthy*. Cambridge: MIT Press.

Riker, W. H. 1962: *The Theory of Political Coalitions*. New Haven: Yale University Press.

Riker, W. H. 1982: *Liberalism Against Populism: A Confrontation Between the Theory of Democracy and the Theory of Social Choice*. San Francisco: Freeman.

Riker, W. H. and B. R. Weingast 1988: 'Constitutional Regulation of Legislative Choice: The Political Consequences of Judicial Deference to Legislatures.' *Virginia Law Review* 74:373–402.

Ritzer, G. 1980: *Sociology: A Multiple Paradigm Science*. Boston: Allyn and Bacon.

Rokkan, S. 1966: 'Norway: Numerical Democracy and Corporate Pluralism.' In R. A. Dahl (ed.): *Political Oppositions in Western Democracy*. New Haven: Yale University Press.

Rosenau, J. N. 1997: *Along the Domestic–Foreign Frontier. Exploring Governance in a Turbulent World*. Cambridge: Cambridge University Press.

Rosenau, J. N. 1998: 'Governance and Democracy in a Globalizing World.' In D. Archibugi *et al.* (eds): *Re-imagining Political Community*. Oxford: Polity Press.

Rousseau, J.-J. 1994 [1762]: *The Social Contract*. Oxford: Oxford University Press.

Sabine, G. H. 1937: *A History of Political Theory*. London: George G. Harrap & Co.

Sales, A. 1991: 'The Private, the Public and Civil Society: Social Realms and Power Structures.' *International Political Science Review* 12:295–312.

Sandel, M. J. 1996: *Democracy's Discontent: America in Search of a Public Philosophy*. Cambridge, Mass.: Belknap Press of Harvard University Press.

Sandel, M. J. 1998 [1982]: *Liberalism and the Limits of Justice*. 2nd edn. Cambridge: Cambridge University Press.

Scanlon, T. M. 1982: 'Contractualism and Utilitarianism.' In A. K. Sen and B. Williams (eds): *Utilitarianism and Beyond*. Cambridge: Cambridge University Press.

Scanlon, T. M. 1998: *What We Owe Each Other*. Cambridge, Mass.: Belknap Press of Harvard University Press.

Schelling, T. C. 1980 [1960]: *The Strategy of Conflict*. Cambridge, Mass.: Harvard University Press.

Schmitt, C. 1928: *Verfassungslehre*. Berlin: Duncker & Humblot.

Schmitt, C. 1988 [1923]: *The Crisis of Parliamentary Democracy*. Cambridge, Mass.: MIT Press.

Schmitt, C. 1996 [1932]: *The Concept of the Political*. Chicago: University of Chicago Press.

Schnädelbach, H. 1990: 'Remarks about Rationality and Language.' In S. Benhabib and F. Dallmayr (eds): *The Communicative Ethics Controversy*. Cambridge, Mass.: MIT Press.

Schön, D. A. and M. Rein 1994: *Frame Reflection. Toward the Resolution of Intractable Policy Controversies*. New York: Basic Books.

Schumpeter, J. A. 1942: *Capitalism, Socialism, and Democracy*. New York: Harper & Row.

Sciulli, D. 1992: *Theory of Societal Constitutionalism. Foundations of a Non-Marxist Critical Theory*. Cambridge: Cambridge University Press.

Sciulli, D. 1996: 'Habermas' Structural Change: Professions and Corporations Today.' Paper, APSA Annual Meeting, San Francisco.

Searle, J. R. 1969: *Speech Acts*. Cambridge: Cambridge University Press.

Sen, A. K. 1970: *Collective Choice and Social Welfare*. San Francisco: Holden-Day.

Shapiro, I. 1996: *Democracy's Place*. Ithaca: Cornell University Press.

Simon, H. 1969: *The Science of the Artificial*. Cambridge, Mass.: MIT Press.

Simon, H. 1976 [1945]: *Administrative Behavior*. 3rd edn. New York: The Free Press.

Skirbekk, G. 1993: *Rationality and Modernity. Essays in Philosophical Pragmatics*. Oslo: Scandinavian University Press.

Skirbekk, G. 1996: 'The Idea of a Welfare State in a Future Scenario of Great Scarcity.' In E. O. Eriksen and J. Loftager (eds): *The Rationality of the Welfare State*. Oslo: Scandinavian University Press.

Skjei, E. 1985: 'A Comment on Performative, Subject, and Proposition in Habermas's Theory of Communication.' *Inquiry* 28:87–105.

Strawson, P. F. 1968: 'Freedom and Resentment.' In P. F. Strawson: *Philosophy of Thought and Action*. Oxford: Oxford University Press.

Sunstein, C. R. 1985: 'Interest Groups in American Public Law.' *Stanford Law Review* 38:29–87.

Sunstein, C. R. 1988a: 'Constitutions and Democracies: an Epilogue.' In J. Elster and R. Slagstad (eds): *Constitutionalism and Democracy*. Cambridge/Oslo: Cambridge University Press/Norwegian University Press.

Sunstein, C. R. 1988b: 'Beyond the Republican Revival.' *Yale Law Journal* 97:1539–90.

Sunstein, C. R. 1990: *After the Rights Revolution. Reconceiving the Regulatory State*. Cambridge: Harvard University Press.

Sunstein, C. R. 1993: 'The Enduring Legacy of Republicanism.' In S. L. Elkin and K. E. Soltan (eds): *A New Constitutionalism. Designing Political Institutions for a Good Society*. Chicago: University of Chicago Press.

Sunstein, C. R. 1995: 'Incompletely Theorized Arguments.' *Harvard Law Review* 108:1733.

Sunstein, C. R. 1999: 'Disagreement Without Theory.' In S. Macedo (ed.): *Deliberative Politics. Essays on Democracy and Disagreement*. Oxford: Oxford University Press.

Taylor, C. 1985a: 'What is Human Agency?' In C. Taylor: *Human Agency and Language. Philosophical Papers 1*. Cambridge: Cambridge University Press.

Taylor, C. 1985b: 'What's Wrong with Negative Liberty.' In C. Taylor: *Philosophy and the Human Sciences. Philosophical Papers 2*. Cambridge: Cambridge University Press.

Taylor, C. 1986: 'Die Motive einer Verfahrensethik.' In W. Kuhlman (ed.): *Moralität und Sittlichkeit*. Frankfurt: Suhrkamp.

Taylor, C. 1989: *Sources of the Self*. Cambridge: Cambridge University Press.

Taylor, C: 1994: 'The Politics of Recognition.' In C. Taylor *et al.*: *Multiculturalism. Examining the Politics of Recognition*. Princeton: Princeton University Press.

Taylor, C. 1995: *Philosophical Arguments*. Cambridge, Mass.: Harvard University Press.

Teubner, G. 1996: 'De Collisione Discursuum: Communicative Rationalities in Law, Morality, and Politics.' *Cardozo Law Review* 17:901–18.

279

Thompson, J. B. 1984: *Studies in the Theory of Ideology.* Cambridge: Polity Press.

Thompson, J. B. 1990: *Ideology and Modern Culture.* Stanford: Stanford University Press.

Thompson, J. D. and W. J. McEwan 1958: 'Organizational Goals and Environment.' *American Sociological Review* 23:23–31.

Tocqueville, A. de 1969 [1835–40]: *Democracy in America.* New York: Anchor Books, Doubleday & Co.

van Mill, D. 1996: 'The Possibility of Rational Outcomes from Democratic Discourse and Procedures.' *The Journal of Politics* 58:734–52.

Vetlesen, A. J. 1991: 'Utkast til en kritikk av Habermas' samfunnsteori.' *Norsk filosofisk tidsskrift* 26:1–29.

Vetlesen, A. J. 1994: *Perception, Empathy and Judgement.* Pennsylvania: Pennsylvania State University Press.

Viroli, M. 1995: *For Love of Country – An Essay on Patriotism and Nationalism.* Oxford: Oxford University Press.

Waldron, J. 2001: *Law and Disagreement.* Oxford: Oxford University Press.

Walzer, M. 1977: *Just and Unjust Wars.* New York: Basic Books.

Walzer, M. 1983: *Spheres of Justice.* Oxford: Basil Blackwell.

Walzer, M. 1985: 'The Moral Standing of States. A Response to Four Critics.' In C. Beitz (ed.): *International Ethics.* Princeton: Princeton University Press.

Walzer, M. 1990: 'The Communitarian Critique of Liberalism.' *Political Theory* 18:6–23.

Warner, M. 1990: *The Letters of the Republic.* Cambridge: Cambridge University Press.

Warnke, G. 1996: 'Legitimacy and Consensus.' *Philosophy & Social Criticism* 22/2:67–83.

Warren, M. E. 1994: 'Deliberative Democracy and Authority.' Paper prepared for delivery at the 1994 Annual Meeting of the American Political Science Association, September 1994.

Weber, M. 1930 [1904–05]: *The Protestant Ethic and the Spirit of Capitalism.* London: Harper Collins.

Weber, M. 1965 [1919]: *Politics as a Vocation.* Philadelphia: Fortress Press.

Weber, M. 1978 [1922]: *Economy and Society*, Vols 1 and 2. Berkeley: University of California Press.

Wellmer, A. 1986: *Ethik und Dialog.* Frankfurt: Suhrkamp.

Wellmer, A. 1991: *The Persistence of Modernity.* Cambridge: Polity Press.

Wellmer, A. 1993: *Endspiele: Die unversöhnliche Moderne.* Frankfurt: Suhrkamp.

White, S. K. 1988: *The Recent Work of Jürgen Habermas.* Cambridge: Cambridge University Press.

Wiggershuas, R. 1994 [1987]: *The Frankfurt School. Its History, Theories and Political Significance.* Cambridge: MIT Press.

Willke, H. 1992: *Ironie des Staates.* Frankfurt: Suhrkamp.

Winch, P. 1958: *The Idea of a Social Science.* London: Routledge & Kegan Paul.

Winch, P. 1964: 'Understanding a Primitive Society.' *American Philosophical Quarterly* 1:07–324.

Wolin, S. 1989: *The Presence of the Past. Essays on the State and the Constitution.* Baltimore: The Johns Hopkins University Press.

Young, I. M. 1979: 'Self-Determination as a Principle of Justice.' *Philosophical Forum* **11**:172–82.

Young, I. M. 1990: *Justice and the Politics of Difference*. Princeton: Princeton University Press.

Young, I. M. 1997: 'Difference as a Resource for Democratic Communication.' In J. Bohman and W. Regh (eds): *Deliberative Democracy*. Cambridge, Mass.: MIT Press.

Young, O. R. 1972: 'Intermediaries: Additional Thoughts on Third Parties.' *Journal of Conflict Resolution* **16**:51–65.

INDEX OF SUBJECTS

INDEX OF PERSONS